EQUALITY PRACTICE

EQUALITY PRACTICE

Civil Unions

and the Future

of Gay Rights

WILLIAM N. ESKRIDGE JR.

ROUTLEDGE

NEW YORK AND LONDON

Published in 2002 by
Routledge
29 West 35th Street
New York, NY 10001

Published in Great Britain by
Routledge
11 New Fetter Lane
London EC4P 4EE

Routledge is an imprint of the Taylor & Francis Group.

Copyright © 2002 by Routledge

Printed in the United States of America on acid-free paper.

Library of Congress Cataloging-in-Publishing Data

Eskridge, William N., Jr.
    Equality Practice : civil unions and the future of gay rights / by William N. Eskridge, Jr.
    p. cm.
Includes bibliographical references and index.
ISBN 0–415–93072–3 — ISBN 0–415–93073–1 (pbk.)
    1. Same-sex marriage—United States. 2. Gay rights—United States. I. Title.

HQ76.3.U5 E85 2001
306.84'8—dc21   2001034964'

IN MEMORY OF NOAH JOLLES

CONTENTS

PROLOGUE AND ACKNOWLEDGMENTS

SAME-SEX MARRIAGE may be an idea whose time is coming. This book is an exploration of the process by which this is occurring in the United States and other developed countries, and of the jurisprudence that either explains or justifies that process. The nation became vividly aware of that process when Hawaii came close to recognizing same-sex marriage, a story told in chapter 1, and Vermont created a parallel institution for same-sex couples in 2000, as explained in chapter 2. Chapter 3 describes similar developments afoot in other countries. There is a virtual stampede for some kind of state recognition of same-sex relationships across the postindustrial world. Within the last two years alone, the Netherlands recognized same-sex marriages; France created *pactes civils* open to different- as well as same-sex couples; Germany established the life partnerships institution for same-sex couples; Canada and several of its provinces amended their cohabitation laws to include same-sex couples; and similar but weaker laws were adopted in Portugal, Belgium, and provinces in Spain and Australia.[1] State recognition of same-sex unions in the West is part of a larger trend whereby the modern state is now offering a menu of government-sanctioned regulatory options from which romantic couples can choose, based in part on the level of commitment they have for or would like to present to each other. Many of these options are available to same-sex as well as different-sex couples. Someday, all such options might be.

I do not intend to present the story told in chapters 1 through 3 as a heroic story of normative triumph, whereby a pervasive inequality has been recognized and is gradually being rectified or ameliorated. I wish that were the story I could tell. Instead, the largely descriptive account is complicated and ambivalent rather than triumphalist. Western democracies radically changed their regimes for relationship recognition in the twentieth century: at the beginning of the century, marriage was the exclusive regulatory regime, with restricted entry and highly restricted exit; at the beginning of the next century, marriage is the main item on a broader regulatory menu, entry is easier, and exit much easier. The most dramatic trend in recent years has been the state's opening up the regulatory menu to same-sex couples, and sometimes expanding the menu to accommodate such couples. These developments in the law are connected with and perhaps driven by three different but interrelated social developments. For convenience, I shall focus on the United States, but similar accounts could be given for other Western countries.[2]

To begin with, Americans do not marry with the frequency they once did, and marriages do not last as long. In 1970, there were 1.1 million multiperson households in the United States consisting of persons who were neither married nor related by blood or adoption. In 2000, the figure was 5.5 million.[3] According to the 2000 census, more than 27.2 million households now consist of one person living alone, a number greater than the 24.8 million households consisting of a married couple with children.[4] In the last thirty years, the percentage of middle-aged men and women who have never married has doubled.[5] Almost half of today's single mothers have never married, and the number of children living with unmarried couples has gone up more than fourfold.[6] The reluctance of more Americans to marry has occurred during a period in which the state and private employers added more benefits to that status. The divorce rate is more than half of all marriages. This last development is most obviously a joint product of shifting tastes, social norms, and legal regulations. The no-fault divorce rules adopted in the 1970s were both a response to shifting tastes and norms and a factor contributing to higher rates of marital dissolution.

For men and women who do choose to marry, the dynamics of the relationship also changed during the twentieth century. The big change is that many more wives have jobs outside the home in 2001 than in 1901. The working wife was a rarity at the end of the nineteenth century, a commonplace at the end of the twentieth.[7] The greater economic opportunities for women have inspired relatively greater equality in decision-making authority within the home and in allocation of household tasks. The trend toward equalization has not yielded anything like complete equality, however. Recent studies suggest that husbands and wives share household duties more than ever before, but wives (including those with jobs outside the home) still do twice as much housework as husbands.[8] There is some perception today, and a stronger one than there was one hundred years ago, that marriage is a much better deal for husbands than it is for wives.[9]

The third, and most ironic, trend is that lesbians and gay men probably do not marry in the great numbers they once did. In 1901, most Americans who had erotic feelings for people of the same sex married people of the opposite sex. Although these arrangements usually did not yield happy marriages, they were rational from the perspective of the "sexual invert" or the "homosexual," as such people were termed. State criminal sanctions and strong social disapproval made it hard to find appropriate partners of the same sex, and disastrous to form openly sexual liaisons with them; marriage was not only the path of least resistance, but also the ideal cover for the invert.[10] This strategy grew less rational for lesbians, gay men, and some bisexuals as gay subcultures grew in visibility and, more dramatically, after gay rights groups won rights for gay people to be left alone and even protected in many jurisdictions. An increasing number of lesbians, gay men, and bisexuals have formed open relationships; the 2000 Census reported 594,391 same-sex partnered households. Many of these households are the situs for childrearing. No one knows, even roughly, how many such households there are in this country. Estimates range from one to five million lesbian or gay households with children.[12] Also, no one knows how many gay and bisexual men and women are married to persons of the opposite sex, but a reasonable hypothesis is that the percentage is much lower than it was one hundred years ago; most gay men and lesbians today want to be partnered with persons of the same sex.

The foregoing social changes have yielded two different impulses toward traditional legal rules, which focused on marriage as an institution with restricted entry and highly restricted exit. The dominant impulse during the twentieth century has been a liberalization of family law: a greater array of choices for couples seeking state recognition of their relationships and easier exit from the institutions of choice.[13] The same-sex marriage movement has been a part of this process. It also reflects a *politics of recognition,* whereby gay people have been petitioning for equal legal treatment of and some degree of social respect for their relationships. Ironically, at the same point when many straight people are opting out of marriage, many gay people want in. The other regulatory impulse has been a traditionalist critique of liberalization: marriage is the only valid form of state recognition, and it has been weakened by the new options for state recognition and by the ease of exit from marriage. The *politics of preservation* reflecting this impulse has not been able to stop massive liberalization but has been energized by the possibility of same-sex marriage. Paradoxically, the minor (and promarriage) liberalization that would be accomplished by recognizing same-sex marriage has turned into an apocalyptic normative struggle between liberals and traditionalists. In the political arena, the latter usually win, but in winning they have sometimes lost. In the United States and elsewhere, traditionalists have headed off same-sex marriage, but at a cost of proliferation of new state-sanctioned institutions for relationships, sometimes including straight as well as gay ones.

The role of law in this normative struggle between the politics of recognition and preservation has been central and fascinating. Courts and legislatures have been important situses for this struggle. The landmark legal development in the United States, thus far, has been Vermont's recognition of *civil unions* for same-sex couples in 2000. Civil unions carry with them the same state-created rights and duties of marriage, but not the name; nor are they likely to be recognized in many jurisdictions outside Vermont or under federal law at the present time. This development ought to generate normative anxiety for the politics of both preservation and recognition. For the former, the Vermont law represented a breach in the long-standing refusal of the state to accord official and pretty much equal recognition to lesbian and gay relationships. The law was, as these critics maintained, a symbolic "promotion" of openly gay relationships (from legally unmentionable to almost normal) and another step in the ongoing decentering of marriage, which had once been the exclusive mechanism for state regulation. For the latter, the Vermont law represented a compromise that was possibly unprincipled and, for some people, reminiscent of the "separate but not really equal" regime of American apartheid. Metaphorically, the statute could be deemed a linguistic segregation: straight people get the dignity of marriage terminology while gay people come in through the back door of civil unions.

The second half of this book explores the jurisprudential features of the Vermont compromise, and others like it in Denmark, France, Germany, Canada, and elsewhere. Chapters 4 and 5 examine the compromise from the perspectives of liberal theory of the state and communitarian theory, respectively. Vermont civil unions and the normative and political debate that preceded the law exemplify virtues and limitations of each kind of theory. For example, liberalism as articulated by John Rawls provides a theoretical basis for appreciating the impulse of the Vermont Supreme Court and the Vermont legislature to eschew sectarian arguments and comprehensive philosophies in evaluating the lesbian and gay couples' rights claims. But liberalism has a harder time appreciating the willingness of both the court and the legislature to consider widely accepted sectarian feelings in crafting a remedy. Conversely, Michael Sandel's communitarianism appreciates the need for accommodation of traditionalist values as the state proceeded to address the needs and interests of its lesbian, gay, and bisexual citizens, but offers an insufficient theoretical basis for recognizing the equality rights of couples who seem so different to many Vermonters.

Gay experience and ordinary legal practice—a genuinely odd couple—suggest a fruitful way of thinking about the Vermont law and others surely to come. Law routinely distinguishes between *rights* and *remedies*. Thus, one may have a right the state must respect, but courts will consider broader social interests before giving rights full and complete remedies. Often, judges will grant provisional but incomplete remedies for rights violations, with an expectation that full remediation may come over time. Gay experience complements the legal point. Lesbians and gay men who come out of their closets ask family members, close friends, and coworkers for their continued love or respect notwithstanding information that may be discomforting. Although some confidants unreservedly accept the gay person's sexual orientation, others need time to come to grips with it. Typically, a compromise works best: the family, friendship, and workplace are preserved, with the gay person still a valued member, but on the condition that she be discreet in a variety of ways. The agreed-to discretion tends to ease up over time, and the result may be full acceptance of the gay person and her partner (if any) as a part of the family, friendship, or workplace community. This is what I call *equality practice*. Equality for lesbians, gay men, bisexuals, and their relationships is a liberal right for which there is no sufficient justification for state denial—but it is not a right that ought to be delivered immediately, if it would unsettle the community.

So equality comes on little cat's feet. The experience in other countries, surveyed in chapter 3, suggests that the path to same-sex marriage is incremental and can be exceedingly slow. Sudden equality for gay people is neither politically feasible nor jurisprudentially desirable if it produces a fierce politics of preservation that undermines the conditions for reciprocity and citizenship in the community. The tried and true path is the one followed by the Netherlands, which recognized same-sex marriages as this book was going to press. First, the state must repeal laws making consensual same-sex intimacy criminal, as that allows lesbians and gay men private spaces for personal flourishing without state interference. Many will "uncloset" themselves to their families, friends, and coworkers. This educative process will help straight people accept the second step, which is state laws prohibiting public and private discriminations against sexual and gender minorities, especially in the workplace. As opponents say, these laws will promote the status of gay people from social outcasts to almost normal members of society; still more people will be openly gay, and some will come out as couples. The third step is state recognition of same-sex relationships—usually without yoking it to the term *marriage*. State laws recognizing same-sex domestic partnerships (California), reciprocal beneficiaries (Hawaii), and civil unions (Vermont) provide gay people an opportunity to celebrate their relationships and provide straight people an opportunity to see that women can form loving and rewarding relationships with other women and men the same with other men. Some straight people will be very surprised to find out how many lesbian and gay families include children. After this kind of experience, it is possible for the government to move to same-sex marriage without creating a rift in the community.

Theoretically, equality practice seeks a law-based synthesis: liberalism instructs us as to rights, communitarianism as to remedies. Such a synthesis exploits the strengths of both theories, but of course can be questioned under both. The liberal can properly object that most jurisdictions will deliver on gay couples' equality rights with the celerity of a sloth, and some jurisdictions will never do so. The communitarian can properly object that recognition of this kind of right for sexual and gender minorities slights the legitimate interests of religious minorities. Finally, as chapter 6 demonstrates, progressives can properly object that equality practice's emphasis on same-sex marriage and "marriage-lite" institutions neglects opportunities for more fundamental changes in American family law. All these objections are well-founded. Equality practice has the vice of messiness and the virtue of workability.

Apart from the neat deployment of law's right-remedy distinction, there is an underlying elegance to the idea of equality practice. The epilogue to this book will trace the trajectory of equality practice as I see it playing out in the medium term and will tie the notion to the larger relationships among laws, public values, and social norms. Equality practice rests upon the supposition, tentatively supported by law's treatment of sexual and gender minorities in the last century, that law, public values, and social norms are interconnected: values and norms influence law, and law influences norms and values. This process is usually in equilibrium: the law adequately reflects public values and social norms as to important matters. That equilibrium can be unsettled by external shocks, such as the social changes described at the beginning of this prologue. When that occurs, new interests and ideas challenge both old law and old norms. People who had been imprisoned and electroshocked as sexual inverts in the early twentieth century are now a social group that has proven, or is proving, itself productive and worthy of human respect, in my opinion. The politics of recognition and preservation are driven by the horribly difficult process of adjusting law and norms to new social forces and concepts. The advantage of equality practice—or something like it—is that it recognizes both the need to accommodate new ideas and the inability of human beings and their communities to do so without a long process of education and personal experience.

The foregoing are the ideas I seek to develop in this book. Like social movements of all kinds, this work is a collective endeavor. I have been writing on the subject of same-sex marriage for a decade, and my ideas have evolved as a result of what I have learned from other intellectuals and from events in this country and the world—events that no one predicted. I have debated this topic with a long list of public intellectuals, among them Professor Walter Berns; Mayor William Brown of San Francisco; Professor David Coolidge; Paula Ettelbrick, Esq.; Professor Nancy Polikoff; the Reverend Louis Sheldon; the late Thomas Stoddard, Esq.; and Professor Lynn Wardle. I learned a lot from all these people and admire their commitment to ideas, even though their ideas are different from mine in most cases. Professor Wardle and I have become something of a traveling road show, and we have developed a warm friendship in the process.

My story of the Vermont civil unions statute is based on my first-hand examination of people who participated in that process and of the primary materials. I appreciate the cooperation of the Vermont Legislative Council, which provided tapes of the legislative proceedings at nominal charge. I especially appreciate the generosity of Beth Robinson, Esq. and Susan Murray, Esq., who provided me with indispensable background material, and of some of the legislators and state officials, who were willing to talk with me or my research associate, Travis LeBlanc. Some of the conversations were off the record.

The Yale Law School provided essential support for this project. Dean Anthony Kronman got me started with a summer research grant. The spectacularly helpful staff of the Yale Law Library helped me with references. As he has done for many at the law school for forty years, Gene Coakley gathered sources for me and cheered me on in this project. John Davie walked me through technical aids such as tape recorders. And Yale law students provided critical research assistance. Joshua Stehlik of the class of 2001 helped me track down most of the international sources I needed for chapter 3. Travis LeBlanc of the class of 2002 found materials, edited chapters 4 and 5, and masterminded Internet and other data searches that enriched my research beyond measure in chapters 1, 2, and 3.

I presented various chapters of the book in faculty workshops at the New York School of Law and the University of Colorado School of Law, and received useful comments from the participants at those workshops. Particularly helpful comments came from Professors Carlin Meyer and David Schoenbrod. Professor Robert Wintemute of King's College in London provided me with advance copies of chapters in his edited book *Legal Recognition of Same-Sex Partnerships*. I have constantly profited from conversations with Professor Wintemute, who is the world's authority on same-sex marriage. Professor Kees Waaldjik of the University of Leiden School of Law kept me up to date on developments in the Netherlands and was an important influence on the pragmatic model that my book advances.

I am perhaps most grateful to the three plaintiff couples in the Vermont case that triggered that state's civil unions law: Stannard Baker and Peter Harrigan, Nina Beck and Stacy Jolles, and Lois Farnham and Holly Puterbaugh. I interviewed all three couples and met two of them. They are wonderful people who have established loving families. They were rather brave to attempt this pathbreaking lawsuit. Ms. Beck and Ms. Jolles did so under particularly adverse circumstances. Early in the course of the lawsuit, their son Noah Jolles died of congenital circulatory problems. He will not be forgotten. His picture is prominent in the couple's living room, where their second child now plays.

CHAPTER ONE

Same-Sex Marriage and the Politics of Sexuality

FOR MOST OF THE TWENTIETH CENTURY, legally recognized same-sex marriage was unthinkable. "Homosexuals" were a despised group, outlaws hunted by the state. The most practical strategy was denial of one's sexual orientation and practices—a lifelong *masquerade*, as people termed it for most of the century. An open relationship with another person of the same sex would have exposed the masquerade, and applying for a marriage license would have been a ticket to prison. After World War II, homosexuals came to see themselves caught in the dilemma of the "closet": the secrecy that protected them also suffocated them.[1] Some of those who felt this suffocation or who had been pushed out of the closet (usually by the state) objected to their treatment by the state. At first, their horizons were narrow. The early homophile movement was largely limited to a *politics of protection*: the state engaged in episodic campaigns to protect children and public spaces against homosexuals, who in turn fought to protect their private spaces and subcultural institutions (bars, clubs, journals) from state intrusion. Under such a regime, same-sex marriage was not a realistic goal.

This politics began to change in the 1960s. Inspired by the civil rights movement, some homosexuals publicly insisted that the state treat them the same as everyone else. The Stonewall riots of June 1969 stimulated thousands of queer people to come out of their closets and create hundreds of organizations insisting that the state not only get off their backs but assure them equal rights other minorities had achieved. The post-Stonewall "gay rights" movement not only demanded that states repeal sodomy laws, but that states and municipalities adopt new laws prohibiting public and private discrimination on the basis of sexual orientation. Nancy Fraser calls this a *politics of recognition,* which she distinguishes from a class-based politics of redistribution. As she notes, "Gays and lesbians suffer from heterosexism: the *authoritative* construction of norms that privilege heterosexuality. . . . The remedy for the injustice, consequently, is *recognition*, not redistribution. Overcoming homophobia and heterosexism requires changing the *cultural valuations* (as well as their legal and practical expressions) that privilege heterosexuality, deny *equal respect* to gays and lesbians, and refuse to recognize homosexuality as a *legitimate* way of being sexual."[2] Once gay, lesbian, bisexual, and transgendered (GLBT) people engaged in a serious politics of this sort, state recognition of same-sex marriage was not only conceivable, but many GLBT people considered it the ultimate goal, the crowning achievement. Lesbian and gay couples' petitions for same-sex marriage were uniformly unsuccessful in the 1970s but won a series of dramatic court victories in the 1990s.

Recognition is not the end of the story, however. Progay politics straightaway begat a countermovement by "traditional family values" (TFV) people for whom gay rights were threatening. Opposition to gay rights has thus become a kind of identity politics for religious fundamentalists and others who fear progay changes in public law as corrosive of their republican vision for America and who view sexual orientation antidiscrimination laws as infringing on their family values and their rights as parents, coworkers, and landlords not to associate with lesbians, bisexuals, or gay men. Theirs is what I call a *politics of preservation.*[3]

Same-sex marriage has been a godsend to the politics of preservation. Not only is it an issue where such a politics can be successful, but it expands the base of that politics: ordinary people who are not concerned one way or the other about gay rights, or who consider the whole matter too icky to contemplate, can be stimulated and recruited into antigay activism by the marriage issue. Thus, after same-sex marriage broke through with a favorable decision by the Hawaii Supreme Court in 1993, the antigay politics of preservation mobilized as never before— persuading the federal government, most states, and even tolerant Hawaii to legislate against "homosexual marriage." Although this second wave of same-sex marriage lawsuits came close to establishing a beachhead in Hawaii, it crashed against the shoals of a preservationist politics stronger than anyone imagined it could be on the eve of the millennium. Ultimately, the Hawaii experience suggests how lawsuits and other mechanisms of the law can affect politics in unpredictable ways. The same-sex marriage lawsuit in that state was agenda-seizing: it contributed to the politics of recognition by stirring the aspirations of GLBT people everywhere in the country, while at the same time fueling the politics of preservation by providing it with an easy object for mobilization on behalf of traditional family values.

FROM PROTECTION TO RECOGNITION AND PRESERVATION: THE FIRST WAVE OF SAME-SEX MARRIAGE LAWSUITS

For most of the twentieth century, it was a crime throughout the United States to have intercourse with someone of the same sex, to solicit or even suggest such an interaction, or to transgress gender-based dress codes. GLBT people were social outcasts and legal outlaws. Most such people were able to closet their sexual or gender variation from the mainstream, but one effect of the closet was that sexual and gender minorities were not able to refute stereotypes and prejudice against them and were not politically active. The early homophile movement focused its energies almost exclusively on a politics of protection—seeking to head off or ameliorate state violence against sexual minorities through official arrests, raids, harassment, and witch-hunts.[4] The most gay people could expect from this politics was *don't ask, don't tell.* In this environment, legally recognized same-sex marriage was virtually unimaginable.[5]

The Mattachine Society of Washington and its leader Franklin Kameny envisioned a different kind of politics in which homosexuals would be treated as free and equal citizens and not as tolerable misfits.[6]

Directly inspired by the African-American civil rights movement, this was a nascent politics of recognition. For homosexuals, this politics required people to come out of their sexual and gender closets, which did not happen on a large scale until the Stonewall riots in June 1969; then the handful of homophile organizations of the earlier 1960s were overwhelmed by hundreds of gay and lesbian groups demanding equal rights.[7] The post-1969 gay rights movement sought not only to repeal state policies penalizing people for their sexual orientations and consensual private activities, but also to assure GLBT people the same rights and obligations straight people took for granted.

Should equality include the right to marry? That was a contentious topic. Most lesbian and gay radicals maintained that the husband-wife marriage with children was "the microcosm of oppression."[8] Radical lesbians drew from feminist theory the criticism that marriage is a patriarchal institution.[9] Traditionally, women lost their legal personhood when they got married, and husbands held near-absolute sway over their wives' bodies as well. The liberalization of marriage freed women to have some legal personhood but still subordinated them to their husbands, who remained practically and often legally immune from most charges of rape, beating, and economic manipulation. Living in Berkeley, California, in the early 1970s, Nina Beck shared this philosophy: her lesbian orientation and feminist philosophy made her unreceptive to legal marriage, even marriage to another woman. Same-sex marriage would just ape the structure of traditional marriage, she felt. It would be better for GLBT people to create their own institutions of love, nurturance, and commitment—families we choose rather than families forced onto us by the state and blood relatives.[10]

Other radicals objected to marriage because of its insistence on monogamy. For these critics, gay liberation was most fundamentally a challenge to America's pervasive sex negativity. By confining sexual expression to one's marital partner—whether of the same or different sex—marriage was reactionary because it was the embodiment of sex negativity.[11] Some sexual-liberty radicals drew from Marxist theory the critique that monogamy objectified the marital partners because it extended "[c]ompetition and exclusive possession, traits of the marketplace, . . . to erotic relations among persons."[12] Like the radical lesbians, the sexual-liberty radicals rejected the idea that gay liberation should be just a politics of recognition. Although the radicals supported equal rights for GLBT people, they maintained that activism ought to be a *politics of transformation*. Hence, lesbians and gay men ought to join women and people of color not only to get outsiders the same rights insiders had long enjoyed, but also to renovate the house in which all lived—not just a place at the table, but a new table.

When the National Coalition of Gay Organizations drew up a list of demands for law reform in 1972, it included as a key item in its agenda "[r]epeal of all legislative provisions that restrict the sex or number of persons entering into a marriage unit and extension of the legal benefits of marriage to all persons who cohabit regardless of sex or numbers."[13] This demand was a compromise between the two kinds of politics (recognition and transformation) that GLBT people were engaged in. The National Coalition did not advocate the abolition of marriage, as radical lesbians favored, nor did it directly attack the monogamy requirement, as the sexual radicals urged, but it did insist on a major transformation of the institution as well as making it available to most gays and lesbians—a compromise that could have appealed to Nina Beck. Thus, the demand spoke not only to the radical critics, but also to the thousands of GLBT people who had a yearning to get married to persons considered by the law to be of the same sex.

Of course, none of the demands of the National Coalition was acceptable to mainstream politics. But one of the demands—for same-sex marriage—could easily be expressed in terms of constitutional rights, by reference to the race discrimination precedents set by the U.S. Supreme Court under Chief Justice Earl Warren. Thus, at the very point when activists were deliberating over the kind of politics gay liberation ought to emphasize and what ought to be its stance toward marriage, lawyers and their gay and lesbian clients were engaging in a preemptive strike. By filing lawsuits challenging their exclusion from marriage laws, same-sex couples not only put their politics of recognition at the forefront of the gay agenda, but also made it harder for more radical proposals to be floated later on. The structure of American public law played a role in a process by which marriage became the situs for cutting-edge gaylegal reform.

The First Wave of Same-Sex Marriage Lawsuits

In the 1970s, the gay politics of protection won state legislative repeal of sodomy laws in most states and police nonenforcement of such laws almost everywhere else, an abandonment of antihomosexual witch-hunts at both state and national levels, and an easing in government censorship of homoerotic publications. At the same time, their politics of recognition also made headway, as the federal government and some states adopted public nondiscrimination policies and many municipalities adopted laws prohibiting sexual orientation discrimination by private organizations.[14] Radicals made virtually no progress in petitioning the law to transform or abandon traditional institutions, but neither did couples desiring to join that institution.

This is not to say that such couples didn't try to crash the institution of marriage throughout the 1970s. Their applications for marriage licenses triggered internal dialogues within state bureaucracies as to whether state law excluded same-sex couples and whether any such exclusion was constitutional. Almost no one dared say that same-sex couples were entitled to such licenses. One of the few exceptions was Cela Rorex, the court clerk in Boulder, Colorado. With the concurrence of the district attorney, she issued marriage licenses to same-sex couples in 1975—and raised such a fuss that the state attorney general intervened to stop her.[15] Colorado refused to honor any of the licenses Rorex issued. More typical was the experience in Vermont, whose clerks obediently followed the state attorney general's written opinion that the "legislature has proscribed homosexual marriage."[16] That was the end of the matter in Vermont during the 1970s, but in other states spurned same-sex couples sued the clerks to get their marriage licenses.

Richard John Baker met his partner, James Michael McConnell, in graduate school. When Baker matriculated as a law student at the University of Minnesota in 1970, McConnell moved there with him and got a job as a cataloger at the university. They asked their priest, "Do you feel that if two people give themselves in love to each other and want to grow together with mutual understanding, that Jesus would be open to such a union if the two people were of the same sex?"[17] The priest felt Jesus would be open to such a union. Baker and McConnell applied for a marriage license, which the state denied. They got married anyway, in a religious ceremony, and then sued the state for legal recognition of their marriage.[18] Shortly thereafter, Manomia Evans and Donna Burkett, a different-race lesbian couple, applied for a marriage license in Milwaukee. When the clerk denied the application, they sued him, and a Wisconsin legislator introduced a bill to amend the marriage law to include same-sex couples.[19] Tracy Knight and Marjorie Ruth Jones, a mother of three, sought a marriage license in Jefferson County, Kentucky. After the district attorney rejected their application, they, too, sued the state.[20]

In contrast, no one went to court claiming that the state was required to give cohabiting or polyamorous couples (of any sexuality) the benefits of marriage. It may be that such radicals found the legal process less congenial, but a legal reason for the asymmetry is that the federal constitutional precedents offered much greater analytical support for the politics of recognition than for the politics of transformation. This is no coincidence, for a politics of recognition is generally pressed upon social groups making claims under the equal protection clause of the Fourteenth Amendment to the U.S. Constitution. That clause says that the states cannot deny any person "the equal protection of the law." Persons arguing that they have been treated unequally must show that their situation is sufficiently similar to that of persons privileged by the law. Where the challengers are minority groups, they must therefore claim that they are "like" the majority in relevant respects. Hence, their posture in equal protection cases is intrinsically assimilationist—a key feature of a melting-pot politics of recognition and a feature discouraging openly transformative strategies.[21]

Lawyers considering whether to file same-sex marriage lawsuits in the 1970s were not only inspired by the civil rights campaign of racial assimilation but found specific support for their vision in *Loving v. Virginia*, where the U.S. Supreme Court ruled unconstitutional a state law barring different-race marriages. Part one of the Court's opinion in *Loving* found the law's race-based classification to violate the equal protection clause.[22] Because the state treated black-white couples differently than white-white or black-black couples, it was discriminating "because of" the race of one of the partners. Race is a highly suspect classification, triggering the most beady-eyed scrutiny from the Court and almost always requiring judicial invalidation. In 1972, Congress passed the Equal Rights Amendment (ERA) by the two-thirds majority needed to send it to the states for ratification. The amendment would have made sex a suspect classification, just as race was. During Congress' deliberations, Professor Paul Freund warned that adoption of the amendment would render same-sex marriage bars constitutionally suspect, by analogy to *Loving*: because the state treated female-female and male-male couples differently than female-male couples, it was discriminating because of the sex of one of the partners.[23] Just as race was the regulatory variable (the item whose change altered the state's treatment of the couple) in the different-race marriage bar invalidated in *Loving*, so was sex the regulatory variable (the item whose change altered the state's treatment of the couple) in the same-sex marriage bar. Giving no persuasive reason why Freund was wrong, the ERA's sponsor denied this conclusion,[24] but it probably played a role in the failure of the ERA to win ratification of three-fourths of the state legislatures. Nonetheless, many states adopted equal rights amendments to their state constitutions, and some attorneys relied on "junior ERAs" to challenge the same-sex marriage bar.[25] Note how this sex discrimination analogy provides no basis for arguing that state refusals to give benefits to cohabiting or polyamorous couples are an invidious kind of discrimination "like" race discrimination.

Litigants in states without junior ERAs (as well as those in ERA states, of course) had access to another constitutional argument. Part two of the *Loving* opinion presented an independent ground for striking down the different-race marriage law. "The freedom to marry has long been recognized as one of the vital personal rights essential to the orderly pursuit of happiness by free men," said the Court. "To deny this fundamental freedom on so unsupportable a basis as the racial classifications embodied in these statutes . . . is surely to deprive all the State's citizens of liberty without due process of law."[26] This holding offered a more direct basis for challenging same-sex marriage bars: they violated the fundamental right to marriage for lesbian and gay couples, essential to those couples' "orderly pursuit of happiness." All of the early litigants made this argument and invoked *Loving* for the broader proposition that traditional prejudices ought not stand in the way of state recognition for unions of excluded minorities—gay people any more than people of color. Again, the fundamental right-to-marry jurisprudence afforded little help to cohabiting or polyamorous couples that might have considered constitutional litigation for state benefits.

Unsurprisingly, judges dared not accept these arguments in the 1970s. "Marriage has always been considered as the union of a man and a woman," the courts unanimously ruled.[27] To the extent that they even bothered to respond to the couples' arguments, judges dismissed the analogy to *Loving*: the different-race couple in the earlier case snugly fit within the traditional biblical and procreative goals of marriage, while same-sex couples did not. Hence, there was no *sex discrimination*, as the same-sex couples were denied marriage licenses because of their failure to fit within the procreative model, not because of their sex. And there was no denial of a *fundamental right*, for the right to marry extended only to people who could theoretically procreate. So the claimants all lost their cases. The gay rights movement lost more than the cases.

Same-Sex Marriage and a New Politics of Preservation

These lawsuits played a significant role in energizing a TFV political movement in the 1970s—and galvanizing a vigorous politics of preservation appealing to traditionalists who disapproved of homosexuals or their "lifestyles." Once openly GLBT people emerged in the public culture, many fundamentalist Christians made central to their faith an anti-homosexual reading of Leviticus 20:13 and Romans 1:26–27.* Biblical literalism reasserted the value of male-female procreative sex within marriage; biblical eschatology refocused on homosexual license as the fulcrum around which civilization would crumble in the millennial holocaust.[28] For some literally, for others figuratively, Satan was homosexualized, and the never-married Christ was homophobialized. For these and other Americans, resentment at increased homosexual visibility interacted with resentment at other changes associated with the sexual revolution of the 1960s: abortion on demand, no-fault divorce, teenage

---

★ Leviticus 20:13 declares a man lying with a man to be an "abomination." Romans 1:26–27 condemns as "shameful" and "against nature" the passionate relations between two women or two men.

pregnancies, sexual cohabitation prior to or in place of marriage, and the availability of pornography to youth. All these changes threatened the family as it was traditionally understood. People began to array their identities around their opposition to these sexual- and gender-liberalizing features of American society. In the south, for example, one's identity as a Baptist had long been rooted in the fact that one was not a Methodist or, especially, a Roman Catholic. In the 1970s, many Baptists found much common ground with Catholics and Methodists, because all were concerned with the decline of the family, the rise in teenage sexual experience, and alarming public expressions of homosexuality.

These like-thinking traditionalists correctly saw that the law was deeply involved in sexual liberalization and the decline of the family: no-fault divorce statutes sent divorce rates soaring, the due process clause swept away one hundred years of abortion statutes, the First Amendment hackled state policing of pornography and offensive speech—and homosexuals were seizing on all these precedents to claim full public equality, and even the right to marry! This alone would have triggered a TFV political movement of some sort. Gay rights issues not only helped the movement draw together different groups to a common cause, but assured that the TFV politics of preservation would enjoy explicit and extensive support from organized religion. The same-sex marriage issue reinforced both features: it was an issue that united all kinds of traditionalists and had special relevance to fundamentalist religions. Not only did priests, ministers, and rabbis perform marriage ceremonies, but procreative husband-wife marriage was considered central to Judeo-Christian morality. Religious leaders had special learning as to the institution and a deep interest in its traditionalist definition.

The nascent politics of preservation following gay liberation was unable to prevent wholesale sodomy law repeals, but it feasted on the issue of same-sex marriage. For example, a coalition of religious traditionalists unsuccessfully opposed sodomy repeal in California in 1976 and were not even able to attract enough support to get a sodomy referendum on the ballot.[29] But when gay activists insisted that sodomy repeal, together with the state's 1971 rewrite of its marriage law to make it gender neutral, established same-sex marriage in the state code, traditionalists got the immediate attention of the California legislature. In

1977, it amended the state code to make explicit that marriage was limited to "one man and one woman."[30] When District of Columbia Councilmember Arrington Dixon in 1977 introduced a bill that might have legalized gay marriage, the Roman Catholic Diocese of Washington, D.C., and various Baptist churches mobilized to oppose the bill, with easy success.[31] Other states similarly responded to the mere possibility of same-sex marriage agitation by amending their laws to reaffirm marriage's traditional definition.[32] Most jurisdictions followed the example of Vermont, which repealed its sodomy law with scarcely a whimper from traditionalists but held fast to its marriage exclusion; the attorney general's opinion went unchallenged in either the courts or the legislature. In states with high concentrations of Mormons and Southern Baptists, the politics of preservation was able to block sodomy reform, and for the most part same-sex marriage dared not speak its name in those jurisdictions.[33]

The early campaigns to head off legislative recognition of same-sex marriages gave the antigay politics of preservation its start. Churches that had rarely been involved in state or local politics were entering the fray and forming alliances with other churches whose members they had once considered devilrous. (Same-sex marriage, in this weird way, contributed to the easing of religious intolerance in America.) By 1977, when California regendered its marriage law, the same-sex marriage movement was spent—but the TFV movement had only just begun. It gained national attention in 1977, when Anita Bryant's "Save Our Children" campaign succeeded in revoking Dade County, Florida's sexual orientation nondiscrimination law.[34] The campaign exemplified the appeal of TFV ideas to a broad array of voters and the ability of organized religion to affect politics. Bryant also developed a winning argumentative strategy: appeal to religious fundamentalists and homophobes with the argument that any legal recognition of gay people as near equals would "promote" sinful "homosexuality," while appealing at the same time to parents that promotion of homosexuality was a threat to their children and indeed was a violation of the constitutional rights of parents to protect their children against perversity.[35] This was the same kind of argumentation deployed by the Moral Majority (a formal coalition of religious leaders and traditionalists) in 1981, when it mobilized the U.S. House of Representatives to veto Washington, D.C.'s attempt to repeal its sodomy and fornication laws.[36] This was the Moral Majority's debut in national politics.

Ironies abound. The early same-sex marriage movement, lured into the open by seemingly applicable civil rights precedents, got smashed in the judicial as well as political process. This not only set back the politics of recognition, but occluded opportunities for a more ambitious politics of transformation. Challenges to marriage as the sole organizing principle for families were not made by gay people but instead were made by heterosexual litigants like Michele Marvin, whose pioneering California Supreme Court victory brought judicial and later statutory recognition to different-sex cohabiting relationships at the same time that gay activists were agitating unsuccessfully for same-sex marriage in that state.[37] More important, same-sex marriage played a significant role in luring fundamentalist churches into the political arena; once in politics, they stayed in politics and flourished in politics. No issue, not even abortion, united them or galvanized their constituencies more than same-sex marriage.

The Domestic Partnership Movement

In light of the negative political feedback and uniform lack of success in the courts, lesbian and gay activists lowered their sights: from the state to the municipal levels, and from full marriage rights to a few rights associated with a new institution that would not be mistaken for marriage. The key move in the politics of recognition for lesbian and gay relationships was from the state level to the municipal level. Demographically, GLBT people gravitated to the nation's large cities, where they were likely to find more people like themselves. The politics of protection they engaged in to reduce police harassment got them politically organized, and in the 1970s lesbian and gay political organizations applied themselves vigorously to the goals of the politics of recognition. Cities adopted ordinances prohibiting discrimination on the basis of sexual orientation long before their states did, because GLBT groups were better organized and had more allies in many cities than TFV groups did.[38] Relatedly, urban demographics earlier on reflected the rise of "nontraditional" families, including single mothers raising chil-

dren, cohabiting men and women, and friends living together as well as
same-sex couples.

Thus, GLBT groups petitioned city councils to create a new institution, *domestic partnership*, that would give some recognition to same-
sex couples.³⁹ The politics of such measures usually went something like
this: With same-sex marriage not a politically viable option, GLBT
activists would join forces with nontraditionalist straight people and
their organizations to petition for municipal recognition of their alternative families. The city council would study the issue or create a non-
partisan commission to do so. Experts would tell the city how
demographics had changed, leaving traditional families to be the exception rather than the rule, and would explain how easy and inexpensive
it would be to provide recognition and some employee benefits to such
nontraditional families. TFV groups in the urban area would complain
that domestic partner recognition would undermine marriage, but most
big cities were ultimately willing to adopt such legislation anyway.

The first major domestic partnership bill was passed by the San
Francisco Board of Supervisors in 1982, but Mayor Diane Feinstein
vetoed it on the ground that it "mimics a marriage license."⁴⁰ In 1984,
the Berkeley City Council adopted the first operative municipal domestic partnership policy, which provided a registry for public recognition
of same-sex relationships; the law was later amended to allow city
employees to obtain health benefits for their registered domestic partners and to require hospitals to permit domestic partner visitation.⁴¹
Berkeley's action was atypical in initially including just same-sex couples; subsequent domestic partner ordinances almost always included
different-sex couples, who became the main beneficiaries of the policy in
most jurisdictions. Berkeley's action was typical, however, in the few
benefits it could offer. A municipal politics of recognition could never
create GLBT marriage, for that was an institution regulated mostly at
the state level. All that cities could do was to provide same-sex couples
with a euphemism, a registry, and a few benefits. The main benefits were
fringe benefits for municipal employees: their partners could sign onto
their health insurance, could be beneficiaries of disability or death
payments, and could have the benefit of employee bereavement or family care leave.⁴² Outside of government employee fringes, the main ben-

efit was mandatory visitation rights for one's partner in a health care institution.

Local coalitions of gay activists and allies obtained similar domestic partnership registries in West Hollywood (1985, implemented in 1989), Madison (1988), San Francisco (1990), Washington, D.C. (1992), Sacramento (1992), New York City (1993, expanded in 1998), Atlanta (1993), Boston (1993), New Orleans (1993), Seattle (1994), Denver (1995), Oakland (1996), St. Louis (1997), and Philadelphia (1998).[43] A number of cities, like Baltimore (1995), Miami Beach (1998), and Pittsburgh (1999), now offer their employees domestic partnership benefits, but without creating a municipal registry. As of 1999, almost eight hundred major corporations offered their employees domestic partnership benefits. Counties followed suit, as did a few states. Massachusetts offered such benefits to state employees through a 1992 executive order, and Vermont extended domestic partnership benefits to state employees as a result of a labor board decision in 1994.[44] In the same year, the California legislature passed a domestic partnership bill. Like Mayor Feinstein a dozen years earlier, Governor Pete Wilson vetoed the bill on the ground that it would be a "foot in the door" for same-sex marriage,[45] but in 1999 Wilson's successor, Governor Gray Davis, signed a statewide domestic partnership law that established mutual responsibilities and some benefits for couples who register.[46]

Although TFV groups have not been able to prevent domestic partnership ordinances and policies from being adopted, they have been able to confine their ambit. For example, in 1992 gay groups pressed the District of Columbia to enact a domestic partnership law that not only provided a registry, fringe benefits for city employees, and hospital visitation, but also spouse-like rights in cases where one's partner is incapacitated or dies or is abusive.[47] Although these few additional benefits would have cost the city nothing to implement, they raised a hornet's nest of traditionalist opposition to the domestic partnership bill that had been introduced by John Wilson, Chair of the D.C. Council. Not only did the Council fail to add the suggested benefits, but it felt compelled to change the whole presentation of the bill. Its title was changed from the proposed "Domestic Partnership Act" to the "Health Care Benefits Extension Act," and the bill was expanded to include health care benefits for pairs of blood relatives, such as an elderly woman and her niece or nephew. After the Council passed this desexualized law in 1992,[48] Congress responded to TFV complaints that the new law would "devalu[e] marriage" and "officially recognize and santion homosexual unions"[49] by prohibiting the District from funding the law.[50] The politics of preservation was a mighty force in 1992.

THE POLITICS OF RECOGNITION BREAKS THROUGH: THE HAWAII SAME-SEX MARRIAGE DECISIONS

Domestic partnership was a potentially attractive starting point for a gay politics of transformation: it recognized the existence and worth of nontraditional families, eased some of the legal discrimination between married and cohabiting couples, and was generally a step toward a liberal, free-choice regime for family law. Although domestic partnership was a small step in the politics of recognition as well, it was hardly satisfying to most lesbian and gay couples who wanted to marry. Thousands of same-sex couples registered—as did many more different-sex couples—but for most committed couples domestic partnership only whetted their appetite for the marriage option. For some, marriage was essential because it offered so many more benefits than the paltry few in domestic partnerships. The famous case of Sharon Kowalski illustrated the risks same-sex couples ran: for years after she was incapacitated in an auto accident, her blood family was able to prevent Karen Thompson, Sharon's life partner, from giving her the only care and therapy that worked for her partial recovery.[51] Municipalities could not provide this kind of legal protection; it was only available through state guardianship, and would be provided as a matter of course if same-sex marriages were recognized.

For others, domestic partnership was an empty option because it did not entail obligations of mutual support or even commitment; exiting a domestic partnership was as easy as filling out a form. Many couples wanted to signal their commitment to one another through marriage. Moreover, the lesbian baby boom of the 1980s, and the smaller "gayby boom" among men, fueled a desire for the *family* commitment often entailed in marriage. When Nina Beck fell in love with Stacy Jolles in 1989, she had changed her mind about marriage: not only had the institution changed in response to feminist criticism, but Nina had changed.[52] She and Stacy (another former radical lesbian) not only wanted to commit to one another, but also to children they would raise jointly; both felt that the legal as well as moral obligations of marriage would signal and cement their mutual commitment. They realized, of course, that same-sex marriage was probably a pipe dream. That changed with a same-sex marriage lawsuit in Hawaii.

POLITICS AND LAW IN THE HAWAII SAME-SEX MARRIAGE LAWSUIT

Ninia Baehr and Genora Dancel of Honolulu, Hawaii, were appalled that their relationship was treated as second class by the state, and a friend told them about William Woods. Woods, the executive director of the Gay Community Center in Honolulu, had been pressing both local and national gay leaders on the issue throughout the 1980s, with mixed success.[53] Woods urged Baehr and Dancel to go to court. After being declined representation by the Hawaii branch of the American Civil Liberties Union (ACLU), Woods persuaded local attorney Dan Foley (who had been affiliated with ACLU-Hawaii) to represent Baehr and Dancel, as well as two other same-sex couples. On May 1, 1991, the three couples sued the state for marriage licenses. Five months earlier, Craig Dean and Patrick Gill had sued the District of Columbia for similar discrimination.* These lawsuits triggered a decade's worth of soul-searching by the gayocracy, the judiciary, and the political process all over the nation.

When the first wave of same-sex marriage lawsuits had been filed, there were no national gaylegal organizations. When this next round of suits were filed, there were at least two—the ACLU's Gay and Lesbian Rights Project and the Lambda Legal Defense and Education Fund—but neither played a positive role in the initiation of those lawsuits. Paula

---

★ Although not involved in Dean and Gill's decision to file their complaint on November 26, 1990, I was enlisted by the Gay and Lesbian Lawyers of Washington (GAYLAW) to represent Dean and Gill during the litigation. The plaintiff's compaint was dimmsed by Judge Shellie Bowers on December 30, 1991. A panel of the District of Columbia Court of Appeals affirmed, over the dissent of Judge John Ferren. See *Dean v. District of Columbia*, 653 A.2d 307 (D.C. 1995).

Ettelbrick, Lambda's legal director, believed that marriage was too patriarchal an institution and urged lesbians and gays to create better ones for fostering their unions.[54] Tom Stoddard, Lambda's executive director, believed that gay people should have all the same rights—including marriage-related ones—as straight people,[55] but worried that the Hawaii and D.C. lawsuits were coming too early. The national ACLU had the same concerns. Given the continuing strength of the TFV movement, or the "Religious Right," as journalists called it, the organizations' concerns were not unfounded. But, as Lambda and the ACLU learned, the national organizations could not always control local activists who insisted on their equality rights. Hence, Baehr and Dancel (the Hawaii case) and Dean and Gill (the D.C. case) filed their lawsuits without any support from the national organizations—and stimulated the imaginations of thousands of same-sex couples who chafed at the disrespect shown by the law to their relationships, unions, and (in their eyes) marriages.

In the wake of *Bowers v. Hardwick*,[56] in which the U.S. Supreme Court had ruled that the Constitution's right to privacy was not violated when states made private "homosexual sodomy" between consenting adults a felony, the second wave of same-sex marriage lawsuits like the one in Hawaii did not press claims under the U.S. Constitution. (People have rights under both the U.S. Constitution and state constitutions. Therefore, if the U.S. Constitution does not protect gay people against state invasions of their privacy, the state constitution might yet be construed to provide such protection.) Although *Hardwick* did not address equal protection claims by gay people, its rhetorical hostility and dramatic holding discouraged such claims: If the state can put a lesbian in jail as a felon for consensual intimacy with another woman, can it not refuse to recognize their romantic partnership as a marriage? Notwithstanding his careful avoidance of a federal claim, Foley did deploy earlier federal precedents as conceptual support for his clients' claims under the Hawaii state constitution. His main argument was that the same-sex marriage bar violated plaintiffs' fundamental right to marry. This was a stronger argument in the 1990s than it had been in the 1970s, because the U.S. Supreme Court had read the right quite broadly.[57] In *Zablocki v. Redhail*, the Court extended *Loving*'s reasoning to hold that deadbeat dads were denied equal protection of the laws when the state refused to allow them to remarry. The Court held that no state restriction of the "'freedom of personal choice in matters of marriage and family life'" can be sustained under the equal protection clause unless the state can show that its restriction is narrowly drawn to serve a compelling social purpose.[58] Just a few years before the Hawaii lawsuit, in *Turner v. Safley*, the U.S. Supreme Court had extended *Loving* to protect the right to marry of state prisoners.[59] The Court's articulation of the right to marry emphasized the unitive rather than procreative goals of marriage. Even prisoners who could not sexually consummate their marriages could derive myriad spiritual and legal benefits from such unions, including "expressions of emotional support and public commitment," "spiritual significance," and "government benefits" such as social security and property rights.[60] Foley argued that Hawaii's privacy and equality jurisprudence recognized a right to marry at least as broad as the federal constitutional right, and that committed lesbian and gay couples had as much of a right to marry as convicted felons did.

Although Foley did not invoke the Hawaii junior-ERA to make the sex discrimination argument for same-sex marriage, he did argue that the same-sex marriage bar was an unconstitutional sexual orientation discrimination. In 1988, two federal judges had ruled that sexual orientation is "like" race for equal protection purposes: it is a fundamental feature of one's hard-to-change identity that has been unfairly penalized by the state in the past and rarely if ever forms the basis for rational state policy.[61] Foley argued that Hawaiian equal protection jurisprudence ought to consider sexual orientation a suspect classification, like race was, and that the gay and lesbian marriage bar was sexual orientation discrimination that was not justified by a compelling state interest.

The Judicial Response: Same-Sex Marriage

Foley's arguments did not prevail with the trial judge; making the same arguments, he filed an appeal to the Hawaii Supreme Court. On May 5, 1993, the court handed down its decision in *Baehr v. Lewin*.[62] To the surprise of the world, the court reversed the trial court's order dismissing the lawsuit and remanded for a factual hearing to determine whether the state could produce a compelling state interest justifying its discrimination against same-sex couples. To the surprise of the world and of the plaintiffs' counsel, Justice Steven Levinson's opinion for the Hawaii Supreme Court rejected the right-to-marry argument, declined to address the sexual orientation discrimination argument, and rested its judgment on an argument no party had raised: the state law was discrimination because of *sex*, which the equal rights amendment to the state constitution rendered just as suspect as race discrimination.[63]

Like other state constitutions but unlike the federal one, the Hawaii state constitution explicitly protects "the right of the people to privacy."[64] In construing that right, Hawaiian courts have generally followed the federal precedents, including *Loving* and *Zablocki*.[65] Justice Levinson explored the federal privacy precedents and found that they recognized a fundamental right to marry, but also that the right was intrinsically linked to procreation, childbirth, adoption, and child rearing. Hence, "the federal construct of the fundamental right to marry . . . presently contemplates unions between men and women."[66] Justice Levinson then concluded that the right of same-sex couples to marry was not sufficiently rooted in the nation's traditions to be added to the fundamental rights protected by Hawaii's privacy right. His opinion on this issue was both incomplete and circular. It was incomplete because it did not adequately consider *Turner v. Safley*'s articulation of the fundamental right to civil marriage as implicating *unitive* goals, without even mentioning its *procreative* or child-rearing goals (which would have been inapplicable to most of the prisoners).[67] The opinion was circular because it rejected the constitutional claim of right by accepting the state's definition of the right. When the Supreme Court decided *Loving*, it had never extended the right to marry to different-race couples, yet it would have been profoundly illogical to have ruled that the couple had no fundamental right because they had traditionally been denied it. *Baehr*'s holding rested upon viewing the right to marry at a high level of specificity—Had this been the traditional nature of the right?—rather than more generally—Are these couples' mutual commitments similar enough to that of couples whose marriages the state has traditionally recognized?

Hawaii's Constitution also assures that "[n]o person shall . . . be denied the equal protection of the laws, nor denied the enjoyment of the person's civil rights or be discriminated against in the exercise thereof because of race, religion, sex, or ancestry."[68] Justice Levinson started with the proposition that Baehr and Dancel's "civil right" to marry had been denied—a holding in tension with the first part of his opinion. He then ruled that the civil right had been denied "because of . . . sex." As scholars had previously recognized, the analytical structure of part one of *Loving* supported the argument that same-sex marriage bars are sex discrimination: the state's different treatment of white-black and black-black couples is race-based discrimination, because the regulatory variable, the item that changes the legal treatment, is the *race* of one of the partners; similarly, the state's different treatment of female-female and female-male couples is sex-based discrimination, because the regulatory variable, the item that change the legal treatment, is the *sex* of one of the partners.[69] Levinson rejected the state's argument that it was denying this civil right because of "the couple's biologic inability as a couple" to procreate (and not because of sex). This argument was "circular," Levinson concluded. Ironically, the state's argument against the sex discrimination claim was circular in the same way that Levinson's argument against the right to marry claim was circular: both the state and Levinson rejected rights claims by narrowly characterizing the rights at stake.

Justice Levinson's opinion in *Baehr v. Lewin* was very bold but not all that bold. It was very bold as the first judicial decision in this country that even questioned the state's long-standing exclusion of same-sex couples from civil marriage. It was also very bold in accepting the sex discrimination argument, revealing Levinson's deep appreciation of feminist theory as well as an open mind about gay marriage. Yet the opinion was timid in rejecting the right to marry argument. Probably, the reason for this timidity was the fear of a Pandora's box. If the right to marry were fundamental, the court would open the door to polygamists, brothers and sisters, and so forth. (All these cases could be decided the state's way, in my view.) By deciding the matter on the basis of the regulatory classification (sex) rather than the fundamental civil right (marriage), the court's holding could not be deployed by other potential litigants, for the regulatory classifications they objected to would be numerosity (polygamists) or blood relation (incest), neither of which was a suspect classification for equal protection purposes.

The Hawaii Supreme Court was unbold in another way: it did not assure Baehr and Dancel a marriage license, because the justices remanded the case for trial on the state's justifications for the discrimination. No one thought the state could meet the requirements imposed by Justice Levinson: the marriage law is "presumed to be unconstitutional" unless the state can show that "(a) the statute's sex-based classification is justified by compelling state interests and (b) the statute is narrowly drawn to avoid unnecessary abridgments of the applicant couples' constitutional rights."[70] The remand served the practical function of giving the state political process an opportunity to react—perhaps by amending the marriage law to include same-sex couples, perhaps by amending the constitution to allow discrimination—before any judgment was reached in the courts. As set out below, the legislature, after much pulling and hauling, reaffirmed one-man, one-woman marriage and created a new institution for lesbian and gay couples.

The *Baehr* case went to trial in September 1996. The state had initially suggested a number of policies that might be advanced by excluding same-sex couples from marriage,[71] including

- "a compelling [s]tate interest in fostering procreation" because "same sex couples cannot, as between them, conceive children" and, in any event, "a child is best parented by its biological parents living in a single household";
- "same-sex couples will have disproportionate incentives to move to and/or remain in Hawaii," which would "distort the job and housing markets" and "alter the State of Hawaii's desirability as a visitor destination";
- "allowing same sex couples to marry conveys in socially, psychologically, and otherwise important ways approval of non-heterosexual orientations and behaviors."

At trial, however, the only justification for which the state produced evidence was that children were best raised in families where there were a mother and father, each of whom was the biological parent of the children.[72] The state presented several expert witnesses who testified about the advantages of such a family for children, but on cross-examination the state's own witnesses cheerfully conceded that lesbian and gay couples can and often do just as good a job raising children.

On December 3, 1996, Judge Kevin Chang ruled that the state had not met its burden of justifying the marriage law discrimination.[73] Judge Chang found that the state had presented no colorable evidence to support any of the proffered justifications—except the argument that the exclusion of same-sex couples from marriage was needed to protect the health and welfare of children. The judge's written opinion examined the testimony of each witness and concluded, as a matter of fact, that "[g]ay and lesbian couples and same-sex couples can be as fit and loving parents, as non-gay men and women and different-sex couples."[74] Contrary to the state, "if same-sex marriage is allowed, the children being raised by gay or lesbian parents and same-sex couples may be assisted, because they may obtain certain protections and benefits that come with or become available as a result of marriage."[75] Judge Chang entered judgment for the plaintiffs and granted their injunction directing the state to cease its discrimination against same-sex couples.

As a routine matter, Judge Chang stayed his injunction pending the state's appeal. Notwithstanding its provisional nature, his order outraged the most devout opponents of same-sex marriage. The Reverend Louis Sheldon, founder of the Traditional Values Coalition, termed it "judicial tyranny. . . . They have stolen marriage." His view that the decision was "our Pearl Harbor" was echoed by representatives of the Christian Coalition, the Hawaii Catholic Conference, the American Muslim Council, Evangelicals for Social Action, and the Church of Jesus Christ of Latter-Day Saints.[76]

The Legislative Response: Reciprocal Beneficiaries, Not Marriage

Soon after the Hawaii Supreme Court decision in *Baehr*, the Hawaii legislature responded with a law reaffirming marriage as intrinsically between a man and a woman and denouncing the court's decision as usurpative judicial policymaking.[77] The next year the legislature created a Commission on Sexual Orientation and the Law to advise the state as to how it should treat same-sex couples as a matter of policy.[78] In 1995, after months of intense fact-finding, the commission concluded that lesbian and gay relationships were productive and worthy of state encouragement for the same reason that straight relationships were. Accordingly, the majority recommended that the legislature extend marriage to same-sex couples or, in the alternative, to create a comprehensive rights-and-duties regime of domestic partnership.[79] Two dissenting members urged the legislature to do nothing or to extend only a few specific benefits to same-sex couples.[80] They objected that "[h]omosexual rights are not civil rights," and they were "concerned about the adverse effect legalizing homosexual marriage will have on the social, sexual and psychological development of children." The position of the dissenters was taken up by at least two religious-based groups organized at about the same time: Hawaii Future Today, formed by the Roman Catholic and Mormon Churches, and Alliance for Traditional Marriage, created by fundamentalist Protestants.

The Hawaii legislature was torn between the desire to accommodate GLBT people, a group loyal to the ruling Democratic Party, and fears of a voter backlash. In 1996, the state Senate passed a domestic partnership bill patterned on that proposed (as an alternative) by the commission, but the House took no action. Opening the 1997 session, House Speaker Joe Souki announced that he would push for both a constitutional amendment to take the issue away from the courts and a statute assuring same-sex couples some of the state benefits and rights afforded married couples. On January 21, the House Judiciary Committee followed the speaker's directive, by reporting H.B. 117 (the constitutional amendment) and H.B. 118 (a bill providing a short list of benefits to *reciprocal beneficiaries*). In the next month, the state Senate offered its own compromise by passing a bill proposing a constitutional amendment allowing the state to reserve marriage to different-sex couples, provided that "the laws of the state ensure that the application of this reservation does not deprive any person of civil rights on the basis of sex." To assure that equality, the Senate also passed a bill creating a new *life partnership* institution with almost all the benefits and obligations of marriage for same-sex couples. At this point, the Senate was insisting on legislation similar to that proposed (as a fallback) by the commission, while the House was insisting on legislation like that outlined in the commission's minority report. The two chambers conferenced during March and April but did not reach agreement until April 16, 1997. Under the compromise, the legislature placed on the November 1998 ballot a proposal to amend the state constitution "to clarify that the legislature has the power to reserve marriage to opposite-sex couples,"[81] and enact a new statute extending "certain rights and benefits . . . to couples composed of two individuals who are legally prohibited from marrying under state law (same-sex couples and blood relatives)."[82]

The House bill was the template for the latter statute, and it was titled the Reciprocal Beneficiaries Act. Adults who were excluded from the marriage law either because they were too closely related or because they were considered to be of the same sex could choose to form a mutually beneficial partnership by filing a form with the state whereby the two parties affirmed that they wanted to be treated as *reciprocal beneficiaries*.[83] Reciprocal beneficiaries would enjoy about fifty of the more than two hundred rights and benefits enjoyed by married couples. They include the following:

- for state and municipal employees, rights to have reciprocal beneficiaries treated like spouses for purposes of health care benefits (for an experimental two-year period), as well as for funeral leave, moving expenses, pension and accidental death benefits;[84]
- worker's compensation benefits in the event of the reciprocal beneficiary's death on the job,[85] as well as the right to collect wages, sick leave, and vacation owed by an employer to one's reciprocal beneficiary at the time of her death;[86]
- the right to take time off from work to care for a reciprocal beneficiary (family leave);[87]
- rights to visit one's co-beneficiary in the hospital and to make health care decisions in case of her incapacity and anatomical gifts in the event of her death;[88]
- notice of and a right to be heard in proceedings for civil commitment of one's reciprocal beneficiary;[89]
- the right to own property as tenants in the entirety, where the parties each enjoy complete ownership just as married spouses do;[90]
- rights to an elective share and (in some cases) avoidance of probate in the event of the death of one's reciprocal beneficiary, again like the death of a spouse;[91]

- assurance that life insurance benefits will be paid to a reciprocal beneficiary upon the death of her insured partner;[92]
- the right to bring a wrongful death lawsuit for loss of care, support, attention, and counsel of one's reciprocal beneficiary;[93]
- exemption from paying a state transfer tax when conveying property between reciprocal beneficiaries (as between spouses);[94]
- protection under the state victim's rights laws the same as that given spouses;[95] and
- protection against domestic abuse.[96]

The reciprocal beneficiary law offered many more benefits and rights than domestic partnership ordinances did (or could offer so long as they were adopted at the municipal rather than state level). In fact, as of 1997, this was the most far-reaching state recognition of same-sex unions ever adopted by an American legislature—and by a wide margin.

Yet the compromise measure was not acceptable to the lesbians, gay men, and their allies involved in the *Baehr* litigation. Not only were reciprocal beneficiaries afforded fewer rights and benefits than married couples, but (like domestic partners) they were subject to no duties and responsibilities entailed in the commitment of two people to one another. The law provided no obligations of mutual support, and made dissolution of the reciprocal relationship as easy as filling out a form. The legislative compromise, in some respects, infantilized lesbian and gay couples, treating them as only interested in the goodies and not in the serious obligations of partnership. The statute was a denigrating response in another way: not only did the legislature implicitly follow the disparaging logic of the minority report of the Commission on Sexual Orientation and the Law and treat lesbian and gay couples as unworthy of marriage, but it insisted on lumping their relationships with the sexless ones of blood relatives who depended on one another for medical care and the like. In short, the reciprocal beneficiaries law gave the *Baehr* plaintiffs no reason to abandon their trial court judgment on appeal. Knowing that a referendum on the legislature's proposed constitutional amendment was ahead, plaintiffs' attorneys Dan Foley and Evan Wolfson pressed on.

THE POLITICS OF PRESERVATION STRIKES BACK:
DOMA AND STATE RESPONSES TO THE HAWAII SAME-SEX
MARRIAGE DECISIONS

Baehr was a great gaylegal victory. But it provoked the biggest antigay backlash since the McCarthy era. After *Baehr*, an issue that had been a curiosity became an apolcalyptic sensation. Traditionalist talk shows, pundits, and politicians roasted same-sex marriage as the next step in the nation's trek toward Sodom and Gomorrah. Some critics made open appeals to antigay feelings: homosexuals were biblical "abominations" and should not be given any "special rights." Other critics bemoaned same-sex marriage for its promotion of homosexuality at the expense of traditionalist marriage. Even the mildest critics made insulting arguments that invoked the worst stereotypes about lesbians and gay men: If two women can marry, why can't I marry my cat?[97] Once two women can be married, why not a man and a harem of women? The public ate up these arguments like famished dieters, and polls consistently showed large majorities of Americans firmly opposed to state recognition of same-sex marriages and unwilling to consider arguments to the contrary.

As the Hawaii courts moved toward their seemingly inevitable conclusion that the state would have to start issuing marriage licenses to lesbian and gay couples, the politics of preservation became a stampede to isolate that state and its judiciary. Hard cases make bad constitutional law—but really bad laws can *un*make constitutional principle. And that is what happened after 1993. In a stunning statutory moment, Congress and the President ignored two hundred years of understanding about full faith and credit and one hundred years of thinking about equal protection to enact the most sweeping antigay law in the nation's history. In a dramatic constitutional moment, the Hawaii Supreme Court backed down in the face of overwhelming popular opposition to same-sex marriage.

State Nonrecognition Laws and the Full Faith and Credit Clause

If same-sex marriage was on the horizon in Hawaii, it might spread to other jurisdictions, in the following way: a same-sex couple married in Hawaii might move to state A and insist that state A recognize their marriage, or a same-sex couple residing in state A might fly to Hawaii to be married and then demand that state A recognize their marriage. Most states follow the celebration rule, recognizing any out-of-state marriage and enforcing its benefits and obligations so long as the marriage was valid in the state of celebration.[98] The celebration rule encourages the foregoing strategy, but virtually all the states recognize exceptions to the rule. Some states have evasion statutes, providing that courts shall not recognize the marriages of state residents who travel to another state to evade the home state's marriage exclusions. Most states will not recognize out-of-state marriages contrary to the state's public policy.[99]

With same-sex marriage on the horizon, and with Lambda openly calling for lesbian and gay couples to travel to Hawaii to get married and then seek recognition of those marriages in their home states, a politics of preservation raised the alarm, in every state of the nation, that Hawaii would export same-sex marriage to that state. TFV groups, especially churches, urged legislative preemptive strikes to head off the possibility that a single same-sex marriage would ever be recognized. The analogy is this: same-sex marriage is like the flu virus; get vaccinated now, before the virus starts spreading. To head off this kind of infectious civil rightsism, traditionalist legislators introduced bills against same-sex marriage in virtually every state legislature; legislators all over the country were inundated with letters, postcards, and phone calls from people panicked at the possibility of same-sex marriages in their states, with little or no effective counter from lesbian and gay people; and such bills rolled through most legislatures like a hot knife through butter, as liberal and moderate legislators ran for cover. Within months of the first *Baehr* decision, Utah amended its marriage law to provide that marriages "between persons of the same sex" are "prohibited and declared void."[100] This *definition of marriage* statute was similar to those adopted in the 1970s, when the issue was first being litigated. Within two years of the decision, Utah further amended its marriage law to direct that its state courts will not recognize same-sex marriages entered into elsewhere.[101] Utah's 1995 law was the first *nonrecognition* statute aimed only at same-sex marriage, but it was by no means the last.

Between 1995 and 2001, thirty-four states joined Utah in legislating against recognition of same-sex marriages in their courts.* The statutory responses took a variety of forms. Most jurisdictions followed the Utah approach of simply directing that same-sex marriages were invalid in their states and would not be recognized.[102] Some states went further. Following Utah, Virginia augmented its 1975 law prohibiting same-sex marriage with a new nonrecognition law, but the nonrecognition law was broader than Utah's: "Any marriage entered into by persons of the same sex in another state or jurisdiction shall be void in all respects in Virginia and any contractual rights created by such marriage shall be void and unenforceable." Michigan defined marriage as an "inherently unique relationship between a man and a woman," prohibited same-sex marriages (in the same provisions where it barred incestuous marriages), and laid out in detail the state's "special interest in encouraging, supporting, and protecting that unique relationship in order to promote, among other goals, the stability and welfare of society and its children,"[103] but in the end adopted a nonrecognition rule much like Utah's: "marriage between a man and a woman is invalid in this state regardless of whether the marriage is contracted according to the laws of another jurisdiction."[104] The most elaborate response was Georgia's, which not only defined marriage to be inherently different-sex and prohibited any kind of legal recognition of same-sex marriages, but tried to nail down any possible evasion. It reads, "No marriage between persons of the same sex shall be recognized as entitled to the benefits of marriage. Any marriage entered into by persons of the same sex pursuant to a marriage license issued by another state or foreign jurisdiction or otherwise shall be void in this state. Any contractual rights granted by virtue of such license shall be unenforceable

---

★ State with nonrecognition statutes, as of September 1, 2001, are (with the date of enactment): Alabama (1998), Alaska (1996), Arizona (1996), Arkansas (1997), California (2000), Colorado (2000), Delaware (1996), Florida (1997), Georgia (1996), Idaho (1996), Illinois (1996), Indiana (1997), Iowa (1998), Kansas (1996), Kentucky (1998), Louisiana (1996), Maine (1997), Michigan (1996), Minnesota (1997), Mississippi (1997), Missouri, (1997) Montana (1997), Nebraska (2000), North Carolina (1995), North Dakota (1997), Oklahoma (1996), Pennsylvania (1996), South Carolina (1996), South Dakota (1996), Tennessee (1996), Texas (2000), Utah (1995), Virginia (1997), Washington (1998), and West Virginia (2000). Most of these states also have definition of marriage statutes, usually adopted in the same legislation. Hawaii in 1994 adopted a definition statute, but did not adopt a nonrecognitionl law.

in the courts of this state and the courts of this state shall have no jurisdiction whatsoever under any circumstances to grant a divorce or separate maintenance with respect to such marriage or otherwise to consider
or rule on any of the parties' respective rights arising as a result of or in
connection with such marriage."[105]

These statutes pose a variety of constitutional and interpretive problems. One problem relates to the *Loving* parallel: the laws are open discrimination on the basis of either sex or sexual orientation. Although
Baehr had accepted the sex discrimination argument, other states did
not take it seriously, nor did they think it conceivable that the U.S.
Supreme Court would accept that argument or ever strike down a law
discriminating on the basis of sexual orientation. *Hardwick* was read for
the notion that GLBT people were essentially outside the equal protection clause. In May 1996, the Supreme Court disabused the states of this
notion. The Court, in *Romer v. Evans,* ruled that an "unprecedented"
Colorado initiative depriving gay people of the protection of local
antidiscrimination ordinances violated the equal protection clause,
because the initiative was so broad in the disabilities it imposed on sexual minorities that it must have been motivated by antigay "animus,"
which the Court held to be an illegitimate state goal.[106] The scope of the
Court's ruling remains unclear, but at the very least it posed problems
for nonrecognition laws as broad as Georgia's, which (like the *Evans* initiative) was unprecedented and seemed to close off state courts to lesbian and gay couples in a limitless array of situations. Georgia could
argue that it only meant to protect marriage and not to express "animus" against GLBT people, but Colorado had made the same argument
without success in *Evans.*

A bigger problem for the nonrecognition statutes lay in the first sen-
tence of the U.S. Constitution's full faith and credit clause. (The clause
assures, "Full Faith and Credit shall be given in each State to the public
Acts, Records, and judicial Proceedings of every other State. And the
Congress may by general Laws prescribe the Manner in which such
Acts, Records, and Proceedings shall be proved, and the Effect thereof.")
Although the policy of the clause is to assure interstate harmony of
rights and obligations, it has not been interpreted to impose severe lim-
its on a state's ability to choose to apply its own over another state's *law*

in its own courts. The main limit imposed by the full faith and credit clause in these situations is that Georgia cannot impose its own law on same-sex couples if the state has no or virtually no interest in or contact with their controversy (aside from technically having personal jurisdiction over the parties).[107] The constitutional analysis changes significantly if Georgia refuses to enforce a Hawaii *judgment* imposing obligations on one party, such as alimony or child support, arising out of a same-sex marriage or its dissolution. The Supreme Court has ruled that the full faith and credit clause does require a state to recognize and enforce valid judgments entered by the courts of a sibling state, even where the legal conclusions underlying the judgment violate the state's public policy.[108] Thus, neither the Georgia statute nor any of the others I have quoted could constitutionally bar the use of a state's courts to enforce a judgment resting on a same-sex marriage.

A final uncertainty is that no one knows exactly how the different state courts will interpret their various nonrecognition statutes. Generally, a court must first determine whether its statute applies to a certain controversy before it will decide whether the law is constitutional, and most cases raising full faith and credit questions are resolved by narrow constructions of state statutes. Consider three fact situations:

1. Same-sex couple lawfully married in state A moves to state B. Partner 1 is killed through the negligence of a drunk driver. Partner 2 sues the driver for her emotional losses, which are allowed under the laws of state B only for spouses of victims. The driver argues that partner 2 is not a spouse.
2. The couple remain in state A but own property in state B. One partner dies without a will, and a probate judgment in state A determines that the surviving partner now owns the property in state B. Blood relatives of the deceased sue in state B to control the property under state B's intestacy laws.
3. The same-sex couple break up and enter into a separation agreement in state A; they later divorce. The separation agreement vests property in state B with partner 1. Partner 2 reneges and sues in state B, on the ground that the property was hers and that the agreement is unenforceable in state B.

Assume that Utah, Virginia, and Georgia are each "state B" for purposes of these examples, and assume that the serious equal protection problems with the statutes are not in play. The state courts in Utah, Virginia, and Georgia would very likely interpret the nonrecognition laws of their respective states to protect the drunk driver in case 1, and the full faith and credit clause (as it has thus far been construed) would pose no bar to such constructions. Case 2 is probably also an easy call: because the full faith and credit clause requires enforcement of interstate judgments, all three states would probably interpret their nonrecognition statutes to be no bar to the enforcement of the state A judgment winding up the estate. Any other result would be a recipe for interstate chaos.

Case 3 is the hardest, because it does not involve an interstate judgment but does involve a contract and a relationship that ought to be governed by the laws of state A; application of state B's law would be an intrusion by state B into the legal relationship created by state A. The Utah nonrecognition statute does not seem to cover case 3, and its courts should not extend the law to it. The Virginia and Georgia nonrecognition statutes seem applicable, on their face; the Georgia law seems tailored to this specific case. But courts in those states might still enforce the separation agreement under state law. Both states follow the choice of law rule that courts in contract cases should apply the law where the contract was made; when the contracting parties are also domiciliaries of the state where the contract was made, this result becomes compelling under most choice of law theories. Hence, in case 3, the nonrecognition statutes clash strongly with an entrenched choice of law rule, and judges might well follow the old rule in that case. This would be particularly appropriate if the judges feared that following the nonrecognition law would violate the full faith and credit clause—and well it might. Any choice of law rule that permits the forum court to prefer its own law to the law of the parties' domicile state, simply because the forum prefers its policy over the policy of the domicile state, is at odds with the policy of the full faith and credit clause.[109] Nonetheless, it is unpredictable how broadly Virginia or Georgia courts will apply their nonrecognition laws; because they are broadly worded statutes, judges might read them to override all other choice of law rules. This indeterminacy is not only inconsistent with federalism and full faith and credit, but also undermines the rule of law, for it makes the partners' legal status highly uncertain. "If there is any one thing that the people are entitled to expect from their lawmakers, it is rules of law that will enable individuals to tell whether they are married and, if so, to whom."[110]

These kinds of arguments were made in Utah and other states adopting nonrecognition laws, but legislators' rush to enact the laws—usually with only perfunctory public hearings and legislative debate—rendered them nothing more than road bumps. Nonetheless, TFV groups were aware of the choice of law problems raised by these statutes, especially the broader ones like the Virginia and Georgia laws. Accordingly, they sought a national solution. They found one in the spring of 1996, when the Republican Party seized upon Hawaii same-sex marriages (still on the horizon) as a wedge issue in their battle to recapture the White House.

The Federal Defense of Marriage Act

In May 1996, after effectively locking up the Republican nomination for president, U.S. Senate Majority Leader Robert Dole joined other senators in introducing S. 1740, the Defense of Marriage Act (DOMA); a parallel bill, H.R. 3336, was introduced in the House by Representative Robert Barr and others. The bill was simple. Section 2 provided that no state would be required to give full faith and credit to "any public act, record, or judicial proceeding of any other State . . . respecting a relationship between persons of the same sex that is treated as a marriage under the laws of such other State . . . or a right or claim arising from such relationship."[111] Section 3 defined the term *marriage*, for purposes of federal statutory and agency law, to mean "only a legal union between one man and one woman as husband and wife," and the term *spouse* to mean only "a person of the opposite sex who is a husband or a wife."[112] President William Clinton immediately signed onto the bill, depriving it of its partisan wedge value, but a bipartisan coalition pushed it speedily through Congress anyway—and over dispositive constitutional objections.

Section 2 of DOMA was unnecessary or, if necessary, unconstitutional.[113] It was unnecessary to the extent the various state nonrecognition laws were valid choice of law statutes, as they would be in situations like case 1 described earlier. To the extent those laws were themselves in violation of sentence one of the full faith and credit clause (quoted earlier), as they would be as regards enforcement of judgments, my case 2, they could not be saved by Congress pursuant to sentence two, its power to "prescribe the Effect" of state acts, records, and judicial proceedings. The drafting history of the full faith and credit clause suggests that the prescribe-effect sentence had as its only purpose the *effect*uation of interstate recognition, consistent with the overall goal of the clause to assure nationwide portability of judgments and other vested rights.[114] No one said it would allow the legislature to dilute the protections of the first sentence. That the prescribe-effect sentence served facilitative purposes is reinforced by the first federal statutes to be adopted, one in 1790 and the other in 1804; both laws merely provided for means of authenticating legislative acts and proving judicial proceedings.[115]

Surely dispositive is the constitutional language itself: if the framers meant to authorize Congress to subtract from rather than *effect*uate the first sentence, they would have drafted the clause the way they drafted Article III, section 2, which gives the Supreme Court appellate jurisdiction "with such Exceptions and under such Regulations as the Congress shall make." Conversely, compare the prescribe-effect sentence with Congress' powers under the Fourteenth Amendment. Section 1 of the Fourteenth Amendment assures all persons the equal protection of the laws; section 5 gives Congress "power to enforce, by appropriate legislation, the provisions of" the amendment. The Supreme Court has held that this enforcement power does not authorize Congress to derogate from or even to add to rights found (by the Court) in section 1.[116] Although the language of the prescribe-effect sentence is not the same as that of section 5, the differences are not material: if I tell you to "prescribe the effect" of my directive, that is no different from telling you to "enforce" the directive, and it is very different from telling you to "create exceptions" to my directive as you see fit. There is much greater textual and historical reason to read section 5 more liberally than the prescribe-effect sentence, and so it would be astounding if the Court did not give the latter at least as stingy a reading as it has recently given the former. Moreover, the same slippery slope concerns that impelled the

Court to give a narrow reading to section 5 augur more strongly against reading the prescribe-effect sentence broadly. Surely Congress cannot prescribe the effect of the full faith and credit clause by legislating that Hawaii judgments should be given less dispositive effect than judgments from other states—yet that would be the sort of unfettered power that a broad reading of the sentence would allow.

Notwithstanding the foregoing constitutional problem, the Clinton Administration, in a letter declining to send a representative to the House DOMA hearing, opined that the measure "would be sustained as constitutional"—but without giving a sentence of reasoning.[117] Six days later, the U.S. Supreme Court decided *Romer v. Evans*. That decision raised serious questions about the constitutionality of DOMA's section 3, which negated possible federal benefits for same-sex married couples across the board—possibly the same kind of undifferentiated discrimination against GLBT people that *Evans* invalidated. The Court's decision also raised some question about the constitutionality of section 2, which seemed like an overwrought reaction to a problem that had not materialized and that if it did materialize would be handled easily enough by the courts, as outlined above. As Andrew Koppelman has demonstrated, *Evans* creates constitutional difficulties for the whole DOMA enterprise.[118] The public justifications for the bill did not fully resolve those difficulties.

In the wake of *Evans*, the U.S. House Judiciary Committee and the bill's sponsors sought to defuse potential equal protection issues by establishing neutral bases for DOMA. To begin with, the committee posited that the federal government has "an interest in maintaining and protecting the institution of heterosexual marriage because it has a deep and abiding interest in encouraging responsible procreation and child-rearing."[119] The committee failed to acknowledge that millions of lesbian and gay partnerships rear children who would benefit from the additional security state-enforced marital obligations would bring to their families.[120] As the committee's report went on, the parents-with-children objective morphed into an argument that marriage was an imperiled institution needing defense from gay rights groups, who were prepared to flood Hawaii with same-sex couples who would then demand recognition of their marriages from sister states. This was a major theme of the House debates. Representative Barney Frank, an opponent of the bill, asked Representative Steve Largent, a sponsor, whether *his* marriage was threatened by the Hawaii litigation. Largent responded that it was not, but that "the institution of marriage" was![121] Largent never identified precisely how marriage was threatened by adding more couples, nor did other legislative supporters or the committee's report.[122]

In my view, the concern of traditionalists such as Largent was that marriage has been weakened by *liberalization*, the trend toward legal accommodation of free choice, such as rules allowing cohabitation and no-fault divorce. Allowing cohabitation undermines marriage by providing an alternate institution for partnering; given the alternative, fewer couples will marry. No-fault divorce undermines marriage by making exit easier; hence, more married couples will break up. Traditionalists were frustrated because they could not roll back these disastrous liberalizations. Allowing same-sex couples to marry was a liberalization they could stop, and so they focused their concerns on that issue. But this is discordant with their stated goal of protecting marriage: admitting same-sex couples into the institution would in the short term strengthen marriage, as it would add new and enthusiastic recruits; it is highly doubtful that same-sex marriage would scare away potential straight couples. By seeking to cement the exclusion of same-sex couples from marriage, the proponents of DOMA were performing a drama whereby gay people were being scapegoated for the decline of marriage for these other reasons or, worse, were being demonized in the name of partisan gain.[123] DOMA was a much better example of antigay "animus" than the Colorado amendment that the Supreme Court invalidated in *Evans*.

"Closely related to this interest in protecting traditional marriage is a corresponding interest in promoting heterosexuality," the House Judiciary Committee opined.[124] This was a deeper reason for the bill. "Civil laws that permit only heterosexual marriage reflect and honor a collective moral judgment about human sexuality. This judgment entails both moral disapproval of homosexuality, and a moral conviction that heterosexuality better comports with traditional (especially Judeo-Christian) morality."[125] This justification paralleled one presented by the state in the *Evans* case: by excluding gay men, bisexuals, and lesbians from the protection of antidiscrimination laws, Colorado claimed it was making a moral judgment denigrating homosexuality. Justice Antonin Scalia agreed with Colorado's argument and maintained that a state ought to be able to tolerate "homosexuals" while at the same time sending signals that their condition is morally degraded. Scalia's view was the minority one in *Evans*, however. The majority of the Court held that imposing a broad array of disabilities on gay people without sounder justification violates the equal protection clause. Especially when the antigay signal is as loosely or even perversely tied to state policy (protecting marriage) as the DOMA sponsors' statements suggest, this kind of argument seems like the kind of "animus" that *Evans* ruled unconstitutional.

On the floor of the House, the supporters recast the case for DOMA in "no promo homo" terms. As one representative put it, "homosexuals" were demanding much more than tolerance; they were "aiming for government and corporate mandated acceptance," which must be resisted because homosexuality is "inherently wrong and harmful to individuals, families, and societies."[126] According to Representative Charles Canady, a key question was "whether the law in this country should treat homosexual relations as morally equivalent to heterosexual relations." He thought not and posed the killer question, "Should this Congress tell the children of America that it is a matter of indifference whether they establish families with a partner of the opposite sex or cohabit with someone of the same sex?" He liked this way of putting it so much he "reportedly" uttered exactly the same quoted language on two successive days of debate.[127] The same no promo homo theme also received some verbal support in the Senate debates: "[W]hen we prefer traditional marriage and family in our law, it is not intolerance. Tolerance does not require us to say that all lifestyles are morally equal."[128]

There were some other purported justifications for the bill, but the no promo homo reason was the most plausible one given by DOMA's sponsors. While the state surely does have a fair leeway to discourage certain ways of life and activities (like smoking), the no promo homo rationale does not, as a matter of logic, save DOMA. To begin with, the state cannot take away fundamental liberties in order to promote favored lifestyles. It can deploy advertisements to warn teenagers about the dangers of smoking, but it cannot forbid smokers from getting married, even if that were a more effective way of deterring smoking. The Supreme Court in *Turner v. Safley* ruled that the state cannot even adopt a per se rule against allowing convicted felons to marry while they are in prison. Moreover, as I have argued in detail elsewhere, the no promo homo argument against same-sex marriage is incoherent except as a direct status denigration of GLBT people, which would violate *Evans*.[129] That is, there is no reliable evidence that denying GLBT people the right to marry will have any of the effects traditionalists suggest—such as more teenagers "choosing" homosexuality (there is no evidence that sexual orientation is a conscious choice) or engaging in homosexual conduct (same-sex marriage would carry a fidelity requirement that ought to diminish such conduct). Thus, no promo homo arguments against same-sex marriage boil down to arguments that gay people are and ought to be second-class citizens. The Supreme Court opened its opinion in *Evans* with its answer to that kind of argument: "One century ago, the first Justice Harlan admonished this Court that the Constitution 'neither knows nor tolerates classes among its citizens.'"[130]

The gentle reader may gasp at this sweeping a conclusion, but the most serious speech of the DOMA debate went even further. Representative John Lewis, one of America's most distinguished civil rights leaders, listened to the debate and observed, "[T]his is a mean bill. [It] seeks to divide our nation. . . . I have known racism. [This] bill stinks of the same fear, hatred and intolerance."[131] DOMA supporters insisted that the bill did not reflect prejudice or bigotry, but they never explained exactly how same-sex marriage would destroy marriage, why other more tangible dangers to marriage were not being tackled before this hypothetical one, and why every single federal law or rule mentioning spouse or marriage had to be yoked to the same antigay policy. (For example, DOMA affects federal conflict of interest laws which direct that a federal official must recuse herself from decisions where her spouse, as well as she, has an interest in the matter. This sensible rule of governance should surely apply to same-sex spouses as well as different-sex ones.) That the bill was rushed through both chambers of Congress, with perfunctory hearings and little if any scholarly basis for the full faith and credit provision, in an election year, is further evidence supporting Representative Lewis's charge.

The supporters' own language further corroborates the Lewis understanding, for the debates were filled with appeals to unfounded antigay stereotypes. Representative Barr, the chief DOMA sponsor in the House, opened the second day of the House debate with this alarm: the "flames of hedonism, flames of narcissism, the flames of self-centered morality are licking at the very foundation of our society: the family unit."[132] Representative Tom Coburn supported DOMA because his constituents felt "homosexuals" are "immoral" and "promiscuous." The issue, he said, "is not diversity"—the issue is "perversity." He warned of the social consequences of homosexuality and the "perversion" it brings.[133] These and other statements were open appeals to false stereotypes about GLBT people: not only are lesbians the least "promiscuous" group in the country, and gay people no more "hedonistic" than straight people, but there is no basis for saying GLBT people are "perverse" except for sectarian interpretations of isolated religious texts. Opening the Senate debate, Senator Robert Byrd urged that DOMA was an emergency measure because of the concerted campaign by homosexuals to force same-sex marriage upon the country.* This was followed by a diatribe on the immorality of homosexuality—a proposition for which Senator Byrd, like the House Judiciary Committee, cited only the Bible.[134] These features of the congressional debate render DOMA more questionable, in one respect, than was the Colorado initiative invalidated in *Evans*: the DOMA debates themselves reveal significant antigay "animus," whereas the Supreme Court had to infer animus from the breadth of the initiative in *Evans*; and the DOMA debates suggest that the measure was sectarian in a way that the Colorado initiative was not shown to be. Laws adopted to satisfy religious factions are in tension with the establishment clause of the First Amendment.[135]

Notwithstanding the foregoing constitutional problems, the Defense

---

★ In support of his alarm, Senator Byrd quoted page after page from my book, *The Case for Same-Sex Marriage* (1996), which argued for same-sex marriage as a matter of constitutional right as well as political justice. I was happy to see that he had read the book so carefully. But I was sad to find him so alarmed, for I grew up in West Virginia, and so he was my senator for years. When I graduated from high school, I received the first Robert Byrd Award, a U.S. Savings Bond for twenty-five dollars, which I still have.

of Marriage Act sailed through Congress by margins of 342 to 67 in the House and 85 to 14 in the Senate. DOMA was signed into law without a whimper by the President in a private ceremony.[136] After DOMA's enactment, more states enacted nonrecognition laws, which are now called "junior DOMAs." As of April 1, 2001, thirty-five states have such statutes (listed on page 38).

The Same-Sex Marriage Referenda in Hawaii and Alaska

As it was chalking up victories everywhere else, the politics of preservation was not idle in Hawaii. Within a year of DOMA, in the compromise legislation described in the previous part of this chapter, the Hawaii legislature voted to put on the November 1998 ballot a constitutional amendment to nullify Judge Chang's judgment in *Baehr*. (This was part of the compromise that added the reciprocal beneficiary provisions to Hawaii law.) The ballot question generated an intense political campaign, with around $1.5 million spent by each side and numerous debates and media advertisements.* The main advocate for the constitutional amendment was Michael Gabbard, the distinguished grayhaired founder of an organization called Stop Promoting Homosexuality (established in 1991) and of the Alliance for Traditional Marriage and Save Traditional Marriage 98. Although a follower of Krishna, Gabbard spoke for many Roman Catholics, fundamentalist Protestants, and Mormons in Hawaii when he outlined the philosophy underlying his campaigns against homosexuality as well as same-sex marriage: "One morning I woke up to a world in which an unnatural, unhealthy, immoral activity, which was taking thousands of lives, was being portrayed in the media as moral, natural, healthy and normal. I believe that all our problems—be they environmental, crime, health, economic, wars, etc.—can be traced to people holding on to and living by [a] hedonistic and therefore selfish world view. . . . This is why [homosexuality and same-sex marriage] is such an important issue to me."[137]

★ The Church of Jesus Christ of Latter-Day Saints—the Mormons—contributed about $600,000 to the campaign in favor of the ballot initiative. Funding for the opposition came largely from the Human Rights Campaign. Both organizations exist largely outside Hawaii.

Because polls consistently reported that large majorities of the electorate (usually about 70 percent) were opposed to same-sex marriage, there was little dramatic tension as regards the outcome of the referendum, but the rhetoric and argumentation were nonetheless that of a tremendous constitutional moment. Echoing the state's defense of its same-sex marriage exclusion and the minority report of the state commission, the main line of public and media argument for amending the constitution was consequentialist: "homosexual marriage" would bring ruin to Hawaii, and especially to its children. In one television ad, a boy was depicted reading a booklet, *Daddy's Wedding,* to another man; a voice then queried, "If you don't think homosexual marriage will affect you, how do you think it will affect your children?"[138] The discourse at the ground level was more openly moralistic. Typical argumentation among voters at the water cooler or lunch table, or from the church pulpit, involved direct appeals to a natural order. Wrote one voter as his reason for opposing same-sex marriage, "I think it's anti-Biblical, not allowed in the Bible."[139] Another: "God made the different sexes so marriage could be between one man and one woman. Socially, we're taught from childhood it's for a man and a woman."[140]

Most voters agreed with this kind of reasoning. In November 1998, with the *Baehr* appeal still pending, the electorate voted by a 69 to 28 percent majority (with 2 percent of the ballots blank or spoiled) to amend the constitution to add this sentence: "The legislature shall have the power to reserve marriage to opposite-sex couples."[141] In light of this constitutional amendment and the legislature's earlier statutory reaffirmations of the exclusion of same-sex couples, the Hawaii Supreme Court vacated Judge Chang's order and directed him to dismiss the lawsuit.[142] Although they had a colorable equal protection claim under *Evans,* plaintiffs and their counsel chose not to refile their case under the U.S. Constitution, for the sensible reason that a far less liberal U.S. Supreme Court would be even more sensitive to the politics of preservation than the Hawaii Supreme Court had been.[143]

If the lessons of the Hawaii same-sex lawsuit were not clear enough, they were confirmed by parallel events in Alaska. Inspired by *Baehr* and by an Alaskan trial court order in 1995 directing the University of Alaska at Fairbanks to provide "spousal" employment benefits to same-sex partners,[144] Jay Brause and Gene Dugan sued the state for a marriage license. Their lawyers argued that Alaska's gender-neutral marriage law already allowed same-sex marriage, but while their lawsuit was pending the Alaska legislature amended the marriage law to make it explicit: no same-sex marriages.[145] Yet plaintiffs' counsel also maintained that Brause and Dugan's exclusion from civil marriage violated the privacy and equality protections of the Alaska Constitution. On February 27, 1998, Superior Court Judge Peter Michalski ruled that the plaintiffs were denied the fundamental right to marry, which the judge reasoned was part of Alaska's privacy guarantee.[146] As Judge Chang had done in *Baehr*, Judge Michalski ordered the state to issue marriage licenses to same-sex couples but postponed the order's effect while the state sought appellate review. The political process was not going to await an appeal, however; its reaction was swift and decisive. Resolutions to amend the Alaska Constitution to override Judge Michalski's decision were introduced on March 2, 1998, and breezed through both chambers of the legislature with more than the two-thirds vote needed to place a constitutional amendment on the November ballot.[147] The sponsors of the amendment supported it as reaffirming the traditional definition of marriage as one man and one woman. In response to arguments that the amendment represented state intolerance of lesbians and gay men, the senate sponsor denied that "tolerance requires us to publicly recognize and sanction and confer special benefits on homosexual relationships."[148]

Although the Alaska campaign was not as nationally publicized as that in Hawaii, it was similarly contentious and well-financed, albeit mainly on the side of proponents, due to a $500,000 donation from the Church of Jesus Christ of Latter-Day Saints.[149] The amendment's opponents, Alaskans for Civil Rights, maintained that the amendment would take away privacy and civil rights from Alaskans. Proponents, the Catholic Bishops of Alaska and the Alaska Family Coalition (which received the Mormon donation), argued that the amendment only confirmed the traditional definition of marriage and therefore deprived no one of rights that they legitimately had.[150] The state's leading newspaper endorsed their position on the eve of the election, saying that because "marriage is a unique institution for historical, cultural, and biological reasons" it "should not be altered by a sudden flash of light in an Alaska courtroom."[151] The voters agreed, by a 68 to 32 percent margin, and the Alaska Constitution was amended to include this new provision: "To be valid or recognized in this State, a marriage may exist only between one man and one woman."[152] In light of the new constitutional language and the plaintiffs' decision not to challenge their exclusion on federal constitutional grounds, Judge Michalski dismissed their lawsuit.[153]

November 1998 seemed to spell the end to the movement for same-sex marriage, or at least the second wave of same-sex marriage lawsuits. Even in states with liberal (Hawaii) or libertarian (Alaska) traditions and receptive judges, state recognition of lesbian and gay unions had been overwhelmed by the power of the politics of preservation. Lesbians, gay men, bisexuals, transgendered people, and their partners were not just officially second-class citizens, they were unofficially "abomination." Even the couples involved in the lawsuits suffered. Ninia Baehr and Genora Dancel moved away from Hawaii and subsequently separated. Craig Dean and Patrick Gill separated also, soon after they lost their lawsuit for same-sex marriage in the District of Columbia (see note on page 26). Gill was a gentle young man, with a kind soul and a generous spirit. He was the nicest person I have ever represented as an attorney. The lawsuit had cost him his job and perhaps also some peace of mind. He took his own life several years after the breakup.

CHAPTER TWO

The Vermont Civil Unions Law

ON JULY 1, 1972, PROFESSOR HOLLY PUTERBAUGH walked into the statistics class she was to teach during the University of Vermont's six-week summer term.[1] Sitting in the front row was a tall, lanky woman whose hair was prematurely graying. Holly fell dead in love at first sight. Although she did not even know the word "lesbian," she knew her feelings for this other woman and sought out her company. Lois Farnham, the student, knew what a lesbian was and knew that she was one, but was blind to the nature of Holly's attention. As the two women went to movies, dined, and took trips together after the class had ended, Lois figured out that she was falling in love with this lively woman whose face lights up the room when she talks. To help her friend understand who she was, Lois gave Holly a copy of Radclyffe Hall's famous lesbian romance *The Well of Loneliness*. Holly caught on immediately. Their romance deepened, and they moved in together. When Lois went away to a conference in the fall, Holly was devastated by how much she missed her partner. Lois was her soulmate. Lois shared that feeling, and on October 20, 1972, the two women committed themselves to be together as partners for life.

Lois and Holly's commitment was not public. There was no wedding ceremony, and no honeymoon, family celebration, or spousal benefits from their respective employers. In 1972, it was a felony in Vermont, as in most other states, for two women to have sexual intercourse, and most people would have considered it "perverted" for two women to love one another the way a woman "naturally" loves a man. There were no laws protecting lesbians or gay men against job discrimination, whether by the private hospitals Lois worked for or the state university employing Holly. Although they were discreet about their relationship, Holly and Lois flourished as a couple. They were involved in many community activities, including the Girl Scouts; cared for several foster children and raised their adopted child together; partnered in creating and operating the Red Shovel Christmas tree business; and maintained close relationships with many family members, whose children considered them a couple. Aunt Holly and Aunt Lois were partners in all senses of the term. They were good old-fashioned Vermonters who minded their own business, helped other people, and did not rock the boat.

Yet almost 25 years after they sealed their union together, Lois Farnham and Holly Puterbaugh, with Stannard Baker and Peter Harrigan and Nina Beck and Stacy Jolles, rocked Vermont, and ultimately the entire country, by suing the state for refusing to issue a marriage license to recognize their committed partnership. In the wake of complete defeats in Hawaii, Alaska, and the District of Columbia, one wondered whether these plaintiffs could succeed where others had not. Yet succeed they did—in a sense. Their lawsuit triggered one surprise after another for all concerned. Its result, which few could have predicted, was unprecedented in the United States—formal recognition of same-sex relationships, with the same state-enforced benefits and obligations as different-sex civil marriage, but with a new name: *civil union.*

THE VERMONT SAME-SEX MARRIAGE LAWSUIT

After the Hawaii voters essentially voided the *Baehr* litigation, family values activist Michael Gabbard said that the same-sex marriage problem had not gone away, for there was a similar lawsuit then pending in Vermont.[2] He was right, and the idea he had doused in Hawaii was burning brightly at the other end of the United States. People like Nina Beck and Stacy Jolles, who had assumed that same-sex marriage was at best a long-term aspiration, reconsidered that assumption after May 1993, when *Baehr v. Lewin* was handed down.[3] Other gay couples, such as Lois Farnham and Holly Puterbaugh, were only generally aware of *Baehr* when it was handed down, but became caught up in its wake later on. But the fact is that *Baehr* opened up lesbian and gay imaginations to the possibility that their relationships might be recognized by the state as civil marriages, and it can hardly be surprising that many of the galvanized ended up as plaintiffs in court. Although the litigation in Hawaii sowed the seeds for Vermont, the latter lawsuit proceeded along somewhat different lines.[4]

The Background of the Vermont Lawsuit

Formed in 1985, the Vermont Coalition for Lesbian and Gay Rights was an umbrella organization of activists seeking legal protections for gay Vermonters. Its primary methodology was fact-based education, showing public officials that actual lesbians and gay men are productive members of the community who are often treated unfairly because of stereotypes and prejudices about them. When Governor Madeleine Kunin established liaisons for lesbian and gay issues in 1986, she chose coalition members to advise her formally. Vermont legislators were also sensitive to the coalition's concerns. In 1989, they passed a hate crime law enhancing the penalties for crimes committed because of the victim's sexual orientation; the legislature later expanded the category to include gender orientation.[5] In 1991, the coalition helped persuade the legislature to adopt a law prohibiting sexual orientation discrimination in public and private employment, public accommodations, education, and housing.[6] In 1993, lawyers associated with the coalition persuaded the state supreme court to allow a lesbian to adopt the child of her female partner, so that both women would be the legal parents of the child, and two years later the Vermont legislature wrote that rule explicitly into the state's family law code.[7] Activists also sought equal rights for gay and lesbian couples—typically a more contentious matter. Still, in 1993, Burlington's Mayor Peter Clavelle persuaded the city council to adopt a domestic partnership ordinance, allowing municipal employees to include same-sex partners in their health-care benefits package. The voters responded two months later, ejecting Clavelle and some councilmembers from office.[8] Yet when a labor board decision extended domestic partner benefits for unmarried same-sex as well as different-sex state employees in 1994, there was little if any protest.[9]

Although each of the foregoing measures required activists to persuade public officials to extend new equality guarantees to lesbians, gay men, and bisexuals, the educative process was somewhat different in each instance. For the antidiscrimination and hate crime measures, activists emphasized the social fact of antigay prejudice and stereotyping and argued that it inspired unjustified discrimination and violence against gay people. For the second-parent adoption and domestic partnership measures, activists emphasized the social fact of lesbian and gay families and argued that they were productive enough to justify some kind of state recognition.

In the wake of *Baehr*, the coalition created a committee to work on the issue of same-sex marriage. Mary Hurlie, Susan Murray, and Beth Robinson of the committee developed a manual of "speaking points" concerning the issue. They then organized a workshop on same-sex marriage at the fall 1995 Queer Town Meeting, where gay, lesbian, bisexual, and transgendered (GLBT) Vermonters gathered every year to discuss issues of common concern. Attorney Jan Platner of Gay and Lesbian Advocates and Defenders (GLAD) in Boston was the main speaker at the 1995 session, which attracted a fair number of interested people, including Puterbaugh and Farnham, whose interest in actually getting married was stimulated by learning about the many legal consequences of marriage.[10] Spurred by this interest, Robinson and Murray in December 1995 formed a separate organization to focus on this issue—the Vermont Freedom to Marry Task Force. The task force's first public meeting was held in the basement of an Episcopal church in Montpelier. Apart from the convenors, only about ten people attended the inaugural meeting; two of them were Farnham and Puterbaugh. With a modest number of interested people, the task force's agenda was similarly modest: to provide education and arguments relating to same-sex marriage so that same-sex couples and their straight and gay allies could speak to churches, gay activist groups, and social clubs about the issue in their local communities. Several dozen people were trained in this way, creating a small but growing network of people energized about the issue.

This group sponsored a small marching contingent in the June 1996 gay pride parade in Burlington. It was at that parade that Peter Harrigan first learned of the task force, for he knew two of the marchers, Michael and Joseph Watson, a gay couple.[11] Robinson and Murray organized a marriage workshop at the fall 1996 Queer Town Meeting, and it was jam-packed, with about eighty people in attendance. An increasing number of people were interested in the issue, and there was substantial consensus among them that lesbians and gay men should be seeking the right to marry. Not only was it unfair that the state denied the rights and benefits of civil marriage to gay and lesbian couples, but the state's refusal of formal equality and its implicit denigration of lesbian and gay relationships ought to be contested—just as it was being contested in Hawaii. Correspondingly, the task force was a beehive of activity in 1996: its members spoke in front of clubs, churches, and other groups all over the state; met with public officials, including the governor and members of the legislature; and developed a video presentation entitled *The Freedom to Marry: A Green Mountain View*. Puterbaugh and Farnham were two of the numerous couples interviewed in the video, illustrating how "normal" such couples are in Vermont: they loved and were committed to one another, suffered the same kinds of setbacks as well as triumphs, and raised children in nurturing environments. With a formal wedding between two women in the background, the narrator enunciated the video's main thesis: "Many lesbian and gay people make lifelong commitments to each other, but lesbian and gay couples do not have access to the protections of civil marriage,"[12] which was obviously unfair in light of their many affinities with different-sex couples. The narrator was Stannard (Stan) Baker, Peter Harrigan's partner, whom producer Joseph Watson had recruited for the video because of his mellifluous voice.[13]

Robinson and Murray had been interested from the beginning in possible constitutional litigation to challenge the state's same-sex marriage bar. As early as 1996, Puterbaugh and Farnham had discussed with lawyers their being plaintiffs in such a lawsuit. Baker and Harrigan, as well as Beck and Jolles, expressed similar interests later on. In late April and early May 1997, each of the three couples went to their local clerks and requested marriage licenses. (All three couples lived in Chittenden County, but they went to different clerks because they lived in different cities and towns.) The clerks in each case were pretty noncommittal about the desirability of same-sex marriages, but all were bound to deny the applications pursuant to the 1975 opinion of the state attorney general construing the marriage law to exclude same-sex couples.[14] On July 22, 1997, Murray and Robinson, with co-counsel Mary Bonauto of GLAD, filed a complaint in Chittenden County Superior Court, seeking an order requiring the clerks to issue the requested marriage licenses. Like the complaint in the Alaska case (discussed in chapter 1), the complaint in *Baker v. State* asserted that the gender-neutral marriage law should be construed to include same-sex couples and that, if it were not so construed, the law violated the Vermont Constitution. As in the Hawaii and Alaska cases, plaintiffs' counsel did not include a claim that the state law contravened the U.S. Constitution.

The lawyers held a press conference the day they filed the complaint. Four of the plaintiffs were there to field questions. Missing were Stacy Jolles and Nina Beck, who were in the hospital with their son Noah Jolles. (Nina was Noah's biological mother and so gave Noah half his genes. Stacy was Noah's other mother and gave him her last name.) Noah had been the inspiration for the couple to join the case as plaintiffs. From early in his life he had circulatory problems, and he was hospitalized in Boston for heart failure on July 20, 1997. With his mothers by his side, waiting for a heart transplant, Noah died on August 29. Murray and Robinson had protected the family's privacy during this difficult period and offered to drop the mothers from the lawsuit, but they declined. "More than anything we were driven by the memory of Noah to continue," they said.[15]

The Trial Court and Supreme Court Decisions

The state moved to dismiss the lawsuit, and the trial judge, Linda Levitt, swiftly ruled on the motion.[16] Judge Levitt's memorandum opinion held that the state constitution did not require heightened scrutiny of the exclusion, because the fundamental right to marry did not apply to same-sex couples as a definitional matter and because the exclusion did not rest upon a genuinely suspect classification.* Therefore, the law's exclusion was permissible if it bore some kind of reasonable relationship to a legitimate state interest. The state offered seven different justifications for excluding same-sex couples from the marriage law. Judge Levitt ruled that the state's asserted interests in preserving a time-honored institution and in ensuring that its marriages be recognized in other states were not legitimate public interests. She found the state's interest in "preserving the legislature's authority to channel behavior and make normative statements through its legislation . . . a difficult statement to grasp," and similarly dismissed the other state rationalizations save one. Because marriage has been a union between one man and one woman who were supposed to generate a family through their mutual procreative activities (sex), the judge accepted the state's interest in "furthering the link between procreation and child rearing."[17] Judge Levitt's reasoning is odd: if the state cannot exclude couples from marrying simply as a reaffirmation of tradition (a reason the judge rejected), it is hard to see how the state can do the same thing to reaffirm the link between procreation and child rearing (the reasoning that saved the law). Surely the state could not deny marriage licenses to different-sex couples who could not bear children, yet that result could be supported by the judge's reasoning. Her rationale could much more easily support a law requiring deadbeat dads to pay up on their child support obligations before remarrying, but the U.S. Supreme Court invalidated precisely such a law in *Zablocki v. Redhail*.[18] This memorandum opinion would carry no weight on appeal.

Plaintiffs' counsel were happy enough to get a quick dismissal at the trial level and filed an immediate appeal, making both statutory and

---

★ Recall from chapter 1 that the state ordinarily has an easy burden in defending a law against constitutional attack: courts will uphold a law if it is a reasonable means to achieve a legitimate state objective, broadly defined to include normative as well as routine governmental goals. If a law deprives people of a fundamental right or discriminates in the provision of such rights (such as the right to marry), the state has a much higher burden: courts will uphold the law only if it is strictly necessary (a less restrictive law will not work) to achieve a compelling state interest, narrowly defined to exclude state desires to instill morals or to save money. The same kind of heightened scrutiny applies when the state uses a suspect classification (such as sex or race) in a statute.

constitutional arguments. Their appeal attracted seventeen *amicus curiae* (friend of the court) briefs. Among the court's newfound friends were the Roman Catholic Diocese of Burlington, Agudath Israel of America, and the Christian Legal Society (all supporting the state) and the National Organization for Women and the American Civil Liberties Union (for the plaintiffs).* The briefs addressed a variety of issues—such as the proper interpretation of the state marriage statute, the status of the right to marry under the Vermont Constitution, and the earlier-noted arguments under the U.S. Constitution. The main question, however, was whether the exclusion violated the Vermont Constitution's *common benefits clause*, which states that "government is, or ought to be, instituted for the common benefit, protection, and security of the people, nation, or community, and not for the particular emolument or advantage of any single person, family, or set of persons, who are a part only of that community. . . ."[19] Plaintiffs argued that their exclusion from civil marriage was inconsistent with the inclusionary principle instinct in this unusual state constitutional provision.[20] Relying on federal equal protection as well as Vermont precedents, plaintiffs insisted that their exclusion required strict scrutiny (see note on page 59) for any one of three reasons: (1) they were denied a fundamental right (2) based upon a sex-

---

★ I drafted a brief for sixteen professors of legislation supporting the plaintifs on statutory and constitutional grounds. The brief was also joined by Professors James Brudney (Ohio State University), Walter Dellinger (Duke University), Daniel Farber (University of Minnesota), Cynthia Farina (Cornell University), Michael Fitts (University of Pennsylvania), Philip Frickey (University of Minnesota), Elizabeth Garrett (University of Chicago), Eric Lane (Hofstra University), Jon Macey (Cornell University), Abner Mikva (University of Chicago), William Popkin (University of Indiana), Daniel Rodriguez (University of California at Berkelely), Jane Schacter (University of Wisconsin), Edward Rubin (University of California at Berkeley), and Nicholas Zeppos (Vanderzilt University).

  Professor Lynn Wardle of Brigham Young University drafted a brief signed by seventeen professors of law and jurisprudence supporting the state. It was also signed by Eric Anderson (University of Iowa), Gerald Bradley (University of Notre Dame), Teresa Collett (Texas A&M University), George Dent (Case Western Reserve), Robert Destro and Bernard Dobranski (Catholic University), Willliam Duncan (Univesity of Nebraska), John Finnis (University of Notre Dame), David Forte (Cleveland State University), Robert George (Princeton University), Russell Hittinger (University of Tulsa), Douglas Kmiec (Pepperdine University), Michael Paulsen (University of Minnesota), Josephine Potuto (University of Nebraska), Charles Rice (University of Notre Dame), and Richard Wilkins (Brigham Young University).

based classification (3) that uniquely harmed a disadvantaged class (lesbians, gay men, and bisexuals). Under heightened scrutiny, general rationales like the trial court's loose connection among marriage, procreation, and child rearing could not be accepted. Hence, the exclusion of same-sex couples was unconstitutional.

The state and its allies argued against any form of heightened scrutiny and maintained that the exclusion was supported by a public-regarding interest. Following Judge Levitt, the state's primary interest was "furthering the link between procreation and child rearing," because same-sex couples typically do not have children and even when there are children they do not have biological links with both parents in the household.[21] The *amici* briefs supporting the state's position had a different focus; several of them maintained that marriage is a "unique institution" whose communion of love between one man and one woman both joins and transcends the lives of each. "Rather than a semantical technicality, the heterosexual dimension of marriage is indispensable to its intrinsic worth. The physical, intellectual, and emotional blending of the male and female produces a bond and a union different from all others."[22] Other briefs focused on alleged consequences of Vermont's recognition of same-sex marriages, especially asserted harms to children.

At oral argument before the Vermont Supreme Court,[23] Beth Robinson opened the appellants' case with an analogy to the California Supreme Court's bold decision in *Perez v. Lippold*,[24] which had struck down that state's different-race marriage exclusion. This was the first judicial opinion to invalidate a miscegenation law and did so at a time (1948) when a large majority of states had such laws. Both *Perez* and *Baker*, Robinson argued, involved the right to marry. In each case it was denied to a couple for an invidious reason (race in one case, sex as well as sexual orientation in the other). In neither case was the discrimination justified by any weighty state policy, or anything other than tradition and prejudice. The California Supreme Court had done the right thing by striking down a popular state discrimination in 1948. The Vermont Supreme Court ought to do the right thing by striking down an equally popular state discrimination a half century later, Robinson argued. In 1967, the U.S. Supreme Court vindicated *Perez* when it declared miscegenation laws unconstitutional in *Loving v. Virginia*.[25] The implicit message of Robinson's argument was that the Vermont Supreme Court would look just as good in 2048 as the California Supreme Court looked in 1998.

Through its lawyers Eve Jacobs-Carnahan and Timothy Tomasi, the attorney general's office defended the statutory exclusion. In an oral argument divided between the two counsel, the state vigorously defended their brief's position that the court should not apply heightened scrutiny in the case and that the analogy to *Loving* and *Perez* was inapt. But Jacobs-Carnahan and Tomasi irritated some of their "friends" in the courtroom by tepid argumentation as to the rational basis for the exclusion.[26] Unlike several of the *amici*, the state did not insist upon the natural law view that only procreative man-woman marriage could create unique human flourishing, nor did the state strongly press its own position that children were better off in households with both male and female role models.

Although the questions from the five-justice bench were evenhanded and inquiring of all three attorneys, the plaintiffs and their counsel (as well as more than a few on the other side) expected the court to invalidate the exclusion. None of the justices seemed to share the state's alarm that the institution of marriage was in peril from lesbian and gay couples, and most of them seemed receptive to plaintiffs' view that their exclusion implicated the couples' civil rights.[27] Justice Denise Johnson, for example, was openly skeptical of the state's position; she repeatedly asked why the exclusion of same-sex couples was not discrimination, a question the state's attorneys seemed unable to answer. Justice James Morse, who had joined Johnson's 1993 opinion recognizing second-parent adoptions, and Justice John Dooley also seemed to view the case as one involving "civil rights," as Robinson sought to frame the case, and not the "defense of marriage," as the state had tried to frame it. Chief Justice Jeffrey Amestoy gave no clear signal of his leanings.

Given the importance of the case, it is no surprise that it took the Vermont Supreme Court about a year to issue its opinion. The court's decision in *Baker v. State*[28] astounded almost everyone when it was handed down on December 20, 1999. The court unanimously ruled that the state had impermissibly discriminated against the three plaintiff couples by denying them the rights and responsibilities routinely given to similarly situated different-sex couples. That was no great surprise inside Vermont, but observers were taken aback by the court's reasoning, which invalidated the law without applying strict scrutiny. Most unexpected was that a four-to-one majority of the court declined to direct an immediate remedy for the unconstitutional discrimination and, in effect, remanded the issue to the legislature to correct the discrimination—either through allowing same-sex couples to get marriage licenses or, possibly, through creating a new institution assuring such couples the same rights and responsibilities as married couples.

Chief Justice Amestoy authored the opinion for the court.* From the language of the common benefits clause, he drew the inference that the Vermont Constitution, more than the U.S. Constitution, was committed to the principles of *inclusion* and *social equality*.[29] The distinctive history of the common benefits clause, which antedated the federal equal protection clause by almost one hundred years, also rendered irrelevant (the chief justice reasoned) the tiered approach developed by the U.S. Supreme Court to apply the equal protection clause. Under a tiered approach, certain classifications, such as race or sex, trigger a heightened scrutiny that few statutes can survive, while most classifications only call for a minimal level of scrutiny that few statutes can fail (see note on page 59). Amestoy read the Vermont common benefits clause as applying in generally the same way whatever the state classification. Thus, the clause polices "artificial governmental preferments and advantages" and assures that "the law uniformly afford[] every Vermonter its benefit, protection, and security so that social and political preeminence would reflect differences of capacity, disposition, and virtue, rather than governmental favor and privilege."[30] In applying this uniform standard for examining state rules excluding some Vermonters from "common benefits," the chief justice examined the government purpose for the exclusion in light of "(1) the significance of the benefits and protections

---

★ Three justices joined Chief Justice Amestoy's opinion. Justice Dooley concurred entirely in its judgment but wrote separately. Justice Johnson concurred in the majority's finding of unconstitutional discrimination but dissented from its refusal to direct that marriage licenses be issued to the plaintiff couples.

of the challenged law; (2) whether the omission of members of the community from the benefits and protections of the challenged law promotes the government's stated goals; and (3) whether the classification is significantly underinclusive or overinclusive."[31]

The chief justice agreed that the state has a legitimate interest in "promoting a permanent commitment between couples for the security of their children," but objected that the exclusion of same-sex couples from marriage was, as to this particular goal, both underinclusive (the state gives marriage licenses to different-sex couples who cannot or do not choose to procreate) and overinclusive (many same-sex couples, including Beck and Jolles, wanted to raise their biological children within a marital household).[32] The bad fit between the legitimate state goal and the statutory discrimination was, Amestoy ruled, unjustifiable in light of the enormous range of legal benefits, rights, and responsibilities associated with marriage and spousehood. The state's main argument was flatly rejected, as were the laundry list of supporting arguments—including protection of children lest they be raised in lesbian and gay households (the main state argument on remand in the Hawaii lawsuit) and tradition and the long history of exclusion of lesbian and gay relationships from state recognition. The chief justice emphatically negated any notion that tradition-based "animus" can be a legitimate state interest and noted that, in any event, Vermont has been at the forefront in denouncing antigay animus and providing state remedies for private antigay discrimination.[33]

The attorney general and several amici had also warned about the "destabilization" of marriage that could occur if gay people could enter the institution. In another odd twist, the chief justice ruled that such an argument could not be a ground for denying relief but that it was "not altogether irrelevant." Because a "sudden change in the marriage laws" could have "disruptive and unforeseen consequences," with attendant "uncertainty and confusion," the chief justice ruled that the existing discriminatory scheme should remain in effect "for a reasonable period of time to enable the Legislature to consider and enact implementing legislation" correcting the discrimination, either by amending the marriage law or creating a new institution for equal recognition of lesbian and gay relationships.[34] Justice Johnson vigorously disagreed with the court's judgment in this respect. The court's "novel and truncated remedy," she maintained, "abdicates this Court's constitutional duty to redress violations of constitutional rights." The world did not end, nor were "uncertainty and confusion" created, when the California Supreme Court required the state to issue marriage licenses to a different-race couple in *Perez*.[35] Drawing upon federal equal protection jurisprudence, she argued that "it is not only the prerogative but the duty of courts to provide prompt relief for violations of individual civil rights."[36] The chief justice responded that prior courts have allowed grace periods for legislative correction of unconstitutional discriminations and that the experience of courts in Hawaii and Alaska illustrates that court judgments that ignore political realities will not, in the end, assure the rights they announce.[37]

In the Wake of the Vermont Supreme Court's Decision in Baker

The Vermont Supreme Court released its decision the morning of December 20, 1999. All six plaintiffs learned of it by the afternoon, when they appeared in a hastily assembled press conference. Their private views were complicated. Of course, they were delighted that the court had unanimously agreed with them that the marriage exclusion was an unconstitutional discrimination, and they were "amazingly moved by some of the writing" in the opinions, as Stan Baker put it.[42] "We were high. Amestoy's words were beautiful," recall Holly Puterbaugh and Lois Farnham. "It was a nice Christmas present." On the other hand, all six were "disappointed" (the word everyone used) that the court did not require the state to issue them marriage licenses. Stacy Jolles agreed, "I continue to be disappointed. We got on the bus but are still being made to ride at the back of the bus." Nina Beck felt that the disappointment should be set against "the fact that this is so much more than anyone else [among lesbian and gay people] has had in the United States before." So there was some basis for "rejoicing."* Attorney Beth Robinson's reaction was particularly interesting. After

---

★ There was a more important cause for Nina Back and Stacy Jolles to rejoice: on November 20, 1999, Nina had given birth to Seth Jolles, the couple's second child together. Seth has enjoyed a healthy infancy.

winning the biggest case of her life, and assuring that the fruits of her and Susan Murray's organizing and advocacy would be in casebooks and law review articles for decades to come, Robinson's immediate reaction was that December 20 was "the worst day of my professional career."

The political reaction was a reverse echo of the ambiguity the plaintiffs had about the court's opinion. That is, politicians of both major parties, afraid to death of same-sex marriage, were relieved that the court left it open for the legislature to adopt an alternate institution for satisfying the common benefits clause. Vermont Governor Howard Dean (a Democrat) and U.S. Senators James Jeffords (then a Republican) and Patrick Leahy (a Democrat) hailed the court's decision for recognizing the civil rights of a minority group but allowing flexibility as to remedy. The governor immediately proposed creating a new domestic partnership institution for same-sex couples, with all the same benefits and duties of marriage but without that traditional name. Within hours of the decision, Vermont House Speaker Michael Obuchowski, a Democrat who favored same-sex marriage, polled his colleagues and reported that domestic partnership was the most viable alternative.[39] Republican state Senator Vincent Illuzzi opposed same-sex marriage but was open to domestic partnership, with all "the same opportunities, rights and responsibilities," as he put it; other conservative senators publicly said they could live with domestic partnership.[40] Very few groups or officials denounced the court's decision. Even Take It to the People, a group founded in 1997 to oppose the same-sex marriage grassroots movement, praised the court for leaving traditional marriage "intact" and took no position on domestic partnership.[41] Roman Catholic Bishop Kenneth Angell praised the court's decision not to require same-sex marriage but rejected domestic partnership as well, for his church viewed it as a "basic threat to the sanctity of marriage."[42]

Popular reaction to the decision was more one-sided and seemed to confuse the ruling with an endorsement of same-sex marriage.[43] Joe Pratt, a sixty-three-year-old electrician, objected to "homosexuals'" pushing their "agenda" onto his community and feared that Vermont would become the next "San Francisco," considered a refuge uniquely attractive to gay people. Graduate student Cecil Abu-Damoah objected that same-sex marriage or even domestic partnership would "encourage homosexuality," a development that would push society "towards our doom." Wim Van Loon feared that the justices were moving too quickly to settle a divisive social issue; his main objection to same-sex marriage was that "a child that grows up with gay parents is going to have trouble." Street preacher Martin Casey invoked the Bible—"That is an abomination against God's word to approve of any way of homosexuality"—and felt that the court's decision was pernicious. Many people, straights as well as gays, had positive reactions to the *Baker* decision, but a poll immediately after the decision found that 52 percent of Vermonters disagreed with the court's ruling in some respect, with only 38 percent in agreement. Nearly half the respondents favored a constitutional amendment to override the court's decision.[44]

ON REMAND TO THE LEGISLATURE: H. 847

The Vermont Supreme Court's decision in *Baker* was a bombshell tossed into the legislative process. On December 20, when the decision was handed down, the legislative session was just about to begin, and its agenda had already been set. The legislature only meets for about four months each year, and the same-sex marriage issue threatened to be more divisive than any other in living memory, but the leaders within the legislature decided to tackle the issue and not defer it if possible. Some of them felt it was their duty under the law; others feared the supreme court would direct the state to issue marriage licenses to the plaintiffs if the legislature were not perceived as moving ahead in good faith; and a significant minority believed that same-sex relationships should be recognized by the state and that this was the best chance they would have to legislate on the matter. Although knowledgeable observers said from the beginning that the likely response would be comprehensive domestic partnership and not same-sex marriage, the path to that result—and the new nomenclature—was anything but straight.[45]

House Judiciary Committee Hearings

Baker stimulated an array of legislative proposals, including proposals to clarify the state marriage laws to assure that they only recognize unions of one man and one woman and to amend the state constitution to override the court.* The serious work of figuring out precisely what to present to the Vermont House of Representatives fell to the House Judiciary Committee. The chair of the committee was Thomas Little, a Republican, and the vice-chair was William Lippert, a Democrat; the committee consisted of five Republicans, five Democrats, and one Progressive. Given this composition, any proposal would have to be bipartisan. A pragmatic moderate, Little felt that the first task was fact gathering. That was not only the proper way to craft important legislation, but it was important for legislators, like Little, who did not have fully formed preferences on the issue of state recognition of same-sex relationships.[46] In that spirit, he drove his committee through twenty-nine days of hearings, including two giant public hearings conducted jointly with the Senate committee.[47] Although only a few hearings were recorded, Little prepared and distributed to committee members a written summary of each week's testimony.[48]

In a framing memorandum to the committee on January 4, Little accepted *Baker*'s premise that the "Vermont Constitution mandates that the stream of rights, privileges and benefits that flows from the status of civil marriage must be made available to all citizens, without discriminating on the basis of sexual orientation." In light of the decision and of citizens' "intense feelings and concerns" about the issue, Little's goal was "not only to keep the Committee's 'eye' on the Constitutional principles, but also to build consensus and avoid divisiveness within the General Assembly and throughout the state."[49] Thus, the committee commenced with a thorough exploration of the Supreme Court's ruling and the three opinions. In the first week, the committee heard from the attorneys representing the plaintiff couples; lawyers in the state attorney general's office; two constitutional law experts at the Vermont Law School; lawyers representing the Mormon and Roman Catholic Churches, amici in the *Baker* appeal; and the director of the Marriage Law Project at Catholic University.[50]

★ Amending the state constitution is an arduous process. The state Senate must propose an amendment by a two-thirds vote, and the House must concur. In the next session of the legislature, the proposal must be passed by both the House and the Senate, and then it is presented to the voters. If they ratify it in the next regularly scheduled election, the amendment becomes part of the constitution.

In the second week of hearings, the committee shifted its focus to the legal and social history of civil marriage.[51] Professor Nancy Cott of the Yale history department presented a detailed survey of the ways in which marriage has changed in the last two hundred years.[52] Most of the changes have involved the liberalization of the institution: women gained legal personhood, different-race and other forbidden relationships became recognized as marriages, and divorce became easier. Moreover, the civic role of marriage has changed. In early American history, when our society was largely rural, the state's primary interest in regulating marriage was the advancement and protection of families. As the country has urbanized, the state's primary interest has shifted toward fostering stable social interactions. Another witness, Professor Lynn Wardle of the Brigham Young University School of Law, took the position that marriage ought to be viewed as normatively unchanging; only "traditional marriage," involving one man and one woman, uniquely contributes to the "stability, quality, and prosperity of our society."[53] He criticized *Baker* for ignoring the natural law of marriage and sending "a false message to the young and vulnerable that marriage doesn't really matter. That is irresponsible and destructive." Wardle objected that recognition of same-sex marriage or even domestic partnerships "will further devalue the institution of marriage" and directly contribute to the failure of marriage and rise of troubled families in the United States.[54] He and other law professors told the committee that the benefits and duties of same-sex marriages or domestic partnerships celebrated in Vermont would not be recognized in most other states. These arguments were reiterated by Bishop Angell's testimony to the committee in early February.

During the third week of the committee's deliberations, it and the Senate committee held a hearing where the general public were invited to speak. Notwithstanding a blizzard that made travel difficult, the public hearing on January 25 drew between twelve hundred and fifteen hundred Vermonters. The blizzard did preclude a vigil against same-sex marriage that Bishop Angell had called for in a public letter to his parishioners that was read in churches throughout Vermont: "We believe . . . that re-defining marriage, expanding it to include other private relationships, will ultimately attack the age-old truth that traditional marriages and stable families constitute the very foundations of our society." The letter also warned against the state's "subsidizing a lifestyle they know to be objectively wrong," presumably referring to the "homosexual lifestyle."[55] Although Bishop Angell was the most outspoken religious figure on this issue, other prominent leaders took a different position. In her letter to Vermont's Episcopalian congregations, Bishop Mary Adelia McLeod took the position that "[h]eterosexual and homosexual people are equally capable of entering into life-long unions of love, mutual support and fidelity. . . . God's great gift of love and expressing that love cannot and should not be denied to those among us who happen to be homosexual."[56] The Methodist Bishop of Vermont, the President of the Vermont Congregational Churches, and the Reformed Jewish Congregations of Vermont also took public stances in favor of state recognition of lesbian and gay committed unions.

At the joint hearing on January 25, the committees were able to hear from more than one hundred witnesses by limiting testimony to two minutes per person. Vermonters opposing state recognition of lesbian and gay relationships, many of them wearing white ribbons signifying purity, framed the matter as one of (not) promoting immorality. The Reverend Jim Lake was typical of opponents. He felt that both same-sex marriage and domestic partnership would make "sexual promiscuity the norm," explicitly equating homosexuality with heterosexual adultery. He urged the state to tolerate individual lesbian and gay people but not to "legitimize" their "sinful" lifestyles.[57] Other witnesses insisted upon the unique nature of man-woman marriage and the "natural complementarity of men and women," which would be violated by sanctioning "unnatural" relationships.[58] Witnesses supporting state recognition— many of them lesbians and gay men living in committed relationships and wearing pink stickers supporting the right to marry—framed the matter as one of mutual commitment and hence not a radical redefinition of marriage. Speaking for eighty-two rabbis, ministers, and priests, the Reverend Gary Kowalski argued, "Marriage can only be strengthened by extending our understanding of marriage through the faithful committed relationships of same-gender couples."[59] Most witnesses favorable to same-sex marriage framed the matter as one involving civil rights. Just as slavery and apartheid were wrong, so was exclusion of lesbians and gay men from marriage wrong. As one ambivalent heterosexual put it, moral doubts should be set aside to assure equality under the law.[60]

If the public hearing did not contribute any new arguments to the debate over same-sex marriage, it did reveal the range and intensity of popular feelings on the issue. A second joint hearing, held on February 1, confirmed this observation.[61] An estimated two thousand people were crammed into the hearing rooms and corridors, and more than one thousand more stood vigil outside the statehouse, in protest against the legislature's considering such proposals. One speaker after another, including Bishop Angell, urged the legislature to follow "God's law" and refuse to sanction unholy unions.[62] The speakers at the second hearing remained highly polarized. Opponents continued to condemn lesbians and gay men as "abominations" and, if anything, raised the level of aggression in their opposition. For example, opponents urged the legislature to initiate proceedings to impeach the Vermont Supreme Court Justices for issuing the *Baker* opinion. The stakes were getting higher.[63]

The Civil Unions Bill, H.847

The House Judiciary Committee met on February 9 to decide what kind of bill to draft. Following *Baker*, Little framed the issue as one of civil rights. "Accordingly, I believe that these [lesbian and gay] families are entitled to the protection of a common set of legal rights and responsibilities." But his judgment was that a "legal benefits act is the right thing for the people of the State of Vermont now, and not an expansion of the marriage laws."[64] Every other committee member—Republican as well as Democrat—agreed with Little's framing the issue as one of civil rights. This was the most significant effect of the committee hearings: a politically heterogeneous group of legislators, including Little, had changed their minds about how same-sex relationships should be treated by the state. Although *Baker* effectively pushed the members into putting the issue on the legislative agenda, it was the evidence that pushed the members into support for legal equality. Democratic Representative Michael Vinton had cosponsored a brief supporting traditional husband-wife marriage in the *Baker* litigation but was dismayed by "how close" the opponents' testimony came to "really bigoted words" and ignorant stereotypes about gay people.[65] Like other members of the committee, Vinton did not view the lesbian and gay witnesses as people whose relationships threatened public order. As Republican Representative John Edwards put it, the key evidence was "compelling stories of gay and lesbian people about who they are, what they stand for, and how valuable they are to our community."[66] One of those gay Vermonters was Representative Bill Lippert, the vice-chair of the committee. Undoubtedly, his presence and his reputation for legislative productivity helped some members see the unfairness of treating some Vermonters differently.

Yet what kind of equal treatment could the committee support? Little proposed an approach that committee members had been calling a "domestic partnership" approach. A civil rights framing of the issue, however, suggested that domestic partnership might be a "separate but equal" arrangement too much reminiscent of apartheid.[67] Referring to her twelve-year marriage to another woman, Donna Lescoe made this argument explicitly during the February 25 public hearing: "I strongly oppose any attempt to construct any type of separate but equal system, whatever you call it, [like] domestic partnership. I've always disliked that term; it makes me feel like the domestic help."[68] As Little now recalls it, Lescoe's testimony turned his mind away from the phrase "domestic partnership," and he resolved to find a better term for the bill he was already working on.[69] Lippert urged the committee to avoid the conceptual messiness and simply amend the marriage statute to add same-sex couples.[70] Representative Steve Hingtgen, a Progressive, specifically rejected domestic partnership on separate but equal grounds.[71] Although essentially agreeing with Little, Republican Representative Michael Kainen said, "the name domestic partnership would be inadequate and we should do our best to provide the symbolism important to same-sex couples." Representative Cathy Voyer, another Republican agreeing with the chair, urged that the provision of equal benefits and responsibilities ought to be made "in a *civil union* package at this time, because we have to be realistic in what can happen within this building and in our society and I don't want to see my community or any other community in Vermont be torn apart because of our decision."[72] This was the first time I saw the term *civil union* used in the public record of the Vermont legislative deliberation.[73]

At the end of the discussion, the committee members voted eight to three in favor of developing a domestic partnership kind of bill rather than a same-sex marriage bill.[74] Little and legislative counsel prepared and circulated a draft of the bill. Committee members, staff, and interested persons commented on the draft bill, and it was continually revised, especially as to terminology. Some of the terms bruited about included *civil accord* and *civil domestic partnership*, as well as the term ultimately propounded by Little—*civil union*. This term was supported by other members of the committee and by lesbian and gay activists, who disfavored the *domestic partnership* term. Agreement (or exhaustion) on this point enabled the committee to report H.847 to the House on March 2. The committee's bill started with a list of twelve factual findings, among them that Vermont is a state where tolerance and equality have always been foundational; "gay and lesbian Vermonters have formed lasting, committed, intimate and faithful relationships with persons of their same sexual orientation"; the state has an interest "in promoting stable, strong and lasting families, including families based upon same-gender couples; those relationships are similar to those of married Vermonters and are entitled to the same legal protections pursuant to the common benefits clause."[75] The bill created two new institutions: *civil unions* for same-sex couples, which carried the same procedures, legal benefits, and obligations as different-sex marriage,[76] and *reciprocal beneficiaries* for Vermonters who want a mutual decision-making partner (of either sex) for life and health decisions, especially in the event of incapacity.[77] Finally, H.847 proposed the establishment of a Vermont Civil Union Commission to study the operation of civil unions.[78]

House Consideration and Passage of H.847

The Vermont House of Representatives debated H.847 on March 15 and 16, 2000.[85] The House leadership and the committee chair did not have the support of a clear majority of the chamber when they introduced the bill but were hopeful a majority could be persuaded during the course of discussion. To oppose their efforts, Representatives Robert Starr, a Democrat, and George Schiavone, a Republican, had formed a Traditional Marriage Caucus when the House reconvened on March 13. Representative Oreste Valsangiacomo, the chair of the Ways and Means Committee and one of the senior Democrats in the chamber, joined the caucus. The caucus's strategy was to press for resolution of the same-sex marriage issue by popular vote rather than legislative deliberation and, failing that, to defeat the bill on its merits.

At the outset, Representative John Robb introduced a joint resolution calling for the Vermont Senate "to adopt a constitutional amendment defining marriage as a legally sanctioned union between a man and a woman."[80] (Only the state Senate can propose constitutional amendments.) The presiding officer referred the resolution to Representative Little's Judiciary Committee, where it languished for the remainder of the session. Once the House took up consideration of H.R. 847, Representative Thomas Koch moved to strike the bill and replace it with a call for a constitutional convention. He and Representative Valsangiacomo urged adoption of the amendment so that a truly popular process could resolve the issue. The chamber defeated the amendment by a surprising 103 to 45 vote, however. A similar fate befell an amendment by Representatives Starr and Schiavone to scrap the bill in favor of an advisory referendum on the civil unions issue.[81] That amendment went down, 56 to 91. As is obvious from these counterproposals, opponents believed that the matter should be decided by popular vote and were confident that their views would prevail. According to opponents, the results of any referendum were foreshadowed by local referenda that had been held in about fifty communities on Town Meeting Day, March 9: there was a distinct minority in favor of same-sex marriage and greater support for domestic partnership, but the large majority of voters favored no big changes in state law.[82] Supporters of H.847 noted that the referenda were mainly held in localities dominated by opponents of gay rights; there had been no referendum in Burlington, the state's largest and most progay city, for example. In any event, many legislators on the fence saw the referendum proposal as an evasion of the legislators' responsibilities under *Baker*.

The next amendment represented H.847's biggest procedural hurdle. Republican Representative Margaret Flory's amendment in the nature of a substitute would have created, instead of a civil union, a *domestic unit* similar to the legislation Hawaii adopted in 1997—open to same-sex couples and related pairs who could have decision-making rights in the event of injury or incapacity. Flory argued that the legislative process was moving too rapidly and should approach the question incrementally: give same-sex couples a few benefits to see how they work, and then extend more benefits in the future. She also noted that her amendment sought "to take sexual activity out of the equation."[83] That is, by associating male-male relationships with those between an aunt and her nephew (or niece), citizens would be less likely to understand the state as sanctioning gay and lesbian sexuality. But Flory's thoughtful amendment was unresponsive to lesbian and gay demands that their *romantic* relationships be recognized.

Critics of the Flory amendment also objected that it would not meet the civil rights requirements of the common benefits clause as construed in *Baker*. Supporters of the amendment rejected a characterization of civil unions as a civil rights issue; it was, they argued, a marriage issue. Indeed, it was insulting to compare antigay exclusions to previous ones based on race. Once that point had been made, Representative Francis Brooks, the legislature's only African-American member, felt compelled to rise. Speaking to a deathly silent chamber, Brooks expressed his view that there were parallels between prior racial exclusions and current exclusions of lesbians and gay men. He regretted that he was still judged by the color of his skin and expressed empathy for lesbians and gay men who felt the same way. "[P]lease consider the human beings that you have decided to place a stigma on," he implored.[84] Although Representative Walter Freed (a prominent Republican) vociferously disagreed, Brooks's remarks brought a tone of seriousness and personal confession to the debate.

At the end of the debate on the amendment, Representative Lippert addressed the chamber, seeking to put his "human face" on the bill, saying, "I've had the privilege of developing a deep, devoted, loving, caring relationship with another man." He went on to say that this relationship enriched his life in the same ways that marriage has enriched the lives of his legislative colleagues: "Gay and lesbian couples deserve not only rights, but they deserve to be celebrated." In light of historic prejudice against gay people, he noted, these relationships are "miraculous." Lippert urged his colleagues to see the committee bill as a matter not just of individual civil rights, but also as a matter of *common* benefits. "We are not a threat to your communities; we are an asset; we are your neighbors, your friends, indeed, we are your family."[85] After he sat down, some legislators were close to tears, and several hugged Lippert.

Representative Robert Kinsey rose to say he had just heard the greatest speech on the floor in thirty years and that he was proud to call Bill Lippert his friend. Although a conservative Republican, Kinsey joined Lippert in voting against the Flory amendment. It failed, 29 to 118.[86]

The next amendment, offered by Progressive Representatives Dean Corren and David Deen, sought to amend the marriage laws to include same-sex couples. Corren reminded his colleagues that Vermont was the first state to renounce slavery; the state ought to be just as eager to embrace an opportunity to assure lesbians and gay men full legal equality. "Separate but equal is not equal," he maintained.[87] A central lesson of *Brown v. Board of Education* is that inequality bearing the sanction of law is particularly unhealthy. With little debate and lukewarm opposition from the committee, the amendment failed, 22 to 125. In the short period after the roll call vote, when legislators can explain their votes, one representative sarcastically intoned two sounds, "Quack, quack." This was a reference to the metaphor afloat in the halls that there was no difference between same-sex marriage and civil unions: if it looks like a duck, walks like a duck, and quacks like a duck, it must be a duck. Ducks popped up all over the statehouse during the debates.

Most of the legislative debate occurred on the question whether H.847 should have a third reading. Representative Little laid out the civil rights case for the bill. The main speaker against the bill was Republican Representative Nancy Sheltra, who objected that state sanctioning of "homosexual" unions would promote the "teaching of homosexuality" in the public schools, "taxpayer-funded homosexual activism," and "homosexual curriculum and reeducation programs and hate speech regulations."[88] Sheltra saw the bill as "legalizing sodomy" rather than loving relationships and encouraging activity that "causes disease and STDs," including AIDS. At this point, a member raised a point of order, and the presiding officer asked Sheltra to stick to the subject of the debate, which she did, arguing that civil unions would contribute to the "tearing down of traditional marriage." Her conclusion: "We are really putting ourselves in a dangerous situation in regards to a judgment from the Almighty God."

After Sheltra's speech, which I found painful to hear even on audiotape, she reportedly motioned to her allies to rise in support of her comments. Instead, she was followed by Representative Mary Mazzariello, who is married with three children, two of whom are lesbians: "They did not choose to be different, Mr. Speaker, and have always cared about the rights of others. . . . Is it fair for us to discriminate against them . . . to ask them to live alone and lonely? We need to allow them the same sorrows, joys, and responsibilities of married couples." As she audibly choked back tears, Mazzariello recounted how she and her husband and children "felt rejected by our church. . . . Please help to remove the stigma and to allow others to enjoy legal relations. Make Vermont the leader in the preservation of family life."[89]

Almost all the speakers for the committee bill drew from their own experiences to support the civil rights framing of the issue. For example, Representative Gaye Symington drew parallels that she and her husband had uncovered between southern resistance to the mandate in *Brown v. Board of Education* and some Vermonters' resistance to *Baker v. State.* She read quotations from southern objections to *Brown*: "the judiciary has overstepped its bounds"; "so-called civil rights"; "this decision threatens a way of life"; "this decision threatens traditions"; "slow down."[90] Representative Robert Rusten recalled that when he was a child, he saw signs that said "Nigger" and "Kike." He asked his parents about those terms; they said those were vile words he should not use, but neither should he challenge the people who did use them. Homophobia, Rusten observed, is similar to racism and anti-Semitism: they are all prejudices, and we all ought to stand up against them. Referring to Representative Lippert's speech, he concluded: "It's not his load to carry anymore; it's ours."[91]

The speeches of Mazzariello, Symington, and Rusten were heartfelt and potentially persuasive to a neutral listener—unlike Sheltra's intemperate speech. My impression is that few of the moderates opposing the bill chose to speak, because they had neither the heart to deny the sentiments voiced by supporters nor the gall to make Sheltra's arguments. Although most of the speakers against the committee bill framed the issue as a referendum on the immorality of homosexuality and their supposed attack on marriage, many of the representatives inclined to vote against it did so for more mundane reasons: strong constituent opposition to civil unions, irritation at the state Supreme Court for foisting the

issue of "homosexual marriage" upon the legislature, discomfort in talking about homosexuality (or sexuality), and a preference for legislating
some benefits now and then adding more later on (the Flory approach).

At the end of the House session of March 15, the members voted 79
to 68 for the third reading of the bill.[92] This was a favorable signal, but
the sponsors were still uncertain about ultimate passage of the bill. To
gather a few more Republican votes, specifically those of
Representatives Bruce Hyde and Richard Marron, the committee proposed a further provision to section 1 of the bill, its findings provision:
"marriage means the legally recognized union of one man and one
woman."[93] On March 16, the House agreed to add this provision and
then took up further amendments raised by critics of the civil unions bill.

The most serious amendment was a proposal to add a "junior
DOMA" providing that same-sex marriages entered in another state or
jurisdiction would be void and not recognized in Vermont (see chapter 1).
Representative Flory argued for the amendment: "If we are not going to
allow same-sex marriages for Vermonters, it looks like we'd want to stick
to that same policy for an out-of-stater."[94] Representative Little responded
to this logical point with the contention that "the defense of marriage
movement," with its antigay overtones, "is not something this state should
endorse." Representative Kainen, another Republican on the judiciary
committee, confirmed what was implicit in Little's objection: "DOMAs
carry that baggage because they're part of a national antihomosexual
agenda. . . . It's the wrong symbolism."[95] Supporters as well as opponents
were surprised that the junior DOMA was defeated by a large margin, 55
to 89. The House also defeated proposals to send the bill back to committee (53 to 92), to give the public more time to comment before enacting the
law (voice vote), and to require partners applying for civil union licenses to
produce evidence that they had been tested for HIV infection (2 to 136).

At the end of the day, the legislators voted 76 to 69 for passage of
H.847.[96] Voting in favor of the bill were 14 Republicans, 57 Democrats,
4 Progressives, and 1 Independent; voting against were 50 Republicans
and 18 Democrats. Female legislators voted 35 to 9 in favor of the bill;
male legislators voted 41 to 60 against the bill. Some of the yes votes were
swayed by Lippert's speech, and some by Brooks's speech and the analogies to civil rights of African Americans. Some, like Representatives

Mazzariello and Kinsey, had lesbian or gay children or close relatives. The no votes reflected views fearful of the effects of the legislation on traditional marriage and intense pressure from constituents. Most of the yes votes realized that "this decision may cost some of us our political careers," as Republican Representative Marion Milne put it, adding, "I will not be silenced by hatred and intolerance."[97] One of the no votes came from Representative Bill MacKinnon, who so strongly favored same-sex marriage that he voted against the committee's bill on grounds that it was a constitutionally deficient separate-but-equal measure.[98]

SENATE DELIBERATION AND ENACTMENT OF THE CIVIL UNIONS LAW

The Vermont Senate Judiciary Committee, chaired by Senator Richard Sears, a Democrat, had not been idle during the House deliberations; for example, the Senate committee co-sponsored the large public hearings on January 25 and February 1. But the Senate had deferred to the House to act first, in part because the prospect for passing a domestic partnership bill appeared more certain in the Senate: if the House acted favorably, as it had done, the Senate was most unlikely to block the way, and the governor had been supportive of a civil union type bill from the beginning. Also, now that the House members had put their necks on the electoral chopping block, the political pressure on the Senate to pass a similar measure was even stronger. Thus, a civil unions law seemed likely on March 16, but the politics of the matter were becoming increasingly volatile, and hostile. The Senate's more predictable path toward voting for the bill was trod amid a growing number of popular landmines.

Senate Judiciary Committee Deliberation and the Polarization of Debate

The polarization of public debate that had begun in February, when the House Judiciary Committee went public with its endorsement of a comprehensive equal rights and responsibilities bill, accelerated after the House passage of H.847. The most accessible evidence of this is the outpouring of letters and other documents by Vermonters to their newspapers and other publications.[99] Most of the published letters opposed recognition of same-sex unions for sectarian reasons. Typical of the thousands of such letters is the argumentation of Blake Frost, that "homosexuality is a perversion, no less than pedophilia and bestiality, and to try to divert from that fact by labeling it love, is a type of perversion in itself." Accordingly, the state should not recognize same-sex unions, and the legislature should give homosexual relationships "no more sanction that any other perversion."[100] Many of the letters associated same-sex unions with promiscuity, AIDS and other venereal diseases, disgusting sexual practices, sex in public, pedophilia, incest, and polygamy.[101] One of the more moderate letters found the consideration of same-sex marriage as a civil right as "the equivalent of proposing laws to give civil rights to alcoholics, habitual gamblers and drug addicts."[102] (All of these, by the way, do have constitutional rights to marry that cannot be abridged because of their addictions) Repeatedly, opponents predicted that state recognition would permanently associate Vermont with Sodom and Gomorrah and bring down the wrath of God on the state and its people.[103]

The Senate Judiciary Committee had witnessed the intensity of oppositionist feelings and rhetoric in the joint public hearings. Although the committee held no new public hearings, its members held open meetings with the public on an individual basis. For example, Sears held a public forum in traditionalist Bennington County, which he represented; the forum was also attended by committee members Richard McCormack (a Democrat) and Vincent Illuzzi (a Republican). In January, Illuzzi had introduced a domestic partnership bill that went just as far as H.847 in giving state recognition to same-sex unions,[104] but by the end of March he was not only opposed to civil unions but was proposing to amend the state constitution to override *Baker*. Many of the Bennington constituents agreed with him—and with intense conviction. Joe Wolfe, a personal friend of Sears, said, "This issue has taken on for some of us aspects of a holy war and holy wars don't go away."[105]

The holy war was also becoming a partisan war. Democratic Governor Howard Dean was in favor of a civil union approach, while Republican Ruth Dwyer, his opponent in 1998, was making the civil union proposal a centerpiece of her campaign to unseat the governor in the November 2000 election. While Republicans and Democrats alike worked under Republican Tom Little's leadership on the civil unions bill in the House Judiciary Committee, the Senate Judiciary Committee was polarized along partisan lines. All four of the Democrats—Senators

Sears (chair), McCormack (the Senate Democratic Majority Leader), Ann Cummings, and James Leddy—were basically precommitted to state recognition, while the two Republicans—Senators Illuzzi and Richard Bloomer (the state Senate Minority Leader, who wanted McCormack's job)—were precommitted to oppose state recognition and to favor a constitutional amendment to override *Baker*.

Between March 17 and April 13, the committee held twenty-three hearings to gather facts and deliberate about H.847. Although most of the witnesses (especially those from the attorney general's office) were neutral or evenhanded, many of the hearings were an arena in which starkly irreconcilable moral visions did battle through the presentations of organized groups on each side: the progay politics of recognition aligned against the traditionalist politics of preservation, just as had occurred in Hawaii. Bishop Angell for the Roman Catholic Church; Michele Cummings and Ruth Charlesworth for Take It to the People; and Professor David Coolidge for Catholic University's Marriage Law Project verbally battled Susan Murray and Beth Robinson of the new Vermont Freedom to Marry Action Committee.[106] Bishop Angell told the Judiciary Committee, "You have no duty, moral or constitutional, to weaken the institution of marriage. If the court thinks otherwise, then let the people overrule the court."[107] He favored a constitutional amendment to override *Baker*. The Reverend Glen Bayley of the Missionary Alliance Church went further in his testimony. Senator Sears objected to letters telling him he would go to Hell if he voted for the bill. Reverend Bayley responded, "But they're not telling you to go there and they're encouraging you to go in a different direction. I do believe you'll be judged. . . ."[108]

The rising tide of acrimony spilled onto the streets of Montpelier. Representative Sheltra organized a protest march on the statehouse for April 6, in order to "claim Vermont for godly purposes." She was joined by Republican presidential candidate Allen Keyes, who had been invited by Senator Bloomer to testify before the Senate Judiciary Committee. Although Senator Sears declined to allow Keyes to testify, he came to Vermont anyway and addressed Sheltra's crowd: "I think the state of Vermont is simply being used right now as a stalking-horse in an effort to destroy the foundation of marriage throughout our society," to encourage "us all to become individuals so enslaved by passions that we have redefined human nature. We cannot accept this new form of slavery," said Keyes, an African American. He argued that homosexuality is a perverse choice—just like rape, pedophilia, and adultery. Hence any discrimination against "homosexuals" is not only admissible but desirable in a moral society. "Shall we forgo all discrimination against people who exploit children? Shall we forgo all discrimination against rapists and people of this kind? Where do you stop in your willingness to say that human sexual behavior is a condition and not a choice?"[109]

The Senate Judiciary Committee was caught between a rock and a hard place. As the civil unions bill progressed toward enactment, the intensity of the opposition escalated, and perhaps the number of opponents as well. A politician's natural instinct in such a situation is to put the issue off to another time or, at least, to compromise. But Sears was honor bound to press forward with a bill now that the state House of Representatives had committed to it; he was also concerned that the state Supreme Court would intervene if the legislature did not act or at least make progress this session. As to compromise, the first and last resort of a politician, Sears and his colleagues found themselves boxed in: the House had already made almost all the compromises the Vermont Freedom to Marry Action Committee was willing to accept; dilution of any benefit or duty would have violated the constitutional floor laid out by the Vermont Supreme Court; and the opponents of the bill were proving quite mobile themselves, as they accused every new compromise of being tantamount to "homosexual marriage" (the now tiresome duck argument).

At its meeting on April 13, the Senate Judiciary Committee discharged the requirements of political honor. It changed the House bill in a number of respects—all of them cosmetic[110]:

- the findings were rearranged and explicitly relied on *Baker* as a reason for adopting the legislation;
- a legal definition of marriage as the "legally recognized union of one man and one woman" was added to the state's Domestic Relations Law;
- assistant town clerks were authorized to perform the duties of town clerks with respect to the issuance of marriage and civil union licenses (some town clerks objected that they were not willing to perform these duties);

- town clerks would be required to tell applicants for civil union licenses that Vermont residency may be required for dissolution of a civil union;
- the membership, terms, and duties of the Civil Union Review Commission were altered; and
- most parts of the law would become operative on July 1, 2000 (moved up from September 1).

The committee rejected the more consequential changes, including[111]:

- Senator Sears' proposal to change the terminology, from *civil unions* to *domestic partnerships*;
- Senator Illuzzi's proposal to exempt churches from offering health benefits to their employees' civil union partners;
- various proposals to make it harder for out-of-state couples to apply for civil union licenses.

After an exhausting and sometimes heated discussion, the committee voted to report the revised bill to the Senate, with the two Republicans in dissent and the four Democrats in the majority.

Senate Debate and Legislative Enactment of the Civil Unions Bill

The Senate floor debate commenced on April 18. Before the Senate took up H.847, it considered several proposals to amend the Vermont Constitution, as the Roman Catholic Diocese, Take It to the People, and other organizations requested.[112] Proposition 6, offered by Republican Senator Julius Canns, would have added this language to the constitution: "That marriage is a special label for a partnership between a man and a woman." Senator Illuzzi offered an amendment to Proposition 6 that would have more clearly overridden *Baker* by adding, "Marriage [is] the legal union of one man and one woman. The General Assembly shall define the legal benefits and responsibilities associated with marriage. No provision of this Constitution shall be held to require that any such benefits and responsibilities be extended by the General Assembly or the judiciary to any grouping of people other than one man and one woman."[113] Senator Gerald Morrissey offered a substitute that would have amended the constitution to provide, "No provision in this constitution shall be held to require that marriage be extended by the judiciary to any grouping or people other than one man and one woman." There were various other minor or technical amendments. The debate over these proposed constitutional amendments reflected the increased passions and higher stakes surrounding the issue.

The sponsors offered slightly different rationales for their proposed constitutional amendments. Senator Illuzzi focused on the defects, in his opinion, of the *Baker* decision: it was unprecedented in its disregard of both the language and original intent of the common benefits clause and was an intrusion into the policy-making role normally played by the legislature. Agreeing with this criticism of *Baker*, Senator Canns also emphasized the threat gays and lesbians posed to marriage and society: "Proposition 6 . . . helps to guarantee the survival of traditional marriage while avoiding the slippery slope of civil unions or domestic partnerships that could slide into same-sex marriage." He rejected the characterization of the bill as adding new civil rights, for lesbians and gay men in the state had all the civil rights other Vermonters had. Instead, they were "demanding special marital status" and were pawns of a national campaign "not to gain civil rights but to compel sexual practices and habits both unacceptable and distasteful [to] the great majority of Vermonters."[114]

Speaking for the committee, Senator Sears favored substitution of the Illuzzi amendment for the Canns amendment, and the Senate did that by a 27 to 3 vote, but he opposed any proposal to amend the state constitution. The point of a constitution is to place certain individual liberties beyond majoritarian control, especially when addressed to an unpopular minority, and *Baker* was a classic application of that precept to state discrimination against lesbian and gay couples. Sears also argued that the Illuzzi amendment would collide with the U.S. Supreme Court's decision in *Romer v. Evans*,[115] which construed the federal equal protection clause to protect lesbians, gay men, and bisexuals against arbitrary targeting in state constitutional amendments (see my discussion in chapter 1). The Supreme Court had emphasized the unprecedented nature of the state constitutional amendment, the broad range of rights and benefits it placed beyond the normal political process for gays and lesbians alone, and the antigay "animus" that the Court thought inspired the amendment. Similar arguments could be made against the Illuzzi amendment, Sears argued. The senator had a larger point to make, and he did so with an anecdote.

A man named Curtis lived in Putney, Vermont, most of his adult life. He was a man of color in an overwhelmingly white state. Curtis asked the senator what he and his colleagues were planning to do to the Vermont Constitution. "Why do you ask?" inquired the senator. "I just wonder whether I'm next."[116] This anecdote is reminiscent of Sir Thomas More's argument in Robert Bolt's play *A Man for All Seasons*, in which he defends the proposition that even the devil is entitled to the rule of law, for once man starts cutting a road through the law to get at the devil, pretty soon there are no legal protections for anyone.[117]

Sears's anecdote also illustrates the pervasive appeal of civil union senators to the experience of racial, ethnic, and religious minorities who have been subjected to discrimination in our history. As one senator put it, "Most of us at some point in time, if we look back, came from a despised minority, and the Constitution protected them."[118] Senator Canns, who is part Native American, vigorously objected to this line of argument, but it resonated with some senators in the middle. Senator Mark MacDonald, a Democrat from conservative Orange County, spoke about conversations he had with constituents who favored amending the constitution. Their arguments were that the state was already doing enough for homosexuals; marriage or civil unions were special rights. "How can people in my villages say those things? And the answer is simple: these are the same things I said last year. My constituents feel the same way I did when this issue was put on the table. It wasn't something I wanted to talk about. Some of the thoughts are unpleasant. Some of them remind me of my high school days and how people I looked up to treated racial minorities."[119] A constitutional amendment was a way to make the issue go away. But the state Supreme Court, MacDonald argued, was right to force the political process to grapple with the issue. H.847 offered Vermonters an opportunity to get beyond prejudiced feelings and easy answers.

Proposition 6, as amended to substitute the Illuzzi version of the proposed amendment, needed two-thirds of the senators to initiate the lengthy process of amending the constitution (note on page 68). It did not draw even one-third, failing 9 to 21.

The Senate then turned to H.847. Senator Sears presented the Judiciary Committee's bill, which changed H.847 in various respects, as discussed earlier. Especially after the chamber's rejection of the constitutional amendments, Sears emphasized the duty of the legislature to comply with the *Baker* court's mandate to equalize the rights of same-sex couples with those of married different-sex couples.[120] Revised H.847 met that mandate. He warned his colleagues that anything falling short of the mandate could stimulate the court, which had retained jurisdiction over the matter, to require the state to issue marriage licenses to the three plaintiff couples. At the end of his presentation, the Senate voted to replace the House version of H.847 with the one drawn up by the Senate Judiciary Committee.

The debate was dominated by supporters of the bill, who gave their personal reasons for viewing civil unions as an important civil right and not as a threat to marriage. Senator James Leddy received a great deal of constituent pressure to vote against "homosexual marriage and homosexual benefits," but he was most swayed by the letter from Helena Blair, a 78 year-old Roman Catholic mother of eight children, one of whom was gay. He read from the letter, "'What were we to do— understand instantly or cast him aside? Accept him in a patronizing way or continue to love him unconditionally?'" The answer was obvious for her son, "'who was just plain born gay. . . . God blessed us with eight children, and my God made no mistake when He created homosexuals and when he gave us our gay son.'"[121] Recognizing this young man's capacity for commitment was only decent and fair, Leddy suggested, and was no threat to his own marriage of twenty-eight years.

Democratic Senator Benjamin Ptashnik recounted how he was brought up to believe that homosexuals were subhuman or at least highly undesirable people. These sentiments filled the letters written to him by constituents. But he had come to reject this view of gay people, who have been subject to the same kind of group vilification in America that Jews, gypsies, and homosexuals suffered from the Nazis. There was a connection between violence against gay people and the incarceration of Ptashnik's family in Buchenwald during World War II, and the connection was that both actions reflected bigotry, in his opinion. He objected to the "negativity and hatred" he heard in much of the oppositionist rhetoric.[122] Senator Elizabeth Ready agreed. She was told more than once, "You're going to Hell. You're an evil person," because she supported equality for lesbian and gay people. The debate gave her an opportunity to say yes to inclusionary, and no to exclusionary, perspectives. She saw a parallel between the lesbian and gay plaintiffs in *Baker* and Rosa Parks, whose refusal to sit in the back of the bus inspired civil rights protesters.[123]

Senator MacDonald was the last to speak before the third reading of the bill. He is an eighth grade social studies teacher. When he tells his students to change seats—including seats they have occupied for only minutes into the semester—they whine and complain because they don't like giving up "their" seats. Sitting in a seat for a few minutes vests the student with feelings of ownership she is reluctant to give up. Adults are the same, he posited; they don't like giving up "their" privileges; they don't like change. In light of this verity, the safe thing to do would be to vote against civil unions, as too close to homosexual marriage (the duck argument); the Senate's Democratic leadership had told MacDonald that he had a pass on this vote, given his conservative constituency. But the senator could not view H.847 as a matter of pure politics. A friend asked him, "'What are you going to tell the kids when you get back to school?' What was I going to tell them—I voted the way I did so it would be easy for me to get reelected?" Was there a fair reason to vote no? MacDonald called his mother, who said, "You'll know the right thing to tell them."[124] He concluded that the right thing—the only course of action he could defend to the kids—was to vote yes on H.847. He did, and so did eighteen other senators. At the end of the legislative day on April 18, the Senate voted 19 to 11 for the third reading of the civil unions bill.

The Senate returned to H.847 on April 19. Because the bill was now certain to pass, the agenda was reconciliation and closure.[125] Senator Sears joined his colleague from Bennington County, Republican Senator Morrissey, in supporting an amendment to make clear that the civil union bill would not infringe on the free exercise and speech rights of religious organizations. Morrissey congratulated Sears for the decorum of the prior day's debate. Republican Senator Jean Ankeny explained why she and many in her "faith community" supported same-sex marriage and felt that the civil unions bill was a giant step in that direction.[126] Democratic Senator Cheryl Rivers spoke of the personal odyssey she and her family had traveled as they struggled with the issues raised by *Baker*. "This subject has required me to confront my own prejudice."[127] Republican Senator Illuzzi offered reconciliation with an edge: "In my view, the war is not over; the battle is lost. But we must still be friends."[128]

Only Senator Canns expressed continued dissatisfaction, as he took offense at his being "stereotyped as a bigot" and the "sex problem" of homosexual relations being treated as a "civil rights problem."[129]

After the foregoing brief debate, the Senate voted 19 to 11 for H.847. All 17 Democrats plus 2 Republicans supported the measure, and 11 Republicans opposed it. All 10 women in the Senate voted for the bill; the men voted 9 to 11 against it. All 6 senators from Chittenden County, including Republican Senators Ankeny and Peter Brownell, voted for the bill. (Chittenden County contains Burlington, the state's largest city. All six *Baker* plaintiffs resided in Chitenden County.) In contrast, the three Republican senators from more rural Rutland County not only voted aginst the bill but repeatedly spoke against it.

Because the Senate had made changes to H.847, the bill returned to the House; both chambers had to pass exactly the same statutory language. Thus, the originating chamber could (1) accept the Senate's changes and send the bill to the governor, (2) refuse some or all of the Senate's changes and return the bill for the Senate to accept its version, or (3) ask for a conference committee to resolve differences. The House sponsors followed the first option, because the Senate changes were not major and because there was insufficient time to follow the second and third options. Notwithstanding the increasingly fierce and polarized public debate, and increased pressure from the Roman Catholic Church to defeat the bill, the managers did not think many members would change their votes. So when the House took up the bill on April 25, they generally rested their case on the March deliberations.

Opponents of the bill made a last-ditch effort to sway ambivalent House members. A small group gathered on the statehouse steps, praying that some members would see the error of their prior yes votes. "Remove from him his desire to be compassionate by believing that which is in fact not true. Prevent this unrighteousness from coming to Vermont," the group implored.[130] Inside the statehouse, the words used against the measure were hardly prayerful. Some members denounced the bill as state promotion of "perversion" and conduct "against the law of nature." Homosexual marriage—which is what the civil unions law had come to stand for in some circles—was nothing but corruption, a corruption of language and of ideas. A state that sanctioned homosexual marriage had fallen prey to sophistic arguments misleading them to believe "depravity is virtue" and "immoral values are ignorance." Representative Sheltra charged that the new law condoned conduct that leads to AIDS.[131] As she read from a tract charging that "homosexuals" were seeking to foist sodomy and disease onto the entire nation, several legislators walked out of the chamber. Her arguments surely atttracted no votes, and probably firmed up votes in support of the measure.

On April 25, the House approved the revised H.847 by a vote of 79 to 68, a slightly higher margin than before. Once both the House and Senate had agreed on the same language, the bill went to the governor's desk. Governor Dean signed it the next day in a private session during the lunch hour. He did not have the customary public ceremonial signing, because he did not want to give the appearance of celebration for an issue that so divided Vermonters, and with increasing ferocity.[132] Representative Little, the person most responsible for the new law, took the same conciliatory stance, conceding "recriminations" on both sides of the issue making it clear "the state is divided, and it will take time to become less divided." Others were more celebratory. Representative Lippert announced, "I couldn't be happier with the results," even though the legislature had not adopted same-sex marriage. The term *civil union* carries "a significance and symbolism that is very appropriate."[133] Many were defiant. A speaker for the Family Research Council assailed the law for encouraging "homosexuals" to believe "that what they are doing is normal and healthy" and to "young people that marriage-based families are irrelevant. It gives people a powerful reason to support other homosexual activist ideas—such as teaching children that homosexuality is the equivalent of marital love."[134]

The six *Baker* plaintiffs were mainly exhausted. They had all attended at least some of the hearings and debates and were all present when the House voted for the bill to become law on April 25. Holly Puterbaugh's initial reaction to the civil union idea was "Yech," but on reflection she considered it a "brilliant compromise," the most that could have been obtained by anybody in the political process.[135] Lois Farnham, as well as Nina Beck and Stacy Jolles, independently expressed to me their strong preference for the term *civil union* as opposed to *domestic partnership*. What Vermont accomplished was unprecedented in American law, and it was good that the legislature came up with a new term to express that advance.[136] Like the four women, Peter Harrigan and Stan Baker were disappointed when the House Judiciary Committee opted for *civil union* rather than same-sex marriage terminology, but they have "since come to believe that the [committee] acted bravely."[137]

Aftermath: In the Wake of the Civil Union Law

Armaggedon did not come on April 26, 2000, when the governor signed the civil unions law, but neither did the tide of antigay acrimony immediately abate. Some opinion polls showed most Vermonters disapproved of *civil unions*, with many of the opponents considering it the main issue they would weigh in the November elections.[138] One or two town clerks resigned in protest over the law, and a few others announced that they would not issue licenses to same-sex couples. Roman Catholic priests and Methodist ministers were forbidden by their denominations from performing civil unions. Most parts of the civil union law took effect on July 1, a Saturday when town clerk offices were normally closed. Some town clerks opened up especially to accommodate the demand for civil unions. Town Clerk Annette Cappy of Brattleboro opened her office just after midnight on July 1, so that Carol Conrad and Kathleen Petersen could receive their licenses—the first lawfully issued by any American jurisdiction to an avowedly same-sex couple.[139]

Farnham and Puterbaugh also received their civil union license that Saturday, through the good graces of Burlington Town Clerk Margaret Picard. Their wedding was held the same day, in the First Congregational Church of Burlington, the Reverends Robert Lee and Adrianne Carr presiding. Their daughter was the attendant, and two hundred friends, coworkers, and coplaintiffs were witnesses.[140] Baker and Harrigan waited to apply for their licenses. Their wedding was at the Episcopal Cathedral in Burlington, on August 13.[141] As this book goes to press, Beck and Jolles have not yet joined in civil union. They remain a committed couple, raising their son Seth and thinking about having another child, but are waiting to see what happens to the civil union law.[142]

Indeed, the backlash that commenced during the legislative deliberations continued after the law took effect. Vermonters irritated at the supreme court's earlier decision requiring greater equity in school funding and legislation implementing that mandate, concerned about the visibility of lesbians and gay men in the state, alarmed about sex education in the schools—these Vermonters, especially the old-timer "wood-chucks," planted *Take Back Vermont* signs in their yards, on their cars, in their workplaces all over the state. "Civil unions are like the straw that broke the camel's back," said Ken Paronto, a Corinth woodchuck. A cluster of unrelated issues arising out of the modernization of Vermont were causing profound anxiety among much of the citizenry. Linda Weiss, a mail carrier who has lived in the town with her female partner for ten years (making her an immigrant "flatlander"), agreed with the description but was concerned about its underbelly: "People are so angry. They're filled with hostility and rage. It's scary to be in a small room with them, or in a small town with them, frankly."[143]

On September 12, 2000, voters in the Republican primary ousted four representatives (Edwards, Milne, Kinsey, Fyfe) and one senator (Brownell) who had voted for the civil union bill. They also nominated Ruth Dwyer to run for governor, with a Take Back Vermont platform, and renominated Senator James Jeffords, who was critical of the Take Back Vermonters.[144] Targeted for political oblivion was Representative Thomas Little, the father of the legislation, who had been considered a rising star of the Republican Party. He won renomination but saw his party slipping away from him. The fall 2000 campaign was conducted in significant part as a referendum on civil unions, with Dwyer vigorously assailing the governor and his party for their support of the new institution. A third-party Progressive candidate for governor not only threatened to split the pro-union vote, but also to deprive Dean of a more than 50 percent majority. If that happened, the election would be decided in the new legislature, which was predicted to be heavily Republican. Once the most popular governor in the nation, Dean was running for his political life because he supported civil unions.

By the time the votes were cast, on November 7, 2000, most Vermonters were tired of the whole business, but they expressed satisfaction with the leaders who had brought them civil unions. The voters reelected Dean with 52 percent of the overall vote, with Dwyer getting only 38 percent, less than she had received in 1998. Lieutenant Governor Douglas Racine, a Democrat who openly supported same-sex marriage, was narrowly reelected. Secretary of State Deb Markowitz was also reelected, notwithstanding heated attacks against her for instructing town clerks that they had a legal duty to obey the new civil unions law. Senator Elizabeth Ready, another pro-union Democrat, was elected State Auditor, as the successor to Ed Flanagan, an openly gay Democrat who lost to pro-union U.S. Republican Senator Jeffords by a 3 to 1 margin.* The Vermont House returned a significant majority for the Republicans, with many pro-union Democrats, such as Diane Carmoli, Robert Kinsey (running as a Democrat after being defeated in the Republican primary), and Mary Mazzariello being defeated by pro tradition Republicans. Representatives Little and Lippert won handily. The Vermont Senate remained Democratic by a 16 to 14 margin, and pro-union by a margin of 17 to 13. Mark MacCormack remained Majority Leader, and Richard Sears would head the Judiciary Committee again. The most public casualty of the Take Back Vermont movement was Orange County's Senator Mark MacDonald, whom the voters returned to the classroom fulltime.

On January 18, 2001, Representative Sheltra introduced the Marriage Restoration Act to repeal the civil union law and void the unions entered into under that law. Representative Flory, the new chair of the House Judiciary Committee, has not lent her support to the repeal measure, but her committee held a series of hearings in early 2001 to consider ways to amend the law to make if more acceptable to traditionalists, who now dominate the committee. The committee reported a bill replacing the civil union institution with a weaker substitute, and the bill passed the House but died in the Senate. The Vermont Supreme Court has terminated the *Baker* lawsuit, but any bill weakening the civil union statute would face a new constitutional challenge. The debate continues in Vermont. As of September 1, 2001, Vermont had issued more than 2700 licenses for couples to join in civil union, 80 percent of whom were from out of state.

★ The most notable result of the election is this: the Republican Party had only local-ized success in exploiting the civil union issue. Not only did Dwyer crash and burn on the issue, but Jeffords's long-standing progay stance made him the biggest winner of all on November 7, 2000. He was the only statewide official of the Republican orientation—until he left the Republican Party in 2001. His departure, which gave the Democrats control of the U.S. Senate, may have been inspired in part by Republican gay-bashing in the civil union debate.

CHAPTER THREE

Comparative Law Lessons for the Same-Sex Marriage Movement

THE DIALECTIC BETWEEN GAY PEOPLE'S politics of recognition and traditionalists' politics of preservation is a transnational phenomenon.
Specifically, the debate in the United States regarding state recognition of
lesbian and gay relationships has parallels with developments elsewhere
in the world, particularly in Canada and Europe. Leaders of the same-sex
marriage movement in the various countries are in constant communica-
tion with one another,[1] and no doubt traditionalists are in contact across
state lines as well. To understand and evaluate the American experience
in Hawaii and Vermont, introduced in chapters 1 and 2 of this book, one
must also consider the experience in other countries.

For one thing, that experience gives us valuable perspective. The
Vermont Civil Unions Law was a major cultural as well as legal event in
the United States but would not have been considered nearly as big a
deal in some other modernized countries. The gaylegal politics of recognition has made greater headway in Canada and most western European
countries than it has in the United States. As this book goes to press in
the summer of 2001, the Netherlands has just recognized same-sex marriages, way ahead of any state in the United States, and important

83

legislation recognizing same-sex unions has recently been ted in Germany, Canada, and France. Correlatively, the traditionalst politics of preservation has been less successful in those countries; fundamentalist religious perspectives are much more prominent in our country than in these others, and so is openly antigay prejudice. At the same time, gay, lesbian, bisexual, and transgendered (GLBT) people are also more prominent in our public culture than they are in Europe and Canada, where they tend to blend into the rest of society. The more tolerant public norms of these other countries have probably contributed to their assimilation of sexual minorities—in contrast to the more acrimonious and public "culture clashes" between sexual minorities and traditionalists in our less tolerant country.

Because Europe and Canada are, from a gaylegal point of view, ahead of the United States in their treatment of same-sex couples, I expected that a close examination of developments in those countries would suggest directions for our own. The more I have explored the matter, the more persuaded am I that the comparative law of same-sex unions casts a deeper and more ambiguous light on our future. This chapter will provide a detailed report of the evolving state recognition for same-sex unions in Denmark, the Netherlands, Canada, Germany, and France, as well as mention of partial recognition in other countries. Experience in other nations suggests, on the one hand, that equal, or roughly equal, recognition for same-sex relationships is on the way but, on the other hand, suggests different possibilities for what that recognition might be. One way to array the possibilities in the menu is by reference to the level of commitment entailed or assumed by the different regulatory schemes.

In the United States, the most common form of recognition is the *domestic partnership* laws adopted in California and many urban centers.[2] These laws assure employment fringe benefits and entail the weakest level of commitment between the partners. *Cohabitation* laws, which impose duties as well as confer benefits on couples, are a more serious state recognition. Such laws have been extended to same-sex couples in many states of this country as well as abroad; the range of benefits flowing to cohabiters is generally much greater in Canada and Europe. A third level of state recognition might be termed *cohabitation-plus* or, after the 1997 Hawaii law, *reciprocal beneficiaries*.[3] This model assumes a higher level of commitment and treats the partners as surrogate decision makers for one another, and as persons entitled to mutual support and employer fringe benefits. Vermont's *civil unions* and Denmark's *registered partnerships* represent another choice in the menu: the couples pledge lifelong commitment, which the state backs up with various obligations and rewards as well as multifarious benefits and rights. This regulatory item is *marriage* without the name, or the portability, that is, the automatic recognition that marriage carries with it to other states and countries. A final, and also novel, option is *covenant marriage*, where the partners signal their long-term intentions by precommitment to more divorce obstacles than states now pose to the dissolution of marriage.

What I have described in the preceding paragraph is the emerging menu of state-recognized commitment options for couples. No state has adopted all the regimes on the menu, and only the Netherlands has extended all its menu options to same-sex as well as different-sex couples. Nonetheless, the menu represents a rough roadmap of the future of state recognition in the United States as well as in Europe and Canada. The consequences of the menu are important for the American same-sex marriage movement and its critics. One consequence is that the developments in other countries help create an aura of inevitability in this country: now that the Netherlands has breached the modern taboo against recognition of same-sex marriage—and with the support of large majorities of the straight population—supporters have taken heart and opponents are counting the days (or decades) until the institution comes to their locales. Supporters need this sense of inevitability, because the comparative law experience also suggests, rather strongly, that same-sex marriage will come to other jurisdictions only in "small steps," as Professor Kees Waaldijk puts it.[4]

But the small steps will vary from state to state. Each jurisdiction recognizing same-sex marriages will come to that point by a different route. This, too, is instructive for Americans. Minority groups, such as lesbians and gay men, in our country are accustomed to winning equality rights from judges. The same groups in Europe have made greater progress by obtaining equality from their parliaments, not their courts.

Even Canada, where gay people have won important constitutional protections, has seen legislators act favorably, enabling popular consolidation of judicial victories. Perhaps the most important comparative law lesson for the same-sex marriage movement is that the experience in other countries suggests robust alternatives to the court-centered strategies for obtaining equality for lesbian and gay couples. Consider the stories of a few of these other countries in some detail.

THE DANISH REGISTERED PARTNERSHIP ACT AS
ONE ROAD TO SAME-SEX MARRIAGE

As the Hawaii and Vermont case studies in chapters 1 and 2 reflect, lesbian and gay activists in the United States have for the most part followed a *court-driven* same-sex marriage model. The model is court driven in that activists' primary strategy has been to appeal to courts rather than legislatures or agencies to equalize the status, benefits, and duties of same-sex couples with those of different-sex couples. It was the Vermont Supreme Court, not the litigants, that sent these issues to the legislature, and there is no reason to believe the legislature in that state would have done anything had there not been a state supreme court decision recognizing the rights of same-sex couples. But now that the Vermont legislature has acted, even if under judicial pressure, lesbian and gay activists have been reconsidering the courts-first strategy in some states. For example, in Connecticut, where I live, same-sex marriage advocates have petitioned the legislature first, and the first hearings on such legislation were held on March 16, 2001. (In contrast, in our neighbor Massachusetts, gay and lesbian advocates and defenders have brought a lawsuit seeking state recognition of same-sex marriages.) Moreover, some benefits of marriage can be obtained administratively, by liberal construction of terms like *family* or even *spouse* to include same-sex partners. Although the Defense of Marriage Act forecloses this strategy at the federal level when the statute or regulation speaks of spouse or marriage, it does not necessarily bar administrative interpretations of other statutory terms to allow some benefits, such as immigration, for same-sex partners.

The American model has also been one that seeks marriage rather than some other goal—such as statewide domestic partnership—that would have entailed piecemeal recognition of selected benefits and the creation of a whole new state institution. Marriage was not the goal of the gayocracy before the 1990s, however. Litigation often yielded piecemeal benefits and duties for same-sex partners, such as the right to succeed to the rent-controlled apartment of one's partner in New York,[5] the right to be appointed guardian of one's incapacitated partner in Minnesota,[6] and the obligation to keep implicit promises of support after breaking up with one's cohabiting partner in California.[7] Even after marriage became the official goal in the 1990s, of course, the results have not fit the model. In Hawaii, same-sex partners ended up with a new institution of reciprocal beneficiaries and piecemeal benefits, with no obligations. In Vermont, the new civil union institution entails the full range of benefits and obligations.

It is interesting to compare the court-driven marriage model characteristic of the American movement with the approaches followed elsewhere in the world. The most successful model thus far has been the *legislature-driven partnership* approach pioneered in Denmark. This approach has thus far yielded a new institution of registered partnerships in six countries, one of which (the Netherlands) has just enacted a law recognizing same-sex marriages.

The Danish Registered Partnership Act of 1989

The same-sex marriage movement in Scandinavia began well before the one in the United States and has already yielded positive results.[8] In Denmark, Martin Elmer, editor of *The Friend*, and the gay Society of 1948 started advocating for state recognition of same-sex unions in the period 1966–68. Unlike American activists galvanized by civil rights litigation successes, those in Denmark engaged in an educational campaign aimed at showing members of Parliament and the general population that lesbians and gay men were often partnered and that those partnerships suffered from the legal benefits denied them because they were not marriages. Friendly members of Parliament introduced legislation to give legal recognition to cohabiting relationships, including those of lesbian and gay people. Instead of adopting that proposal, Parliament established a Marriage Committee in 1969.

Notwithstanding this early start, little headway was made in the

1970s.[9] Lesbian and gay activists themselves met with the Marriage Committee but were uncertain as to what to ask for. Elmer and most leaders of the Society of 1948 favored same-sex marriage, but radical feminist and gay groups that proliferated in the early 1970s objected to marriage as reactionary and patriarchal. They favored creating new institutions. In 1973, after vigorous grassroots discussions and study, the Society of 1948 voted to demand legal recognition of same-sex *partnerships*—not marriages, but a new institution with the same rights, benefits, and duties. However, the Marriage Committee, populated with unsympathetic legislators and administrators, was not inclined to go along. In 1973, the committee issued its first report. With only one member dissenting (Else-Merete Ross, a member of Parliament), the committee concluded that homosexual couples faced many needless legal disabilities but ruled out recognition of their relationships on par with marital ones, because both the public and international opinion would be outraged at such a departure from the traditional definition of marriage.[10] In response to the committee's discouraging signal and intensified criticisms of marriage within the lesbian and gay community, the Society of 1948 gave up on marriage and petitioned the Marriage Committee in 1976 for recognition of cohabitation rights for all couples. In 1980, the committee substantially rejected this proposal as well.[11]

The Landsforeningen for Bøsser og Lebiske (the successor to the Society of 1948) responded to this rebuff by having friendly members of Parliament introduce legislation in 1981. Their bill would have created registered partnerships that would have most of the benefits but few of the obligations of marriage. A progressive party, the Radical Liberals, introduced its own simpler registered partnership bill in 1984; the measure would have assured registered partners of all the same benefits and responsibilities of marriage, without the name. This bill died, but Parliament did create a Commission for the Enlightenment of the Situation of Homosexuals in Society, which included gay representatives. The commission concluded that lesbians and gay men suffered unfairly from their unequal treatment and in 1987 recommended adding sexual orientation as a basis for hate speech and public accommodation discrimination claims; Parliament immediately enacted the recommended laws.[12] But the commission's final report, issued in January

1988, recommended (by a 6 to 5 vote) against establishing a registered partnership system, still fearing public and international reaction.[13]

Notwithstanding this recommendation, representatives of the Social Democrats, the Socialist People's Party, and the Radical Liberals introduced a bill in Parliament to create registered partnerships along the lines proposed in 1984. The governing party opposed the bill, arguing that it was premature and would unsettle opinion in Denmark and elsewhere. Members of the Christian People's Party (CPP) opposed the measure as "a bomb" that would destroy marriage and promote "unnatural" homosexual conduct. The bill was reintroduced in November 1988, after new elections and after a poll showed most Danes in favor of the measure. The parties agreed to allow their members to vote their consciences. The debate turned into a religionfest. CPP opponents of the bill declared it "fundamentally against that which this Christian society is built upon." Supporters responded that the bill was supported by Christian valorization of "the ability to love," and the Danish Christian tradition of "charity and tolerance."[14] On May 26, 1989, the legislators voted for the bill, 71 to 47, with five abstentions. The Danish Registered Partnership Act went into effect on October 1.[15]

The Danish law gave registered same-sex partners all of the same benefits and same responsibilities that the law gave to different-sex married couples—except for those associated with children. Thus, registered partners were not permitted to adopt children, including one another's children, nor to have access to state-provided artificial insemination services.* Also unlike different-sex marriage, at least one of the registered partners must be a citizen of and permanent resident in Denmark; there is no involvement in celebration or divorce by the official state clergy; and registered partners' rights and duties are not portable to other countries unless those countries themselves agree to it. Notwithstanding all these residuals of inequality, lesbians and gay men heralded the law as a major advance. The first partnerships registered on October 1 of that year; among the first couples were Axel and Eigil Axgil, two of the leading gay rights activists in the country.

★ The Danish Parliament repealed the first of these restrictions in Act No. 360 of June 2, 1999. The restriction on artificial insemination remains in effect (as of June 2001).

Following the Danish Model: Registered Partnerships in Other Countries

The Danish law was essentially copied by five other states in the 1990s: Norway (1993), Sweden (1995), Greenland and Iceland (1996), and the Netherlands (1998).[16] Deferring discussion of the Netherlands to the next section, consider here the interesting stories of how the Danish model contributed to the adoption of similar laws in Norway and Sweden in particular.

Although Norway's public culture is more religiously oriented than Denmark's, gay men, bisexuals, and lesbians have been able to live more open lives in Norway. The Det Norske Forbund (or Norweigian Society) of 1948 (DNF-48) was able, for example, to persuade the government not only to decriminalize consensual sodomy but also to equalize the age of consent for same-sex and different-sex couples in 1972, several years ahead of the rest of Scandinavia.[17] Although political conditions were ripe for persuasion as to same-sex relationships, DNF-48 was torn between members who wanted recognition of same-sex marriages, and those who wanted to dismantle marriage altogether. Although they remained divided as to relationships, DNF-48 and radical groups united in persuading the government in 1981 to adopt a new law making it a crime to disparage or refuse to serve people based on their sexual orientation.[18] This was the first national antidiscrimination law in the world for lesbian and gay people. The government's commitment to changing public attitudes also impelled it to accept gay men and lesbians into the nation's armed forces and even to subsidize educative organizations.

It was not until 1988–89 that the lesbian and gay rights groups formed a reasonably united effort to seek legal recognition of their relationships. One advance was a result of coalition politics: Parliament's adoption in 1991 of the Joint Households Law, which provides for support obligations and inheritance of joint property for adult couples (including same-sex couples) who have cohabited for more than two years. In the meantime, Norway's gay rights organizations were pushing for something like the Danish law. They immediately confronted an obstacle. The Christian People's Party (CPP), strongly opposed to any significant state recognition, was a coalition partner in the new government formed after the 1989 elections. Following its Danish counterpart and the Danish legal model, DNF-48 pushed for a private bill creating a new institution of registered partnerships. Such a bill was introduced in 1990 and supported by legislators from the Labor, Left Socialist, and Progress Parties. After almost being killed by the CPP, the bill made slow progress and was referred for study to the Ministry of Children and Family Affairs.

The Ministry's 1992 report took the position that lesbians and gay men were worthy citizens of Norway whose relationships should be fostered by the state in the same manner as different-sex relationships were fostered. Acknowledging the views of the National Council of the Church of Norway that marriage has traditionally been founded in procreation between the marital partners and in "the natural, transcultural awareness of sexual polarity," the Ministry concluded that "marriage is also a legal contract that regulates the financial situation of the two people who live in a close economic union and become dependent on each other."[19] The "reciprocal economic and legal needs of two people of the same sex who live together in a committed relationship will be virtually the same as those of a married couple" in this respect. The Ministry saw legal recognition of same-sex partnerships as having several salutary benefits. The law would allow same-sex couples to signal to one another and the community that they are forming a committed relationship; such commitment means that "greater efforts are made to avoid a break-up if the relationship undergoes a crisis."[20] Not unimportantly, the law would "mean a public acceptance of homosexual relationships" and would "encourage more gays and lesbians to come out, and thus reduce the problems created by their need to hide their own nature and live in isolation." With more "out" lesbians and gay men, unproductive social prejudice would erode, the Ministry argued.[22] Notwithstanding this reasoning in favor of lesbian and gay partnerships, the Ministry choked on adoption by these couples. Given the lack of knowledge about the effects of the partnership on children—and implicitly bowing to public and parliamentary resistance—the Ministry summarily concluded that "it is not pertinent to discuss this matter" and went along with an adoption exclusion.[23]

Although this was a powerful endorsement, DNF-48 and its parliamentary allies still faced a hard struggle: unlike the other countries in Scandinavia, Norway has two parliamentary chambers whose assent is needed for legislation, and religion-based opposition was fierce.[23] Opponents argued that the registered partnership law would condone homosexual conduct, would undermine the institution of marriage, and was unnecessary, as the most legitimate needs of lesbian and gay couples could be satisfied through more modest changes in the law. Unlike Denmark, there was an organized grassroots (the People's Movement against the Partnership Law) as well as parliamentary (CPP) opposition to the proposal. In both arenas, however, the opponents suffered from one strategic catastrophe after another. For example, Anders Gåslund, the leader of the CPP's youth organization, came out as gay in protest to his party's attack on the bill. Notwithstanding the intense opposition, the proposal squeaked by narrowly: the Odelsting (akin to the U.S. House of Representatives) passed it by a 58 to 40 margin on March 29, 1993, and the Lagting (Senate) voted for it 18 to 16 on April 1.

Sweden followed a slightly different path from either Norway or Denmark. Like the other countries, Sweden had a well-organized gay rights movement; sodomy had been decriminalized in 1944. Unlike Denmark's, Sweden's Parliament in 1973 endorsed the idea of cohabitation between same-sex partners at the same time it was giving legal recognition to cohabiting partners. In 1977, Sweden created its first Commission on Homosexuality, which in 1984 issued a report describing the lives and aspirations of lesbian and gay persons and couples and documenting the antigay and discriminatory attitudes held by most straight people. The report urged that the government conduct an educational campaign, adopt laws prohibiting private discrimination (there was no state discrimination against gay people in employment or the armed forces), and give same-sex couples all the rights afforded different-sex cohabiting couples. The report accepted the notion that homosexual couples had much the same needs as heterosexual ones but sadly concluded that "present-day judgements with regard to marriage are so firmly rooted that it is hardly possible to speak of marriage between two individuals of the same sex, without defining marriage in a different way from that practiced today."[24] In response to the report, Sweden adopted the Homosexual Cohabitees Act of 1987, which extended the mutual support and inheritance rights provisions of earlier cohabitation legislation to same-sex cohabiting couples.[25]

So Sweden was just as much a pioneer as Denmark: the cohabitation law was the first of its kind anywhere in the world, but its limitations became more pronounced after Denmark adopted its registered partnership law in 1989. Sweden's Parliament created a Homosexual Partnership Commission in 1990, and the commission issued its report in 1993. The report supported a registered partnership law to recognize and reinforce the mutual commitments made by lesbian and gay couples, to extend to those couples the economic security of legal benefits as well as obligations, and to influence social attitudes, which had already softened in response to earlier progay legal reforms.[26] The commission rejected arguments that legal sanction for lesbian and gay relationships would have deleterious effects on marriage, society, or civilization and characterized such arguments "as an expression of the moral panic which can occur in times of upheaval and change."[27] Like its counterparts in Denmark and Norway, the commission felt that there was not sufficient evidence to support state encouragement of lesbian and gay families with children.

Following the pattern of its neighbors, Sweden's Parliament took up the issue on a private bill basis: members could vote their consciences. The Christian Democratic Party, which was part of the ruling government, was the situs of most opposition; it deemphasized the immorality-of-homosexuality argument, however, and only argued that the legislation was unnecessary and would weaken marriage. On June 7, 1994, Parliament voted 171 to 141 in favor of the Registered Partnership Act.[28] Like its Danish model, the Swedish law extended to same-sex registered partners almost all the same benefits and obligations of different-sex marriage, with the main exception being rights of adoption, joint custody, and artificial insemination, and requires that at least one partner be Swedish. (Parliament in February 1999 created a commission to study lesbian and gay families with children and to reexamine the custody, adoption, and insemination issues.) The Swedish law was different in requiring towns to appoint a separate official to perform a partnership ceremony and in explicitly recognizing same-sex registered partnerships entered in other countries.

Greenland, a self-governing dependency of Denmark, accepted the registered partnership law, with some reluctance, in 1994, and the new law took effect in 1996.[29] Iceland followed the other countries in 1996. Its law created "confirmed partnerships" and differed mainly in allowing couples joint custody of the children either partner brings to the family.[30] Registered partnership legislation has been introduced in Finland, Latvia, and Spain, but no action has been taken in any of these countries as of June 2001. Proposals for registered partnerships were the basis for compromise legislation adopted in Germany and Portugal in 2001, and they are discussed later in this chapter.

Expanding upon the Danish Model: The Netherlands

The biggest convert to the Danish model was the Netherlands.[31] Like its neighbors to the north, the Netherlands had a gay community that had long been organized—first as the Cultural Leisure Committee (COC) in 1946, whose members were closeted. COC went through several name changes as it became a more activist group. Since 1971, when it took on its current name, the Netherlands Association for the Integration of Homosexuality COC (NVIH-COC) has spearheaded a dizzying agenda of successful reform proposals, including[32]

- a statute equalizing the age of consent for homosexual and heterosexual intercourse (1971);[33]
- revocation of homosexuality as a ground for rejection for military service (1973);
- state recognition of NVIH-COC as a registered corporation (1973);
- parliamentary approval of asylum for people persecuted because of their homosexuality (1981);
- the opening up of most institutions of artificial insemination to lesbians and same-sex couples (1980s and 1990s);
- state sponsorship of a study into the causes of antigay discrimination, followed by statutes adding sexual orientation to the country's list of hate crimes (1992), and generally prohibiting sexual orientation and other forms of discrimination in employment, housing, medical care, and access to goods and services (1994).[34]

With these advances in civil equality, NVIH-COC and activists in the 1990s pressed strongly for recognition of same-sex relationships—essentially the last major inequality left on the statute books. Unlike the gay rights groups in Scandinavia, NVIH-COC was dealing with a left-of-center government receptive to its goal of full equality.

TABLE 3.1. **PARTNERSHIP REGISTRATION IN FIVE COUNTRIES, 1990–2000**

	Denmark	**Norway**	**Sweden**	**Iceland**	**Netherlands**
1990 (MM/FF)	746 (573/173)	n.s.	n.s.	n.s.	n.s.
1991 (MM/FF)	258 (171/87)	n.s.	n.s.	n.s.	n.s.
1992 (MM/FF)	218 (139/79)	n.s.	n.s.	n.s.	n.s.
1993 (MM/FF)	185 (124/61)	n.s.	n.s.	n.s.	n.s.
1994 (MM/FF)	197 (105/92)	294 (203/91)	n.s.	n.s.	n.s.
1995 (MM/FF)	194 (119/75)	98 (64/34)	333 (249/84)	n.s.	n.s.
1996 (MM/FF)	199 (106/93)	127 (80/47)	160 (101/59)	n.s.	n.s.
1997 (MM/FF)	178 (101/77)	118 (75/43)	131 (79/52)	33 (16/17)	n.s.
1998 (MM/FF)	197 (84/113)	115 (71/44)	125 (79/46)	12 (5/7)	4626 (1686/1324)
1999 (MM/FF)	298 (161/137)	144 (82/62)	144 (77/67)	11 (6/5)	3256 (897/864)
2000 (MM/FF)	n.a.	n.a.	179 (109/70)	n.a.	2922 (815/785)
Total (MM/FF)	2908 (1831/1077)	892 (573/319)	1072 (694/378)	57 (27/30)	10,804 (3398/2973)

Source: Professor Kees Waaldjijk, University of Leiden Faculty of Law.

In 1996, the government introduced a registered partnership bill and established a commission to study the implications of recognizing same-sex marriage. In December, the lower house of Parliament voted by more than two to one for the measure, and it was adopted in 1997. The Dutch registered partnership law followed the Danish model in most respects: registered partners had almost all the same benefits and obligations of marriage, but not the right to adopt children. Unlike the Danish law, the Netherlands statute made it easier for registered partners to divorce: they could either go to court, as married couples do, or dissolve their union by mutual agreement. Also, the Dutch law required that both partners be Dutch citizens or have a "valid residence entitlement" in the Netherlands (thus excluding tourists and asylum-seekers). Most important, the Dutch law allowed different-sex as well as same-sex couples to register. As table 3.1 shows, almost five thousand couples (a third of them different-sex) registered in the first year, and more than ten thousand couples in the first three years—many more couples than had registered in all the Scandinavian countries for all the years of their statutes' operation!

In August 1996, while the partnership bill was progressing, the government established a committee to study the possibility of extending marriage to same-sex couples. The Kortmann Committee issued its report in October 1997. Like those of Scandinavian countries, this report found that lesbian and gay people lived in committed relationships that would profit from legal recognition. The report found little need even to address the religious arguments that had been prominent in the north but, instead, paid more attention to the presence of children in lesbian and gay households.[37] Unlike the study commissions in the other countries, the one in the Netherlands voted 5 to 3 for same-sex marriage and for adoption by same-sex couples. The government was receptive to both proposals. On July 8, 1999, it introduced separate bills for same-sex marriage and adoption in the lower house of Parliament.[36] The government's explanatory memorandum affirmed "the principle of equal treatment of homosexual and heterosexual couples," which the legislation sought to advance.[37] The marriage bill left registered partnerships in place, with the option of converting one's partnership into a marriage. Citing the large number of couples who have registered, the government concluded that "there is a need for a marriage-like institution devoid of the symbolism attached to marriage."[38] All the rights and duties of marriage were, of course, applicable—except that the presumption that a child born to a married woman is the progeny of her spouse would not apply when the spouse was another woman. "It would be pushing things too far to assume that a child born in a marriage of two women would legally descend from both women. That would be stretching reality."[39]

On September 12, 2000, the lower house of Parliament voted 109 to 33 in favor of the government's same-sex marriage bill and by an uncounted but substantial majority in favor of the adoption bill as well. The Liberal and Labor Parties that formed the government supported these measures, as did several deputies of the Christian Democratic Party. The bills then proceeded to the upper house, which approved them on December 19. Her Majesty Queen Beatrix signed the bills into law on December 21, 2001, and they were published on January 11, 2001.[40] The new law went into effect after a further statute was adopted by Parliament and signed by the Queen.[41] Once that occurred, the Netherlands became the first modern western state to recognize same-sex marriages as a matter of law. As amended by the Act on the Opening Up of Marriage, Article 30(1) of the Dutch Civil Code now provides, "A Marriage can be contracted by two persons of different sex or of the same sex."[42] A new Article 77a sets forth procedures by which couples can convert their registered partnerships into marriages. Shortly after midnight, April 1, 2001, Amsterdam Mayor Job Cohen presided over a wedding ceremony that converted the registered partnerships of four lesbian and gay couples into marriages, as allowed by the new law. The couples rejoiced as Christian protesters outside picketed their ceremony.

STATE RECOGNITION OF SAME-SEX UNIONS ELSEWHERE: OTHER ROADS TO SAME-SEX MARRIAGE?

Thus far, the Danish model has flourished in northern European countries with small ethnically homogeneous populations and a tradition of separating religion and politics—countries a lot like our state of Vermont, whose civil unions are similar to registered partnerships. Most of the world is not like Denmark, the Netherlands, and Vermont, however.[43] Lesbian and gay relationships are not currently relevant to the public law agenda of most developing countries, such as the overpopulated ones of Asia and the population-depleted ones in sub-Saharan Africa. The mix of modern and premodern culture and politics in those countries is not hospitable to a potent lesbian and gay rights movement. Even where conditions allow a modest rights movement for gender and sexual minorities, as in Latin America, it is in most places not yet robust enough to challenge core cultural and religious attachments to marriage as the only way to think about relationships. The same is true of the Middle East, whose Islamic politics render homosexuality a taboo topic.

The exception is, of course, the one non-Islamic country in the Middle East: Israel. Israel's politics is suffused with religion, including homophobic versions of Judaism, yet also with a pragmatic tolerance reflected in some of the boldest judicial decisions I have seen on the topic.

Europe outside of Scandinavia and the Netherlands has moved more slowly on the issue. Some countries have recognized same-sex unions as a form of cohabitation, as Sweden did in 1987; several are considering registered partnership proposals. Recognition as a form of cohabitation has been the choice, so far, in Belgium, Portugal, and Hungary. The most interesting development has been in France, which created a new institution called *Pactes civiles*, similar to the reciprocal beneficiaries law created in Hawaii (see chapter 1). In late 2000, Germany followed with a law recognizing "life partnerships," also a hybrid generated by the politics of compromise. The European Union (EU) ought to be a vehicle for wider and stronger legal recognition, because it is committed both to nondiscrimination on the basis of sexual orientation and to assuring free movement of persons (and couples?) within the union,[44] but thus far the European Council and, more surprisingly, the European Court of Justice have been timid in pressing countries to recognize same-sex unions.[45] The Netherlands' legislative activities in the last five years have proceeded on the assumption that the EU would not recognize same-sex unions or marriages anytime soon. But, if most of the European countries coalesce around registered partnerships, updated cohabitation, or same-sex marriage, the organs of the EU (as well as the European Court of Human Rights) will surely pressure outlying states to follow.

One European country offering virtually no recognition is the United Kingdom, which has a culture that is both puritan and prurient and a politics periodically infused with doses of moralism. (The UK is the most frequent situs for lesbian and gay complaints of violation of European treaty and convention obligations.) Correspondingly, most English-speaking countries have been slow to give legal recognition to lesbian and gay relationships. Thus, virtually no progress has been made in India, Pakistan, Gibraltar, and New Zealand. Where there has been progress, as in the United States, Canada, and South Africa, it has been painfully incremental, and the result of judicial pressure. An exception to this generalization is Australia, where court cases have been unsuccessful, but a pioneering cohabitation and domestic relations law was adopted in 1999 by the province of New South Wales (where Sidney is located).[46]

The French-German Model: Legislature-Driven Cohabitation-Plus

The Danish registered partnership law almost immediately triggered legislative proposals in France.[47] Bills were introduced to create *Contrats de partenariat civil* in 1990 and *Contrats d'union civile* in 1992. (Note the semantic anticipation of Vermont's civil unions by the 1992 proposal.) Both proposals were open to different-sex as well as same-sex couples, and to nonromantic as well as romantic couples. In 1993, the French Parliament adopted one part of the latter proposal when it made social welfare benefits available to dependent cohabitees, regardless of sex.[48] Simultaneously, couples were litigating for the benefits of *concubinage*, French statutory rights of cohabiting couples. In 1997, the French Cour de cassation held in *Vilela v. Weil* that the surviving person whose partner had died of complications associated with AIDS could not succeed to the partner's lease, a right he would have had if they had been a cohabiting different-sex couple. The court ruled that "concubinage can only result from a stable and continuous relationship having the appearance of marriage, therefore between a man and a woman."[49] The case reflected the involvement of AIDS groups as well as gay rights groups in the French movement. AIDS and gay rights groups devised a proposal for a *Contrat d'union sociale* (CUS) that was introduced in the National Assembly and Senate in early 1997. This bill focused on romantic couples, but a subsequent proposal, the *Contrat d'union civile et sociale*, applied to any two persons, including relatives. Various other proposals were floated.

The parties of the Left campaigned in 1998 on a platform that promised legal recognition of same-sex relationships and won a smashing victory. In May 1998, the victorious parties introduced a bill proposing to create *Pactes civils de solidarité* (PaCS), which would allow different-sex as well as same-sex couples to assume mutual responsibilities for one another, similar to the CUS. The parties of the Right were able to block the legislation when it came to the floor on October 9, because the Socialists in particular were absent from the chamber, suggesting ambivalence in light of the subject matter and the rising popular opposition. In September, the prime minister's office was flooded with thousands of letters against "the unspeakable and repugnant proposal for homosexual marriage" due to a campaign orchestrated by a fundamentalist Christian group. The Conference of Catholic Bishops, which termed the proposal "useless and dangerous," and the Association of Catholic Families and the Families of France conducted what two authors have called "the last homophobic crusade."[50] Emboldened by the popular religious opposition and the Socialists' timidity, deputies of the Right vigorously attacked the bill when it was revived and extensively debated between November 3 and December 9. Deputy Christine Boutin opened the debate with a Bible-based criticism of homosexuals; her colleagues compared homosexuals to "zoophiles" and argued that the bill would be "a return to barbarism."[51] Notwithstanding these barbs, a majority of deputies voted for the bill's first reading on December 10.

On January 31, 1999, Boutin led a demonstration of almost 100,000 people against the bill. Professor Daniel Borrillo reports that the marchers carried signs reading, "The homosexuals of today are the pedophiles of tomorrow," "No nephews for the big aunties," and "Jospin [the Prime Minister] take care of your rear end!" Throughout the march, people reportedly shouted, "Burn the fags at the stake!" In response to countersigns from ACT-UP Paris, an AIDS organization, the crowd cried out, "Filthy fags—Burn in Hell!" In this context, the Senate rejected the PaCS bill but proposed a new law extending concubinage to same-sex couples (overriding *Vilela*). On second reading in the National Assembly, the deputies voted to create PaCS and to revise the concubinage law to include same-sex couples. The Senate still refused to go along, and was able to delay the bill so that it died at the end of that parliamentary session in June.

When Parliament reconvened, the parties of the Left insisted on the bill, and the Senate's delaying tactics were no longer able to stop it. On October 13, 1999, the National Assembly passed the PaCS law in a party-line vote, 315 to 249. Deputies and senators on the Right filed an immediate petition to the Conseil constitutionnel, arguing that the new law violated the French Constitution. The Conseil upheld the law on

November 9.[52] The law was promulgated by the President on November 15.[53] The new law adds same-sex couples to the established institution of concubinage and creates a new institution, the PaCS.

A PaCS is "a contract concluded between two adult individuals, of different sexes or of the same sex, to organize their life in common [*vie commune*]."[54] Entering into a PaCS is as easy as entering into a contract: you and your partner fill out a PaCS form, submit it to the town clerk, and you are "PaCSed," as they say. Although same-sex as well as different-sex couples can PaCS, there are some limitations: both partners must be adults; neither can be married; one cannot enter into a PaCS with one's parent, grandparent, child, grandchild, mother, father, son, daughter-in-law, brother, sister, uncle, aunt, nephew, niece, and so forth; but one *can* PaCS one's cousin. In upholding the law against constitutional attack, France's Conseil constitutionnel gave it an interpretive gloss that imputes a romantic and possibly sexual component to the PaCS. The Conseil construed *vie commune* to mean not just *une communauté d'interêts* (common interests), but also *une vie de couple* (life as a "couple"). The requirement of a (sexual?) life as a couple can explain the particular prohibitions that track French incest law.

Partners joined by a PaCS undertake to help one another "mutually and materially," and they are jointly liable to third parties for debts contracted by either of them "for the necessities of their daily life and for expenses relating to their common residence."[55] Unless otherwise agreed, movable and immovable (real and personal) property purchased by the partners after the conclusion of the PaCS is presumed to be jointly and equally owned, with a right of survivorship.[56] The partners may choose another regime, either in the PaCS agreement they submit to the county court or in each document granting them title to each item of property. The partners are subject to joint taxation of their combined incomes after three years in a PaCS.[57] If one partner is the official tenant of the partners' common residence and abandons the residence or dies, the lease continues for the benefit of, or is transferred to, the other partner—reversing the Cour de cassation's decision in *Vilela*. If one partner cannot claim social security benefits in any other capacity, he can benefit from the other partner's (public) health and maternity insurance coverage.[58] Partners enjoy the same rights as spouses to request a transfer for the partner left behind when the other partner is transferred to another city for professional reasons (if both partners are civil servants), to simultaneous vacations (if they are working in the same company), to two days of bereavement leave if one partner dies, and to the return to the surviving partner of the capital of certain social security contributions made by a deceased partner.[59] The new law says nothing about sexual fidelity, inheritance rights, or obligations and rights toward children of either partner.

A PaCS is almost as easy to dissolve as to create. If the partners agree to dissolve their PaCS, they can do it almost immediately, and without the aid of an attorney. (In France, even more than in the United States, divorce is a lengthy process and requires court appearances and usually legal representation; women object that the process is slanted against their interests.) Even if one partner objects, the other partner can still dissolve the PaCS by providing notice to the objecting partner, and the union dissolves three months later. The law does not say what alimony or quasi-contractual rights partners might have in the event of a dissolution, and this issue is sure to be litigated.

Although the PaCS law was the government's response to lesbian and gay demands for equal marriage rights, it is open to straight couples as well. Informal estimates suggest that as many as 40 percent of the more than fourteen thousand couples PaCSed in the first four months of the law's operation were different-sex couples.[60] Note the different nature of PaCS for different couples. For lesbian and gay couples, the PaCS is the closest they can come (in France) to marriage, and most couples have celebrated their unions like marriages. For straight couples, however, the PaCS is a possible alternative to marriage, a middle ground for the couple critical of marriage's patriarchal past or leary of its obligations and difficulty in termination.

The adoption of the PaCS law by the French Socialist government placed increased pressure on the German Socialist government, which had been elected at about the same time and with the same promise for legal recognition of same-sex relationships. The "Red-Green" (Socialist-Environmental) coalition government had been unsuccessful in persuading the upper chamber of the German Parliament (the Bundesrat) to accept such legislation. In 2000, Minister of Justice Herta Daeubler-

Gmelin proposed two bills, only one of which required Bundesrat approval. The conservative Christian Democratic Union (CDU) vigorously opposed recognition of same-sex unions. "This is unconstitutional and an outrage to German culture," said its leader, Norbert Geis. Roman Catholic Cardinal Joachim Meisner wrote, "The bill gives privileges to homosexual relationships and thus represents the active sponsorship by the state of what is in the Church's view immoral behavior."[61] The other leading parties enthusiastically supported the measures—the Socialists, the Greens, and the liberal Free Democrats.

On November 10, 2000, the day after the anniversary of both Kristallnacht and the fall of the Berlin Wall, the Bundestag (the lower chamber, controlled by the Red-Green coalition) approved both bills. The primary bill sought to establish a new institution, the registered *life partnership* (*Lebensgemeinschaft*), for lesbian and gay couples. Under the bill, registered couples would be entitled to many of the benefits of marriage, including hospital visitation, immigration and naturalization (for registered partners of a German national), some coparenting rights, joint tenancy, inheritance rights, pension and health insurance, as well as primary obligations—that is, mutual support and a formal process for dissolution of the life partnership, with the possibility of a judge-imposed directive for continuing financial support. The bill excluded adoption rights, however. This bill did not require Bundesrat approval. The second part of the government's package would have given registered partners more of the state-supported financial benefits of marriage—namely, those governed by the labor, tax, and welfare codes. This bill *did* require upper chamber approval, because the Bundesrat must concur with any taxing and spending proposal. On December 5, the CDU-controlled Bundesrat approved the first bill and vetoed most of the second. The CDU members raised both fiscal and moral objections to the failed second bill, which was framed as state subsidization and vigorous support for gay marriages. The life partnership law went into effect in January 2001. Just before this book went to press, traditionalists went to court to challenge its constitutionality.

As in so many other matters European, France and Germany have moved in virtual lockstep on the recognition of lesbian and gay partnerships. Although the laws differ in their details, the two countries have ended up with similar measures. Neither country has gone as far as Vermont, Denmark, or the Netherlands in according all the benefits and duties of marriage to the new institution, but the new statutes go well beyond the legal regime recognized by cohabitation laws. In particular, the apportioning of state social benefits to the new institutions by both countries and the inheritance and coparenting rights accorded by the German law go well beyond standard cohabitation regimes. Moreover, the process by which same-sex unions were recognized was an exclusively legislative process: left-leaning governments were elected in both countries on platforms promising recognition, and those governments delivered a diluted version of their promise, in the teeth of intense opposition from the leading traditionalist party and the Roman Catholic Church. A similar process transpired in Portugal, where the leftist government delivered legislation in March 2001 that accorded same-sex couples a modest array of benefits already accorded different-sex cohabiting couples.

The Israel–South Africa Model: Court-Driven Benefits

The United States is hardly the only country where lesbian and gay relationship rights have been recognized by judges. Two other countries illustrate how judges can jump-start a politics of recognition but also how such a politics will have limited effect until or unless the parliament gives the judicial decisions teeth.

A highly religious society, Israel was without a public presence for lesbians and gay men until 1975, when the Society for the Protection of Personal Rights was formed. (It is now called the Association of Gays, Lesbians and Bisexuals in Israel.) After a slow start, Israel has recently been quite receptive to equality claims by sexual minorities. As late as 1988, sodomy between consenting male adults was a crime. In that year the Knesset repealed the consensual sodomy law. The Labor Party government enacted a law protecting gay people against employment discrimination (1992), established a Knesset committee on lesbian and gay rights (1993), and ended the exclusion of lesbians, gay men, and bisexuals from the nation's highly regarded armed forces (1994).[62] None of these measures related to same-sex unions, but they may have helped prepare the way for the judicial bombshell of May 4, 1994.

On that date, a panel of Israel's High Court of Justice delivered its decision in *El-Al Israel Airlines v. Danilowitz*.[63] El-Al's collective bargaining agreement assured fringe benefits, including free airline tickets, to the "spouses" of employees, as well as persons who who are "commonly known as" or "reputed to be" spouses. Jonathan Danilowitz requested an airline ticket for his male domestic partner, and when El-Al refused he sued for relief under the Employment (Equal Opportunities) Law of 1992. Affirming the lower courts, the High Court of Justice ruled that the law required El-Al to treat Danilowitz's partner the same as it treated different-sex spouses and common law spouses. Justice Aahron Barak delivered the opinion for the Court. He started with the principle of equality, which he declared "the basis for our whole constitutional regime" in Israel. As regards the collective bargaining agreement, Danilowitz and his partner were similarly situated to a husband and a wife, because the benefit was based upon the notion of a "shared life" of love and cooperation. "Is partnership between two people of the same gender different in terms of partnership, fraternity, and management of the social cell than partnership between different-gender people?" Barak asked. "Are the shared lives of two persons of the same sex different from those of two persons belonging to opposite sexes?"[64] The answer was no. There was no reasoned basis for denying the same benefit to Danilowitz and his partner, and the Employment Law directed that discrimination on grounds of his sexual orientation was an invalid reason. A concurring opinion by Justice Dalia Dorner went even further than Justice Barak's opinion, for she argued that the general principle of equality in Israeli labor law mandated equal treatment of Danilowitz's partner even without the directive of the 1992 Employment Law.[65]

The judgment in *Danilowitz* stimulated a national debate as to the proper stance the state should take to lesbian and gay unions.[66] It has also generated more lawsuits, of course. The next important case involved a man who sued the government to obtain pension payments to which family members of deceased army personnel are entitled; the claimant was of the same sex as the deceased. The first decision in *Steiner v. Pensions Officer* was by the Magistrate Court in Tel-Aviv, and it went against the claimant.[67] The judge ruled that it was not possible to include a homosexual lover as a "family member" within the meaning of military law. Such a reading would be contrary to the laws of nature and Israel's Basic Law, which the judge believed should be informed by Biblical precepts. On appeal to the Tel-Aviv District Court, Steiner prevailed. Judge Shaul Aloni ruled that the *Danilotwitz* understanding of equality requires the law to recognize Steiner as the "reputed spouse" of the deceased.[68] The appeals judge suggested that excluding Steiner from the pension benefits would be both sex discrimination and sexual orientation discrimination. The government settled the case after this judgment and subsequently agreed to treat Steiner as if he were the deceased family member for all purposes. Other litigation in Israel's family courts has and will grapple with the question of how broadly to read the precepts announced in *Danilowitz*.

While the courts have been a virtual beehive of activity, the Israeli Knesset has not been. The election of a more traditionalist government in 1996 precluded any comprehensive legislative reexamination of state nonrecognition of same-sex unions, but a broad reading of *Danilowitz* would suggest that the equality requirement is inherent in Israel's constitutional tradition and therefore not a matter for legislative derogation. In April 1998, Israel's Civil Service Commission extended spousal benefits and pensions to the domestic partners of lesbian and gay state employees. That move left the armed forces as the only leading employer in Israel not to recognize same-sex partners for those purposes.[69] It remains to be seen whether the new government of Ariel Sharon, elected in 2001, will override this decision.

The approach taken by Justices Barak and Dorner in *Danilowitz* has been followed in a number of other countries. In a minor step forward, the British House of Lords cited *Danilowitz* when it found a right of a same-sex partner to inherit a protected tenancy.[70] Shortly after *Danilowitz*, the Hungarian Constitutional Court ruled in March 1995 that the state could not discriminate against same-sex couples in its law granting many of the benefits of spousehood to different-sex domestic partners living together in a common household. Although the Court ruled that the state could limit marriage to a man and a woman, the state could not exclude lesbian and gay couples from new institutions by which the state sought to foster pair-bonded relationships. "An enduring union for life of two persons may constitute such values that it should be legally acknowledged on the basis of the equal personal dignity of the persons affected, irrespective of the sex of those living together," the Court said."[71]

Developments in South Africa have been almost as dramatic, and potentially more far-reaching. The South Africa Constitution of 1996 prohibits the state from discriminating on the basis of sexual orientation (as well as race, sex, color, religion, and other classifications).[72] In 1998, the Pretoria High Court relied on this constitutional protection to invalidate a state agency's refusal to extend health care benefits to the partner of a lesbian employee. The Court reasoned that homosexual and heterosexual relationships deserve equal respect as well as benefits from the government.[73] The South African Constitutional Court confirmed this liberal construction of the Constitution in December 1999, when it invalidated the immigration law's exclusion of privileges to same-sex couples that it gives to different-sex couples. Gays and lesbians in same-sex life partnerships are as "capable as heterosexual couples of expressing and sharing love in its manifold forms. . . . They are as capable of constituting a family," the Court reasoned.[74] The Court has vigorously applied the equality principle of the South African Constitution and might be expected to press for further legal reform if political conditions permit.

The Canadian Model: Court-Driven Cohabitation-Plus

Canada has long been the most gay-tolerant of the world's English-speaking countries. Like Europe and the United States, Canada had a small but vigorous gay-rights movement in the 1960s. Like Europe but unlike the United States, Canada repealed its various sexual offence laws relating to consensual homosexual intimacy in 1969, and did so without creating separate ages of consent for homosexual and heterosexual intercourse (unlike most of the European countries).[75] As in the other western countries, lesbian and gay rights groups proliferated in the 1970s—and argued internally over their agenda. There was much greater consensus in favor of seeking laws prohibiting discrimination against gay people than there was for any particular form of state recognition for same-sex relationships, and so activism focused on the former, with some success at the provincial level. Ontario and Quebec, for example, prohibited sexual orientation discrimination early on, but the western provinces did not. Nor did the Canadian national human rights act, adopted in 1985. Section 15, the equality provision of the Canadian Charter of Rights and Freedoms, which became Canada's human rights constitution in 1982, did not mention sexual orientation as a suspect classification, but was drafted in such a way that the listed categories were presumably not exhaustive.*

Strategists for lesbian and gay litigation groups argued that sexual orientation is an "analogous ground" to those listed in section 15 as a basis for a discrimination claim under the Charter. An important situs for their argument in the 1990s was cohabitation litigation. With Ontario leading the way in the 1970s, and with some judicial prodding, Canadian provinces granted many of the benefits and some of the obligations (like alimony) of marriage to different-sex cohabiting partners.[76] These cohabitation laws did not include same-sex partners, however. In 1994, for example, Ontario's legislature rejected Bill 167, which would have included lesbian and gay couples as "cohabitants" entitled to many of the benefits accorded married couples in the province's code.[77] The federal government followed suit, extending (for one example) the spousal allowance in its Old Age Security Act to include "a person of the opposite sex who is living with the person, having lived with that person for at least a year, if the two persons have publicly represented themselves as husband and wife."

James Egan and John Nesbit, pioneering activists who were Canada's most famous gay couple, asked that this allowance be extended to Nesbit. The two men had been partners since 1948 and considered themselves married. They argued that their exclusion was "discrimination" under section 15 of the Charter. In *Egan v. The Queen*,[78] the Canadian Supreme Court unanimously held that sexual orientation discrimination is analogous to the kinds listed in section 15—but Egan

---

★ Similar to most of the provincial antidiscrimination codes, and the later-adopted federal code, section 15(1) of the Charter assured "[e]very individual . . . the right to the equal protection and equal benefit of the law without discrimination and, in particular, without discrimination based on race, national or ethnic origin, colour, religion, sex, age or mental or physical disability."

and Nesbit still lost the case. Four Justices ruled that the statute did not effect a true "discrimination" because it separated married and near-married people from unmarried people. This rational distinction naturally required the different treatment of Egan and Nesbit, because "marriage is by nature heterosexual."[79] A fifth Justice accepted that there was discrimination but ruled for the government because it was justified by the state's substantial interest in providing for the security of families as traditionally understood.[80] Four Justices dissented.[81]

Although the result in *Egan* reflected the persistence of one man/one woman definitions of marriage and family, the unanimous holding that sexual orientation is an analogous ground for heightened judicial review was significant. To begin with, it would be the death knell for any kind of state discrimination outside of relationship recognition. Thus, *Egan* seemed to ratify the 1992 holding of the Ontario Court of Appeals requiring sexual orientation to be "read in" the Canadian Human Rights Act, which Parliament amended to that effect in 1996.[82] The Supreme Court explicitly ratified that reading in *Vriend v. Alberta*,[83] which not only reaffirmed *Egan*'s holding that sexual orientation was an analogous ground, but also signaled that the Supreme Court (with no dissent) was prepared to apply section 15 aggressively. Although *Vriend* was a case of employment discrimination and not of relationship recognition, lawyers in the various human rights bureaus of the provinces (such as Joanne Rosen in Ontario's Human Rights Commission) as well as gay rights lawyers (such as Martha McCarthy and Joanna Radbord of Toronto) read the decision to make relationship discrimination problematic.[84]

McCarthy and Radbord immediately sought to apply the principles of *Vriend* to partner issues. "M." and "H." were female partners whose lives were economically as well as emotionally intertwined. When M. left the family home upon their separation in 1992, she sought an order of support under Ontario's Family Law Act, which considered cohabiting different-sex partners to be spouses for support purposes. Representing M., McCarthy and Radbord argued that the failure to include same-sex cohabiting partners violated section 15 of the Charter. Their argument prevailed at every level. In *M. v. H.*, Justices Frank Iacobucci and John Cory wrote tandem opinions for the Supreme Court, as they had in *Vriend*. Justice Cory's opinion ruled that M. and H.'s sexual orientation was not only the basis for their different treatment, and a basis arousing special concern because of the history of antigay prejudice and infair treatment, but was in this family law context a discrimination under section 15.[85] Justice Iacobucci's opinion rejected the state's justification for the discrimination. The purpose of the spousal support statute was to provide for an equitable resolution of economic disputes arising when financially interdependent partners break up. While that goal surely applies when husbands and wives break up, especially if there are dependent children, Justice Iacobucci felt it also applies to lesbian or gay couples who also became economically interdependent, as M. and H. had.[86] The government further justified the discrimination on the grounds that it protected children. Justice Iacobucci pointed to ample evidence that lesbian and gay couples were raising children in Canada as a result of adoption, surrogacy, and artificial insemination. "[I]t seems to me that the goal of protecting children cannot be but incompletely achieved by denying some children the benefits that flow from a spousal support award merely because their parents were in a same-sex relationship."[87]

The Court's remedy in *M. v. H.* was to rule the challenged discrimination invalid but to suspend operation of its ruling for six months, so that the legislature could remedy the invalidity. (The Vermont Supreme Court would follow this Canadian strategy nine months later in *Baker v. State*, which is discussed in chapter 2.) The Ontario legislature responded with an omnibus bill that added a new category to its family law: "same sex partners" and "households" were given the same rights and obligations as "spouses" in those statutes where spouse included different-sex cohabiting partners.[88] This was a more grudging response than France would come up with later in the same year, and much more grudging than Vermont's response to a similar judicial decision the year after that. The government's public rationale asserted that the law "protected" marriage against homosexual intruders.[89] M. and her attorneys witnessed the legislative debate. "Our client wondered aloud if any of the politicians had even read the Court's decision. Watching the MPPs do crossword puzzles and pass around family photos during the self-congratulatory debate, it was difficult to answer in the affirmative."[90]

Accordingly, M.'s attorneys moved for the Supreme Court to rehear the case in light of the new law and to declare it inconsistent with the earlier mandate. The Court denied the motion, and assessed costs against M.'s attorneys.[91]

As these twists and turns were occurring in Ontario, Ottawa was not idle. In June 2000, the national Parliament passed the Modernization of Benefits and Obligations Act.[92] The law amended sixty-eight federal statutes to extend benefits and obligations to same-sex couples on the same basis as common law opposite-sex couples. The government explained that the bill does not create same-sex "marriage," as that institution should be limited to different-sex couples. Instead, the bill would create a new institution called "common-law partners," which would be defined as "in relation to an individual, . . . a person who is cohabiting with the individual in a conjugal relationship, having so cohabited for a period of at least one year." One benefit covered is the "spouse's allowance" under the Old Age Security Act; thus, the new law overrode the result in *Egan*. For unmarried opposite-sex partners, the new law represents a symbolic demotion from spouse to common-law partner in those statutes. For same-sex partners, the new law represents a symbolic promotion from no legal status to common-law partner with dozens of statutory benefits and obligations. The federal law also creates a melange of institutions in Canada for same-sex couples: they are common-law partners (along with unmarried opposite-sex partners) at the federal level, same-sex partners in Ontario (where unmarried opposite-sex partners remain spouses), *conjoints de fait* or de facto spouses in Quebec (along with unmarried opposite-sex partners), and spouses in British Columbia (along with unmarried opposite-sex partners).[93]

Within months of the end of *M. v. H.*, attorneys McCarthy and Radbord were back in court. In *Halpern et al. v. Wong et al.*, eight same-sex couples are suing the Toronto Clerk of the Court, the Attorney General of Ontario, and the Attorney General of Canada for declining to issue them marriage licenses. Their argument is that the different treatment of same-sex and different-sex couples by the provincial and national marriage laws violates section 15. As this book goes to press, the plaintiffs and defendants are exchanging affidavits and discovery of expert witnesses.* On July 20, 2000, the government of British Columbia has filed its own petition with the Supreme Court of British Columbia, seeking a declaration that exclusion of same-sex couples from civil marriage violates section 15 of the Charter.[94] On January 14, 2001, the Reverend Brent Hawkes, the senior pastor of the Metropolitan Community Church of Toronto, officiated at the marriage of two same-sex couples, Elaine and Anne Vautour and Kevin Bourassa and Joe Varnell.[95] Governor-General Adrienne Clarkson sent her congratulations, which were read from the pulpit. Because the two couples had published banns at their church on three successive Sundays, the marriage certificates issued by Reverend Hawkes were registered by the province. Although no legal consequences will follow from that registration, this was the first open same-sex marriage to be legally registered by a modern state in North America.

IMPLICATIONS OF THE COMPARATIVE LAW EXPERIENCE AND THE EMERGING MENU OF OPTIONS FOR STATE RECOGNITION

Even a cursory overview of political and legal debates and resolutions concerning same-sex unions in other westernized nations is intrinsically interesting. Because these countries are demographically and culturally similar to the United States today, their experience sheds some light on the accounts I gave in chapters 1 and 2 about the same-sex marriage movement in the United States. In all these countries, there has been a vigorous gay politics of recognition since World War II, which in the last generation has stimulated a politics of family preservation. Nothing has brought out the intensity of that politics more than the possibility of same-sex marriage. That politicians in France, Canada, Denmark, Sweden, the Netherlands, Germany, Hungary, and Israel have been embarrassed to discuss romantic commitment among people of the same sex and have cowered in the face of popular outrage helps us understand the behavior of judges and legislators in Hawaii and Vermont. The experience in all these other countries suggests that opposition to same-sex marriage is more deeply rooted than support for sodomy laws or even opposition to antidiscrimination laws.

★ I am an expert witness for the plaintiffs in this litigation; my affidavit analyzes the history of same-sex marriage.

The most apparent agent is homophobia. We all harbor such feelings, to some extent. Same-sex marriage mobilizes the deepest foundations of homophobia—sex negativity and gender conformity.[96] Many people are both fascinated and disgusted by nonprocreative sexual practices. Such people are willing to look the other way so long as those practices are conducted in private—hence the downfall of consensual sodomy criminal laws—but their disgust is fully alerted when lesbians and gay men or nonconforming straight people "flaunt" their "deviance." Same-sex *marriage* is per se flaunting because it is both public and sexual, given the intrinsically romantic nature of marriage in our culture. This is why so much antigay marriage rhetoric is violent: people are literally hysterical that sexual deviance would go public, and that their state would "sanction" or "promote" it. Sex is not all there is to it, however. A lot of westerners have become comfortable with oral or anal sex, so long as it is performed by a man and a woman, and remain disgusted with the same motions performed by two men or two women.* Rigid gender roles undergird homophobia as well. Many people find security in the inherent differences between men and women—all of which tend to originate in their different procreative functions.[97] Homosexuality is inconsistent with this kind of thinking, and same-sex marriage turns it on its head.

Another source of concern has to do with the perceived decline of our romanticized institution of marriage. Western middle-class people adore the lifetime commitment to a sexual soulmate entailed in our construction of marriage. That feature of the institution—which never existed quite as we imagine it did—is in apparent decline, in part because of marriage's pervasive liberalization. No-fault divorce and other changes treat marriage more like a contract between autonomous individuals, rather than as a union of two soulmates. Such legal changes have the effect of weakening marriage, in the sense that the mutual commitment has become increasingly contingent: "till death do us part" has given way to "till the sex dies" or even "till I get tired of you." Concerns

---

★ Consider this thought experiment. President William Clinton's political career survived the knowledge that he was periodically fellated by Monica Lewinski. This would not have been the case if the President had been fellated by a male aide.

about the weakening of marriage inspire many people to be overprotective. Thus, when lesbians and gay men seek to join the institution, some people are immediately wary about yet another "liberalization" of the institution. And more liberalization suggests further decline. The foregoing chain of reasoning seems profoundly irrational, because no-fault divorce is a completely different kind of free choice rule—it does make it easier for couples to break up—than same-sex marriage. Although people make the connection, another agent is at work—a cognitive agent that shows how the defense of marriage concern and homophobia are more deeply related to one another.

A lot of the concern about same-sex marriage is based on semantic or cognitive investments in customary usages. That is, people understand the long-standing definition of marriage as entailing a linguistically or even normatively natural form. Changing one's conception of marriage would then be a big cognitive as well as linguistic shift.[98] Most Americans associate male-female marriage not only with procreation, but also with the complementarity of the sexes, romantic love till death do us part, and the ideal of a happy childhood presided over by mom and dad. At a higher level of abstraction, different-sex marriage is closely associated with such concepts as unselfishness and citizenship, because the best examples we can imagine of other-regarding conduct involve romantic love between married husbands and wives, matched only by the parental love that the (married) mother and father show their offspring. At the highest level of abstraction, marriage and the complementarity of the sexes are key conceptual underpinnings for the binariness of human thought. Either/or as well as both/and tropes are best exemplified by the man-woman and husband-wife dyad. Same-sex marriage, for many people, destabilizes patterns of thinking that go beyond the construction of family.

So same-sex marriage will not come overnight. But the other lesson of my comparative survey is that it will come, even if at a glacial speed. When you look at the politics of preservation over long periods of time and across national borders, you see that Armaggedon-like rhetoric gives way to acquiescence once lesbian and gay relationships start getting recognized by the state. Public norms can change even in populations with private antigay attitudes. Semantic endowments can be tipped over by law, even if this takes a long time to happen. The comparative law of same-sex unions can tell us a lot about the path to legalized same-sex marriage: it is step-by-step and incremental, inevitable in some jurisdictions, impossible elsewhere in the short term, and sedimentary in the sense that new institutions are being piled on top of old ones. Consider these points in some detail.

Incrementalism and the Step-by-Step Principle

Table 3.2 offers a survey of the major progay legal changes adopted in the countries discussed in this chapter, and a few more for comparative purposes. As Professor Kees Waaldijk of the University of Leiden first suggested, the overriding lesson of table 3.2 is that legal recognition of same-sex relationships comes through a step-by-step process, as a series of "small changes."[99] Such a process is *incremental* and *sequential*: it proceeds by little steps taken in a particular order. A country will not give legal recognition to same-sex relationships until that country has first decriminalized consensual sodomy and equalized the age of consent for homosexual and heterosexual intercourse, and then has adopted laws prohibiting employment and other kinds of discrimination against gay people. Note how this pattern not only fits the Netherlands, Denmark, Sweden, Norway, Canada, Israel, and France, but also fits the stories of Hawaii and Vermont. Those two states were ripe for relationship recognition because the prior steps had been taken. The only state with comparable protections for lesbians and gay men is California, which in 1999 adopted a statewide domestic partnership law. Although same-sex marriage was not politically possible in any of these states for now, they all—like France, Denmark, and Canada—adopted statutes giving greater recognition to lesbian and gay unions than any other American state has done.

The recurrence of the same pattern in country after country, and in several American states, suggests this paradox: law cannot move unless public opinion moves, but public attitudes can be influenced by changes in the law. For gay rights, the impasse suggested by this paradox can be ameliorated if the proponents of reform move step by step along a continuum of little reforms. Step-by-step change permits gradual adjustment of antigay mindsets, slowly empowers gay rights advocates, and can discredit antigay arguments. Consider each reason.

TABLE 3.2. **PROGAY CHANGES IN THE LAW, SELECTED COUNTRIES**
(THROUGH SEPTEMBER 2001)

Country	Sodomy Repeal	Equal Age of Consent for Same-Sex Relations	First big Sexual Orientation Anti-Discrimination Law	Legal Benefits for Same-Sex Cohabitors	Registered Partnership Legislation	Adoption by Same-Sex Partners	Same-Sex Marriage
Netherlands	1810	1971	1992		1998	2001	2001
Denmark	1930	1976	1987		1989	1999	
Iceland	n.k.	1992	1996	1996	1996	Proposed	
Sweden	1944	1978	1987	1987	1995		
Norway	1972	1972	1981	1991	1993		
Belgium	1792	1985	Proposed	2000	Proposed		Proposed
Finland	1971	1998	1995		Proposed		
Canada	1969	1969	1996	2000			
Spain	1822	1988	1995		Proposed		
Catalonia	1822	1988	1995		1998		
Aragon	1822	1988	1995		1999		
Portugal	1945	1945	Proposed	2001			
Israel	1988	1988	1992	1997			
France	1791	1982	1985	1999			
Germany	1969	1994		2000			
Hungary	1961			1995			
South Africa	1998	1998	1997	1999			
Australia	1997	1997	1989				
N.S. Wales	1973	1973	1977	1999			
Russia	1993	1997					
United Kingdom		2000					
England	1967						
Scotland	1980						
N. Ireland	1982						
Brazil	1823	1823					
India							
China							
Argentina							

Sources: ILGA, *World Legal Survey* (www.pga.org, as of November 1, 2000); *Source*: Professor Kees Waaldjijk, University of Leiden Faculty of Law; William N. Eskridge Jr., "Comparative Law and the Same-Sex Marriage Debate: A Step-by-Step Approach to State Recognition," 31 *McGeo. L. Rev.* 641 (2000) (app. 1). Dates in the table signify when a new law took effect, which in some cases is a year or two after its enactment.

Paul's experience on the road to Damascus is exceptional; human beings rarely change their fundamental attitudes overnight. But one's anti-gay attitudes—or one's willingness to express or act on them—can change as the surrounding culture changes. If you are sickened by "homosexuals," you are unlikely to support gay marriage, but you might favor sodomy decriminalization for practical reasons, such as your belief that the state is wasting its time snooping around people's bedrooms. Yet sodomy decriminalization and a lessening of public condemnation of homosexuality will embolden some of your gay friends, family members, and coworkers to come out of their closets. You may be shocked at first, and you can assimilate them as exceptions to your dislike of homosexuals, but your antigay attitudes may soften as you enter middle age.[100] Over time, your interaction with gay people might open you up to acquiescing in antidiscrimination laws, if your experience has been that gay coworkers are okay and that antigay workers are troublemakers. You could still oppose same-sex marriage, but even this attitude might bend when your daughter partners with another woman and your spouse and other children accept her and integrate her partner into the extended family. As each step in the progression toward gay equality encourages more people to be openly gay, not only can middle-aged homophobic attitudes change, but the attitudes of new generations might start out less homophobic. These changes will support gay equality. The foregoing is, admittedly, only one among several possible scenarios. Because the homophobe may have a traumatic experience that confirms his dislike or simply ignores or denies positive information, his preexisting antigay attitudes may be completely resistant to change.[101]

Even if underlying attitudes do not change, legal incrementalism can contribute to gay equality. Consider how sodomy decriminalization paves the way for the adoption of antidiscrimination laws. Not only does it remove a logical objection to such laws,[102] but it facilitates the political conditions for such laws. Repeal of sodomy laws emboldens some gay people to come out of their closets and emboldens the uncloseted to organize themselves politically and press for other equality assurances. The more openly gay people there are *and* the better organized they are politically, the greater attention officials will pay to their arguments for equal legal entitlements, even if popular attitudes are otherwise unaffected.

Another way incrementalism facilitates gay equality is by building up a battery of falsified predictions. Opponents typically argue that progay measures will have catastrophic consequences—promiscuity, child molestation, erosion of families. These ills do not in fact occur when states adopt gay equality measures, in part because the predictions are irrational to start with, and in part because the changes are so small. When sodomy laws are repealed, gay people do not much change their sexual practices, as repeal comes after years of nonenforcement. Predictions of doom have been particularly untrustworthy in the same-sex mariage debate. Registered partnership laws in Europe have been so modestly used (see table 3.1) that they could not be held responsible for ripple effects in society. In fact, as Darren Spedale's study of the matter has documented, registered partners in Denmark have a divorce rate lower than that of married couples, and the overall divorce rate in that country has fallen since the law went into effect.[103] Not only do traditionalists lose some credibility when they repeatedly misstate the effect of progay changes in the law, but some nonhomophobic traditionalists will come to doubt the power of their own worldview.

The Progressivity Thesis and the Inevitability of Same-Sex Marriage

The foregoing incremental and sequential process is also *progressive*: each step in it is a step toward formal equality for lesbians, gay men, bisexuals, and transgendered people. The decriminalization of sodomy makes it easier to adopt antidiscrimination laws, which in turn make it easier to recognize same-sex unions, for the reasons developed above. This is a breathtaking thesis only if viewed in the short term. Fifty years ago, it would have been preposterous to think that consensual sodomy would be widely decriminalized in the United States, as it is today. Thirty years ago, extending antidiscrimination protections to gay people in the workplace would have been unthinkable, whereas today such protections are commonplace, especially in Europe. Fifteen years ago, it would have been visionary to think that a government would create a registry and benefits for same-sex partnerships, such as now exist in nine countries and four American states, and insane to believe that same-sex marriages would be recognized by the state, as they are now by the Netherlands. Now that one country has acted so decisively, and God failed to send the locusts down, others will follow, just as they followed Denmark after it recognized registered partnerships. This process might take years, it might take decades—but it will take place.

A skeptic can reasonably object that this is a whiggish approach to history. Not only can external shocks (wars, depression) derail the project I have described, but the cognitive barriers described earlier in this chapter will make it impossible, the skeptic might suggest. I concede the possibility of derailing external shocks and the enormous power of cognitive barriers. The former introduces an element of unpredictability. The latter suggests that same-sex marriage will, in the foreseeable future, be localized in states or nations where economic and social circumstances undermine sex negativity and rigid gender roles. Consider what it is that distinguishes the most progay countries in table 3.2 from the most antigay countries. The primary, interconnected variables are modernization, urbanization, and opportunities for women outside the home. Urbanization correlates positively with gay equality for a variety of reasons: sexual and gender minorities have greater freedom in big cities to form subcultures; urban life discourages large families and offers women more opportunities outside the home, which undermines traditional gender roles; as procreation declines and social opportunities multiply in urban settings, sex for pleasure becomes relatively more acceptable. Clustering of human beings in urban, suburban, and exurban areas appears to be a robust trend in industrialized, technology-driven modern states, and this trend will continue to open up opportunities for women outside the home. These developments will undercut attitudes that form the basis for homophobia—namely, gender rigidity and sex negativity.[129] Thus, even without a step-by-step approach to gay equality, popular attitudes ought to evolve in gay-friendly ways because of urbanization and the greater economic independence of women.

That legal recognition of same-sex marriage is inevitable does not mean that it will be universal. However long it takes to recognize same-sex marriage in Denmark, it will take longer in the United Kingdom, which still does not protect gay people from discrimination, and much longer in Argentina, in which consensual sodomy is still a crime. Although I think same-sex marriage is an idea whose time is coming, I also think that it will not come to some jurisdictions for a long time, and maybe not ever. Countries in Northern Europe and states in the Northeastern United States are most likely to lead the way, given their readiness under the step-by-step principle, but it is really unclear how many countries or states will recognize same-sex marriage even in the medium term and even if urbanizing trends continue.

There is another variable that makes the matter less predictable. Why are the Scandinavian countries so much more progay than comparably urbanized countries like England? And the United States, which also offers many opportunities for women? A secondary variable is whether fundamentalist religion plays an important role in the public culture of the country or state.[105] In America, those states where the aggressively antigay Southern Baptist Convention and the Church of Jesus Christ of Latter-Day Saints have the most members are the most antigay in their policies. Internationally, countries where organized religion has become politically domesticated (Scandinavian nations and the Netherlands) are most likely to have progay policies. Countries where religious involvement in politics is viewed with suspicion (France, Germany) are likely to have intermediate policies, and countries with active involvement of religions in politics (Latin America and the Moslem world) generally have antigay policies.

Unlike increasing urbanization, which seems predictable in the medium term, the role of fundamentalist religion in public culture is much less predictable. No one has ever successfully predicted the trajectory of religious enthusiasm. Indeed, that trajectory might be influenced by gay people's efforts to secure equal rights. As gay rights and openly gay people have become part of the public culture, fundamentalist religions in the United States have not only been energized in their efforts to confront that development, but have reordered their religious beliefs to make homophobia doctrinally central rather than peripheral. Thus, it is quite possible that recognition of same-sex marriages in one or a few jurisdictions could massively reenergize religious fundamentalism and trigger a national or transnational backlash against gay rights. If that occurred, the United States and the world could end up with a long-term division between those jurisdictions that recognize same-sex marriages or unions and those that do not.

The Sedimentary Precept and the Emerging Menu for State Recognition

Each step toward same-sex marriage is typically (but not always) *sedimentary*: rather than displacing earlier reforms, the new reform simply adds another legal rule or institution on top of an earlier one.[106] In this way, the same-sex marriage movement has contributed to a transformation in the options the state offers to different-sex as well as same-sex couples. Thus, when Sweden enacted its registered partnership law, it did not revoke the legal rights of cohabiting same-sex couples. The French PaCS law included cohabitation rights for same-sex couples as part of the elaborate process through which the law emerged. The Canadian same-sex marriage lawsuit would probably leave cohabitation rights in place. The new Dutch same-sex marriage law leaves intact the 1998 law creating registered partnerships for same-sex as well as different-sex couples. These examples suggest that the experimentation in social policy triggered by the same-sex marriage movement can, and perhaps should be expected to, create new institutions and tinker with existing institutions. Sometimes the new institutions will be available to all couples, as the French PaCS and Dutch registered partnerships are.

The same-sex marriage movement is part of a larger evolution in the way the state regulates human coupling. Today in the Netherlands and France, and tomorrow in many other jurisdictions, couples of all kinds will have a *menu of options*. One way to conceptualize part of that menu is around the degree of unitive commitment expected or entailed in the partners' relationship. Drawing from legal regimes already created in the United States and Europe, the menu looks something like the following. I have arrayed the items on this particular menu from lowest to highest level of commitment, and from least to most like our romantic fantasy vision of traditional marriage.

1. Domestic Partnership (Employment Benefits without Necessarily Much Commitment). Municipal ordinances in the United States and the 1999 statewide law in California have provided a useful model that is being followed by many business enterprises: any employee who is willing to sign a form identifying a significant other (of any sex) ought to be able to add that person to the health care, life insurance, and other benefits provided by the employer to married employees. Being someone's domestic partner may reflect romantic as well as nonerotic love, but it reflects a level of commitment only slightly greater than being a friend. The emphasis is on employment benefits, but there is some symbolic recognition that the relationship is consequential to both parties and ought to be rewarded with a few benefits. At this level, there is no legal obligation imposed on the partners, however. They might be highly committed to one another, but that is neither a premise nor an expected effect of state recognition.

2. Cohabitation (Economic Obligations as well as More Benefits). Canada and most European countries impose support obligations on and offer some state benefits to couples who have cohabited for a substantial period of time.[107] Two people can be domestic partners without living together and with no expectation of a long-term relationship; cohabitation usually suggests both the reality of some legs on the relationship and the expectation for more. The assumption of greater commitment entails greater interdependence, which the state both rewards and obligates. The cohabiting household is treated by the state as a unit for purposes of economic security for each partner. Thus, a cohabitation regime will generally impose duties of support on the couple, especially if there is specialization within the household, where one partner works outside the home and builds up her outside earning capacity, while the other partner sacrifices some of hers so that the household can run smoothly and children can be cared for properly. European and Canadian laws also provide legal presumptions of joint property ownership and tenancy, family and bereavement leave, and sometimes wrongful death claims for cohabiting partners.

3. Cohabitation-Plus (Unitive Rights as well as Economic Obligations and Benefits). The arrangement in the previous paragraph is the old version of cohabitation rules. The last ten years has seen them expand, and the compromises entailed in legislative wrangling over same-sex marriage have stimulated further innovations. France's PaCS, the German life partnership, and Hawaii's reciprocal beneficiaries illustrate a new kind of cohabitation regime; because the terminology varies so much from state to state, we can generically term this *cohabitation-plus.* The regime created by these laws both assumes and creates a greater level of commitment than do domestic partnership or cohabitation. As with domestic partnership, the couple must register but, unlike domestic partnership, usually must go through a more formal process of dissolution. As with cohabitation, the state not only imposes duties of mutual support but also provides benefits to encourage the partners' economic unity. What the French, German, and Hawaiian regimes most distinctively add is unitive rights—namely, rules treating the partners as coupled and granting them financial and other benefits that reflect their unity as to matters like health care decisions when one partner is incapacitated, organ donations after death, and mandated bereavement or sick leave for one's partner. In an ideal system, cohabitation-plus would also entail rights to enter the host country to be with one's partner. Obviously, this regime signals as well as entails a higher degree of mutual commitment than the first two.

4. Civil Unions (Family Rights and Obligations as well as Unitive Rights, Economic Obligations, and Benefits). After or instead of cohabiting, many couples decide to commit to a longer-term relationship. Some of those couples want full-fledged state recognition, like that accorded marriage. The Netherlands, the Scandinavian countries, and Vermont allow these couples to become registered partners or join in civil unions. The state will encourage this long-term commitment with employment and other benefits, will help the couple carry out their purposes with the unitive rights and interdependence benefits, will underline the commitment's seriousness with obligations of mutual support and fidelity and with the added difficulty of legal divorce proceedings in the event of a breakup, and will reenforce family ties by giving the partners mutual rights over their adopted or biological children.* What the state does not give in these civil union or registered partnership laws is the name *marriage* and its interstate and international portability. That is, Alabama will recognize a French *marriage* but probably not a *PaCS*.

★ Thus the civil union option follows Vermont rather than Scandinavia in the matter of ensuring that children are part of a unified family. In 1999, Denmark amended its registered partnership law in this direction, and the Netherlands adopted a similar reform in 2001, at the same time it enacted its same-sex marriage law.

5. Marriage (The Name as well as Intangible Obligations, Unitive Rights, Economic Obligations, and Benefits). The traditional way couples in western culture commit to a long-term relationship, of course, has been marriage. Under the sedimentary precept, the state will continue to support as well as recognize marriage, with all the rights and duties entailed in civil unions as well as the trademarked name and the international portability. The progressivity principle explained above suggests that marriage will be extended to same-sex couples who choose it, but many of them (as well as some different-sex couples) will choose civil unions, cohabitation (plus), or some other form for ideological or personal reasons. Marriage will continue to be the focal point of family formation, because of its deep history and religious overtones. But the commitment it signals will continue to be diluted by the possibility of divorce without a showing of fault.

6. Covenant Marriage (All of the Above, plus It's Harder to Exit). Even though I strenuously disagree with tradtionalists' opposition to same-sex marriage, I agree with them that no-fault divorce has rendered marriage a less reliable precommitment device. If the state is going to experiment with institutions exacting less commitment from couples than marriage does, why not create (or reestablish) an institution with greater commitment? This is the idea entailed in *covenant marriage*: the state provides all the same rights and benefits of ordinary marriage, plus all the obligations and duties, but makes it harder for couples to enter or to dissolve the relationship. For example, Louisiana's pathbreaking statute requires a couple desiring to enter into a covenant marriage to receive extensive counseling and to swear an oath of mutual love and fidelity for life. A couple joined in a Louisiana covenant marriage can divorce only on grounds of serious fault (such as adultery or abuse) or after two years of separation.[108] Covenant marriage both assumes and includes a higher level of commitment from the couple than easy-entry, easy-exit marriage does.

Table 3.3 summarizes the regulatory regime encoded by each institution on my list. Consider a few further thoughts about the foregoing menu of regulatory options. For starters, this is only a partial menu, assuming both a romantic tie between the partners and a level of presumed commitment. Other kinds of state-sanctioned institutions are

TABLE 3.3 **A MENU OF PARTNERSHIP RECOGNITION OPTIONS**

	Domestic Partners	Cohabitation	Cohabitation-Plus	Civil Unions	Marriage	Covenant Marriage
Employee Health Benefits, etc.	✓	✓	✓	✓	✓	✓
Joint Property Ownership— Lease Sharing		✓	✓	✓	✓	✓
Family and Bereavement Leave		✓	✓	✓	✓	✓
Wrongful Death Claims		✓	✓	✓	✓	✓
Mutual Support		✓	✓	✓	✓	✓
Social Security and Other State Benefits			✓	✓	✓	✓
Surrogate Decision- making Capacity			✓	✓	✓	✓
Inheritance Rights			(✓)	✓	✓	✓
Joint Parental Rights over Partner's Kids			(✓)	✓	✓	✓
Taxation			(✓)	✓	✓	✓
Joint Adoption				✓	✓	✓
Fidelity Requirement				✓	✓	✓
Dissolution through Judicial Proceeding					✓	✓
Interstate/ International Portability				✓	✓	✓
Symbolic Tie to Traditional Marriage					✓	✓
Counseling Requirement before Dissolution						✓
Fault-Based Dissolution						✓

possible—such as Vermont's new reciprocal beneficiary law, whose focus is intergenerational dependence. It was aimed to help the niece caring for her elderly aunt or the son giving care to his mother. As Professor Martha Fineman has argued, the law ought to support vertical (caregiving) relationships, not just horizontal (romantic) ones.[109]

Additionally, the partners themselves can edit the state's menu and create their own legal regime as long as they have access to legal services. Domestic partners or cohabitants can create some of the obligations and benefits of marriage by contracts, wills, and joint tenancies, while married partners can opt out of or tailor some of the obligations through prenuptial agreements. The items arrayed in table 3.3 are *off-the-rack rules* automatically available to the couple simply by their registration for one of the different categories. Most couples, especially working- and middle-class couples, have neither the resources nor the foresight to create their own legal regime.

Finally, there is nothing about the options laid out here that precludes the state or couples from creating new institutions of family formation. For example, couples could mix and match the existing institutions: persons A and B could be domestic partners sharing a variety of economic benefits, but the surrogate decision-maker in the event of person B's incapacity could be person C, her niece, whom she has designated as her reciprocal beneficiary. The state could also create new institutions or (more radically) could delink existing institutions such as marriage from the many benefits associated with it. These ideas are not mere speculations. One effect of the politics of recognition associated with the same-sex marriage movement, and of the politics of preservation resisting the same, is that legislatures as well as courts all over the world are experimenting with family law and creating new legal forms. Just as domestic partnerships were unknown thirty years ago, and civil unions were unheard of until last year, so the institutions in 2020 will include some terms that would surprise us today.

CHAPTER FOUR

Civil Unions and Liberal Jurisprudence: Equality Practice

MOST OF THE CRITICISM OF *Baker v. State* and the ensuing civil union law in Vermont came from traditionalists who assailed these moves as compromising the institution of marriage or promoting homosexuality. Some of the criticism, however, came from liberals who assailed these moves as falling short of full legal equality for gay, lesbian, bisexual, and transgendered (GLBT) people—in essence creating a separate but equal regime for gays. In important respects, the civil union law is inconsistent with the premises of the liberal state as applied to same-sex couples: it treats them differently from different-sex couples, and for reasons that are hard to justify without resort to arguments grounded in status denigration or even prejudices. Justice Denise Johnson dissented from *Baker*'s reluctance to require the state to issue marriage licenses to same-sex couples. The majority's concern with "disruptive and unforeseen consequences," she argued, was the same kind of concern raised by segregationist states opposing judicial remediation of apartheid in the 1950s and 1960s. "The Supreme Court's 'compelling answer' to that contention was 'that constitutional rights may not be denied simply because of hostility to their assertion or exercise.'"[1] In the Vermont legislature, Representative Steve Hingtgen opposed any compromise on the ground that it "validates the bigotry" against lesbians, gay men, and bisexuals. "It does more than validate it. It institutionalizes the bigotry and affirmatively creates an apartheid system of family recognition in Vermont."[2] Johnson and Hingtgen raise pertinent issues: Does the institution of civil unions violate the liberal norm of equal treatment? Is the analogy of civil unions and *Baker* to racial segregation and *Plessy v. Ferguson* apt in any respect?

One goal of this chapter is to interrogate civil unions from a liberal perspective. Although I reject the analogy to segregation and the separate-but-equal tag, even the biggest supporters of civil unions concede they are "different but equal," a concept that I find inconsistent with the premises of liberalism as set out by John Rawls in particular. To be sure, the civil unions law satisfies the liberal conception of equality better than the original Danish and Dutch registered partnership laws and the new Canadian cohabitation law—all of which were landmarks in gay people's politics of recognition. But, like those other laws, the civil unions law entails unequal status and some inequality of rights. Indeed, if one considers the U.S. Defense of Marriage Act (DOMA), same-sex unions don't come close to the goal of equal benefits and obligations. The Vermont legislation is a compromise of liberal principles; given constitutional problems with DOMA, it is unclear at this time how big a sacrifice it is.

The other goal of this chapter, however, is to initiate an interrogation of liberal jurisprudence from a civil union perspective, a process that will continue in chapter 5. For now, I want to take liberal theory on its own terms. Even someone friendly to liberalism, as I am, has to think about it in a more complex way. The case of Vermont illustrates a central tension between liberal theory and liberal practice, which lawyers would express as a tension between *right* and *remedy* or (more abstractly) between the *substance* of equality and the *procedure* required to get there. In a heterogeneous polity, immediate equality is usually not attainable, but sometimes *equality practice* is. The chapter will conclude with intuitions from lesbian and gay experience that provide liberal-sounding reasons for equality practice.

CIVIL UNIONS AS A MODEST SACRIFICE OF
LIBERAL PRINCIPLES

Liberal theories maintain that the state exists to provide a context within which its members can flourish. The state properly creates public goods (like roads), prevents people from hurting one another or unnecessarily interfering in one another's affairs, provides a constructive forum for individual development, and (by some accounts) inculcates virtues of toleration and cooperation in the citizenry.[3] As Rawls has famously argued, the state seeks to make it possible for each individual citizen to pursue his conception of the good life and to be neutral as to the question, "What is the best conception of the good life?"[4] Thus, the liberal state is not permitted to hurt people or treat them differently because they are unpopular or even objectionable, so long as they are not positively injuring other people or depriving them of their recognized liberties.[5] To the contrary, the liberal state has an obligation to purge itself of laws reflecting political judgments that a class of harmless citizens should not have the same opportunity as everyone else to pursue their conception of the good life.[6]

Important to Rawls's theory (and to many other versions of liberalism) is the idea of *public reason* among people sharing in equal citizenship.[7] Political dialogue, he maintains, must be confined to discussion of shared political values such as the general welfare, justice for everyone in the polity, protection of future generations, and so forth. Public reason in our political argumentation is satisfied "only when we sincerely believe that [these kind of] reasons . . . are sufficient, and we also reasonably think that other citizens might also reasonably accept those reasons." Citizens are being reasonable when, "viewing one another as free and equal in a system of social cooperation over generations, they are prepared to offer one another fair terms of cooperation."[8] Public reason provides a way to judge whether an exclusionary policy (such as the legal bar to same-sex marriages) is politically arbitrary, which is a very different inquiry than whether a private policy (like religious marriage) is morally arbitrary.

Liberal premises do not necessarily require the state to recognize any two people's marriages, nor to attach legal obligations and benefits to such interpersonal commitments,[9] but once the state has made a policy decision to recognize and even encourage marriages (because they contribute to human flourishing), the state may not arbitrarily deny that recognition and bundle of regulations. For example, the state presumptively cannot give marriage licenses to same-race couples but deny them to different-race couples. Although many religions have traditionally viewed the distinction as morally necessary, there was never a good public reason for the distinction; the human flourishing and family values embodied in marriage applied just as well to different-race couples. The U.S. Supreme Court elevated this liberal principle to a constitutional rule in *Loving v. Virginia*,[10] which held that the state could not bar different-race marriages. The primary ground for the Court's holding was that the law was an invidious discrimination on the basis of race, which is a suspect classification inconsistent with public reason. Under the Court's liberal reading of the equal protection clause, the state cannot deny marriage licenses to a black and white couple because of the race of one partner. Today, the Court's liberal jurisprudence considers sex a quasi-suspect classification, namely, one that is presumptively arbitrary and requires strong justification when deployed by state policy. Andrew Koppelman has argued that, by analogy to miscegenation, state recognition of same-sex marriage is required by this liberal sex discrimination jurisprudence. Just as it is race discrimination for the state to deny marriage licenses to black and white couples because of the race of one partner, so it is sex discrimination for the state to deny marriage licenses to female-female couples because of the sex of one partner.[11] Koppelman's argument takes the liberal case for same-sex marriage and shows how it is mandated by the Court's constitutional jurisprudence.

An alternative holding of *Loving* was even broader: the Court said that the state presumptively could not deny couples the "fundamental" right to marry without strong justification. The Court has elaborated on this principle by holding, in *Turner v. Safley*,[12] that the state presumptively cannot deny convicted felons the ability to marry, even during their confinement in prison. The Court reasoned that the extensive bundle of individual and partnership rights and benefits entailed in marriage is just as important for felons as for civilians. This is a demanding liberalism, and one wonders how far it reaches. The Court says that state restriction on the "freedom of personal choice in matters of marriage and family life" can only be acceptable if it is "supported by sufficiently important state interests and is closely tailored to effectuate only those interests."[13] Some restrictions can pass this test. For example, the state can deny marriage licenses to minors under the supposition that a minor does not have the maturity of judgment to consent to the life-changing commitment of marriage. This supposition is reasonable because it reflects what Rawls calls an *overlapping consensus*: people from a variety of moral and philosophical perspectives have found the idea persuasive. Fundamentalist Christians as well as agnostic utilitarians, sociologists and child psychologists as well as natural law philosophers have, for their own different reasons, come to agree that our society flourishes best when it tells adolescents wanting to get married that they must wait. Although not so easy a case, the state can plausibly maintain that marriage licenses should not be given to closely related persons, such as siblings or uncles and nieces, because the possibility of marriage between close relatives risks undermining the family as a safe haven where children can receive emotional support without sexual attachment.[14] In both these cases, there is a public, rather than sectarian, reason for the restriction on civil marriage. (In both cases churches could recognize such marriages even if the state did not.)

Can the liberal state deny marriage licenses to polygamous partners, typically one man and two women? This was once the main argument against same-sex marriage recognition—it would require the state to recognize polygamous marriages as well.[15] From the perspective of Rawlsian liberalism, the case against polygamy is less clear than it used to be. John Stuart Mill believed liberalism hostile to laws making polygamy a crime but disapproved state recognition on the ground that polygamy has third-party effects harmful to women.[16] Most feminists and traditionalists would agree with Mill's analysis, but this once consensus view may have eroded in recent years. Some women as well as men have testified that plural marriages provide them with the environment they consider most conducive to their flourishing. In our society, polygamy would make it harder for some men to find wives but easier for many women to find husbands, a boon especially in some communities of color.[17] A modern Millian would doubt that women who share their husbands with other women would find happiness, because the bargaining position of the man within marriage would be so much greater. By the way, this liberal argument against polygamy is one of the best arguments for same-sex marriage. If women had options other than to marry men, their bargaining power within male-female marriage would be greater, and wives might actually start getting the equal treatment our society has long claimed that they should have.[18]

The state that cannot legitimately deny different-race couples or even convicted felons marriage licenses ought not deny two adult women the same basic right, and its associated state benefits and obligations.[19] Rawlsian liberalism would reject outright the notion that the state can deny two women the right to marry simply because third parties consider lesbian relationships morally objectionable or desire to disrespect such relationships. These are not good liberal reasons for denying some people state benefits and obligations presumptively owed to all people. Rawls has recently criticized opponents of same-sex marriage for appealing to comprehensive (i.e., sectarian) reasoning for the bar; such arguments are not made with the good faith effort to persuade lesbians and gay men of the injustice of their exclusion. But Rawls does admit arguments grounded upon the "orderly reproduction of society over time," including "orderly family life and the education of children."[20]

Although few leading opponents of same-sex marriage are readers of Rawls, their public arguments in Vermont and elsewhere have deemphasized natural law and religious appeals and have emphasized instead an argument that different-sex marriage is the only appropriate environment for an orderly family life and the rearing of children. Lesbian and gay households, they maintain, are not as stable as straight families, are oversexualized, and have been shown by some researchers to produce children who are odd and dysfunctional.[21] In their respective same-sex marriage litigations, courts in Hawaii and Vermont rejected this line of argument as factually unsupported and, implicitly, as sectarian.[22] Social scientists who have studied mom-and-mom households with children have found no material differences in the well-being of the children, compared with those reared in straight mom-and-dad households.[23] Because most of the studies have involved small samples and none has been able to sample randomly, these conclusions remain provisional. But the consensus of the studies certainly forbodes against claims that same-sex marriage will have third-party effects on children. Rawlsian liberalism cannot accept the state's arguments for excluding lesbian and gay couples from the institution of civil marriage.[24]

In its prefatory text, Vermont's Civil Unions Law recognizes that the liberal state cannot discriminate against same-sex couples and that including them within the state's family law regime is consistent with the purposes of those legal benefits and duties.[25] Following *Baker*, the law posits as its central goal "to provide eligible same-sex couples the opportunity 'to obtain the same benefits and protections afforded by the Vermont law to married opposite-sex couples.'"[26] And the law itself specifically assures same-sex couples the same statutory benefits and obligations as different-sex couples and meticulously integrates civil unions into Vermont's family law. The most thoughtful officials in Vermont—from Representative Tom Little, who chaired the House committee that drafted the bill, to Representative Steve Hingtgen, who ultimately voted for it notwithstanding his earlier reservations, to Governor Howard Dean, who risked his political career by signing the bill into law—believed that this law, on balance, satisfies the obligations of liberalism. Yet it is clear that the law does not assure the full equality liberalism would seem to demand. Consider the equality problems with the civil unions law.

1. Unequal Status. The statute forthrightly concedes that it "does not bestow the status of civil marriage" on same-sex couples, even though the legislature clearly had the authority to do that. The law justifies its choice as one that "will provide due respect for tradition and long-standing social institutions."[27] On the face of it, this is a significant compromise of liberal principles. The legislature acknowledges that marriage is a matter of status as well as rights and duties. Socially, the married couple has long had a special, and generally privileged, status in American society. That privileged status remains reserved for different-sex—presumptively heterosexual—couples. Same-sex couples, who are acknowledged to form similar commitments and families, get another institution that is presented as marriage without the name. This can easily be viewed as second-class citizenship, and one whose only justific

tion is "tradition," namely, the belief that marriage has long been limited to unions between men and women.[28] Tradition standing alone is
not a liberal justification for a polity's treating some citizens differently
from others.

The most plausible Rawlsian argument for the civil unions law is
that the state can provide a separate institution for same-sex couples on
the ground that they differently contribute to the "orderly reproduction
of society over time." Marriage is for couples who can procreate
together and so is the institution that combines unitive and procreative
human goods; civil union is for couples who can only enjoy the unitive
good together. This argument cannot be sustained, however. As
presently constituted, marriage is available to sterile couples or couples
who have no desire to procreate or who engage in contraception or
abortion to prevent it. Conversely, many lesbian couples and some gay
male couples procreate as a couple.* Admittedly, the former need an outside sperm donor and the latter need a female surrogate—but that does
not set them apart from a growing number of straight married couples
who procreate in the same way. A Rawlsian liberal must also confront
the following argument: Could Virginia have created a separate institution for different-race couples to avoid giving them marriage licenses
after it lost the *Loving* case? Would a different-race civil union have satisfied the liberal requirements of the Supreme Court's mandate? Surely
not—and properly not, Rawls would insist.**

There is a disturbing parallel between the civil unions law and the
segregation of railroad cars upheld by the U.S. Supreme Court in *Plessy*

★ Consider the matter from the point of view of Rawls's *original position,* where the
decision maker does not know what status or sexual orientation she will have in the
state that she is planning. If such a person decided to have one institution that combines procreation and unity between the parties (marriage) and another that just has
unity (civil union), then the latter ought to include different-sex couples unable or
unwilling to procreate.

★★ If the *telos* of marriage, its fundamental goal, were procreation, a Rawlsian might
well disapprove the different-race civil union while going along with the same-sex
civil union. In modern society, however, the *telos* of marriage is unitive (the sterile
couple can enjoy the full fruits of marriage's primary feature), and the procreative
features of marriage do not necessarily entail that the partners each contribute biological material to children raised within the marital family (the couple adopting
children enjoy the full fruits of any procreative feature of marriage).

v. Ferguson.[29] Just as Louisiana a century ago gave blacks and whites separate and (assertedly) equal railroad cars, so Vermont now gives gays and straights separate and (assertedly) equal legal forms for their committed relationships. In each case, the separate forms were defended on grounds of formal equality: blacks got a railroad coach, just not the same one whites enjoyed; gays get state recognition for their committed relationships, just not the same one straights enjoy. In each case, the minority objected that separation, viewed in its social context, symbolically reflected and deepened a functional inequality—whose relevance the state denied. Dissenting in *Plessy*, Justice John Harlan argued, "Everyone knows that the statute in question had its origin in the purpose . . . to exclude colored people from coaches occupied by or assigned to white persons."[30] Analogously, the Vermont statutory reaffirmation that "marriage consists of a union between a man and a woman" had its origin in the purpose to exclude homosexual people from the institution of marriage occupied by or assigned to straight persons.[31] In each case, the state bowed to private prejudices in creating a symbolic discrimination and invoked tradition to justify it. Just as the U.S. Supreme Court deferred to Louisiana's discretion "to act with reference to the established usages, customs, and traditions of the people,"[32] so the Vermont legislature exercised its discretion to give "due respect for tradition and long-standing social institutions" to create a new institution rather than admit lesbian and gay couples into marriage.[33]

The next part of this chapter will explore the analogy in greater depth, but for now my point is that liberal concerns about *Plessy* parallel those with same-sex unions. Each regime acquiesces in tradition-based distinctions that connote second-class citizenship for the historically subordinated group. And each legal regime has the possible effect of fortifying customary understandings that treat the minority as damaged goods. Indeed, there is an ugly linguistic parallel between current state denials that same-sex unions can be "marriages" and previous state denials that people of color can be "citizens." This linguistic despotism is eerily announced in a reported claim by a slave master: "I will make you know that I am master of your tongue. . . ."[34] State efforts to erase the association of "lesbians and gay men" with "marriage" (and, with it, "love", "commitment," and "family") reflect a similarly illiberal attitude.

2. Unequal Benefits and Duties (Interstate Recognition). In at least one sense, civil unions flunk the separate-but-equal rule of *Plessy*. That is their lack of interstate portability. Would a Vermont couple joined in civil union be able to move to Massachusetts or Maine and enjoy the same rights and duties as a Vermont married couple that moved to the same place? As of June 2001, thirty-four states have adopted "junior DOMAs," that is, statutes providing that their courts should not recognize same-sex marriages validly entered into in another jurisdiction or state.[35] The laws generally proclaim that same-sex marriages will neither be valid nor be recognized within the jurisdiction; recall the examples quoted in chapter 1. Subject to constitutional challenges, these laws would in almost all cases prevent same-sex couples married in Vermont from taking advantage of the legal benefits of marriage. Junior-DOMA states would probably not treat civil unions any more liberally. Because Maine has a junior DOMA, it would probably not recognize the civil union of our hypothetical couple; courts in other junior-DOMA states (heavily concentrated in the south and west) would be even less likely to recognize their union.

Nor is it clear that states without junior DOMAs would recognize the union. In Missouri and Maryland, which still have laws rendering sodomy between consenting adults a crime, courts might rule that recognition would be contrary to the state's public policy, which is a well-recognized exception to the obligation to recognize out-of-state marriages.[36] Some of the other states might rule the same way based on the traditional definition of marriage. A handful of states, on the other hand, would probably recognize such unions. New Mexico, for example, has a statute requiring its courts to respect marriages valid in the state of their celebration and is less likely than Missouri to invoke the public policy exception, because the state does not criminalize sodomy between consenting adults. Massachusetts is a better possibility. Although the state still criminalizes the "crime against nature," the law is being challenged and probably will be invalidated or construed as inapplicable to conduct between consenting adults.[37] And Massachusetts, like Vermont, has adopted laws protecting lesbians, gay men, and bisexuals against a wide range of discriminations.

For now, it is plausible to say that a Vermont same-sex marriage would probably have been recognized in a few other states. If Vermont had amended its marriage law to include same-sex couples, it is likely that a few states would have recognized those marriages when couples engaged in transactions or even relocated in their jurisdictions.* Would any of the states that would have been willing to recognize Vermont same-sex marriages *not* be willing to recognize Vermont same-sex civil unions? For example, if one partner in our Vermont-to-Massachusetts *married* couple is killed by a negligent motorist, there is a good chance that Massachusetts would allow the survivor to sue for her own anguish and as the presumptive representative of the decedent's estate. The odds might go down—no one knows how much—if the couple were joined in civil union, rather than married, in Vermont. The new institutional form might provide one additional reason for a court to hesitate in extending the special legal protections of the state marriage law to a couple when those same protections are denied to same-sex couples who live their whole lives in the state. Although the extent of the problem is indeterminate, Vermont's decision to recognize same-sex unions but not marriages has a potential effect on the portability rights of same-sex couples.

3. *Unequal Benefits and Obligations (Federal Recognition).* To the liberal it is highly disturbing that a Vermont couple entering into a civil union are not equally situated with a married couple as regards benefits and obligations afforded by federal law. Spousehood or being married entitles persons or couples to 1049 benefits and duties under federal statutes and regulations, which the U.S. General Accounting Office has arrayed into the following categories:

- social security, food stamps, and other welfare programs;
- veterans' and various other military and civilian benefits;
- federal employment benefits;
- tax rules;

★ To continue my parallels with *Loving* and *Plessy*, the situation of a Vermont same-sex couple is akin to that of a different-race couple during apartheid. That is, the couple's marriage would be recognized in some states but not others. Indeed, some couples were considered different-race in some jurisdictions (those following the "one drop of black blood" rule) but same-race in others (those requiring significant black lineage).

- immigration and naturalization rules, including advantages for spouses of American citizens;
- regulations pertaining to Native Americans;
- intellectual property and commercial transaction rules;
- rules requiring financial disclosure and recusal on grounds of conflicts of interest, considering both oneself and one's spouse;
- criminal law provisions, especially those relating to family violence;
- agricultural loans, guarantees, and programs;
- federal natural resources law; and
- miscellaneous other laws.[38]

DOMA provides that, for purposes of federal statutes and regulations, "the word 'marriage' means only a legal union between one man and one woman as husband and wife, and the word 'spouse' refers only to a person of the opposite sex who is a husband or a wife."[39] Although DOMA does not explicitly say whether a same-sex civil union can be treated as a "marriage" for purposes of federal law, or whether civil union partners can be "spouses," it can and probably will be read to preclude federal agencies and courts from treating civil unions like marriages.

If DOMA were read this way, the inconsistency between state treatment of same-sex unions and different-sex marriages becomes much greater: not only do lesbian and gay couples suffer the symbolic disrespect associated with separate-but-equal regimes, but they do not even get an institution that is close to equal in terms of benefits and duties. The situation of gay people would flunk *Plessy*, which theoretically required at least formal equality. That civil unions are separate but ridiculously unequal in this way is no fault of Vermont's, of course, for the state could not have altered the rules dictated by the 1996 federal law. Indeed, DOMA would more clearly deny benefits and obligations if Vermont had adopted same-sex marriage. The liberal's complaint is therefore with the federal government, whose law treats citizens very differently without any neutral justification.[40]

Indeed, Rawls's liberal theory of justice provides philosophical support for the constitutional conclusions I reached in chapter 1. Even if it is admissible to say that the state can provide a separate institution for same-sex couples, on the ground that they differently contribute to the "orderly reproduction of society over time," it would be inadmissible for other states or the federal government in the liberal system to refuse to recognize unions properly entered into in the celebrating jurisdiction. Concededly, a Rawlsian reading of the full faith and credit clause tends to merge with such a reading of the equal protection clause: neither kind of inequality is just. Hence, both provisions of DOMA are profoundly illiberal: section 2, which may authorize the states to violate the full faith and credit clause, and section 3, which requires the federal government to discriminate. The stated justifications for DOMA were equally illiberal. As chapter 1 documents, the main justification was that of "no promo homo," which compounds the liberal objection that DOMA takes sides in the private culture clash between gays and traditionalists. No promo homo is on its face no effort to justify the discrimination neutrally, and statements in the *Congressional Record* associating lesbians and gay men with promiscuity and hedonism are precisely the sort of disrespectful arguments disallowed by liberal public reason.

The defense of marriage argument, also made to justify DOMA, was at least an effort to tie the statute to a possible neutral state goal, but DOMA supporters never explained how same-sex marriage *actually* imperiled the institution. Some of DOMA's most influential supporters, such as President Bill Clinton, Senate Majority Leader Bob Dole, and House Speaker Newt Gingrich, were unable to say a single word to support the law's central normative claim. Supporters who spoke to this issue, like Representatives Robert Barr and Steve Largent, were unable to articulate a coherent argument. An ungenerous inference is that they were all pandering to antigay prejudice. A more generous inference is that the reasons for the measure were generalized concerns with the drift in American public norms, a drift that would be exacerbated by recognizing same-sex marriages.

SUBSTANTIAL EQUALITY AND THE INAPTNESS OF THE APARTHEID TAG

I am a classic liberal and a gay person who supports legal recognition of same-sex marriages. My last book criticized the twentieth-century legal regime that created an "apartheid of the closet" for GLBT people.[41] Yet I do not think the civil unions law creates an apartheid, as Representative Hingtgen charged. Nor do I believe the analogy to *Plessy* holds up. Formally, the law neither separates citizens nor equalizes their entitlements. Functionally, the law ameliorates rather than ratifies a sexuality caste system. The racial apartheid adopted by southern state legislatures and upheld in *Plessy* was very different from the new institution suggested in *Baker* and adopted by the Vermont legislature. Similarly, it is greatly unfair to tag the civil union measure as "separate but equal." Governor Howard Dean suggested that the institution is "different but equal," which is a fair characterization. For the reasons already developed, this still does not satisfy the strenuous requirements of liberalism, but its failure is modest and, for some jurisdictions, temporary.

The Inapt Analogy to Apartheid

The socio-legal backdrop of apartheid is a Rawlsian nightmare. During Reconstruction (1866–77), the southern states were readmitted to the union upon the condition that they would assure black people (the former slaves) free and equal citizenship as required by the Thirteenth and Fourteenth Amendments. Hence, the constitutions and laws of those states did not initially require segregation of the races, a practice that some of the Reconstructors considered antithetical to the equality principle of the Fourteenth Amendment.[42] After Reconstruction ended, southern states backslid, adopting laws and amending their constitutions to create the legal foundations for apartheid. Segregation of the sort upheld in *Plessy* was at least a compromise of the equality baseline set during Reconstruction and, as practiced, a betrayal of the goals of Reconstruction. In short, apartheid was a major setback in the politics of recognition for African Americans and their allies.

Contrast the sociolegal background of same-sex unions (chapter 1). For most of the twentieth century, lesbian and gay people were outlaws, potential felons on the basis of their consensual activities and social outcasts if their identities were revealed. Even after gay rights activists initiated a serious politics of recognition following the Stonewall riots (1969), the focus of legal reform remained repeal of sex crime laws and enactment of antidiscrimination laws, not state recognition of same-sex relationships. Gay rights leaders all but abandoned same-sex marriage as an issue in the 1980s, even before the Supreme Court announced a gay-hostile constitutional baseline. In *Bowers v. Hardwick*,[43] the Court ruled that the state could make "homosexual sodomy" between consenting adults a criminal felony. *Hardwick* is a Rawlsian nightmare for lesbians, gay men, and bisexuals—our parallel to *Plessy*, or even to *Dred Scott v. Sandford*,[44] in which the Supreme Court held that African Americans could not be U.S. citizens. Just as *Plessy* accepted an apartheid, where people of color were physically separated from white people, so *Hardwick* accepted an apartheid of the closet, where gay people were psychically separated from straight people.

Socially, politically, and constitutionally, *Baker* bears a closer kinship to *Brown v. Board of Education*, which declared apartheid a violation of the equal protection clause.[45] *Baker* is to *Brown* as *Hardwick* is to *Plessy*. Like *Brown* and unlike *Plessy*, *Baker* reflects an advancement of gay people's politics of recognition, from the outlaw status reflected in *Hardwick* to the status of substantially equal citizens before the law. Like *Brown*, which insisted on functional as well as formal equality for blacks, *Baker* required functional as well as formal equality for gays. But, like *Brown II*, the second Supreme Court decision in *Brown*, which allowed the political system the opportunity to create a regime of equal benefits for black schoolchildren "with all deliberate speed," *Baker* deferred to the political system to create a regime of equal rights for same-sex couples. The Vermont legislative response, the Civil Unions Law, came much more rapidly than the response of southern states and school districts in the wake of *Brown*. Chapter 2's account of *Baker* and the civil unions statute suggests that the official deliberation was generally faithful to Rawls's conception of public reason. Unlike the *Hardwick* Justices, the *Baker* Justices treated lesbians, gay men, and bisexuals as worthy citizens and seemed genuinely interested in their inclusion and flourishing. Unlike the DOMA Congress, the legislature that adopted the Vermont Civil Unions Law deliberated about same-sex marriage or unions in a way that treated GLBT people as citizens whose distinctive as well as normal lives merited respectful analysis. With several exceptions, the legislative critics of the civil unions bill made arguments that appealed to public reason. Representative Margaret Flory, a thoughtful opponent, avoided sectarian arguments about homosexuality and argued instead that the legislature ought to move in a more incremental manner, meeting the main needs of lesbian and gay couples immediately and then deciding later how much more to fill in.

Substantial Equality of Civil Unions and Marriage

Plessy ratified a regime that took away rights from people of color, such as the freedom to ride in the railroad car of their choice. A later case, *Cumming v. Richmond County Board of Education,*[46] extended *Plessy* to public education and denied black families choice as to schooling as well. Although these cases announced a constitutional rule of *separate but equal,* there is no doubt that *separate* rarely meant anything close to equal, especially in the context of public schools. The schools for black children were greatly underfunded, and in practice there was gross inequality in the education provided the different classes of citizens.

Contrast *Baker,* which insisted that same-sex couples wanting state recognition be given the same benefits and rights as different-sex couples who want state recognition. Following *Baker,* the Civil Unions Law gives partners joined in civil union a variety of state-supported rights and benefits that they did not have before the law was adopted, including the rights to

- receive maintenance and support from their partners;[47]
- access to state courts and rules for division of property and child custody upon divorce, as well as for remediation of spousal abuse;[48]
- priority of inheritance if their partners die without wills, as well as legal capacity to hold property as tenants in the entirety;[49]
- bring lawsuits for wrongful death of partners and seek damages for loss of consortium and emotional distress;[50]
- visitation and notification when their partners are hospitalized;[51]
- make or revoke anatomical gifts by partners;[52]
- the joint care and parenthood of children born to one of the partners during the union;[53]
- adopt children jointly with their partners, or adopt the children their partners bring to the union;[54]

- be free of discrimination on the basis of being married;[55]
- victims' and workers' compensation benefits as a family unit;[56]
- family leave and public assistance benefits under state law;[57]
- immunity from testifying against their partners, if they choose to invoke it;[58]
- equal treatment as married couples under state and local tax laws;[59] and so forth.

This is a long list of rights and benefits, and I could have made it longer. Compare this list with the benefits and duties conferred by the 1999 French and 2000 German laws recognizing same-sex unions, discussed in chapter 3. These rights and benefits of civil unions narrow, and for some couples will eliminate, the gap between rights accorded married different-sex couples and those of unioned same-sex couples.

Family law scholar David Chambers has organized the cluster of state-sanctioned benefits and rights of being married in a helpful way.[60] Some state regulations, such as the first six in my list above, require private parties to respect or be accountable to the emotional and personal interconnection of the couple joined in civil union. These *interdependence* rules create a presumption that each partner acts for the well-being of the other partner. Such rules can sometimes be achieved through wills, powers of attorney, and negotiations with third parties, but special state laws make it easier for married or civil-unioned partners to take it for granted that hospitals, blood relatives, employers, and even one another will treat each as the family of the other. Other regulations, such as the next two in my list, regulate the ability of both partners to adopt children and to be considered parents of children born to either of them during the course of their marriage or civil union. These *parental rights* regulations, which vary widely among the states, would usually be more useful for lesbian and gay couples than straight couples, because the former can have children together only by adoption or by a legal presumption for children born within the relationship. The last five items on the list above, as well as the first item, are regulations whereby the state will treat the partners joined in civil union as an *economic unit* for purposes of their own internal accounting, their commercial dealings with third parties, and their obligations (taxes) to the state.

However one categorizes the array of rights and benefits that accrue to both married and civil-unioned couples in Vermont, their overall purpose is a liberal one, "a facilitating function—offering couples opportunities to shape satisfying lives as formal equals and as they, rather than the state, see fit."[61] Within the confines of Vermont law, the civil unions statute has not only conferred rights and benefits that are the same as those conferred by state law on married couples, but those rights and benefits subserve the classical goal of liberalism, facilitating people's abilities to structure their committed relationships. This full formal equality within Vermont contrasts with the formal inequalities introduced by federal law and by the laws of other states if they do not recognize civil unions, and with the functional inequalities created by social hostility to same-sex unions.

Civil Unions and Liberal Values

A final difference between the separate-but-grossly-unequal regime of racial segregation and the different-but-substantially-equal regime of civil unions is that the latter seeks to and probably will advance liberal values. Segregation of the races in railroad cars and public schools was part of the larger social program of apartheid. The massive separation of the races in all avenues of public life—drinking fountains, swimming pools, colleges, restaurants, rest rooms, hotels, workplaces—had the intended effect of inculcating racist values. Most of the people who grew up under apartheid harbored irrational beliefs (e.g., that human beings of African ancestry were materially different from human beings of European ancestry) and accepted the social as well as political subordination of minority races as natural. The acceptance of irrational stereotypes and social subordination both reflected and generated deep and complex racial prejudices.[62] The dismantling of legal apartheid has not ended racial prejudice, stereotypes, or social subordination, but social science surveys suggest that this move has helped ameliorate all three. Surveys of white people over the latter half of the twentieth century—the period when de jure segregation ended and de facto segregation eroded—demonstrate that the popularity of negative stereotypes about people of color has plummeted and that their material status has improved (both absolutely and vis-à-vis whites) and suggest that whites have more positive feelings and less inclination to discriminate against blacks than they did before *Brown*.[63] While these surveys offer only provisional conclusions and need to be read critically,[64] even the critics believe that progress has been made and that white people harbor diminished prejudice-based attitudes, believe fewer stereotypes, and discriminate against people of color less deliberately in 2001 than they did in 1951.[65]

With a few exceptions, most scholars praise *Brown* not only for moving the law in a liberal direction, but also for contributing to a sociolegal regime where liberal values of rationality, mutual respect, and tolerance among black and white people could flourish.[66] One way that *Brown* contributed to liberal values was by facilitating and later being read to require racial integration. Social psychologists have formed a consensus that the best strategy for ameliorating prejudice is cooperation between ingroup and outgroup members, working on an equal status basis in pursuit of common goals.[67] If the state itself refuses to discriminate, its tolerant policy will create many opportunities for this kind of cooperation among soldiers, teachers and students, researchers, and ordinary bureaucrats working together and with private actors to accomplish routine state goals. If the state can also reduce discrimination by private employers and public accommodations through antidiscrimination laws and the like, it can have an even bigger impact. Not only does intergroup cooperation contribute to better understanding about outgroup members, but it also fosters feelings of empathy for them. The former reduces stereotyping, the latter ameliorates prejudice.

In this respect, too, *Baker* is much more like *Brown* than like *Plessy*. With the addition of the Civil Unions Law, Vermont's regulatory regime is one where liberal values of rationality, mutual respect, and tolerance among gay and straight people can flourish a little bit further. At the dawn of the millennium, Vermont not only conducts its public business without discrimination on the basis of sexual orientation but requires private employers, public accommodations, and schools to do the same.[68] Like other states, Vermont takes a strong legal stand against hate crimes, enhancing the penalties for offenses motivated by race-, sex-, or sexuality-based prejudice.[69] It is one of the few states to have adopted statutes explicitly allowing same-sex partners to adopt one another's children or recognizing same-sex unions.[70] Not surprisingly, Vermont has one of the lowest levels of antigay violence and discrimination in the United States.

Theories of prejudice suggest how Vermont's newest move, same-sex unions, ought to contribute, modestly, to the rational and tolerant society of that state in a way that antidiscrimination laws do not. Antigay prejudice is among the deepest in American society, and stereotypes about gay people among the most outlandish. There is some social science support for the proposition that prejudice is most intense when ingroup people view the outgroup as challenging the ingroup's cherished norms and values.[71] From this notion, the campaign for same-sex marriage could in the short term contribute to antigay prejudice, if straight people saw the campaign as one designed by "predatory homosexuals" to appropriate marriage for the "gay agenda." But once same-sex marriages, or civil unions, are actually recognized by the state and straight people come to know the married or civil-unioned couples, both stereotypes and prejudice ought to decline, albeit slowly.

There is some evidence that this is occurring, unevenly, in Vermont. In the abstract, most Vermonters did not want their state to recognize same-sex marriages or civil unions, and I doubt that the average legislator disagreed. The deliberative process and the commitment of both proponents and opponents to the ideal of public reason had the effect of changing people's opinions. The Vermont House Judiciary Committee's eleven members heard weeks of testimony, some of it from same-sex couples and parents of lesbian and gay Vermonters, and a lot of it by dispassionate, reasoned observers. That testimony transformed the views and feelings of some of the committee members; the committee voted 10 to 1 for the civil unions bill, and the only dissenter favored full rather than substantial equality for gay people. That nine-vote margin by the committee members—almost half of whom were Republicans—was greater than the margin of passage in the whole chamber (76 to 69). One of the committee members, Democratic Representative William Lippert, was openly gay, but the others were not. Probably most of them did not understand how a woman could romantically and sexually love another woman, but they came away from the experience not only with an appreciation of lesbian and gay humanity, but also of their commitment to the same family values that the legislators did understand. As Republican Representative John Edwards put it during the committee's deliberations, "It is time that we put the prejudice behind us," a conclusion he reached after he listened to "the compelling stories of gay and lesbian people about who they are, what they stand for and how valuable they are to our community."[72] Exit polls in November 2000 suggest that most Vermonters agreed with Edwards: a slender majority favored the civil unions law, and the number of fierce critics had declined sharply since April of that year, when it was signed by the governor.

So if DOMA (chapter 1) was a failure of public reason, the Vermont Civil Unions Law (chapter 2) was substantially a success. In DOMA deliberations, legislative opponents frequently invoked sectarian arguments denigrating gay people, while they rarely did so in the civil union debate. The President and most of the members of Congress supporting DOMA were too ashamed to make any public argument for their position, for in their hearts they knew that Representative John Lewis was right when he said "this is a mean bill" that "seeks to divide our nation."[73] Especially in the early stages of deliberation, legislators opposing the civil unions bill forthrightly stated their reasoning, and generally did so respectfully and often self-deprecatingly. To say, as many of the Vermont skeptics did, that they were just not ready for state-sanctioned homosexual unions or that they feared other states would retaliate against Vermont is a more modest and conciliatory stance than that taken by almost all of the public defenders of DOMA, who arrogantly presented themselves as saviors of the institution of marriage.*

EQUALITY PRACTICE: THE COMPLEX RELATIONSHIP BETWEEN RIGHTS AND REMEDIES IN A LIBERAL DEMOCRACY

Given the substantial equality assured by the Vermont Civil Unions Law and its positive contribution to liberal values as well as a minority group's politics of recognition, analogies to *Plessy* and racial apartheid are out of

---

★ There was also an element of hypocrisy in the DOMA debate that I did not find in the Vermont deliberations. The chief public supporters of DOMA—President Clinton, Senate Majority Leader Dole, and House Speaker Gingrich—not only failed to explain how same-sex marriages threatened the institution of marriage, but these "defenders" of marriage were the highest ranking adulterers in the United States. Most of the congressional supporters of DOMA are opponents of other measures that would more predictably strengthen marriage, including restrictions on divorce and tougher rules against spousal abuse.

line. Unfortunately, my earlier point also remains valid: by creating a differently named regime that will not deliver all the benefits and rights of marriage, civil unions do not satisfy the strictest demands of liberal principle. (Recall the analogy to *Loving v. Virginia* and the Rawlsian objections to a law creating a new institution of civil unions just for different-race marriages.) But should the liberal have voted against the Civil Unions Law, as Vermont Representative Bill MacKinnon did? The answer to that, it seems to me, ought to be no. The liberal should have supported the law. If the civil unions statute is not equality, it is at least *equality practice*. Full equality along Rawlsian lines ought to be the goal for a liberal polity, but a polity that is a democracy and whose citizens have heterogeneous views about important matters is one where immediate full equality is not always possible, not practical, not even desirable. In this final section of the chapter, I want to develop the contours of a problem inherent in liberal democracy—namely, the tension between liberal rights and pragmatic remedies. There are a number of ways to handle this tension. Although most liberal theorists are not aware of it or ignore it, I urge liberals to consider this lesson of lesbian and gay experience: the process by which equal rights and respect are achieved is just as important as the rights themselves. A process that forces minority rights onto an unwilling populace will often not "stick" in a democracy; a process that is incremental and persuades the people or their representatives of the acceptability or even desirability of minority rights is much more likely to stick. The incremental process will take a lot longer, but it will also be more lasting. The idea of equality practice, suggested by lesbian and gay coming-out stories, suggests a *pragmatics* that ought to be incorporated in real-world liberalism.

Strategic Compromise of Liberal Principles in a Heterogeneous Democracy

Representative Tom Little, the chief architect of the Vermont Civil Unions Law, defended the compromise to his committee: "Leadership untempered by a practical assessment of the world we live in is not sound leadership. What is achievable in this general assembly and this body politic, is a broad civil rights bill and, speaking for myself, that does not cross the threshold of marriage."[74] His stance was politically shrewd. Among the choices confronting Representative Little's committee were the following:

A. Amend the marriage law to include same-sex couples.
B. Create a parallel institution for same-sex couples, with all or many of the same rights and benefits of marriage.
C. Do nothing, or as little as possible.

In my view, a majority of the committee, after listening to the testimony, was at least theoretically open to option A.[75] Yet in February 2000 the committee voted 8 to 3 for pursuing option B, and reported a bill embodying option B by a 10 to 1 vote in March. In the short term, this was not only rational from their point of view, but rational from the perspective of a liberal gay person, such as myself or Representative Lippert (the vice-chair of the committee), who favors same-sex marriage.

Assume that Little's own preferences were fully liberal and that he personally favored A. Voting without consideration of views outside his committee, he would have proposed A. But in politics, as in life, people vote *strategically*—that is, they take account of other people's reactions and vote for the option that when others have acted will best accord with their preferences.[76] In February, Little knew that a plurality and probably most Vermonters favored option C, that a large majority of the Vermont House of Representatives favored either option C or option B, and that Governor Howard Dean favored option B and might have vetoed option A. In the short term, if the committee chair had mobilized a bare majority of the committee to report a same-sex marriage bill—as Little could probably have done if he were so inclined—Vermont would have ended up with option C, for an option A bill would have been defeated. Every member of the committee was strongly opposed to option C, yet that is what they would have ended up with if the committee had pursued its preferred option. The best *is* sometimes the enemy of the good.

Little could have pursued another strategy, of course. He could have gotten the committee to report option A, but with option B as a fallback. This strategy would have had the advantage of revealing to his colleagues outside the committee how strongly impressed the committee members were by the testimony they heard. Some minds might have been changed, but even if the chamber defeated the committee's proposal it could still have voted for option B, the next best choice. This alternative strategy would not have been a good one either, and it might have been disastrous. The Vermont House debates were anguished enough when only option B was before its members; forcing the representatives to confront option A would have required them to make a harder choice—between full equality and the wrath of the electorate. Faced with the worst array of choices, some House members might have blamed the committee and fallen back on option C instead. The academic liberal flourishes on making hard public choices; the liberal in politics dies by them.

Thus, giving the House option A with a fallback option B would not have improved the odds of option A being adopted, would have posed some risk of ending up with option C, and (most important) would have guaranteed that the next legislature would have been filled with a lot more supporters of option C. The legislature's choice of civil unions, option B, was controversial enough. Four of eight Republican House members targeted for voting in favor of civil unions were defeated in the September 12 primary; Representative Little himself won only 60 percent of the vote against a political unknown. One state senator was knocked off in the primary for his support of same-sex unions. Democratic Governor Dean found himself locked in an intense battle for reelection against a Republican whose main issue was the governor's support for "homosexual marriage." Little, Dean, and others who supported the Civil Unions Law had the credible response that they supported a compromise, the least that the Vermont Supreme Court would have found acceptable and not quite the same thing as "gay marriage." If Little had forced his colleagues in the Vermont House to take a public position on same-sex marriage, he would have imperiled his strongest allies in the upcoming election, and there is little doubt that more of them would have been defeated. Even legislative *consideration* of same-sex marriage in 2000 would have polarized the electorate and yielded a traditionalist backlash more than their adoption of the civil unions statute did. In that event, not only would the next legislature and governor have been able to repeal the law, but they might have had enough votes to propose a constitutional amendment overriding *Baker*. In this nightmare scenario, pushing for option A, the best choice, would not only have resulted in option C, the worst choice, but would have run the risk of hardwiring option C into Vermont constitutional law. This is precisely what happened in Hawaii.

Likewise, this nightmare scenario is the reason the Vermont Supreme

Court pulled its punches in *Baker*.[77] The justices on that court were aware of the fate of earlier same-sex marriage rulings in other states. In 1993, the Hawaii Supreme Court held that the state bar to recognition of same-sex marriages was sex discrimination under the state constitution, and a trial court on remand ruled that the state had not justified the discrimination, leaving it unconstitutional.[78] An Alaska trial judge found his state's same-sex marriage bar unconstitutional as well.[79] In November 1998, voters in both states overrode the court decisions by adopting amendments to their state constitutions that encoded different-sex marriage as the constitutional as well as statutory norm (see chapter 1). More than two-thirds of the voters in both liberal Democratic Hawaii and libertarian Republican Alaska supported the overrides. Enforcing liberal constitutional principles, judges in both states had required option A—and the electoral backlash not only insisted on option C but took option A off the judicial and legislative agendas for the foreseeable future. Aware of this background, the *Baker* Court hedged its constitutional ruling, leaving the legislature free to choose some version of option B, which would stand a greater chance of political survival.

Dissenting from this compromise, Justice Denise Johnson invoked the liberal principle she found in the U.S. Supreme Court's desegregation case law, "'that constitutional rights may not be denied simply because of hostility to their assertion or exercise.'"[80] I admire her principled and courageous opinion but as a scholarly liberal must concede that the desegregation cases carry a more ambiguous message. The cases from the beginning displayed a sharp disconnection between liberal rights and practical remedies. For example, Chief Justice Earl Warren's opinion in *Brown I* was a potentially far-reaching statement of liberal principle: the public school system cannot discriminate on the basis of race. But this was immediately followed by *Brown II*, which required the political process to remedy the constitutional violation, but "with all deliberate speed."[81] District judges in the south required very little actual desegregation until the late 1960s, when federal legislative action and the futility of local compliance impelled the Supreme Court to require more intrusive remedies. In the desegregation cases, judges at all levels were playing a less aggressive strategic game than Representative Little and the *Baker* Court: the judges were settling for option C (doing nothing) until they felt political conditions were receptive—and then judges often settled for option B (partial integration) rather than C (full racial integration). The judicial foot dragging is much debated; many academics decry its sacrifice of rights, while others argue the powerlessness of judges to do more.[82]

Even the Supreme Court's rejection of different-race marriage bars in *Loving* reflects the power of strategic calculations to delay the implementation of unquestionably correct liberal rights. The openly racist Virginia statute first came to the Court in 1955, right after *Brown*. The Court remanded the case to the state court to reconsider its holding in light of *Brown*.[83] The Virginia Supreme Court reaffirmed the validity of the statute on the ground that traditionalist fears of a "mongrel race" and other consequences of different-race marriage were sufficiently rational to pass constitutional muster; this was a decidedly illiberal justification, but the U.S. Supreme Court in 1956 dismissed the appeal from that ruling.[84] Some liberals were appalled by the Court's action, because it was not only unprincipled, but was a retreat from the greatest principle the Court had ever announced, antiapartheid. Defenders of the Court maintained that dodging the different-race marriage issue in 1956 was necessary to protect the result in *Brown*.[85] Southern racists were mad enough about the threat of school desegregation; they were virtually hysterical at the prospect of different-race marriage, and their prejudice was shared by many northerners and people of color. To preserve option B (*Brown II*), the Court was willing to postpone enforcement of option A for more than a decade (*Loving*), at which point half the states that had miscegenation statutes had repealed them.

Political theorists might find the lag between rights and remedies disconcerting or even shocking, but lawyers deal with this phenomenon on a daily basis. One might have a *right* to the same treatment as one's colleague, but the *process* of coercing, or persuading, a reluctant third party to recognize that right or a court to *remedy* its denial is complicated in several ways. One is temporal. If there is disagreement, especially in good faith, as to the nature or even existence of one's right, it will require time, perhaps a long time, to work through and resolve that disagreement. The deeper the disagreement the longer the time required to resolve it. Another complexity is that official legal decision makers—judges, arbitrators, and bureau chiefs—are often willing to compromise as well as delay the full recognition of rights on grounds of practicality. For example, it is common for judges to defer injunctive relief because the social harms outweigh the individual good likely to result from issuing the proposed injunction.[86] It is routine for arbitrators, mediators, and bureaucrats to compromise rights on grounds of practicalities.

Law's routine distinction between rights and remedies suggests a broader lesson for the modern state: its constitution may promise liberal rights that its political system cannot immediately deliver and that its judiciary dare not insist upon.[87] Different-race marriage was such a right in the 1950s and 1960s, the right of state prisoners to be free of unconstitutional prison conditions was such a right in the 1970s and 1980s, and same-sex marriage is such a right today. This is a deep conundrum that must be acknowledged by political as well as legal theory, a conundrum that has proven highly discouraging in the school desegregation cases.[88] But it did not prevent the judiciary from sweeping away antimiscegenation laws. That the political and judicial system cannot practically implement such rights immediately does not mean that they are without legal significance or are politically empty.

A court's or a legislature's announcement of an equality right serves an expressive function at the very least. In the international context, human rights are typically articulated and endorsed long before they can be fully implemented, yet the official announcement of such a right contributes to the creation of a public norm to that effect. Public values and norms can influence private as well as public conduct. More important, they can embolden their intended beneficiaries to demand better treatment from private as well as public authorities.

Equality Practice: A Pragmatic Implementation of Liberal Equality

Gaylegal experience in both the United States and other countries provides some support for the foregoing analysis, at least as a descriptive matter. Recall table 3.2 (in chapter three), which tabulated changes in the law relating to sexual minorities in various countries during the last century.[89] As Professor Kees Waadijk has argued, comparative law information provides insight into the movement toward same-sex marriage in general and in his country, the Netherlands, which recently enacted legislation legally recognizing same-sex marriages.[90] One lesson that Waadijk and I would draw from the table is that legal recognition of same-sex marriage comes through the step-by-step process outlined in chapter 3. Such a process is *sequential* and *incremental*: it proceeds by little steps. Registered partnership laws have not been adopted until a particular country has first decriminalized consensual sodomy and equalized the age of consent for homosexual and heterosexual intercourse; then has adopted laws prohibiting employment and other kinds of discrimination against gay people; and, finally, has provided other kinds of more limited state recognition for same-sex relationships such as giving legal benefits to or enforcing legal obligations on cohabiting same-sex couples. That the Netherlands has just recognized same-sex marriages was facilitated by its prior recognition of, and successful experience with, registered partnerships.

The recurrence of the pattern suggests a paradox: law cannot liberalize unless public opinion moves, but public attitudes can be influenced by changes in the law. For gay rights, the impasse suggested by this paradox can be ameliorated or broken if the proponents of reform move step by step along a continuum of little reforms. Chapter 3 explored pragmatic reasons why such a step-by-step process can break the impasse: it permits gradual adjustment of antigay mindsets, slowly empowers gay rights advocates, and can discredit antigay arguments. The step-by-step approach to achieving the liberal goal of full equality that is suggested by the American pragmatist tradition in philosophy and by our experience with the race cases (*Loving*) also finds support in gay experience.

Coming out of the closet to one's friends and family has in the last two generations been the defining moment or cluster of moments for many lesbians and gay men.[91] Coming out is an expression of identity and an association of the individual with the gay community, but it is also an invitation to equal treatment: you have been my parent/friend/coworker, and I want you to continue to be my parent/friend/coworker now that you know more about me. This is an invitation sometimes declined and sometimes accepted unconditionally. Most often, however, the invitation is accepted with conditions, such as a tacit insistence that the lesbian or gay person be discreet in her discussions of sexuality.[92] The conditions themselves may change over time, as the parent/friend/coworker becomes accustomed to the lesbian or gay person's identity and as she talks about the issues the coming out raises. Is it unprincipled for the open lesbian or gay person to trim her openness in order to accommodate the needs of other persons? In my view, no. Even most of us who would prefer completely equal treatment as an aspiration ought to settle for conditional equality out of humane respect for other people's feelings. Especially when loved ones are willing to accommodate our identities as gay people, we ought to accommodate their identities as gay-ambivalent people. For many, this accommodation becomes a permanent compromise of equal treatment. But it need not be.

Philip Bockman's short story, "Fishing Practice," recounts the shock his disclosure yielded for his parents. His father, who was the first to know, implored the author to soften the blow of disclosure to his ill mother by agreeing to see a psychiatrist. This Bockman agreed to do. That he was seeking professional help made it easier for his parents to deal with this new knowledge, and each parent privately expressed continued love, but not yet comfortableness in talking about the subject. Young Bockman was impatient, "Once, I expressed my frustration to my father about 'the silent treatment.' 'We're trying,' he explained. 'Please give us time.' He smiled, and I was reminded of an incident from my childhood, at about the age of six. He had taken me fishing. He hauled in one fish after the other, while I caught none. At the end of the day, I burst out crying. Kneeling beside me, he told me gently, 'Don't be too sad. Remember, it takes a long time to get good at something. Be patient. Don't think of today as fishing, just think of it as fishing practice.'"[93] After several years, Bockman brought his lover home to meet his parents, who welcomed the friend but still did not feel comfortable talking about homosexuality. Still later, after his mother's death, the author found his father positively affirming and finally willing to talk. Bockman's coming out of the closet with his family occurred over a period of discursive time, not in an instant road-to-Damascus revelation.

The same fishing-practice dynamics are needed for a political culture, even an aspirationally liberal one, to come to terms with new identity knowledges. The dynamics of gradual racial integration, step-by-step advancement of gay rights, and the process leading up to Vermont's Civil Unions Law is equality practice. Like liberal rights themselves, this is an aspiration that may or may not be realized: equality practice that moves too swiftly, as same-sex marriage apparently did in Hawaii and Alaska, may yield a counterproductive backlash, but one that moves too slowly risks entrenching a grating inequality. In my liberal view, Vermont got it right, but the views that really count are those of Vermonters themselves. And those views are still being formed.

Pragmatic Liberalism and the Conditions for Equality

Equality practice poses a normative problem for liberal theory. What stance *should* the liberal take toward the failure of the political system to remedy a denial of rights? One approach is the *liberal pragmatism* of Judge Richard Posner.[94] He takes private attitudes and prejudices as a limit on the ability of law to implement liberal rights and urges the liberal to wait until those attitudes change. This stance ought not be attractive to a Rawlsian, because it is too ready to sacrifice rights when remediation is too conflictual. Also, Posner's particular theory is too passive as to private illiberal attitudes: not only does the state often bear some responsibility for such attitudes, but the state can affect those attitudes and, more important, can influence the kinds of arguments that are acceptable in public debate. Rawls's idea of public reason insists that the liberal state deem certain kinds of arguments out of bounds, and gaylegal experience suggests that this is not an impractical aspiration. Given the experience in Vermont and the comparative law survey in chapter 3, there is a basis for believing that state insistence on public reason as a condition of debate has an effect on the conduct of the debate. Notwithstanding the perseverance of private homophobia or anxiety, countries adopting equality measures have seen a shift in public discourse about lesbian and gay relationships and have been increasingly willing to recognize them legally.

The opposite stance would be disavowal: equality practice may be inevitable and even admirable in some ways but is not defensible under liberal premises, as set forth by Rawls. Recall Chief Justice Jeffrey Amestoy's opinion in *Baker*, which defied exclusionary tradition when it articulated a constitutional right for same-sex couples but then invoked that tradition in fashioning a remedy.[95] A Rawlsian could plausibly reject this deployment of tradition as incoherent with liberal principles, and comfortably conclude that the court's equality practice is a great advance in the direction of liberal equality but must be faulted for not going all the way. Initially, I must object that this is an idealized liberalism. Any liberal who insists that recognition of rights—such as the right to marry—proceed through the legal process has already accepted a delay between the existence of a liberal right and its implementation. The point of equality practice is that the more disconnected a right is from our specific legal traditions, as same-sex marriage is, the more time the legal process needs to effectuate it. In the Netherlands, it only took three years to move from registered partnership to same-sex marriage—faster than many court cases are heard in this country. In Vermont, the shift would certainly take a lot longer, and it might never come. Can a strict liberal accept a compromise that might never advance to full equality?

Probably not, but there is a Rawlsian reason to accept a long gap between rights recognition and implementation, under certain circumstances. The fishing practice analogy in Bockman's story worked because all the participants were respectful of the other's perspectives and of the fact that the parents needed learning time to assimilate that perspective. Like the family dynamics in the story, public reason in state deliberations depends on reciprocity: all citizens and officials invoke public-regarding justifications with the understanding that each is giving up her own parochial justifications and is trying to learn from the other participants.[96] The Vermont House Judiciary Committee deliberations met these conditions for public reason, for it was a heterogeneous group whose members studied the matter exhaustively and argued respectfully and reasonably. Their conclusion was that the primary needs of lesbian and gay couples, including dignity and public respect, could be met by a new institution with the name *civil union*. The committee not only considered but internalized the lesbian and gay perspective—including the fact that many lesbians and gay men do not want to be associated with the institution of "marriage" and its patriarchal baggage (see chapter 6). Two of its three strongest supporters of same-sex marriage, Representatives Lippert and Hingtgen, voted for the civil unions bill when it was reported to the House of Representatives and made passionate speeches for it on the House floor. Their motivations included not just respect for their colleagues and a judgment that civil unions were the closest they could come to marriage under the circumstances, but also the notion that the political process has a learning curve, to which civil unions in practice could contribute.

The Rawlsian liberal could reject the foregoing argument on the ground that the committee members compromised their commitment to public reason when they acquiesced in the illiberal attitudes of the rest of the legislature. (Recall the strategic analysis above.) A Rawlsian could concede that equality practice advances the liberal project but is also an unprincipled sacrifice of public reason. If I am right about this, equality practice not only exposes a big gap between liberal aspiration and the likely operation of a political system, but also suggests a big problem with Rawlsian theory, for it would then ignore the dynamics of public education. There is no sound justification for viewing public reason statically. A lesson of lesbian, gay, and bisexual experience is that coming out of the closet changes the circumstances of discourse and opens up the possibility of candid and equal conversation—but typically after a process of observation and learning, and sometimes after a process of conflict and even emotional turmoil.

There is a third way of evaluating equality practice, that of *pragmatic liberalism*.[97] The goal of such a theory would be full equality for citizens in the strictest liberal sense, but with recognition that equality cannot be imposed upon the citizenry and must be worked for within a political system of heterogeneous preferences. As chapter 1 demonstrated, the same-sex marriage movement teaches us that process matters and that equality cannot be shoved down unwilling throats, especially by the judiciary. So liberalism in operation cannot ignore pragmatic features such as those entailed in equality practice. If a goal of liberalism is the inculcation of the values of tolerance and mutual respect, the way in which liberal projects are accomplished must be consistent with these values. For the judiciary or the professoriate to tell traditionalist citizens that their time-tested family values count for *nothing* in the same-sex marriage debate is a time-tested path to political alienation or revolt. The genius of Vermont's equality practice is that the state insisted that traditional family values give way to the recognition of lesbian and gay rights—at the same time that the state insisted that lesbian and gay family values give way to accommodation of traditionalist anxieties for the time being. Once civil unions in action reveal to Vermonters that lesbian and gay relationships are serious and loving (and fraught with the same problems as marital unions), the state might be ripe for graduation from equality *practice* to equality *simpliciter*.

CHAPTER FIVE

Equality Practice and the Civic Republic

LIBERALISM, PARTICULARLY JOHN RAWLS'S THEORY, has been the object of sustained intellectual criticism by communitarian or civic republican thinkers. The most prominent critic has been Michael Sandel.[1] If Rawls takes the autonomous individual as his starting point, Sandel starts with the citizen connected with her community. Rawls organizes the relationship between the citizen and the state around rights, Sandel around responsibilities. For Rawls, the autonomous individual has obligations because she chooses them, whereas for Sandel her obligations flow from her membership in communities. Both thinkers believe the object of politics should be deliberation for the public good, but they differ as to what kinds of arguments are admissible in such deliberation. In the civic republic but not the liberal democracy, for example, reasons inspired by religious communities can count as public-regarding arguments. The conversation between liberals and communitarians or republicans is not just academic. It has traction in the real world, as illustrated by Vermont's experience with the civil unions issue.

Gay rights debates have superficially echoed the Rawls-Sandel divide, with progay speakers emphasizing equal rights and denying a role for the state in personal value choices, and pro-status-quo speakers emphasizing that the state should support and inculcate traditional family values. The Vermont civil unions debate recounted in chapter 2 had this feature. The lawyers for the plaintiffs in *Baker v. State*, the same-sex marriage lawsuit, argued for marriage as a constitutional equality right that even convicted felons enjoy. Their legislative allies framed the matter as a civil rights issue: lesbian and gay people should be given all the same legal benefits and obligations as straight people; the state should make no judgments about their lifestyles; civil marriage should be disassociated from religious marriage.[2] The state in *Baker* defended the plaintiffs' exclusion from marriage as justified by tradition, popular morality, and the legislature's discretion to promote only what it believed was the best family arrangements for the rearing of children.[3] Rejecting the civil rights framework of the civil unions' sponsors, legislative opponents presented the issue as a matter of the common good: What is the nature of marriage? Wouldn't recognition of homosexual unions undermine the valuable institution of marriage? Should the state be promoting homosexuality? The legislative opponents also maintained that the same-sex marriage controversy had been thrust onto the state by yuppie "flatlanders" (new Vermonters) and their allies in the unelected judiciary.[4] "Take Back Vermont" for the "woodchucks" (the longtime Vermonters) by giving the people an opportunity to vote on a constitutional amendment overriding *Baker*, they argued.

The pattern described above even more strongly characterized the Hawaii and Alaska judicial and legislative deliberations about same-sex marriage in 1993–98, the post-1993 state legislative debates regarding statutes refusing to recognize the anticipated Hawaii same-sex marriages, and the congressional debate about the Defense of Marriage Act in 1996 (all discussed in chapter 1). What was most striking and novel about the Vermont debate, in fact, is that it went beyond the accustomed pattern. As the debate wore on, lesbian and gay activists and their allies increasingly argued that recognition of gay and lesbian relationships was justified by the common good. Although the *Baker* plaintiffs relied analytically on liberal equal protection ideas in the federal cases, their constitutional claim rested on the state *common benefits clause*, providing that "government is, or ought to be, instituted for the common benefit, protection, and security of the people, nation, or community, and not for the particular emolument or advantage of any single person, family, or set of persons, who are a part only of that community."[5] The "common benefit," they contended, was defined by explicit reference to a principle of inclusion, which the same-sex marriage bar offended.[6] At the two big public hearings held by the legislature's judiciary committees, the speakers favoring state recognition of same-sex unions repeatedly spoke to its substance: lesbians and gay men formed loving and committed relationships that were worthy of state recognition.[7] In the Vermont House and Senate debates, legislators rushed to the podium to share their love and respect for their lesbian daughters, gay friends, and homosexual neighbors—and their legitimate demands to be treated as equal citizens. Although the bill's sponsors, Representative Tom Little and Senator Richard Sears, stuck to rule of law and liberal arguments in their main presentations for the bill, Sears was willing to admit, without much hesitation, that the bill would "give sanction to the long-term relationships" of lesbians and gay men.[8] Both he and Little treated this as a matter-of-fact good thing.

In my opinion, the arguments from common good and citizenship made a difference. Those arguments provided the rhetorical high points of the debate and persuaded a few wavering legislators, especially in the Vermont House of Representatives. This chapter will consider the arguments for and against same-sex marriage as a matter of the common good. As I first argued in 1996, the case for same-sex marriage ought to be made as a matter of substance as well as a matter of right.[9] Same-sex marriage is good for many gay, lesbian, bisexual, and transgendered (GLBT) people and is on the whole a good idea for the larger community. These arguments for same-sex marriage have been met with the following interconnected communitarian or civic republican responses. Substantively, critics argue, same-sex relationships can never achieve the profound human good that different-sex procreative marriage can and so should not be promoted by the law to almost-marriage status. As a matter of process, critics point out that this traditionalist common good argument has achieved a democratic legitimacy, as citizens have consistently agreed with it in opinion polls. Voters in both liberal Democratic Hawaii and conservative Republican Alaska voted by more than two-to-one margins against same-sex marriage after a fair and informed public debate in 1998. As in chapter 4, the examination in this chapter will be the debate itself more than the cogency of any of the particular arguments.

Scrutiny of the traditionalist responses and deliberation about how to evaluate their dispute with lesbian and gay activists expose several theoretical difficulties with communitarianism, as elaborated by Sandel and others. One difficulty is the *incommensurability problem*. The common good is an elusive thing when citizens approach the debate from incommensurable normative frameworks. By incommensurable normative frameworks, I mean conceptual frameworks that start from irreconcilable axioms or that operate under incompatible criteria for evaluation. Debates about Charles Darwin's theory of evolution have had this quality. Person A approaches the matter from a comprehensive religious theory assuming that the Bible is the Word of God and evaluating ideas about life according to their consistency with the Bible. Person B approaches the matter from a scientific theory assuming that phemomena like life have materialist explanations, and evaluates competing explanations according to standard criteria of replicability and falsification. Persons A and B can debate Darwinian evolution until the cows come home, and it is likely they will make no progress. Neither has anything to say to the other.

What does the community do when there is a problem of incommensurability? The inclination of most communitarian thinkers is to take the status quo as the baseline and require those seeking changes in the status quo to persuade most other community members that their change is desirable. As a practical matter, a status quo bias is often useful and is sometimes the only workable starting point. But it carries a big cost in a fast-changing society. Under some communitarian tests, we would still ignore Darwinian evolutionary theory and would teach our schoolchildren Bible-based accounts of creation and life, at least in those communities where the Darwinian approach remains controversial. Moreover, a status quo bias exposes two other kinds of theoretical difficulties with most forms of communitarian theory. One is an *endowment problem*. It is well known among social scientists that human beings place an added value on things they possess that they do not place on the same things they do not possess.[10] Thus, if person A "owns" a coffee mug, she will ask for five dollars to give it up, even though she would only offer four dollars to acquire the same mug owned by someone else. The endowment effect extends to nontangible rights as well as tangible goods. Recall from chapter 2 Senator Mark MacDonald's account of how his students resisted efforts to have them change seats, even minutes after they had occupied them on the first day of class; his intuition was that one reason for the resistance was that the students had endowed the seats they had chosen with value. The endowment effect is one way to understand the value of status relations: the privileged are likely to resist the promotion of status outliers, because they have endowed their privilege with tremendous value which will be lost upon any realignment.[11] The endowment problem means that the conservatism of a status quo bias is quite powerful—and potentially paralyzing and wasteful when society would be better off, on the whole, by making a change. (Recall the discussion in the prologue of the changes in society that have given rise to the same-sex marriage movement.)

Communitarians properly respond that deliberation toward the common good will sometimes overcome the incommensurability and endowment problems. People will listen to one another, change their minds, and perhaps even alter their comprehensive theories in light of evidence from the real world. This is unlikely as to issues of social status and morality, for reasons that I term the *reciprocity problem*. Like liberalism, republicanism assumes that deliberating citizens will treat one another with respect and will presume they are willing to learn something from different points of view. This condition typically fails when one group of interlocutors has been historically subordinated and is engaged in a politics of recognition, as described in chapter 1. In that event, discourse regarding social status and morality is likely to be dominated by those who are advantaged by existing status endowments, and often the outsiders' perspective and evidence will be ignored or marginalized. Insiders and their allies are also, in such circumstances, able to prevent the outsiders from obtaining social space to falsify the arguments and assumptions of those supporting the status quo; this makes the arguments for the status quo hard to refute. Especially when the outlier group has been subject to historical prejudice as well as political marginality, the reciprocity problem not only ensures that civic deliberation will not resolve the incommensurability and endowment problems, but presents the possibility that deliberation might reinforce or exacerbate those problems. It is typical in a responsive politics of preservation that the embattled "have" groups not only refuse to listen to the "have-nots," but dig in even more deeply and might even turn on them. Moreover, there is some reason to believe that the incommensurability problem will itself preclude reciprocity. Most discussion of an issue setting one incommensurable philosophy against another will occur within subgroups whose members are like-thinking, whether they be church groups opposed or lesbian and gay groups in favor of same-sex marriage. Discussion about a divisive issue among like-thinking people has a tendency to polarize opinion. Thus, people skeptical of same-sex marriage will emerge from a church meeting alarmed, while people supporting same-sex marriage will emerge from a gay rights meeting appalled by social reluctance.[12] This dynamic not only makes reciprocity unlikely, but creates a risk that deliberation will actually polarize the community.

It is in these and like circumstances that Rawlsian liberalism can claim potential advantages over Sandelian republicanism, but my main point here is that the civic republic can deal with these problems constructively. Though this was set forth in the last chapter as a liberal notion, this chapter considers the value of equality practice from a communitarian perspective. Equality practice in general, and the civil unions compromise in particular, is a way to ameliorate the social endowment, reciprocity, and perhaps even the incommensurability problems. The Vermont Supreme Court's *Baker* decision can be read as a communitarian advance. Interpreting the state constitution's common benefits clause to create a presumption of inclusion, the court softened the social endowment problem by placing the burden of persuasion on those denying same-sex couples equal treatment by the state. The court's declaration of equal rights, combined with its open-ended remedial order, required the political process to listen to lesbian and gay couples, who realized in turn that their voices would be marginalized if they were not responsive to normative concerns of legislative moderates like Representative Little. The Vermont justices were surely aware of the problem of incommensurable philosophies and, essentially, fudged it through a procedural gambit—a *forced dialog* where the two groups each had something to lose by refusing to accommodate their differences. Under such circumstances, moderates within both groups were empowered to reach out to the other group, and a compromise was possible.

I shall conclude this chapter with a theoretical synthesis. Others have noticed that liberal and communitarian theories have more in common than are accounted for by starkly abstract presentations, and thus much of the literature has sought practical or theoretical common ground. My synthesis is different. Assume that liberal and communitarian theories really are different, and that they offer different virtues and difficulties. The practicing lawyer suggests that each ought to play an important role in the nation's political and constitutional culture. The conditions for citizenship in western democracies entail our commitment to recognition of liberal rights justified by public reason, but the implementation of those rights entails a deliberative process that considers a broader communitarian array of arguments and values. In a nutshell: Rawlsian rights and Sandelian remedies.

THE COMMON GOOD AND INDIVIDUAL CHOICE

The liberal posits autonomous individuals with their own unique preferences, and a state that is neutral as to the goals and lifestyle choices of its citizens. The role of the state is to assure a realm in which all humans can make meaningful choices and can flourish in their own way (subject to the flourishing of their neighbors). As chapter 4 maintained, liberal theory is particularly hospitable to same-sex marriage or, more broadly, to a menu of relationship options, including marriage, all of which are open to gay as well as straight couples. Almost all the serious intellectual arguments against same-sex marriages are grounded in communitarian assumptions about individuals embedded in families and about communities and politics as majoritarian deliberation. Consider the three main objections to liberal rights-based arguments for same-sex marriage. First, the great human good of marriage is only available to procreative unions of one man and one woman, and there can be no right to same-sex marriage, as the idea is an oxymoron. Second, same-sex marriage would be state promotion of households that are not good for the flourishing of the partners or for the proper rearing of children. Third, allowing homosexual couples into the institution would undermine marriage. I have examined these s[ ] objections in detail elsewhere.[13] My main enterprise here is to ev[ ] debate itself. This evaluation exposes some challenges for civi[ ] canism as an operational philosophy.

The Human Good of Marriage

Traditionalist natural law thinkers maintain that heterosexual intimacy within marriage constitutes the only form of ethically acceptable sexual expression, as only penile-vaginal (procreative) sex within a committed marriage creates a common moral good.[14] The sex must be penile-vaginal, with ejaculation by the male, because that is the form that can lead to pregnancy, the reproduction of humankind. The procreative intercourse must also be within the marital relationship; any other sexual expression is the instrumental deployment of the body worthy only of animals. Other philosophers have responded that same-sex intimacy and marriage can contribute toward a *unitive* community of friendship and love, the justification St. Augustine gave in *De Bono Conjugali* for valorizing intercourse between a husband and wife who cannot procreate. Just as the sterile straight couple can create a common good in marriage, so can the lesbian or gay couple.[15]

The common good created by the marital partners can, potentially, be a powerful argument for same-sex marriage. Some people find it hard to believe that two gay men or two lesbians can find the same kind of mutual enjoyment and committed love that a straight man and woman can enjoy—but the evidence of human lives suggests that they can. Much of the public debate in Vermont involved same-sex couples, including the six *Baker* plaintiffs, testifying about their mutual love and commitment and the constructive lives they had built as families. I have interviewed all three plaintiff couples and met two of the couples in person. I talk about their stories in chapter 2. There is no different-sex couple that would honor the institution of marriage any more than these three. Not only have they formed households of love and commitment, but their partnerships have been productive situses for rearing children (for two of the couples) and for community service (all three couples). The legal benefits and duties of marriage would be just as useful for these couples as for the most admirable different-sex couples.

Social scientists have shown us that these Vermont couples are no aberrations. The most ambitious comparative study, by Philip Blumstein and Pepper Schwartz, examined samples of (1021) straight, (493) gay male, and (335) lesbian couples. The researchers found that all three groups of couples derived significant satisfaction from their relationships, with the lesbian couples deriving the greatest measured satisfaction.[16] In an eighteen-month follow-up, Blumstein and Schwartz found that more of the married straight couples were still together than were the lesbian or gay male couples, who of course could not marry.[17] Blumstein and Schwartz's findings, including greater satisfaction by the lesbian couples, have been replicated by subsequent studies published in leading peer-reviewed social science journals—most notably by Professor Lawrence Kurdek's ambitious five-year longitudinal examination of 236 married, 66 gay male, and 51 lesbian couples.[18] These studies lend provisional support to the theses that lesbians and gay men do form committed relationships and (more speculatively) that lack of state recognition undermines their longevity. I am not aware of a similarly large-sample, long-term empirical study that has reached different conclusions.

Not a single traditionalist philosopher has been persuaded by this kind of argument.[19] They all insist that the *real common good* (or the *right*) in sexual unions must entail a procreative effort within a recognized marriage, and therefore women's hedonic enjoyment of lesbian unions cannot count.[20] This response, in turn, has been persuasive to no liberal philosopher that I can name.[21] Many lesbians and gay men consider the response disrespectful. Mary Becker takes it to be sexist. "The only sexual act considered potentially moral—because *noninstrumental*—routinely results in male emission and orgasm but rarely (if that is all that occurs) in female orgasm."[22] Her critique is, I'm sure, offensive to traditional natural law philosophers.

The divide between traditionalist natural law and its critics is not simply a liberal/communitarian divide, for some of the critics are communitarian. Instead, it reflects incommensurable criteria and worldviews. Traditionalist natural lawyers reject hedonic or utilitarian criteria and posit a nonfalsifiable criterion of procreative marriage; if you do not accept their axiom, they have nothing to say to you, nor you to them. This debate appears to be a failure of Rawlsian public reason, for traditionalist natural law is in most of its articulations what Rawls calls a "comprehensive doctrine" that, as to matters of marriage and sexual intimacy, denies the legitimacy of other forms of discourse.[23] When most other citizens do not share the assumptions of the comprehensive doctrine, there is scant possibility of reasoned discussion. This is the above-noted incommensurability problem: how to structure public deliberation in a way that facilitates genuine and nonalienating dialog among citizens whose identities are invested in different comprehensive worldviews.

The civil unions debate in Vermont shows how this philosophical problem can lead to political train wrecks. On the whole, the debate in the legislature was constrained by an effort by all concerned to follow Rawlsian public reason, and as a result the debate was more civil and more illuminating than any other that an American legislature has conducted regarding lesbian and gay relationships. The public hearings were not constrained in this way, and the discussion about the common good produced not a single novel point and, instead, degenerated into painful accusations. Reverend Jim Lake was typical of opponents. Both same-sex marriage and domestic partnership would make "sexual promiscuity the norm," said he, explicitly equating homosexuality with heterosexual adultery. Lake urged the state to tolerate individual lesbian and gay people but not to "legitimize" their "sinful" lifestyles.[24] Other witnesses insisted upon the unique nature of man-woman marriage and the "natural complementarity of men and women" which would be violated by sanctioning "unnatural" relationships.[25] Most of the opponents explicitly invoked religious arguments or quoted directly from the Bible. Charles Brett, for example, spent most of his allotted two minutes reading Scripture and closed with a warning that the "wrath of God" would be visited on Vermont if it gave any legal sanction to people the Bible condemned as "abomination."[26] Several lesbian and gay people in the statehouse were frightened for their physical safety as they listened to opponents. Some supporters, in turn, argued that denying lesbian and gay marriage was akin to slavery and suggested that opponents were just as bigoted as the old southern opponents of desegregation.[27] Even when supporters did not use such language, opponents reasonably interpreted their remarks as charges of bigotry.

The gentle reader should not conclude that citizen Brett was speaking for the natural law philosophers who opened this section; in my view he does not. But he does reflect the reciprocity as well as incommensurability problems with communitarian discourse—its tendency to polarize interlocutors engaged in status debates, especially when outliers have traditionally been disrespected. Brett was unquestionably addressing the common good, and a key feature of his common good seems to be the demonization of homosexuals. A virtue of liberalism is its insistence that people like Brett avoid disrespectful sectarian arguments and express their appeals in the language of values that most others share; this reflects their norm of reciprocity. During the Vermont legislative deliberations, there was a Rawlsian moment when the presiding officer of the Vermont House reprimanded Representative Nancy Sheltra as she was launching into a speech about how homosexual activity has nothing to do with loving relations and everything to do with "disease and STDs," particularly HIV.[28] Reminded of the chamber's norm, Sheltra returned to her better-reasoned arguments. Civic republicans can and ought to set similar debating limits. An operational problem for both philosophies is how to police the corrosive appearance of prejudice in public discussion. Reverend Lake's and Representative Sheltra's comments associating homosexuality with promiscuity constitute an open appeal to incorrect stereotypes (lesbians as a group are remarkably nonpromiscuous) and antigay prejudice (gay people are commonly marked as sexualized animals who should be shunned, attacked, or exterminated). Their particular religious spin renders the natural law position not only incommensurable with utilitarian or progressive positions, but hurtful and divisive as well.

Lesbian and Gay Unions as Situses for Human Flourishing

Judicial review ameliorates the incommensurability problem, because such review requires a "neutral" justification for state discriminations that cannot be met by sectarian reasons. Because of this kind of judicial monitoring of the potential incommensurability problem with the natural law kind of argument, neither Hawaii nor Vermont invoked it as a justification in their same-sex marriage lawsuits. Both states instead maintained that same-sex marriage is suboptimal for children, who need to be raised in households where there is both a mommy and a daddy.[29] This argument has the virtue of being liberal as well as republican: the state has an obligation to promote good households for raising children (republican); indeed, if the state promotes inferior households, it is sacrificing the interests and rights of children to the rights of the homosexual parents (liberal). The argument has the vice of being factually unsupported.

The *Baker* litigation illustrated this vice. The main reason why plaintiffs Nina Beck and Stacy Jolles wanted state recognition of their marriage was for the security of their son Noah. The additional public commitment of each woman to the other would reinforce the security of their joint commitment to Noah. No more committed parents have ever walked the earth than these two women. The state did not know these women or any lesbian or gay parents like them when it charged that they were relatively unfit to raise children. The state's charge was irresponsible unless supported by some kind of systematic evidence gathered by neutral observers—which was not the case. Unlike Hawaii, which flew in child psychologists and a sociologist to testify in support of the state's argument at trial, Vermont cited no body of scientific evidence supporting its common benefit argument, either at trial or on appeal. Nor could Vermont rely on the Hawaii experts, who on cross-examination freely agreed that "same-sex parents can, and do, produce children with a clear sense of gender identity" and "have the potential to, and often do, raise children that are happy, healthy, and well-adjusted" and that, "in general, gay and lesbian parents are as fit and loving parents as non-gay persons and couples."[30] None of the state's experts was aware of a single scientific study showing that children raised in lesbian or gay households tended to turn out badly, and Judge Kevin Chang, the trial judge in the Hawaii case, ruled that "[t]he sexual orientation of parents is not in and of itself a indicator of the overall adjustment and development of children" and "[g]ay and lesbian parents and same-sex couples can be as fit and loving parents, as non-gay men and women and different-sex couples."[31] The judge also found that "if same-sex marriage is allowed, the children being raised by gay or lesbian parents and same-sex couples may be assisted, because they may obtain certain protections and benefits that come with or become available as a result of marriage."[32] The Vermont Supreme Court in *Baker* took the same position as Judge Chang.[33]

The Hawaii trial court's findings reflect a careful review of the expert witnesses in the case and are amply supported by published materials as well. Dozens of empirical studies have compared the development of children raised by lesbian or gay parents or households with those reared by straight parents or households.[34] No study that I have seen supports the proposition that same-sex households have harmful effects on children, and the large majority of the studies specifically support the idea that lesbian and gay families can raise children competently. Although most of the studies state at the outset that they offer only provisional conclusions given their small and necessarily nonrandom samples,[35] a recent meta-analysis correcting for small sample size (but not for nonrandomness) found that the data "indicate no [harmful] difference between homosexual and heterosexual parents."[36] On developmental criteria such as self-esteem, adjustment to new circumstances, and emotional disorder, the children raised in same-sex parental households are not significantly distinguishable from children raised in different-sex parental households. The few studies that have compared two-mother households with single-mother households have found that children raised in the former are better adjusted than children raised in the latter, whether the single parent is straight or lesbian.[37] These studies do not support the proposition that children raised in same-sex households will be indistinguishable in their attitudes and values, but they do show that such children do not "suffer" from their upbringing.

The child-rearing argument is a lavender herring yet continues to be made with enthusiasm, and this reflects a deeper problem with a tradition-based communitarianism. Its ability to solve the incommensurability problem by considering criteria—like the well being of children—that reflect overlapping consensus is undermined by the aforementioned social endowment problem with the inquiry. Because they are precommitted to the status quo, traditionalists will be unwilling to admit the validity of evidence that cuts against their worldview; this is the common phenomenon of *cognitive dissonance*.[38] The dissonance problem, of course, also afflicts those people agitating for change. The likelihood of mutual dissonance suggests another kind of danger in arguments for the common good when issues of identity politics are at stake. If deliberators were candid, they would have to admit that, as to most of the hard issues like same-sex marriage, we do not know what would better contribute to the common good, because we have incomplete information and are wantonly speculating about the future. But once debate focuses on the common good, incompletely informed and speculative arguments are made with increasing certitude on either side. The adversary process of making appeals to the common good muddies the waters at the very least.

The same-sex marriage debate illustrates how it can do worse damage than water-muddying. Lynn Wardle, the main academic defender of the child-rearing argument, maintains that children will be harmed in lesbian and gay households because (1) lesbian and gay parents engage in extra-marital conduct that sets an immoral example, (2) the children of such households tend to depart from and to be confused about traditional gender roles, and (3) the children will tend to become homosexual themselves and may even be molested by their gay parents.[39] As Carlos Ball and Janice Pea have shown in detail, there are no factual bases for Wardle's claims that these children tend to be confused, grow up to be gay, or are molested.[40] Wardle's molestation assertion is particularly striking, as the social science evidence shows that molestation is overwhelmingly a male activity, with straight men just as prone to it as gay men, and lesbian as well as straight women the least prone.[41] Added to his shaky factual claims is the striking way Wardle's argumentation rhetorically tracks prejudice-based antigay rhetoric, namely, (1) the hysterical focus on "dirty," promiscuous sexual activities such as sodomy and extramarital sex, (2) the narcissistic insistence on rigid gender identities, and (3) the obsessional focus on the "predatory homosexual" seeking to recruit new homosexuals.[42] This is a politics of preservation with a hard edge.

Notice how substantive but speculative arguments about the common good have rapidly degenerated into hurt feelings and mutual alienation in these cases. As a gay man, I am wounded by Wardle's insistence that people like me are presumptively unfit or even predatory parents, and it upsets me when Wardle (completely unaware) falls into antigay stereotyping to make some of his points. So I not only refute Wardle, but also show how his arguments figure into prejudice-based discourse. Wardle, in turn, is wounded by my response, for it can be read to make him out as a bigot or a panderer to prejudice, which he is not. Not only will he be unpersuaded by my argument, but it is just as likely to cause him to hold to his views more firmly. Notice how this phenomenon of mutual alienation can occur between interlocutors (Wardle and me) who actually like one another, and on issues that are relevant under either liberal or communitarian premises.

Does Marriage Need Defending from Gay and Lesbian Couples?

Because it was embodied in the Defense of Marriage Act (DOMA), the most famous argument against same-sex marriage is that it would undermine "real" marriage.[43] Critics of this argument complain that it reflects misplaced anxiety: same-sex marriage is being scapegoated for the sky-high divorce rate caused by changing social norms and no-fault divorce. How does modestly extending marriage to same-sex couples hurt anyone else's existing marriage or even marriage as an institution? Representatives dissenting from the House Judiciary Committee's recommendation of DOMA put it this way, "The notion that allowing two people who are in love to become legally responsible to and for each other threatens heterosexual marriage is without factual basis. Indeed, when pressed during Subcommittee and Committee debate, majority Members could give no specific content to this assertion. . . . There are of course problems which men and women who seek to marry, or seek to maintain a marriage, confront in our society. No one anywhere has produced any evidence, or even argued logically, that the existence of same-sex couples is one of those difficulties. . . . [W]hen Congressman Schroeder attempted to offer amendments that deal more directly with threats to existing heterosexual marriages, the majority unanimously and vehemently objected."[44] Critics also point out that marriage has never been a static institution; it has changed as society has changed.[45] Each fundamental liberalizing change in the institution—from granting women legal independence to recognizing different-race marriages—has brought charges that marriage is being undermined.[46] Even when they have no response to this criticism, the defenders of marriage remain unpersuaded, in part because of the incommensurability problem.

There are three other reasons why people are unpersuaded. One has nothing to do with marriage and everything to do with gay people: state recognition of same-sex marriage would be a "promotion" of homosexuality and homosexuals.[47] Marriage implicates status, which is the key dispute between a politics of recognition and a politics of preservation. Thus, lesbians and gay men want the right to marry in part because it conveys some societal respect for their relationships, while many traditionalists don't want them to have the respect that married straight couples have traditionally enjoyed. One does not have to be a raging homophobe to be moved by this status concern. One consequence of the social endowment effect is that one's identity becomes invested in long-standing privileges that one takes for granted.[48] The removal of the long-standing privilege is, for some, an assault on their identity. Thus it is that arguments presented as contentions about the common good may be driven by concerns about relative status and even the stability of one's social identity. Liberalism backed up by judicial review is an antidote to the social endowment problem, for it takes a tough approach to the equality baseline and does not tolerate status denigration without a showing of third-party effects. Communitarians have not rallied around a comparably sharp-edged approach, and so status arguments will abound in a civic republic, but under the aegis of the common good. Many communitarians, including Sandel, emphasize and even romanticize tradition and its institutions.[49] To that extent, they make it harder for victims of the social endowment problem to make headway in our polity.

Because of this problem, it is hard for outsiders to break into an established institution, but it is doubly hard when the institution is perceived to be in decline, as marriage is. In imposing a "junior DOMA" by executive order, Mississippi's governor said that "same-sex marriage makes a mockery out of the institution of marriage, which is already embattled."[50] This decline is perceived as a consequence of the shift in family law from a traditionalist focus on obligations of each spouse to the family, to a liberal focus on the autonomy and rights of each spouse. Recall chapter 3's discussion of the evolving menu of state options: at the same time countries and states are recognizing same-sex unions, they are creating new institutions (sometimes open to different-sex couples, as in the Netherlands and France) that can be seen as alternatives to marriage. Just as liberal no-fault divorce rules undermine the longevity of marriages, the new liberal alternatives will encourage some couples never to marry. So liberal principles have placed marriage in a double bind: less often entered, more often exited. This does have consequences for the environment in which children are raised. In the last thirty years, the percentage of middle-aged men and women who have never married has doubled.[51] Almost half of today's single mothers have never married, and the number of children living with unmarried couples has gone up more than fourfold.[52] The divorce rate is more than 50 percent of all marriages.

I am doubtful that we can identify with confidence all the factors that have contributed to these numbers, nor am I sure about their consequences for the common good. What we can deduce with confidence is that denying lesbians and gay men the right to marry will *not* shore up (1) the incidence of marriage, (2) the longevity of marriage, or (3) the likelihood that children will be raised in a marital household. Instead, same-sex marriage will very probably work the other way for at least two of these factors: (1) more people will marry, and (3) children raised in lesbian and gay households will be more likely to have the protections of marriage. As to (2) marriage's longevity, the experience of Denmark has been positive: same-sex registered partnerships entered after 1989 have had much lower breakup rates than different-sex marriages, and the marital divorce rate in the country has fallen since 1989.[53] Put the matter another way. Gay people have nothing to do with the exit problem caused by no-fault divorce. As to the entry problem caused by the new menu, that is as much a consequence of traditionalist opposition as lesbian and gay demand for same-sex marriage. Due to intense opposition, supporters of same-sex marriage must proceed in baby steps, which has meant that they have supported these new institutions as a way to appease traditionalists fearful of a big status shift. Because most lesbian and gay activists are opposed to discrimination in any form, they do not object if their new institutions are opened to straight couples, as in France and the Netherlands. Most dramatically, gay and (especially) lesbian couples are raising children in unprecedented numbers, and so they account for a big chunk of the category of children living with unmarried couples—whose numbers would drop overnight if same-sex marriage were recognized by the state.

The third and most important reason the defense of marriage argument has legs is that it is correct in one sense: same-sex marriage would "change" marriage in a few ways, at least symbolically and perhaps practically as well. The most obvious change would be to undermine the gendered nature of marriage. The requirement that marriage must be of a man and a woman maps conveniently (and not coincidentally) onto patriarchy: man is the boss and works outside the home, and woman raises the children and works inside the home. This pattern has persisted even when the wife also has a job outside the home, for the working wife comes home to a second shift of housework. Same-sex marriage would symbolically undermine this structure, because it would be a union of gender equals. Such unions are less likely to divide tasks outside/inside the home; both wives would usually do some of the housework and have jobs outside the home, for example.[54] But even same-sex households where one partner works outside the home and the other raises the children would symbolically undermine the gendered nature of marriage, because the roles would be severed from gender: the partner working outside the home would be a woman.[55] Same-sex marriage would, in these ways, contribute to greater equality of women even in different-sex marriages.

Perhaps the most important effect of same-sex marriage for women, however, would be to give them an option they do not now enjoy. Marriage in our society remains a major boon for husbands, who live longer and make more money than their single counterparts and extract more advantages from marriage than their wives do.[56] One reason why wives accrue fewer of the advantages of marriage than husbands is that wives' exit options are much more limited, especially for wives committed to their children. Knowing this, husbands take harder bargaining positions within marriage, and wives give in repeatedly to their husbands' demands.[57] A potentially big advantage of same-sex marriage, as a matter of the common good, is that it would provide women with another option for living a coupled life or raising children: partnership with another woman. Recall the evidence, recounted above, that two women can do a better job raising children than single women and just as good a job as a woman and a man. If same-sex marriage were a realistic option for women with children, more wives could credibly insist on more equal terms from their husbands. Even before marriage, the woman would be in a better bargaining position if a number of her competitors took themselves out of the market by marrying other women.

Some readers will be skeptical of this proposition. Don't women "naturally" love just men? Not necessarily. Some women naturally love other women. Frankly, some women can go any which way.[58] Moreover, one can enter a same-sex marriage without having sex with one's partner. Why can't two women who love one another as friends and companions join as partners in raising their children together? There are straight women who have had enough heterosexual intercourse by the time they focus on child rearing and would rather raise the children with someone who understands them better and shares their values. Some women do this now in marriages to gay men. Why not to other women?

Other readers will be horrified by this possibility, because they consider
the gendered nature of marriage necessary to the institution or, if the
truth be told, useful for civilizing men or advancing their interests.[59] This
belief is speculative and, in my opinion, driven by self-interest—but then
so also is my theory, for it cannot be tested until same-sex marriage is
recognized for a period of time, and I am an advocate for same-sex marriage. How can we arbitrate between two positions about the common
good that are both self-interested and speculative? Again, liberalism has
an advantage, for its insistence on equality breaks the tie.

DEMOCRATIC DELIBERATION AND THE
REQUIREMENTS OF CITIZENSHIP

However far apart they are as to substance, liberals and republicans are
closer together as to process, particularly the process of deliberation. Most
of the claims made by Professors Amy Gutmann and Dennis Thompson
in their book on *Democracy and Disagreement* would be acceptable to
both liberals and communitarians. The core idea of *deliberative democracy* is that "when citizens or their representatives disagree morally, they
should continue to reason together to reach mutually acceptable decisions."[60] Reasoning together requires a Rawlsian reciprocity: we should
presume that people disagreeing with us are reasonable and honest people
(like us) who deserve to be reasoned with and treated with respect. In the
civic republic or the liberal democracy, a citizen ought to rely on public-
regarding reasons and should not press positions merely because they
serve one's own self-interest. Disagreement between liberals and communitarians has focused mostly on the ambit of debate allowed by public reason. Rawls would rule out arguments grounded upon a comprehensive
philosophy such as most religions express, while Sandel would rule them
admissible.[61] Most GLBT people would be more sympathetic to the liberal
stance, but I am not concerned with that important debate here.*

Instead, I am interested in other features of deliberative democracy
that liberals and republicans have not debated as much: the appropriate

---

★ My 1996 book *The Case for Same-Sex Marriage* made both liberal and communitarian arguments and assumed, without defending, the proposition that religion-inspired
arguments are admissible in public discourse.

role of popular referenda and judicial review in a deliberative democracy and the proper conditions for deliberative democratic discourse. Speaking *very* generally, one might say that communitarians are more favorably disposed to direct democracy than liberals, and less favorably disposed to judicial review. The civil unions debate in Vermont echoed these allegiances: liberals supporting civil unions were friendly to the Vermont Supreme Court's *Baker* decision, while communitarians sought to override the decision by submitting the issue to a popular referendum to amend the constitution, which liberals resisted. Few thinkers in either group have written much about the conditions for deliberative democratic discourse—which was an important theme in the Vermont debates and will be my starting point here. A communitarian as well as liberal justification for judicial review is that it can play a role in assuring the conditions for deliberative democracy.

The Conditions for Reciprocity

Communitarians and liberals alike normatively privilege democratic outcomes, but few interrogate the operation of democratic participation or deliberation.[62] And with regard to issues affecting minorities, no one has carefully examined the ability of democratic deliberation to solve the problem of reciprocity and inculcate a capacity of citizens and their representatives to presume that people disagreeing with them are reasonable and honest people who deserve to be reasoned with and treated with respect. Gaylaw can shed some light on minorities' difficulties with reciprocity and on the consequences of this for democratic deliberation.

The experience of GLBT people in the United States has been one of suppression, periodic persecution, and political marginality. For most of the twentieth century, every state made it a serious felony for consenting adults of the same sex to engage in oral or anal sex with one another; state and municipal law made it a lesser crime for people to cross-dress, engage in unspecified lewd behavior, or engage in any form of "indecency."[63] With criminalization, by the way, came potential disenfranchisement: if you were convicted of a crime of moral turpitude (which consensual sodomy and most of the other crimes were), you could not enter the United States or become an American citizen, were unfit for federal or state employment, were barred from enlisting or being drafted into the United States armed forces, were not supposed to serve on juries, and lost your right to vote.[64] Because same-sex intimacy was per se criminal, it went without saying that lesbian and gay romantic relationships, including deeply committed long-term ones, were not recognized by the state. Given these disabilities, there were very few people who were open about their sexual or gender variation or about their homosexual relationships. This is the phenomenon of the closet, an institution with pervasive political consequences. Not only were homosexuals and the like demonized by the political process, but they were unable to resist their demonization or refute the foundations of antihomosexual policies either politically or socially.

Today, after a generation of activism, the United States has evolved into three different polities for gay people: as a matter of formal law, a third of the country still endorses the political and social closet and has not changed much from the depiction in the prior paragraph; another third has revoked the main antigay laws but has done nothing to protect gay people from private violence and discrimination, which are in part a legacy from earlier state discrimination and violence; and a final third has revoked antigay laws and has adopted some sexual orientation antidiscrimination measures, thereby encouraging people to come out of their closets.* As a social matter, things have changed even more slowly. A large percentage of the population, in all parts of the country, admit to harboring antihomosexual prejudices.[65] Unfounded stereotypes about gay people are not only invoked and accepted, but regularly show up in serious academic writing by professors I believe to be unprejudiced.[66] Lesbians are routinely denied rights, such as military service or state recognition of their unions, for reasons that have less relevance for lesbians than for straight people but that owe their origin to exaggerated or unfounded beliefs about gay men.[67]

In the United States as a whole, and in most jurisdictions, gay people are treated badly by the state and at the hands of private homophobes. The communitarian status quo bias therefore preserves an unjust situation

---

★ The first third is concentrated in the rural and small-town South and West; the second third occupies most of the Midwest and Great Plains and includes some urban areas in the South and West; the last third is concentrated in the Northeast and West Coast.

for a significant number of citizens, and that philosophy's commitment to democratic deliberation is unsatisfactory because of the incommensurability, social endowment, and reciprocity problems discussed above. The short of it is that sexual and gender minorities are at an enormous political disadvantage in seeking equality rights that almost everyone else takes for granted. To begin with, they are underorganized. Political organizing is ordinarily hard to achieve, because political benefits are public goods shared by all members of a group, whether they make sacrifices to achieve the good or not. Because most lesbians and gay men are socially and politically in the closet, they are less likely to engage in political activism than other minorities.[68] This effect is only partly counterbalanced in most jurisdictions by the law-based incentive for them to organize: legal stigma gives otherwise disparate GLBT people a common focus of great intensity, given that most of their social disabilities have some link to law. While lesbians and gay men remain substantially unorganized in states like South Carolina, Oklahoma, and Idaho, they have partly overcome both the closet and the free rider problem in states as different as Hawaii, California, Florida, Illinois, New York, and Vermont.

Even when gay people get organized, however, they find the path to reform through the political process blocked for several interconnected reasons:

- a heavy *burden of inertia* rests upon any group trying to change the law, because the legislative process is too busy to consider most proposals and contains many vetogates where measures can be blocked;
- the burden of inertia is even heavier when status is involved, because of the *social endowment problem*, which for lesbians and gay men has been hardwired into the polity by generations of legal rules and condemnations;
- the pervasiveness of antigay *prejudice* makes it harder to get on the legislative agenda, form alliances with other groups, and hold onto promised allies—while making it easier for antigay measures to get on the agenda;
- belief in antigay *stereotypes*, even by unprejudiced legislators, requires an enormous educational effort to counteract;
- both prejudice and stereotypes render opponents of gay rights

unusually *intransigent*, again in combination with the social endowment effect; and

- the possibility of a *popular override*, either through a referendum or a failure to reelect, will scare away moderate legislators and render potentially friendly legislators unreliable allies.

One might wonder how lesbians and gay men have ever achieved any reforms through the political process. When they have, it has only been through an arduous and often humiliating process, and usually just to obtain political crumbs.

Illustrating the disadvantages lesbians and gay men face in the political process is the "democratic deliberation" surrounding DOMA, briefly described in chapter 1. The possibility of Hawaian same-sex marriages (which never materialized) aroused a national campaign to counteract it. DOMA sponsors portrayed homosexuals as "immoral" and "promiscuous" and warned of the social consequences of "homosexuality and the perversion" it brings.[69] Faced with a potential wedge issue in a presidential election year, potential allies ran for cover. Weak or even frivolous arguments for the bill went unanswered, and the most massive antigay discrimination ever enacted in this country whizzed through Congress by five-to-one margins. The DOMA process failed not only the reciprocity requirement of deliberative democracy, but also the deliberation requirement. A Congress that could not pass budget resolutions in a timely manner took up DOMA immediately and passed it in record time, without the normal study and debate associated with major legislation. Constitutional problems were either ignored or papered over. It is doubtful that DOMA was a measure conducive to the common good, for the reasons discussed above.

Democracy and Judicial Review

DOMA arguably met the requirement of democracy, for large majorities of the American people opposed same-sex marriage. If there was any doubt about that, it was erased by the overwhelming popular votes for constitutional referenda overriding trial court same-sex marriage decrees in Hawaii and Alaska in 1998. The Hawaii vote, in particular, demonstrated that a community with a tradition of tolerance and many equality protections for sexual orientation minorities could be receptive to the defense of marriage argument. On the one hand, the groups supporting the referendum had a clear communitarian message, that "[i]ndividual rights run amok can cause great harm to other individuals and, in particular, to families. There has to be a balance between individual rights and community rights."[70] The Hawaii referendum campaign relentlessly focused on an important feature of the common good, namely, the future of the family, and voters understood the choice they had and unmistakably chose to override the same-sex marriage right for reasons they associated with family and community. To that extent, the referendum was a republican success.

On the other hand, the Hawaii experience raised some deliberative red flags. Decades of homophobic messages from state and social sources have entrenched antigay stereotypes and prejudices in many people, rendering even tolerant citizens unreceptive to any reciprocal dialog on issues like same-sex marriage. The campaign for the constitutional amendment overriding the right to same-sex marriage appealed to these stereotypes and prejudices, usually under the aegis of religious-based arguments. The public head of the campaign was Mike Gabbard, the host of a Sunday radio show, "The Gay Deception," which portrayed homosexuals as diseased and predatory. He did much of his anti–gay marriage work through Save Traditional Marriage, which ran advertisements suggesting that same-sex marriage would lead to other "unnatural" alliances, as between humans and animals, and would encourage homosexuals to recruit for their "agenda" in the schools.[71] The Hawaii Christian Coalition raised hundreds of thousands of dollars and distributed flyers as well as media ads calling for God-fearing people to support the referendum; among the messages attributed to the coalition were the following:

- "some, but not all, homosexuals are pedophiles, preying on children" and will "recruit children to their lifestyle";
- "God destroyed Sodom for sodomy. . . . Let's not incur God's wrath" by allowing same-sex marriages;
- "The institution of marriage, as we know it, created by God, will come to an end throughout the world in six months to one year" after Hawaiian marriage licenses are granted to homosexuals.[72]

In the final days of the campaign, the Alliance for Traditional Marriage ran ads equating same-sex marriage with bestiality and incest.

Communitarians and liberals might agree that the Hawaii campaign violated the deliberative norms of reciprocity and public reason. The challenge is what to do about this phenomenon, for it is pervasive in antigay referenda: opponents of gay rights invoke the common good, especially the good of children and the family, and deploy antigay stereotypes to mobilize votes for their initiatives and referenda, which have close to an 80 percent success rate in the last generation; no other category of referendum topics comes anywhere close.[73] We have seen the same kind of problem with anti-civil rights referenda targeted at gains made by people of color.[74] The typical liberal response is that the norm of equal treatment cannot be sacrificed because popular majorities have speculative fears about the symbolism or consequences of civil rights, and that norm should be enforced through judicial review.[75] Communitarians have taken no firm position on this issue, but most seem rather skeptical of aggressive judicial review such as that in the Hawaii and Vermont same-sex marriage cases. In my view, civic republicans ought to take a harder line, with the liberals, in favor of judicial review. The Vermont experience provides a reason why.

It is exceedingly hard to amend the Vermont Constitution. Unlike the Hawaii process, where the legislature can send an amendment to popular vote immediately, the Vermont process requires supermajority votes in two successive legislative sessions before an amendment can be presented to the people for a vote. The lengthy period and the supermajority requirement meant that the Vermont Supreme Court was able to trump the social endowment effect with rights, consistent with liberal theory. But, consistent with republican theory, the court did so provisionally, referring the matter to the legislature for remediation of the discrimination. The ensuing legislative debate occurred in the shadow of the Vermont Constitution. That fact alone rendered reciprocity possible even if not inevitable. Legislators listened to lesbian and gay families in part because they had to, but the court could not force the legislators to believe the couples and their advocates. As the legislative debates established, under conditions of substantial equality lesbian and gay people could be persuasive; their stories revealed values and commitments in their lives that belied stereotypes, shamed prejudices, and (most important) raised doubts about the social endowment of marriage only with different-sex couples. Many legislators, in good faith, found their stories counterbalanced by other values, such as the risk to the community or simply the need to go more slowly, but enough moderates were persuaded otherwise to allow the civil unions bill to attain majorities in both chambers. One advantage of the liberal path followed by Vermont is that it enabled deliberation to escape some of the drag resulting from the social endowment effect and traditions of antigay stereotyping and prejudice.

Another advantage is that the debate enabled the petitioners to falsify at least some of the speculative arguments made by opponents. As the Vermont judges and legislators realized all along, the voters would have an opportunity to make their preferences known, but by the time they voted, in September and November 2000, the civil unions law had been in effect for a number of months. The more extreme speculations, as to God's immediate wrath, had not been borne out, nor had the more reasonable ones, such as the fear that Vermont would become a homosexual haven. About one thousand couples registered between July 1 and November 7, 2000. A majority were from out of state. Virtually all of them were nice people who really did love one another and rejoiced in the opportunity to celebrate that commitment. Most Vermonters were impressed by that. Although polls throughout the summer had shown only 35 to 40 percent of Vermonters supportive of civil unions, the Associated Press exit poll showed Vermonters more favorably disposed on election day, with a surprising 27 percent enthusiastic about the law and an additional 25 percent supportive, as against 32 percent opposed and only 14 percent angry. Query: What were the "preferences" of Vermonters regarding civil unions—their views before July 1, or their views after one thousand couples had peaceably joined in civil union? Communitarian theory ought to be receptive to the idea that minority groups need a chance to show the citizenry that equality measures for them do not undermine the common good. Ironically, and precisely for the reasons James Madison articulated in *Federalist* number 10, immediate democratic feedback does not conduce toward the long-term project of republican deliberation.[76] Correlatively, judicial review can facilitate conditions for democratic deliberation by assuring marginalized groups opportunities to make their cases and falsify charges made by opponents appealing to entrenched attitudes.

Equal Obligations and Citizenship

The foregoing is hardly the end of my communitarian story. The Hawaii experience was not a republican wipeout, for the legislature that placed the constitutional amendment on the 1998 ballot at the same time enacted the Reciprocal Beneficiaries Act described in chapter 1.[77] As of 1997, that law was the most generous state recognition of same-sex unions in the United States, assuring lesbian and gay registered beneficiaries more than fifty rights and benefits traditionally associated with marriage. Whatever deliberative deficit I found in the 1998 referendum might be matched with the surplus in the 1997 statute, which took lesbian and gay interests into account and arguably advanced the cause of lesbian and gay rights. That lesbians and gay men were publicly disappointed in the law—certainly a letdown after hopes for marriage had been so high—should not be dispositive.*

A number of things about the compromise ought to concern communitarians, however. Unlike marriage, Vermont civil unions, or Danish registered partnerships, the Hawaii reciprocal beneficiaries measure subtly disrespected lesbian and gay citizens by presenting them with a bundle of *rights and benefits* and denying them the *duties and obligations* associated with state-recognized marriage. That is, the state promised to honor reciprocal beneficiaries' rights to make decisions for one another and receive benefits but did not impose obligations on the couples. Getting out of the reciprocal beneficiary relationship is as easy as filling out a form, so there is none of the legal expense, waiting period, or potential support obligation that goes with marital divorce proceedings. As an item in the menu from which couples could choose, based on their level of commitment, the reciprocal beneficiary option, like the French *pacte civil*, is fine. What is disturbing is that this is the highest level of commitment Hawaii offers to lesbian and gay couples.

The reason this is disturbing owes more to communitarian than lib-

---

★ Some features of the process riled gay rights leaders, who felt that the Hawaii Senate, which favored a comprehensive domestic partner bill, gave in too easily to the House, which wanted a constitutional referendum and a watered-down partnership bill. The final package included both things the House wanted, essentially. Also, there was some last-minute watering-down of the health care benefits that would accrue to reciprocal beneficiaries.

eral theory. Liberals focus on rights of persons vis-à-vis the state, some communitarians focus on obligations owed by people to the state and to their neighbors.[78] In many philosophies and religions, obligation is just as important as right. For instance, a bar or bat mitzvah is a ritual whereby the child in the Jewish tradition assumes adult responsibilities; the term *mitzvah* has a general meaning that Robert Cover identified as an "incumbent obligation."[79] For most western philosophies, children have many rights, but only adults have responsibilities. This has bearing on adulthood in the civic republic. Republican citizenship entails both rights and duties: the state must treat the citizen with respect and evenhandedness, but the citizen owes duties of service to her colleagues and her community. Indeed, rights and duties are interconnected. As one of our earliest political philosophers, Francis Lieber, put it, "[t]he very condition of right is obligation; the only reasonableness of obligations consists in rights. . . . Let us, then, call that freedom of action which is determined and limited by the acknowledgment of obligation, Liberty; freedom of action without limitation by obligation, Licentiousness."[80] Treating lesbian and gay unions as rights without obligations not only infantilizes the couples, but also dovetails with the popular view that homosexuality is inherently licentious. Furthermore, it is in derogation of our republican citizenship.

Chief Justice Roger Taney recognized this connection in *Dred Scott v. Sanford*. To support the proposition that men of African descent could not be "citizens" for federal jurisdictional purposes, Taney relied first on the fact that people of color had always been excluded from the United States armed forces: the framers' generation did not see fit to impose military obligations on black men, because they were not considered citizens, and that refusal of obligation supported denials of rights.[81] The Reconstruction amendments reversed Taney's holding and established that people of color were full citizens. Following from that proposition were the corollaries that neither the state nor private persons could interfere with black people's performance of their obligations as citizens: the duty to vote, to serve on juries, and to serve in the armed forces.[82]

Connected with Taney's argument from military service was the further fact that the antebellum South generally did not recognize marriages among slaves. Denying marriage recognition was one way that the law signaled or confirmed the degraded status of slaves: they were not considered mature or even human enough to assume the obligations of marriage. Dissenting in *Dred Scott*, Justice Benjamin Curtis relied on the fact that Dred Scott had legally married (with his master's consent) as evidence of his emancipation, because "the law does not enable [anyone] to assert a title to the married persons as slaves, and thus destroy the obligation of the contract of marriage."[83] In nineteenth century America, it went without saying that citizenship entailed the right to marry, which in turn was considered an institution fundamental to the well-ordered state. As Lieber argued, marriage was important for reasons beyond procreation and child rearing; it was the foundation for the civic republic, which thrived on the self sacrifice, capacity for sympathy, and patriotism that companionate, romantic marriage inculcated in its participants.[84] Indeed, influenced by Hegel, Lieber drew from marriage his ideal model of a public community in which citizens achieve liberty, not from the state, but through the state and the obligations they owe it.[85] So when Reconstruction guaranteed African Americans citizenship it also assured them the civil right of state-recognized marriage, a point explicitly made by the sponsor of the Civil Rights Act of 1866.[86] The Lieber (Hegelian) view of marriage as a cocoon of citizenship runs through the Supreme Court's marriage decisions, from the polygamy cases of the late nineteenth century to the privacy cases of the late twentieth.[87]

Communitarian obligation is the reason why it was important to African Americans' citizenship that they be amenable to the civic obligations of voting, jury and military service, and marriage. This is the same reason lesbians and gay men have found it important to insist on equal duties regarding jury and military service—and the equal right to marry and assume important obligations with one's soulmate. From the community's point of view, it has a been a very good thing that people of color vote, serve on juries and in the armed forces, and marry people of their choosing, including people of other races. Integration and the easing of divisive mental attitudes is only possible if people of different races can participate on equal terms in the great republican institutions, including marriage. It would also be good for lesbian and gay couples to participate in the institution of marriage, for over time this would help integrate sexual orientation minorities into America and provide interconnections among straight and GLBT people.

EQUALITY PRACTICE AND THE CIVIC REPUBLIC

Let us return to Philip Bockman's short story that inspired the idea of equality practice.[88] In chapter 4 I told Bockman's story from a liberal perspective, where the gay man asserted his individuality and negotiated new terms of discourse that his coming out stimulated. Consider his coming out story from a communitarian perspective. The young Bockman's identity was grounded in his family, relatives and friends, and neighborhood, perhaps also within a local church and Boy Scout group. But the young man who realizes he has erotic feelings for other males confronts a dilemma that includes his family and friends as well as himself: How can he participate as an authentic member of these small communities without being honest about his feelings? Maybe he is confused, but maybe these feelings are deep. The response of most gay men and lesbians in the twentieth century was the closet: hide your feelings so that you could partake in community affairs. The closet has had incalculable consequences for young men and women—not only alienation and unhappiness, but also suicide and violence.[89] Many, and perhaps most, of these women and men married someone of the opposite sex, community-approved choices that generally yielded unhappy marriages, bitter divorces, and sometimes harm to the children.[90]

Bockman was unwilling to hide in the closet, and he confided in his friends and parents. They all then had their own choice: to accept Bockman as he was re-presenting himself, to reject him personally and perhaps exclude him from their subgroup, or to accept him with conditions, what Bockman analogized to "fishing practice" and what I call equality practice. The last is often the best path. It allows the gay person to enjoy a great degree of acceptance under conditions of honesty, while allowing his subgroup to assimilate the new information and work out a normative reconciliation over time. Like liberal approaches, equality practice anchors on the proposition that the individual needs to be treated with respect and accommodated by the community. Unlike most liberal approaches, equality practice allows room for traditional and religious views to influence the terms of accommodation. Now consider equality practice as a legal or political approach to the same-sex marriage issue in particular and to culture clashes more generally.

Registered Partnerships and Civil Unions as Equality Practice

The Danish and Dutch registered partnership laws and the Vermont civil unions statute exemplify the idea of equality practice, as well as its potential virtues and drawbacks. In the face of strong evidence that lesbian and gay families would benefit from state recognition, a majority of the legislatures in each of these states believed that the government should recognize those unions. The discursive baseline was equality, and the legislature insisted that any derogation be supported by a factual argument grounded in normative premises shared by most of the population and the country's tradition. Gay rights advocates were able to advance such arguments, grounded in Danish, Dutch, and Vermont traditions of inclusion and tolerance. The main opponents argued from religious or natural law premises that were not as widely shared, namely, the view that procreative marital intercourse was a unique and the highest human good. Some of the opponents argued from premises that were widely shared, such as the norm that the state should assure a nurturing home for children, but made factual assertions that were erroneous, unduly speculative, or based on stereotypes and prejudices. Without disrespecting lesbian and gay citizens, and without being disloyal to the country's own traditions, a majority of the legislature in each state did not believe it could credit such arguments. The first half of this book demonstrates that these kinds of arguments are typical of opponents in the same-sex marriage debate. State decision makers ought to send a strong signal that arguments traceable to antigay stereotypes or prejudice are simply not cognizable in public discourse.

At the rights recognition stage, the presumption should rest with the equality demand. Just as the family and community ought to presume against excluding their lesbian and gay members because of their sexual orientation, so the political community ought not disrespect its lesbian and gay citizens by excluding them from the fundamental duties and benefits of full citizenship. The burden should be on opponents to support denials of equality, even if it upsets traditionalist citizens. But when the question shifts to how to implement equality of treatment, arguments that are speculative and deferential to traditional endowments ought to be given due weight if made in good faith. It takes awhile for people to get used to equality. When Bockman's father appealed for him to downplay the sexual orientation issue for his mother's sake, the author trusted the good faith of his parents and agreed to all sorts of accommodations. Bockman's parents showed their good faith commitment to an equal relationship by accepting him as their gay son, and he showed them his commitment by going along with their requests. The Danish, Dutch, and Vermont laws had this quality: many fearful straight people accorded lesbians and gay men respect by recognizing their unions, but gay people returned the respect by supporting the registered partnership or civil union compromise.

Sometimes the compromise is painful—as it was for Danish and Dutch gay people who went along with a measure that denied them adoption rights. Was this a sacrifice of equality? Yes, but only provisionally so, for the Danish experience with registered partnership has been so favorable that the Parliament repealed the restrictions on adoptions by registered partners. Even more dramatically, the Netherlands has just enacted laws recognizing same-sex marriage and allowing such couples to adopt children.[91] These experiments have been successful, because they provided a minority group with an opportunity to show that the norms underlying civil marriage could apply to their relationships and to falsify speculative factual arguments made against their equality proposal. Moreover, now that the Danes and Dutch have seen legally recognized same-sex partnerships in action, the social endowment effect has eased for many of them. Attitudes in the Netherlands have changed most decisively, for a large majority of the Dutch now support same-sex marriage![92]

What if the Danish registered partnership and Vermont civil union laws prove to be the end points rather than provisional resting points on the road to same-sex marriage? That is possible, and that is part of the price we pay when we live in a community. Although I believe that states like Vermont will recognize same-sex marriages once the social endowment effect eases and preferences change, it might take a long time for that to happen—but that is fine. It took a lifetime for Philip Bockman to be able to talk with complete candor to his father about his sexual orientation. Conversely, it is possible that the desire of lesbian and gay couples to formalize their mutual commitments will erode, and the demand for same-sex marriage will dry up or will be redirected into other channels. I would be delighted to follow the evidence. That's the great thing about states as laboratories of social experimentation: we can all learn from them, and we all ought to be open to changing our minds based on what we learn.

Equality Practice as a Mediation Between Liberal and Republican Theory

As a theory, equality practice bears similarities to the *pragmatic liberalism* discussed in the last chapter, and to the *liberal republicanism* propounded by other authors.[93] Theoretically distinctive to equality practice are its deployment of lesbian and gay experience, gaylegal and feminist theory, and simple legal process ideas to arbitrate the liberal/communitarian debate. Gay experience and gaylegal theory contribute the core concept of equality practice, as elaborated above, but my thinking about gay rights issues has been pervasively influenced by feminist theories. Cultural and other feminist theorists have been, in my view, the most persuasive critics of America's discourse of constitutional rights. Critics as diverse as Suzanna Sherry and Mary Ann Glendon maintain that the all-or-nothing discourse of rights is not the most productive way of doing constitutional law; a jurisprudence of needs would examine and balance the legitimate needs of differently interested citizens.[94] Such a jurisprudence would seem particularly friendly to legislative action creating a menu of commitment options such as that outlined in chapter 3, for example.

Gay and feminist thought suggests the contours of my approach, but legal process theory suggests a Solomonic way of thinking about it more concretely: Rights recognition ought to be liberal in focus, remedies communitarian.[95] This is precisely the way Chief Justice Jeffrey Amestoy viewed the matter in his *Baker* opinion: arguments of deference and tradition (classic legal stand-ins for the social endowment effect) would not defeat the equality demand that the same-sex marriage bar be overturned, but they could be considered in fashioning a remedy.[96] The Vermont legislature saw matters the same way: the state was obliged to recognize equal rights for lesbian and gay couples and so was obliged to recognize their unions and assure couples of all the obligations as well as rights of marriage, but created a new institution out of deference to the special role reserved for marriage in the eyes of many citizens whose views were entitled to respect.

Equality practice mediates between liberal and communitarian theories quite neatly. We have already seen how much potential overlap there is among the most thoughtful proponents of each theory as to the importance of equality as well as tolerance norms as a goal of state policy and reciprocity as a condition of public deliberation. What continues to divide the theorists most sharply are the admissibility of arguments drawn from comprehensive philosophies (admissible for communitarians, but not for liberals) and the proper balance between judicial review and direct democracy (liberals emphasize the former, republicans the latter). Rights recognition should be dominated by Rawlsian public reason and backed up by judicial review, but remediation should be informed by a larger inquiry and democratic feedback. Where a minority has been traditionally suppressed, and unfairly so from a liberal perspective, the judiciary has special obligations to make sure their views are heard. (The legislature, of course, has the same duty but is less likely to fulfill it because of the day-to-day pressures of ordinary politics.)

Equality practice mediates in a subtler and deeper way as well. Although both liberals and communitarians defend their political philosophies by reference to American political traditions and to the future prosperity of our society, both tend to examine rights debates from a narrow temporal frame: What's the best resolution right now? Equality practice suggests that the proper frame is a temporal *stream* rather than a temporal *point*. Rather than full equality right now, it's equality over time. Rather than defer to or defy tradition, it's let's see how tradition evolves in light of a new practice. Moreover, equality practice is conditional—open to what actually happens over time. Rather than certain equality, it's equality if your view of the world is borne out. Rather than deference to or defiance of tradition, it's let's see whether this experiment can be assimilated into our culture's traditions.

There is an additional virtue to equality practice that is distinctively republican. Liberal insistence on immediate equality, especially through judicial review, can exacerbate the incommensurability, social endowment, and reciprocity problems by polarizing public deliberation about a divisive issue. If traditionalists believe that "homosexual rights" have been forced down their throats through an undemocratic process, they are less likely to abandon their natural law frame of reference and, if anything, are likely to retreat into subgroup deliberations which will intensify antigay feelings. This is a communitarian train wreck, deepening divisions and distrust within the community. The public's input into the Vermont civil unions debate had this feature: letters to the editor, conversations at some of the town meetings, and testimony at the two public hearings reflected little reciprocal give and take and increased hostility between warring camps. Such an experience depletes a community's needed social capital, the reservoir of trust among all citizens.[97] Equality practice can help a community cope with this kind of divisive politics, by reassuring both groups that their perspectives are being heard and by lowering the stakes of the debate. It also can create conditions for less divisive debate in the future by setting in motion a social experiment and allowing citizens of all persuasions to learn from its operation.

Equality Practice in Other Contexts

The traditionalist reader might wonder whether equality practice represents some kind of homosexual Trojan Horse, an effort to corrupt traditionalist political philosophy from within. Please be assured, this is a genuinely republican proposal. Indeed, this is a proposal that ameliorates critical problems facing communitiarian theories (incommensurability, social endowment, reciprocity) without abandoning those theories' many virtues (democratic legitimacy, civic engagement, collective wisdom). Such a proposal is sure to be rejected by normative extremists on both sides. That is another virtue of the approach. Equality practice *works*. It is the best explanation of the actual operation of American constitutional law in several contentious areas, and it has often worked fairly well for this country—or at least better than alternative approaches. Consider three tough examples.

Most American jurisdictions have dealt with consensual sodomy laws as a matter of equality practice. In most major states there was a public debate about this issue, starting in the 1950s or 1960s.[98] Liberals maintained that consensual sodomy ought not be a crime; traditionalists felt it violated fundamental moral goods and feared that deregulation would promote homosexuality. Given the intensity of this moral debate, states were politically reluctant to deregulate. With the rise of lesbian and gay cultures and the perception that most straight couples engage in oral or anal sex themselves, states have strong incentives to deregulate. Most states have mediated this tension through equality practice. New York moved relatively early but is otherwise typical. In 1950, at Governor Thomas Dewey's behest, New York's legislature demoted consensual sodomy to a misdemeanor and reduced its potential sentence.[99] In the 1960s and 1970s, changing social mores and pressure from lesbian and gay activists inspired the police to let up on their enforcement of the consensual sodomy law. In 1980 the New York Court of Appeals ruled that the law was an unconstitutional invasion of people's privacy.[100] The legislature finally repealed it in the year 2000, without a whimper from traditionalists.

From a progressive point of view, this lengthy process is superficially suboptimal, as it left lesbians and gay men as metaphorical social outlaws for an inordinate period of time—in violation of their constitutional rights. From a traditionalist point of view, this process is suboptimal, as it ultimately "promoted" same-sex intimacy to a higher status and paved the way for further gaylegal advances in the public sphere. But from the point of view of the community as a whole—the communitarian focus—this equality practice had the virtue of allowing the state to learn something and to respect both gays and traditionalists at each step along the way. Key to the ultimate deregulation was the fact that many traditionalists abandoned their prior view that same-sex intimacy ought to be criminal, and some traditionalists softened their view that it was immoral, in light of their knowing and working with openly lesbian and gay people in their daily lives.

Desegregation, my second example, is a much harder case. The "all deliberate speed" formula of *Brown II* is widely considered a failure, even after the Supreme Court speeded up compliance between 1969 and 1975.[107] School districts have spent large sums of money, and children have been reassigned from the neighborhood schools that are widely viewed as the best situses for public education, but without impressive amounts of actual school integration or sufficient improvement in the education of previously segregated African-American children. To the extent that the Supreme Court's desegregation campaign was an equality practice, it was not a smashing success. The Court is open to second-guessing as to how it proceeded. For example, it might well be that the Court's school desegregation activism should have waited until the Court, and perhaps Congress, had given teeth to the Fifteenth Amendment's guarantee that the right to vote would not be denied on the basis of race. If local political processes had better reflected the concerns of racial minorities, the federal courts could have (as the Vermont Supreme Court was able to do in *Baker*) insisted that state and local legislatures come up with as well as implement reform plans. One reason for the failure of *Brown II* remedies is that local political processes were too often uncooperative, and people believed that federal judges were forcing unwanted policies onto their localities. In short, incrementalism alone is not sufficient. Equality practice will be successful only if the minorities benefitting from it are politically salient, and the norm entrepreneurs and their state allies pressing for equality are exceedingly clever as well as persistent.

On the other hand, the failure of *Brown II* is not necessarily the failure of equality practice, for the other modes of proceeding could have been even worse. A hard-hitting *Brown I* approach, insisting on equality rights *now*, would probably have yielded more turmoil, more immediate white flight, and perhaps also more violence. A lenient communitarianism, such as that reflected in *Plessy v. Ferguson* (the Supreme Court opinion overruled by *Brown I*), would have also been worse, for it would have lent the moral authority of the state to the idea as well as the practice of a racial caste system. In my view, the failures of *Brown* are not failures of equality practice, but of America's continuing dysfunctions in matters regarding race.[102]

My final example has to do with the constitutional politics of abortion. A robust argument for the right of a woman to choose an abortion is equality: the burden of childbearing, and usually of child rearing, falls on women, and pre-1971 prohibitions did not take account of this unequal burden and the extraordinary effects it had on women's health, intellectual development, employment opportunities, and role within the family.[103] A purely liberal theory of equality could support an absolute right of the mother to choose an abortion, at virtually any point in her pregnancy. That the fairly liberal disposition of the U.S. Supreme Court in *Roe v. Wade* took the matter away from the states and substantially vested the decision with the mother, was expected to settle the matter.[104]

It did not, because the Court and its supporters were unable to show that the fetus is not itself life with cognizable rights, and because the liberal stance was not sufficiently sensitive to the community interest in preserving potential life. Unlike the long public debate over consensual sodomy laws, states did not slowly abandon their policies under liberal constitutional interrogation. Instead, like public resistance to school desegregation, states sought to evade *Roe* through new prohibitions and more indirect policies like denials of state funding for abortions or requirement of medical testing before having an abortion.[105] Unlike both sodomy repeal and desegregation, the abortion issue has continued to mobilize strong moral arguments and social forces on either side.[106]

The foregoing dialogue and continuous stream of regulatory laws culminated with the Supreme Court's decision in *Planned Parenthood v. Casey*, which reaffirmed *Roe*'s central holding that the mother has a liberty interest in the control of her body and her life, but which recalibrated that right to allow a significant amount of state regulation—especially rules requiring the mother to consult with others before she goes through with the procedure.[107] Equality practice suggests that the Supreme Court should have been attentive to both sides in this extraordinarily serious and important debate, and the Court's compromise seems worthy as well—a judgment influenced by Mary Ann Glendon's showing that this has been the drift of regulatory discussion in Europe.[108] Equality practice also suggests that the Court's original disposition in *Roe* would have been more productive if it had been more tentative, like the Vermont Supreme Court's approach in *Baker*. Consider a pre-*Roe* contrast.

Just before *Roe*, Judge Jon Newman had voted to strike down the Connecticut abortion statute on the ground that its original nineteenth-century rationale, to protect the mother's health, had been overtaken by changed circumstances.[109] Judge Newman's approach would have had the liberal advantage of recognizing the woman's right and sweeping away the old statute, but the communitarian virtue of allowing the legislature to fashion a remedy by addressing the issue anew; that communitarian process, in turn, would have been one where the social endowment effect of the state's long-standing abortion law would have been ameliorated by the law's having been overturned. On the other hand, Judge Newman's approach would have had the disadvantage, for some, of being insufficiently radical. This is the main challenge to equality practice as a model for public discourse, including constitutional discourse, and for same-sex marriage as a liberal aspiration. The next chapter will take up the radicals' challenge.

CHAPTER SIX

Equality Practice as a Postmodern Cultural Form

STATE RECOGNITION OF SAME-SEX MARRIAGES is an idea whose time is coming. Liberals can and ought to support it as required by principles of formal equality and justice (see chapter 4). Communitarians can and ought to support it as required by the common good (see chapter 5). As the United States inches closer to state recognition of same-sex marriage, people are coming to appreciate how it is both radical and conservative. The idea is radical because it challenges the conception of marriage, gender roles, and sexuality held by most Americans. It is conservative because it accepts the value of civil marriage—interpersonal commitment reinforced by state benefits and backed up by state obligations—and offers it as one positive aspiration for gay and lesbian couples. Either the radicalism or the conservativism is morally horrifying to most Americans and many intellectuals.

Hence, same-sex marriage has drawn fire from both the Right and the Left. *Traditionalist* critics, whom I have attended to in the earlier chapters of this book, consider same-sex marriage too radical and insufficiently attentive to the unique value of different-sex marriage, long recognized in western history. *Progressive* critics, the focus of this chapter, consider same-sex marriage an insufficiently radical challenge to oppressive traditions and too accommodating to mainstream values. The same-sex marriage debate has, therefore, been triangular: defenders of same-sex marriage respond to traditionalist objections on the right hand, and progressive ones on the left.

The three positions in the debate generally link up with three different kinds of thinking and argumentation. Traditionalists' reasons for rejecting same-sex marriage are at bottom *premodern* in form or essential content. A premodern analysis reasons from nature, history, or authority, including scriptural authority. It often insists on distinctions based on historically or religiously grounded status differences. As I have shown in earlier chapters, the most internally coherent and intelligible justification for opposing same-sex marriage has been of this kind: because marriage is by nature (or by definition or linguistic usage, etc.) different-sex, same-sex marriage is impossible or oxymoronic.[1] Secondary justifications invoked by traditionalists during the Hawaii and Vermont debates started with the propositions that "homosexuals" are a depraved or inferior group and "homosexuality" is a degraded status and contended that state recognition of same-sex relationships would be unacceptable state endorsement or promotion of a degraded status or an invitation for wavering adolescents to join the depraved group.[2] Although traditionalists pose other kinds of problems with same-sex marriage, discussed below, these are their core concerns.

Defenders of same-sex marriage sometimes answer traditionalists on their own terms, suggesting that nature or tradition is more open to same-sex unions or marriage than is commonly supposed.[3] Implicitly, defenders of same-sex marriage also insist that lesbians, gay men, bisexuals, and transgendered people are not depraved, and that sexual or gender variance ought not be a necessarily degraded status, at least as a matter of law. But most of the time, proponents make different kinds of arguments—*modernist* ones. The modernist presumption is that people should not be treated differently because of traditional status distinctions. Even for social outcasts, the baseline is equal treatment, subject to exceptions or exclusions justified by a person's lack of fit with criteria grounded upon the policy reasons for the state benefit or obligation. So the case for same-sex marriage is that lesbian and gay couples fit within the marriage policy's unitive goal and that excluding such couples rests upon no neutral state policy.[4] To exclude same-sex couples because they cannot procreate is incoherent with the goal of state marriage statutes, which freely allow marriages by different-sex couples who do not or cannot procreate, and so cannot be a nonstatus basis for state line drawing. Because marriage is an important cluster of benefits and obligations offered by the modern regulatory state, but whose exclusions are defined by reference to traditional rather than functional criteria, same-sex marriage is at the cutting edge of our culture's odd amalgam of modernist and premodern thinking about matters of family, gender, and sexuality.[5]

Some people argue against same-sex marriage, not because it violates a natural law or because it would not fit the conditions of many lesbian and gay couples, but because it represents a strategic mistake on the part of sexual and gender minorities as a social movement. Their arguments tend to be *postmodern* in form. Some readers will be unfamiliar with this term, and it does have a protean quality. Postmodernism, as I am using the term, is not as concerned with interrogating the veracity of truth claims as it is with interrogating the strategies and the process by which truth claims are put forward, manipulated, adjudicated, and deployed. Progressive exercises in postmodern analysis seek to understand how these strategies and processes fit into larger *power relations* and *practices of subordination*. Most progressives have little quarrel with modernist arguments for same-sex marriage, on their own terms. But many progressives do not consider those arguments conclusive within a broader framework.

A postmodern inquiry would examine the debate itself, to see how reformist rhetoric, arguments, and strategies might play themselves out in ways that are counterproductive or even reactionary. One might ask how the terms of the debate might affect the people involved in it, and whether this particular debate represents the best approach for changing the status quo. The exchange of modernist and premodernist truth claims in the same-sex marriage debate creates a discourse that can profoundly affect people, perhaps more than the actual resolution of the contending claims. Postmodern criticisms of same-sex marriage typically maintain that the process by which this "reform" is achieved, or the discourse resulting from that process, carries with it dangers for the supposed beneficiaries and their allies—such as sacrificing their distinctiveness for conformity with traditional mores.[6] The fact that the debate occurs within the context of the law, itself a conformist discourse, generates even more risks that gay people themselves will suffer unforeseen consequences of arguments that "their" purported speakers put forward. Most important, by focusing political energies on the difficult project of integrating nonconforming couples into marriage, progressives are foregoing the opportunity to challenge other features of the legal regime, such as its focus on sexual fidelity between two persons and its failure to support caregiver relationships as profoundly as it supports romantic ones.[7]

This chapter will analyze the interesting interconnections and dynamics of the same-sex marriage debate as a three-pronged one. Lawyers defending same-sex marriage have focused almost entirely on the premodern and modern arguments, and have slighted the postmodern ones. There may be good reasons for this. Some of the postmodern objections are too obscurely or contentiously expressed, or rest upon insufficiently widespread normative assumptions, to receive due attention in the process of public reason for a deliberative democracy. Be that as it may, some progressive critics make arguments that should be considered by thoughtful supporters of same-sex marriage. The issue ought to be contemplated from a postmodern perspective. Specifically, sexual minorities ought to be aware that state recognition of same-sex marriages would be the introduction of a regulatory regime into lesbian and gay households choosing that option, and there are some scenarios where choices would be socially circumscribed in the wake of "reforms" like this one. These are all valid possibilities to consider in the debate within progressive communities.

Does this line of thinking augur against lesbian and gay petitions for civil marriage? Not necessarily. This chapter will also suggest some postmodern arguments for same-sex marriage and the menu of options that is developing in western democracies. More important is the insight that state recognition will not itself be useful for lesbians and gay men without further ideological struggle, in part because same-sex marriage will itself trigger a political debate about the menu outlined in chapter 3: What choices will be made available to couples? What kind of state regulatory regime is entailed in each choice? Thus, the equality practice introduced in the previous two chapters will not end with full and equal state recognition of same-sex unions. Equality practice ought to include feedback from lesbian and gay groups seeking to open up state recognition to a variety of new forms for recognizing human partnerships. Because this entails an ongoing conversation about who we are as a people, and who among us are "in" or "out" of "mainstream" discourse, equality practice can also be viewed as a postmodern cultural form. And it is a potentially attractive postmodern phenomenon, to the extent that it participates in or even facilitates the transition from traditional marriage-only to a variety of state-sanctioned institutions, available to same-sex as well as different-sex couples.[8]

PERVERSE STRUCTURES OF THE SAME-SEX MARRIAGE DEBATE

Traditionalist critics consider same-sex marriage too radical and insufficiently attentive to the traditional status of different-sex marriage, while progressive critics consider it an insufficiently radical challenge to oppressive traditions. Notice how the traditionalist and progressive critiques mirror one another. Likewise, the specific responses made by the differently situated critics reflect parallel tropes and argumentative moves. Thus, traditionalist justifications for continued exclusion perversely mirror progressive justifications for much greater inclusion.

For example, supporters of same-sex marriage insist upon formal equality: lesbian and gay couples ought to be treated the same as straight ones.[9] This seems simple and just, but both kinds of critics object that formal equality for lesbian and gay couples would *normalize* lesbian and gay couples in unproductive ways. Such normalization would assertedly promote homosexuality or homosexual relationships, which the traditionalist finds inferior to heterosexuality or heterosexual relationships,[10] or would standardize gay lives around committed coupling, which many progressives find too confining.[11] Supporters maintain that same-sex marriage would denormalize traditional gender roles within marriage, even if just incrementally. Naysayers fault the gender-role argument through strategies of *denial*: traditionalists deny that natural gender roles *should* be sacrificed,[12] while some progressives deny that same-sex marriage *will* have any such effect.[13] As to the argument that same-sex marriage would extend useful state benefits and obligations to same-sex couples and would encourage commitment, the critics bemoan the possible *regulatory effects* of such a move. Traditionalists say it would undermine the state's effort to encourage different-sex marriage,[14] while progressives say it would introduce too much state involvement in some and perhaps many gay and lesbian relationships.[15] Table 6.1 maps the arguments for same-sex marriage and the mirror-image responses by traditionalist and progressive critics.

Table 6.1 is a starting point for understanding other structures—and ironies as well as paradoxes—of the same-sex marriage debate. One such feature is the *slippage between symbolic and consequentialist arguments* by most of the debaters. The central commitments of each camp are symbolic or expressive. Defenders of same-sex marriage are alumni of gay people's politics of recognition and consider equal marriage rights or equal menu rights to be the ultimate recognition of gender and sexual minorities as equal citizens.[16] Critics of same-sex marriage are likewise driven by symbolic commitments, either to the sanctity of different-sex marriage (the traditionalists) or to a more radical attack on our society's excessive valorization of the status of being married (progressives). While these are the central commitments, most of the published argumentation has been consequentialist—in part to satisfy conditions of reciprocity in public debate. Critics have increasingly directed their analysis to the bad consequences formal equality would generate, both for their own constituencies and for the country as a whole. Defenders respond that same-sex marriage would not necessarily have such malignant consequences and insist that it would instead have good consequences. Mark this irony, but there is another one that's even neater.

Although the debate now appears to be primarily consequentialist, no one actually knows the consequences, especially the long-term consequences, of state recognition for same-sex marriage. Who can tell what will be "normalized" by same-sex marriage: Homosexuality? Marriage? Commitment? Lesbians with children? What would be the effect on gender roles in the medium or long term? What costs would be imposed on same-sex couples? Or on single gay men and women? How many would be affected? While the experience of Denmark (with registered partnerships) and of the Netherlands (with same-sex marriage) or Vermont (with civil unions) might provide us with information about such effects, my hunch is that experience in these states will support the conclusion that legal recognition per se has few if any demonstrable effects in the short or

TABLE 6.1. **ARGUMENTS FOR AND AGAINST SAME-SEX MARRIAGE**

Case for Same-Sex Marriage	Traditionalist Arguments against Same-Sex Marriage	Progressive Arguments against Same-Sex Marriage
Formal Equality: Same-sex couples ought to be treated the same as different-sex couples.	*Normalization*: Equal treatment would normalize homosexuality or homosexual relationships, which are either bad or, at least, not as good as heterosexuality and heterosexual relationships.	*Normalization*: Equal treatment would normalize lesbian and gay couples, denigrate uncoupled lesbians and gay men, or contribute to the standardization of same-sex relationships.
Regulatory Benefits and Duties: Marriage recognition would assure lesbian and gay couples of tangible benefits, as well as reinforcement of interpersonal commitment.	*Regulatory Costs*: Legitimating an alternate lifestyle, same-sex marriage would undermine different-sex marriage.	*Regulatory Costs*: Introducing the state into same-sex partnerships, same-sex marriage would undermine the liberty of lesbians, gay men, and bisexuals.
Critique of Gender Roles: Same-sex marriage would help erode rigid gender roles (woman = wife and child-rearer; man = husband and breadwinner) within marriage.	*Denial*: Woman's natural role is to be married to a man, and vice-versa. (Woman's natural role is to bear children in the context of marriage to a man.) The state cannot change that.	*Denial*: State recognition of same-sex marriages would have scant effect on gender roles. (It would further marginalize the most radical gender-benders.)

medium term. Whether I am right about this hardly seems to matter, because the different stances either take a long-term perspective in which everything is up for grabs, or they would immediately do so if there were a persuasive demonstration of no short-term effects. The protean nature of the actual arguments suggests that the debate most fundamentally concerns the symbolism attendant to the clashing politics of recognition and preservation described in chapter one. So everyone talks about consequences, but the consequences are strongly filtered through the debaters' symbolic precommitments: formal equality (defenders of same-sex marriage), old-fashioned heterosexual marriage (traditionalist critics), or decentering marriage from its position as the centerpiece of state regulation (progressive critics). Because most people's positions are driven by their underlying commitments, few are really open to changing their minds. This feature of the same-sex marriage debate has generated the various compromises described in the earlier chapters: Vermont's civil unions, Germany's life partnerships, France's PaCS, Hawaii's reciprocal beneficiaries, and Denmark's registered partnerships.

Another feature of the same-sex marriage debate is its *odd triangulation*. I have already remarked about the weird symmetry among the arguments deployed by differently situated critics, and table 6.1 formally expresses that comparison. My suggestion is *not* that traditionalist and progressive critics are making the same points or even thinking in the same ways. They certainly are doing neither, as evidenced by the different relationships among the three kinds of arguments. Contrast the relationships among arguments between (1) the defenders and the traditionalists, (2) the traditionalists and the progressives, and (3) the defenders and the progressives in the same-sex marriage debate.

For legal and political purposes, the central subdebate is between defenders of same-sex marriage and traditionalist critics. Although the latter are inspired by premodern natural-law-type theories, they realize that their position must also be defended along modernist lines as well, because such arguments are the lingua franca of public discourse in modern democracies. In the United States, judicial review enforces this regimen, for judges are typically skeptical of state policies supported by nothing but tradition or sectarian philosophy. The U.S. Supreme Court has specifically ruled that measures inspired by antigay "animus" or sectarian religious views violate the Fourteenth and First Amendments to the U.S. Constitution, respectively.[17] This feature of constitutional law has had a *channeling effect* on political discourse. Accordingly, traditionalist allies in the legislature or the attorney general's office shy away from open appeals to status denigration or Biblical authority. The rhetorical clash between same-sex marriage proponents and traditionalist opponents has increasingly been fought on modernist turf. Zealots who decry "homosexuals" as God's "abominations" have been shoved into the background, and even the more respectable definitional arguments have given way to contentions that same-sex marriage would be bad for children and would undermine the political economy of marriage as an institution. This phenomenon works to the disadvantage of opponents, because their modernist arguments are relatively weak pretexts for their natural law position. For example, their claims that same-sex marriage would hurt children raised in such households has been witheringly reviewed by the modernist experts in child psychology,[18] and their other modernist claims usually fare no better.[19] Nonetheless, their position prevails in most places, for the time being, because of old-fashioned homophobia and nervousness about changing an established institution.

Although they have very different visions of morality and state policy, there is no subdebate per se between traditionalist and progressive critics of same-sex marriage. Their relationship grows out of mutual appropriation and demonization. Traditionalist critics appropriate progressive talk about sexual liberty and gender revolt to demonize same-sex marriage as a betrayal of the fidelity and commitment features of marriage. Even though progressives do not "represent" the point of view held by most lesbians, bisexuals, and gay men, radical declarations that marriage is an outdated institution or should be opened up to threesomes are seized by traditionalists as examples of the *real* "homosexual agenda." Progressive critics, in turn, appropriate the most reactionary features of traditionalism (patriarchy and sexual puritanism) and demonize same-sex marriage as buying into those features of mainstream culture. Again, note the weird parallelism of the two differently situated criticisms.

The subdebate between supporters and progressive critics of same-sex marriage has been rhetorically asymmetrical. Progressive critics slight modernist argumentation and insist on postmodern starting points such as the following: Our identities are contingent and always in the process of formation. That process is one of struggle and resistance. It can be obstructed or distorted by modernist as well as premodernist discourses. While the latter deny human subjects any freedom from their received social role, the former promise freedom but deliver norms of standardization and responsibility that can be just as confining. Accordingly, the liberal ideal of formal equality is a false hope: formal equality for a minority group presents itself as improving the status of the group, but that improvement rests upon the minority's acquiescing in the norms of the majority; such acquiescence is acceptable to that portion of the minority that is already most like the majority; ergo, formal equality has the consequence of debasing the minority insofar as its people give up part of their uniqueness and of splitting the minority into those advantaged by assimilation and those who find themselves even more marginalized.

Because the main debate is with traditionalists, proponents of same-sex marriage have devoted little attention to the debate within progressive, particularly queer,* communities. Unfortunately, they have generally responded to the postmodern questions with the same modernist answers they provide in the main debate. The progressive critics, in turn, ignore or deny the legitimacy of modernist arguments and seize upon any concession by defenders of same-sex marriage to their mainstream and traditionalist critics. For example, defenders respond to traditionalist arguments that marriage is different-sex in nature by showing how well same-sex couples fit the relevant modern policy goal of marriage—commitment to one another in a unitive partnership. Progressive critics cite this response as proof that the same-sex marriage movement seeks to normalize all queer people around the minority who prefer marriage-like arrangements.[20] The same dynamic repeats itself in connection with the regulatory costs and gender role arguments. Table 6.2 is another mapping of the same-sex marriage debate along this structural dimension, namely, the triangulated debate, where liberal responses to the traditionalists are held up as establishing the dangers of a same-sex marriage strategy.

POSTMODERN ARGUMENTS AGAINST AND FOR SAME-SEX MARRIAGE

Table 6.2 and the dynamic it illustrates ought to concern all progay as well as queer thinkers. Same-sex marriage proponents should be more attentive to the arguments of progressive critics. Any failure of mutual engagement misses opportunities to learn useful things about the best path toward reform. Morever, there are ramifications of this nonengagement in the mainstream debate. Not only do progressive critiques perversely mirror traditionalist critiques of same-sex marriage, but traditionalist opponents episodically seize upon the progressive critiques to show that same-sex marriage proponents are misrepresenting the consequences of same-sex

---

★ I am using the term *queer* in the sense the critics do, to describe sexual and gender minorities who radically resist the modes of thought of the mainstream, and not just its openly discriminatory policies. "Queer theory" by writers such as Eve Kosofsky Sedgwick or Judith Butler exposes paradoxes and hypocrisies within mainstream reasoning, even when it ostensibly supports gay—and other—"rights."

TABLE 6.2. **THE ARGUMENT FLOW IN THE SAME-SEX MARRIAGE DEBATE**

Traditionalist Starting Point: Conservative Arguments for Keeping the Status Quo	The Gaylegal Respone: Liberal Arguments for Same-Sex Marriage Recognition	The Progressive Critique: Why Liberal Gay Arguments Are Not Queer
Difference: The procreative goal is essential to marriage. "Homosexuals" don't belong, unless they convert to heterosexuality.	*Sameness*: The unitive goal of marriage is one that same-sex couples can enjoy just as much as different-sex couples.	*Difference*: The sameness argument marginalizes most queer people. Normalizing around marriage is coercive and ignores radical strategies.
Status: "Homosexual marriage" would undermine "real" marriage, an institution already under siege from liberalizing state "reforms" such as no-fault divorce.	*Choice*: Gay marriage is no threat to the institution. It is unfair not to allow same-sex couples to have access to the state benefits and duties of marriage.	*Status*: Buying into state-sanctioned marriage undermines our capacity for sexual choice for state recognition invites state meddling in the sex lives of all queer people.
Role Fixity: Husband and wife are essential roles in marriage, and they can only be filled by man and woman, respectively.	*Role Flexibility*: Rigid gender roles are neither necessary nor just in modern society. Same-sex marriage would challenge, and perhaps undermine, this premise of sexism.	*Role Fixity*: Although rigid gender roles are bad, same-sex marriage will do little to undermine them. It may reinforce the outlaw roles ascribed to some queer people.

marriage; this traditionalist strategy, in turn, presses proponents into more assimilative, and allegedly antiqueer, rhetorical strategies. This is not a good dynamic, and I want to resist its pull. This part teases out the differences among traditionalist (premodern), liberal (modern), and progressive (postmodern) discourses about same-sex marriage. Among other things, this shows the error traditionalists make when they seek to expropriate postmodern arguments for reactionary purposes. More important, I want to suggest ways the same-sex marriage movement should attend to progressive critiques. Most important, I shall pose some provisional postmodern arguments in favor of same-sex marriage.

The Normalization Argument

Different deployments of the term *normal* help us understand the different stances in the same-sex marriage debate. For the traditionalist, normal is what history or religion tells us is natural for the human subject. Most traditionalists insist that the only natural (and therefore only normal) marriage roles are those of husband engaged in procreative intercourse with his wife. Hence, same-sex marriage is abnormal. Treating it as normal is not equality, it is *abomination*. Modernists are voluntarist. Each person has her own individual needs, and we all ought to be able to choose what is normal for ourselves. What is normal for me might be abnormal for you, and the liberal state ought to accommodate a diversity of tastes and needs. Some postmodern thinkers, most famously Michel Foucault, have maintained that there is a subtext to this ostensibly libertarian text in the regulatory state, namely, the modernist tendency to encourage or arrange choices through a process of normalization.[21] Rather than dictating a person's choices through insistence on natural law roles, the state participates in a social process whereby the statistical norm organizes people's thoughts about a matter of concern to them, from diet to etiquette to relationships. Thus, state recognition of same-sex marriage would make marriage more normal than it otherwise is today. The gentle but unpostmodern reader may wonder: Is there anything wrong with that?

Yes, say Paula Ettelbrick and Nancy Polikoff (among others), because normalization can be a coercive process.[22] By their account, state recognition of same-sex marriage would be a strong signal valorizing only those kinds of relationships among gay people—and thereby marginalizing lesbian couples who choose not to marry, gay men who prefer multiple partners, and bisexual and gay people who for various reasons are not coupled. These critics also worry that the people left behind will be disproportionately gay or bisexual women, people of color, and working-class folks. I question that factual assertion.* Other

---

★ There is no empirical basis for accepting—or rejecting—this proposition, and there is no good reason in theory why gays of color, lesbians, and working-class gays would not marry. Most of the plaintiffs in the reported cases are from one of these groups, and the Vermont same-sex marriage movement, described in chapter 2, was organized by lesbians and counted women as the large majority of its members. Lesbian couples have been found by social scientists to describe greater satisfaction than gay male or straight couples from committed relationships. Working class and indigent couples would find the protective benefits of marriage particulary useful, but many of the burdens of marriage, such as disqualification from some social benefit programs, would fall disproportionately on such persons.

critics, such as Janet Halley, say they are ambivalent about whether ethical value "may or may not emerge" from normalization but nonetheless maintain that, if same-sex couples marry, "the unmarried/married distinction would become simpler and more powerful as a mode of social ordering. Unmarried adults, and their sex lives, would become *weirder*."[23] That would seem to have ethical and presumably coercive ramifications for these "weirder" people.

The standard liberal response to these arguments looks to the preferences of sexual minorities. Romantic love and the aspiration of mutual commitment know no sexual orientation in this country. Popular polls say that most bisexuals, lesbians, and gay men want to have the right to marry.[24] This reflects the social fact that most gay people are not as radical in their aspirations as Polikoff and Ettelbrick. It probably is the case that most gay people want to be normalized—by which they mean treated as regular people and not weirdos. This is not a satisfactory answer from a postmodern point of view, however. The current preferences of gay people might actually reflect the triumph of normalization, not truly unconstrained choice. Because sexual and gender nonconformists have never been given free choices in our society and have been subjected to the moral drumbeat "everyone should be married," there is no telling what their ideal choices would actually be. The role of progressive activists is to insist that more real choices be available.

In evaluating the normalization line of thinking, it is productive to think about how same-sex marriage might fit into the overall struggle for social toleration or acceptance of gay people. Same-sex marriage could be desirable from a progressive point of view if it would, in the long term, contribute to greater social acceptance of people who are today considered "sexual nonconformists." Here's the logic of this possibility. As Cheshire Calhoun has recently argued, the underlying but powerful normalization in the debate is not married/unmarried, but heterosexual/homosexual.[25] According to opponents, lesbians, bisexuals, and gay men are weird, and recognizing their marriages would be *really* weird. Much of the population is resistant to same-sex marriage because of homophobia, which of course is harmful to all gay people. By admitting gay people into a fundamental mainstream institution, same-sex marriage would contribute to the *de*normalization of heterosexuality.

Moreover, it is erroneous to assume that the struggle for same-sex marriage precludes the creation of other institutions for recognition of same-sex unions. As the same-sex marriage movement in Europe and the United States suggests (in chapters 1 through 3), the compromises that proponents make on the path toward same-sex marriage have created and will continue to create new institutional norms for thinking about human relationships. Responding to demands for same-sex marriage, the Netherlands Parliament enacted a law recognizing registered partnerships, granting almost all of the rights, benefits, and obligations of marriage but not the name.[26] Unlike the pioneering Danish statute, the Dutch law made registered partnerships available to different-sex as well as same-sex couples, and about a third of the Dutch registrants have been different-sex couples (see chapter 3, table 3.3). Like the laws in Sweden and other countries, the Netherlands' new statute did not disturb laws recognizing specified rights and responsibilities between cohabiting same-sex as well as different-sex couples. When the Netherlands in 2001 recognized same-sex marriages, the new law left the registered partnership institution in place for different-sex as well as same-sex couples.[27]

As part of a compromise that proposed a constitutional amendment allowing the legislature to bar same-sex marriages, the Hawaii legislature adopted a law in 1997 creating a new institution of *reciprocal beneficiaries*, which provided a structure for same-sex couples to cooperate economically but without the marital requirements of monogamy and mutual support.[28] In 1999, the French government created the new *pacte civil de solidarité* (PaCS), which allows couples to assume mutual responsibility for one another's debts and needs and which is available to couples of all sorts—including different-sex as well as same-sex couples.[29] As in the Netherlands, this new institution did not entail the abolition of others already in place for cohabiting couples. In 2000, Vermont's legislature created, as part of the civil unions statute, another new institution somewhat like the French PaCS. Different-sex as well as same-sex couples in Vermont can become *reciprocal beneficiaries*, whereby each has the express right to make decisions for the other if she or he is incapacitated, and each has an implicit responsibility to act in the interests of the other partner.[30] The new reciprocal beneficiary law is limited to partners already related to one another by blood, marriage, or adoption and so is not aimed at romantic partners, as the French PaCS law is, but it might be deployed by romantic couples and certainly introduces a new legal institution for recognizing close relationships. Like the French PaCS, the Vermont reciprocal beneficiary idea offers both same-sex and different-sex couples legal possibilities that did not exist before lesbian and gay liberals agitated for state recognition of same-sex marriage. These laws argue strongly against the suggestion that state recognition of same-sex marriage means that the state will normalize all of its regulations around marriage and marriage alone.

As I argued in chapter 3, the same-sex marriage movement is part of a larger evolution in the way the state regulates human relationships. Today in Vermont, Sweden, the Netherlands, and France—and tomorrow in many other jurisdictions—couples of all kinds will have a menu of options, with state-provided protections and obligations for each option. Recall the potential list from table 3.3:

- *domestic partnership*, providing unmarried partners of employees with the same health and other insurance benefits accorded to spouses of employees;
- *cohabitation*, where the partners are taken to assume certain responsibilities to one another as well;
- *cohabitation-plus* or *reciprocal beneficiary*, whereby the law recognizes the ability of one partner to make decisions on behalf of, and the responsibility to make them in the interests of, an incapacitated partner;
- *registered partnership*, which entails all or almost all the same benefits and obligations of marriage, but not the name or the portability;
- *marriage*, with unitive duties as well as benefits, but with easy exit through no-fault divorce; and
- *covenant marriage*, with the rights and duties of marriage, plus greater difficulty in exiting.

Perhaps surprisingly, the same-sex marriage movement and its traditionalist opponents have generated a series of social experiments in various states which not only provide different options for couples who do not desire to marry, but provide different models for state recognition of relationships. This kind of dynamic is the *equality practice* I have been exploring in the previous two chapters, and it suggests a complication in the normalization process. Vermont now recognizes four forms of relationships: domestic partnership, for state employees; reciprocal beneficiaries, for different-sex as well as same-sex partners who want to share decision-making responsibilities; civil unions, for same-sex couples; and marriages, for different-sex couples. Because there is a much broader array of state-sanctioned unions, *marriage* is actually less normal than it was before the 1990s, and being unmarried is less abnormal. But for the same reason, state-recognized *couples* are more normal, and being uncoupled is more abnormal. So the concern under the emerging regime is, for now, more a concern about normalization around coupling than normalization around marrying. Thus, Foucault's normalization idea explains—better than any traditionalist has been able to do—how Vermont civil unions and French PaCS and Danish registered partnerships *might* undermine marriage, by making it less normal. Ironically, this postmodern idea has great analytical power for traditionalists—but mostly as an argument against the evolving menu of options for state-recognized relationships and less as an argument against same-sex marriage per se. Indeed, by making marriage more normal for a wider range of people, same-sex marriage would actually contribute to what the traditionalists say they are trying to do—support marriage as a preferred institution.

Does the normalization analysis retain similar power for progressives? Under this analysis, the struggle for same-sex marriage has benefitted couples of all sorts—including couples who would not marry even if they could do so. If there is a normalization concern with the emerging menu, it is primarily a concern for the single person of any orientation. Is he or she now more marginalized in Vermont than before the civil unions and reciprocal beneficiaries law? This, too, is not as simple as the critics would make it out to be. It is ironic but possibly telling that the same-sex marriage movement has achieved visibility and modest success at precisely that point in time when marriage has weakened as a normalizing force. One-tenth of middle-aged women and one-sixth of middle-aged men have never married[31]—many of them because they are lesbian, gay, bisexual, or transgendered. On the one hand, this under-mines the suggestion that same-sex marriage will marginalize uncoupled lesbians, gay men, bisexuals, and transgendered people. As a single person well-accepted by my "married" lesbian, gay, and bisexual friends, I am not as pessimistic as the happily partnered Ettelbrick that normal-ization will ostracize people like me. The reason is that state-recognized (or church-recognized) relationships do not carry as much normative force as they did a generation ago. Generally, the normalization objec-tion—wielded with equal enthusiasm by traditionalist as well as pro-gressive critics of same-sex marriage—is a concern that is way too speculative to give much weight in the debate, at this time anyway.

On the other hand, the connection between traditionalist and pro-gressive deployment of normalization concerns does suggest, to me, that the most important normative question, and point of vigorous contest, is not whether the state should recognize same-sex marriages, but instead is whether same-sex marriage should then obviate the need for lesbian and gay couples to have domestic partnership or civil union pos-sibilities available to them. For example, firms that now offer fringe ben-efits to the domestic partners of their employees could drop that policy if lesbians and gay men could marry: if you want the fringe benefits, you can get married. This would have important consequences for straight and gay couples who prefer not to marry but want employer benefits. Although countries and states and firms that already have domestic partnership policies or registered partnership laws will probably keep them, at least in the short term, even if same-sex marriages were recog-nized, things are much less clear for the longer term and therefore ought to be an arena of political contestation. I call this the *channeling* func-tion of law,[32] and this is the most important potential consequence of normalization, however it is conceptualized. I shall return to this idea at the end of this chapter.

The Gender Role Argument

Nan Hunter maintains that same-sex marriage "could also destabilize the cultural meaning of marriage. It would create for the first time the possibility of marriage as a relationship between members of the same social status categories."[33] Drawing from evidence I compiled, Nancy

Polikoff responds that most of the historical examples of culturally or legally recognized same-sex marriages did not destabilize gender roles within the marriages or the societies in which they were located.[34] This is a valid use of the historical evidence and overall an astute point. My study from which Polikoff draws, however, sought only to show how same-sex unions and even marriages had been recognized in various cultures, thereby undermining the argument that such marriages were impossible or had never existed in human history. Reflecting the dominance of men in preindustrial societies, the large majority of the same-sex marriages I surveyed were male-male marriages that did ape male-female marriages. None of my examples, however, fit the situation in western culture today: industrialization and technology have freed women and men to rethink gender roles, and same-sex marriage exploits that cultural opening.

As traditionalists insist, same-sex marriage would be a dramatic shift in the way western culture thinks about marriage—and, I should submit, gender roles. Prior historical evidence is not dispositive as to that issue. More pertinent are contemporary studies showing that lesbian and gay households in western society do follow more egalitarian and distinctly less gendered divisions of labor.[35] Thus, two women raising a family together, like Holly Puterbaugh and Lois Farnham in the Vermont marriage case, are more likely to share household tasks and have jobs outside the home. Moreover, there is emerging evidence that such households manage conflicts differently, and more productively, than different-sex households. John Gottman and Robert Levenson's twelve-year (1987–99) study comparing a nonrandom sample of forty straight, twenty gay, and twenty lesbian couples found that the lesbian and gay couples negotiated differences differently than the straight couples.[36] Based upon taped interactions among the couples that were evaluated by separate decoders, the researchers concluded that the same-sex couples handled conflict more congenially and with greater affection than the different-sex couples. Gottman speculates that one reason for the more fluid process of conflict resolution is that gay and lesbian couples are less burdened by gender anxieties about power disparity. Although the conclusions of this study are highly provisional given the small and possibly unrepresentative samples, it does suggest a good reason why the state ought to give some value to relationships that systematically deny traditional gender roles.

Moreover, Hunter's gender-role argument does not depend upon the possibility that same-sex couples will actually abandon the traditional division of labor (breadwinner vs. housekeeper) within marriage. In a woman-woman marriage where tasks are divided up along traditional lines, a woman will be doing the accustomed male role of working outside the home. In a man-man marriage where tasks are divided up along traditional lines, a man will be doing the accustomed female role of keeping house. It is this symbolism that represents the deeper challenge to traditional gender roles. The symbolism can be expressed in the argot of normalization. Once female-female and male-male couples can marry, the wife-housekeeper/husband-breadwinner model for the family would immediately become less normal, and perhaps even abnormal over time. The wife as someone who derives independent satisfaction from her job outside the home would immediately become a little bit more normal.[37]

Some postmodern critics of same-sex marriage denigrate the gender-role argument as a strategy whereby "same-sex marriage in this culture might slightly improve things, if not for queers, then, indirectly, for women married to men," as Michael Warner puts it.[38] Shouldn't queer people be happy to advance the indefensibly subordinate role of women in our society, whatever the women's sexual orientations? Isn't it a narrow progressivism that considers only "what's in it for us" and does not care about larger social goals? Perhaps progressivism means not helping women who choose to join an allegedly "oppressive" institution (marriage), and if that's what progressivism means, include me out. In my opinion, gay men as well as lesbians ought to be allies of straight women, and we ought to celebrate rather than dismiss any empowerment of women that might flow from same-sex marriage recognition. In any event, there are theoretical reasons to consider the symbolism more broadly significant.

It is a postmodern commonplace that gender is a social construction, and one whose binariness is a key feature of compulsory heterosexuality.[39] Judith Butler takes that point further and maintains that gender is "performative—that is, constituting the identity it is purported to be. . . . There is no gender identity behind the expressions of gender;

that identity is performatively constituted by the very 'expressions' that are said to be its results."[40] Gender is as gender does. Under this view, the display of two women married to one another is particularly significant, for every day and in public view at least one of the women will be performing in ways that everyone knows do not fit with women's traditional roles. Although the marriage ceremony itself is a powerful bit of western choreography, it is the day-by-day performances that make same-sex marriage potentially most destabilizing of gender role. If gender is the linchpin of compulsory heterosexuality, its destabilization over discursive time ought to contribute to the destabilization of antigay and perhaps also antiqueer attitudes and regulation.[41]

The destabilization can even occur once same-sex marriage becomes part of public discourse, without any legal action. Queer people of all kinds have been given opportunities to be heard and "seen" in ways not possible before the same-sex marriage debate hit the western world. Mary Coombs provides a dramatic example of how this can happen. She reminds us that many of the pioneers and activists of same-sex marriage in western culture have been and are transgendered people.[42] Many male-to-female transsexuals have been married to women before and after their sex change therapies and operations. Has their sex changed? Their gender? Their sexual orientation? Were these people heterosexual before and homosexual after their operations? If the state insists on their heterosexuality and that their marriages are not same-sex marriages after their operations, as courts in England and the United States have generally held,[43] the legal system has yielded a wonderful pastiche of gender: a woman is married to a person with female sex organs, female hormones, female attire, but whose male chromosomes enable the state to pretend that she is filling the male sex role so that the marriage can still be considered different-sex. Pastiches like this one not only expose the arbitrariness of denying same-sex couples marriage licenses, but also the arbitrariness of sex and gender as rigid regulatory categories.

Transgendered people are showing up increasingly in marriage cases, and they are destabilizing the categories essential to maintain the barrier to same-sex marriage.[44] A recent example is the decision of the Texas Court of Appeals in *Littleton v. Prange*.[45] Lee Cavazos was born with male genitalia but from early in her life identified as female; as an

adult she changed her name and went through sexual reassignment sur-
gery and hormone treatment to match her body with her gender. She
legally married Jonathan Littleton, and they lived as spouses until his
death. As the surviving spouse, Christie Lee Cavazos Littleton sued the
doctor who allegedly caused her husband's death, pursuant to a wrongful death statute. The doctor challenged her standing to sue on the
ground that she was not the lawful spouse of the decedent. Although
Christie had a marriage certificate, the Texas court ruled her marriage
invalid because it was not one man, one woman. Although her birth certificate was changed to reflect her sex as female and her name had been
legally changed, the court further ruled that Christie Littleton was a
man. The judges reaffirmed all the normalizations American society has
traditionally maintained: marriage must be man-woman and heterosexual, and you are the sex of your original body and birth certificate. But
the intellectual struggle the judges had to engage in, and the logical con-
tortions within their published opinion, reveal many of the holes in
those norms, even from within their normative universe. The *Littleton*
opinion is normalization with edge.

The Regulatory Costs Argument

Nitya Duclos first detailed many of the ways in which legally recognized
marriage imposes costs on the partners that may be particularly unwelcome to lesbian and gay couples, especially those who are not of the
middle class.[46] For example, some state welfare or other security benefits
are reduced or eliminated if the recipient has a spouse who can support
her economically. Also, marriage, unlike domestic partnership, entails
mutual fidelity and support obligations and usually involves the state if
the couple wants to dissolve their relationship. The state involvement in
one's relationship and the terms of its dissolution would be unwelcome
to some couples, if not at the time of their marriage, at least at the time
of their breakup. Duclos did not claim that the regulatory costs are pro-
hibitive, just that they complicate the formal equality argument for
same-sex marriage. Her point remains relevant and important.
Following Duclos, I have suggested that couples who desire the many
legal benefits of marriage need to consider very carefully the legal regulations as well, especially the regulation of marital dissolutions.[47] In

other words, marriage is not for everyone, and civil marriage's many regulations do not make sense for a lot of couples.

Janet Halley presses this theme more aggressively. She warns that potential state interventions in same-sex marriages include enforcement of adultery and antinepotism rules and of support duties; breaking up entails a potentially destructive operation of expensive state divorce procedures.[48] (This is a shorter version of the list of possibly problematic state regulations that Duclos had presented or that I had suggested.) The point of Halley's list is obscure. If its point is to sound an alarm that same-sex marriage will invite increased state attention to lesbian and gay families, it is overstated. A list of potential state interventions into the lives of same-sex couples married to one another is not a great deal more impressive than one detailing the potential state interventions into the lives of cohabiting but unmarried same-sex couples: enforcement of fornication rules and of implicit contractual or quasi-contractual agreements of support; arbitration of disputes within the household; protection of the rights of blood family members to make decisions for an incapacitated partner and to inherit his possessions if he dies without a will; enforcement of the rights of an outside biological parent to children raised in the household; and so forth. I think the biggest variable is whether the couple is raising children together. If lesbian couples with children break up, the state often plays a major role in deciding custody, visitation, and support issues—even though the couples are not married.[49] Overall, the regulatory costs argument reminds us that the state pervasively—even if for the middle class it is most of the time just potentially—regulates households, married or not. Some of the state's intrusions (backing up blood relatives claiming decision-making or inheritance rights) are more likely to occur in nonmarital households, others (like divorce proceedings) in marital households.

A queerer variation on Duclos's caution is the argument that the organized demand for same-sex marriage somehow enables or encourages the state to nose around in the lives of unmarried as well as married sexual minorities. According to Michael Warner, "as long as people marry, the state will regulate the sexual lives of those who do not. It will refuse to recognize the validity of intimate relationships—including cohabiting partnerships—between unmarried people. . . ."[50] Note the extravagant causal claim and the dubious factual assertions. The second quoted sentence is erroneous. Canada, the Netherlands, France, Germany, and Sweden now statutorily recognize cohabiting partnerships (including same-sex ones) as well as marriages. California, Georgia, and other states recognize cohabiting partnerships (including same-sex ones) as a matter of common law without any conflict with their marriage statutes. Moreover, proposals for same-sex marriage in the Netherlands (where the proposal just became law), Canada, and Sweden have not suggested that recognition for cohabiting partnerships be revoked.[51] Warner's first quoted sentence is true but incomplete and inconsequential. There is no inevitable connection, nor does the author demonstrate one, between continued state recognition of marriage and state regulation of extramarital sexual behaviors. Even as increasing numbers of straight people postpone or avoid marriage, the state not only remains intent on regulating everyone's sexual lives, but some of its regulations are more vigorous than ever before—such as rules against rape, including same-sex rape; unwelcome sexual touching short of rape; sexually harassing conduct in the workplace or at school; sexual relations between an authority figure and a patient, student, etc.; and sexual interactions between adults and minors.[52] Indeed, the state's assertive regulation of private sex lives has entered married people's bedrooms even more dramatically than those of unmarried people. In my lifetime, all the states in the United States have revoked or limited the exemption married men traditionally enjoyed against prosecutions for raping their wives, most states have created programs to police other kinds of sexual violence and abuse by one spouse against another, and many states prosecute molestation of children by their fathers and stepfathers more aggressively than ever before.[53]

Katharine Franke offers an interesting parallel that might be read to suggest gay people have something to fear from state-sanctioned marriage. In an ongoing historical study, Franke is showing that recognition of slave marriages after the Civil War was often the occasion for the state to impose its conceptions of sexual fidelity and monogamy on unions that had been more flexibly organized before the law entered the picture.[54] Should lesbian and gay communities expect similar consequences from state recognition of their unions? I doubt it, in part because the normative force of marriage is waning today, just as it was waxing in the late nineteenth century. Consider also the extraordinarily different contexts of state recognition of slave marriages in the 1860s and of gay marriages in the 2000s. Unlike slave unions, which were wholly outside the law in the American South before 1865, lesbian and gay unions in the 1980s and 1990s have often been recognized as cohabiting relationships, domestic partnerships, and registered partnerships in other countries and parts of the United States, without any sign that recognition has stimulated any other kind of state nosiness. Indeed, state recognition of same-sex unions has not been possible until the state let up on its suppression of gay sexualities, once again unlike the situation in southern states after the Civil War. Finally, the nineteenth-century state enforced fornication and adultery laws (the main mechanisms for oppression of former slaves) vastly more than the state does today; the main state mechanism for invading the families of sexual nonconformists today is to take away custody or visitation rights to their children. Same-sex marriage would offer no greater state opportunities for that kind of discipline than the current regulatory regime and, if anything, would offer a little more security for lesbian and gay couples to protect their child-rearing rights. Although posing an intriguing parallel, Franke's study has no strong implications for the same-sex marriage debate.

More broadly, postmodern critiques of causal thinking engender skepticism about the fears of critics like Warner, who claim that same-sex marriage will instigate a state mobilization around sex-negative regulations. A postmodern insight is that nothing happens as a direct result of top-down stimuli (including laws); social change occurs from the bottom up, as a multitude of discourses and power exchanges go on simultaneously.[55] This insight undermines the ability of postmodernists to make consequentialist arguments, including most variations of the normalization argument discussed in the previous section as well as the sexual repression argument here. Thus, a thoroughgoing postmodernist should not be surprised that the decline of state-sanctioned marriage among straight people and the willingness of the state to recognize nonmarital unions (the menu sketched above) have occurred at the same time that the state is increasingly attentive to the sex lives of everyone— including married people! The topography of state activity is much more complex than simple normalization and sexual repression arguments make it out to be. To put it too simply (still), the eruption of public discourse about and increasing toleration of individuated sexual variety has contributed to counterdiscourses about the harms that "sexuality unbound" poses to vulnerable people—employees, children, spouses, single mothers, and so on. The same-sex marriage movement plays little if any role in this complicated dynamic.

The postmodern critique of causal thinking ought to add a note of sobriety to the overheated same-sex marriage debate. All sides overstate—some writers hysterically so—the ability of the state to normalize people around state-sponsored goals. Whether one's preferred goal is civilized commitment (proponents of same-sex marriage), sexual liberty (some progressive opponents), or compulsory heterosexuality (traditionalist opponents), the state's endorsement will not advance that goal in a linear way, and under some circumstances could even undermine the goal. On the other hand, the state together with other institutions can have some effect on social norms, and the symbolic importance of state recognition or nonrecognition of same-sex marriages is sufficient to sustain enthusiasm for the various perspectives discussed in this chapter.

There is value in the critical focus on the regulatory implications of marriage for lesbian, gay, and other queer families. We should consider not just the risks and benefits of a strategy that involves the state, but we should also consider the worthiness or utility of the values we want the state to endorse, at least symbolically. From the beginning of this debate, I have maintained that interpersonal obligation and commitment is a valuable thing for the state or lesbian and gay communities to valorize. I have traditionally emphasized modernist arguments for that proposition: the aspiration of mutual emotional as well as sexual dependence on and commitment to the welfare of another human being is what most gay people think they want, produces great personal satisfaction, and completes them as human beings.[56] Traditionalist and progressive critics of same-sex marriage have left this argument relatively unchallenged, and most of them would like for it to be irrelevant in light of their normalization arguments. Apart from the problems with normalization arguments against same-sex marriage, I now add this postmodern argument in favor of interpersonal commitment.[57]

One condition giving rise to postmodern thinking is the ways in which the communications and transportation revolutions have allowed us to be fluid and many-sided. The emerging post-industrial society has enabled the *protean self* to emerge for large numbers of people who assume different identities in the many different contexts they face and whose personal fluidity reflects the fluidity and disruptions of their social and political environments.[58] Unlike our grandparents, we are unlikely to get a job in the town where we grew up. Unlike our parents, we are unlikely to stay in the same job or the same city for most of our careers, and our friends are dispersed across several cities. Unlike us, the next generation is unlikely to stay in the same job or the same city for more than several years at a time, and many of them will switch careers and friendship networks the way we trade in our used cars. This fast-paced and mobile society yields a dizzying array of choices each day. I can be a different person when I am making deals in a Toronto law office than I will be when I attend the opera in Paris or teach law students in New Haven or conduct a reading group for gay attorneys in Washington, D.C.

The protean self is most available to westerners with money and mobility, and such people have a range of choices unprecedented in human history, but that very multiplicity and fluidity has yielded a self that is fractured and nostalgic as well as protean. In a world of multiple identities and wide choices, the fractured self yearns for human connections that last—history and genealogy, ethical and religious traditions, and intimate bonds, including and particularly longstanding bonds of family.[59] This yearning is ambivalent, for the protean self both aspires to and fears the stability and reliability offered by interpersonal commitment. As Mitt Regan has argued in detail and from postmodern premises, there is presently no western institution that better captures the hopes and fears of the fractured selves of gay as well as straight people than the institution of marriage.[60] Although the protean self ensures that marriages are no longer "till death do us part," the romantic desire to marry maintains a postmodern hold on Americans and other westerners. As a strategy for some stability within a world of flux and for commitment amid shifting alliances, marriage beats the alternatives. In my view, marriage will continue to exercise a normative attraction for many people of all orientations. Lesbian and gay couples ought to be able to share that human good. Surprisingly, there are a good many progressive, even radical, postmodern arguments for this old-fashioned institution.

EQUALITY PRACTICE AS A POSTMODERN CULTURAL FORM

Step back once again from the same-sex marriage issue and think about the debate that has been instigated by progressive critics. What I am deeming *postmodern* criticisms unsettle the modernist presentation of same-sex marriage by situating it in a theoretical dynamic whereby the apparent advantages of this legal reform—respect and dignity for cultural outsiders and regulatory benefits—can just as easily be inverted to become horrible disadvantages—deeper marginalization of many outsiders even as some move to the inside and potentially devastating regulatory costs. Some of the critics present same-sex marriage as a big mistake; others content themselves with raising questions. A common assumption made by these critics is that individual subjects and groups, including their tastes and preferences, exist in a dialectical relation to social context and social structure. No subject is separate from external social and legal conditions. Thus, instead of accepting the liberal assumption that the individual is the analytic starting point of social theory, or the communitarian assumption that the common good is the appropriate goal, critical thinkers conceive that individuals are formed and transformed in their social relations, and that social relations and law are arenas of constant political contest and dispute.[61] Note how this structure of thought also can support traditionalist criticisms of same-sex marriage: if adolescents are formed through the signals sent them by the state and society, and if you as a parent do not want your teenager to be a "homosexual," then you need to head off "homosexual marriage."

Coming out of the closet can be viewed, from a postmodern point of view, as a dialog following the gay person's re-presentation of his sexuality. When gay author Philip Bockman, introduced in chapter 4, came out to his father, he destabilized old relationships and posed risks that he would lose precious connections with his blood family. The moment of coming out to a loved one is a rupture: it is an exciting new beginning as well as an end to old assumptions. Bockman's story suggests that coming out is a process and not a moment. The process entails ongoing conversations with loved ones. Seeking to preserve preexisting relationships, Bockman's conversations focused on the mutual accommodations he and his parents would make regarding the management of his identity within the family. The terms of those accommodations were not preset. They were agonized and struggled over. This is what inspired my idea of *equality practice*.

Equality practice can be understood as a postmodern cultural form in which the polity struggles over the terms under which new attitudes and new minorities are to be accommodated without needlessly sacrificing the community's social capital. Citizen attitudes change as a result of that conversation, but will not change overnight. Nor will people swallow radical revisions in cherished mores and institutions. But just as Bockman's family was willing to accommodate his sexuality, so the polity will be willing to accommodate its sexual minorities. For the polity as for the family, piecemeal accommodations are easier to do than massive alterations. A gay man's ambivalent parents may reiterate their love for their son but prefer that he not discuss his sexuality. Soon enough, the parents will start asking him about his boyfriend. Then they will want to meet the boyfriend and will invite him to family gatherings. An increasing number of old-fashioned parents grow to treat the gay partner as a son-in-law. Similarly, the polity may start with toleration of discreet "homosexuals." After further education, the polity will allow openly gay people to be public servants and schoolteachers. Lesbians and gay men will have a place at the table. The place is fully equalized when the polity feels comfortable (enough) setting a place for two.

This step-by-step process is equality practice. It does not entail immediate equality. Equality practice is a moderate cultural form, which sets it apart from more radical philosophies of separatism or revolutionary change. Viewed this way, equality practice suggests further postmodern justifications for the broader same-sex marriage movement. By that I mean the process by which gay people are working for their inclusion in state-recognized institutions of all sorts, from domestic partnerships to same-sex marriage. At the same time, equality practice suggests some cautions that the ongoing normative struggle for same-sex marriage ought to consider important. Return to the three kinds of progressive critiques of same-sex marriage: normalization, regulatory costs, and displaced beneficiaries. Equality practice deepens the postmodern responses to each critique that I developed earlier in this chapter.

1. Homo Normalization. Recall my complications to progressive normalization charges. If critics insist that state recognition of same-sex *marriage* would normalize marriage and its associated notions of commitment, they should also admit that *same-sex* marriage would normalize lesbian and gay unions. Over time, same-sex marriage would even normalize homosexual intimacy. Equality practice and its accompanying menu of state-sanctioned relationship options invert the progressives' charge. Countries like Canada and France have responded to the sexual liberation movement with a variety of state-sanctioned relationships, thus far not including same-sex marriage. These countries have *denormalized* marriage. Marriage as the situs of coupledom now competes with French cohabitation and PaCS for the attention of straight as well as gay couples. Governments have mediated the claims of gay people and traditionalists by creating or expanding nonmarital institutions. By this process, the fiercest defenders of traditional marriage and the most eager petitioners for entry have combined to undermine the monopoly marriage once enjoyed in public policy.

These new institutions are little social experiments that ought to have some attraction to a progressive agenda. The same-sex marriage movement offers progressives opportunities for pressing the state to create institutions that are more friendly to the interests of women and of unconventional lovers. Thus, their stance ought not be reflexively hostile to the advocates of same-sex marriage. Instead, progressives ought to support those petitions and then be prepared to seize the moment when compromise proposals are floated, to assure that new institutions meet the needs of people and do not supplant the preexisting ones. From a progressive point of view, the risk is not that the state will recognize same-sex marriages, but that in doing so the state will cut off previous as well as future institutional experiments. Vermont provides a recent example, unfortunately. Five years before the civil unions law, the legislature enacted a statute allowing folks to adopt the children of their same-sex partners. The state supreme court applied this law to prevent judges from applying equitable principles to protect the interests of "de facto parents" who did not go through the formal (and not costless) adoption process.[62] This is an example of the channeling effect of law and should remain a concern.

Another virtue of the incremental normalization occasioned by equality practice is that it offers a better strategy for eroding social homophobia than radical strategies offer. Homophobia is resistant to logical argumentation and can be exacerbated by angry confrontation. Like other kinds of prejudice, it is intensified when its objects are perceived as threats to cherished values.[63] The in-your-face queer is likely to confirm rather than disrupt antigay attitudes. Social scientists have found that the homophobe is most likely to adjust his attitudes if someone close to him—especially a family member or a coworker—comes out to him *and* engages him personally by showing him that gay and straight people have much in common, including shared values.[64] As a public declaration of commitment, same-sex marriage is not only a coming out experience, but it is the coming out of the gay pair as a couple, reaffirming the same kind of values husbands and wives exchange in mainstream society. Moreover, every same-sex marriage—whether sanctioned by the state or not—stimulates a dialectic within families, workplaces, and communities. While the initial reaction to such coming out is often avoidance or silence, the ongoing conversations following a gay marriage can and frequently do change people's attitudes about the couple and about gay people generally. That this is a painfully slow process should not obscure the fact that this is the only process that reliably operates to diminish homophobia. So even if unmarried gay people lose ground because of incrementally greater normalization around marriage, they might still be better off if same-sex marriage contributed to more tolerant public norms generally.

2. *Linkages Between Straight Women and Gay People.* The daily performances of lesbians joined in civil union and raising children or of two gay domestic partners contribute to the antihomophobia project described in the previous paragraph. But an equally important performative feature of same-sex marriage is the way it undermines the traditional choreography of gender. In my view, erosion of rigid gender roles is great for gay people as well as for straight women—and indeed for

straight men as well. Others are not so optimistic. Recall Michael Warner's dismissal of the gender role argument for same-sex marriage on the ground that it would help married women and not queer people. The process of equality practice helps us understand how productive this phenomenon might be, at least over time.

Assume that the big beneficiaries of Vermont civil unions are straight married women who are inspired to demand more equitable household and employment arrangements from their actual or prospective husbands. Gay people should be happy about that for reasons of their shared humanity with these beneficiaries, but also for a more selfish reason. Among the greatest allies of lesbian and gay rights are women (including married women) who have careers outside the home.[65] Many such women are just personally empathetic to lesbian and gay concerns, but a more general reason for their support is that they appreciate and may endorse the way that same-sex couples undermine traditional gender roles within the home and family. This common project allies the interests of women with careers outside the home with those of lesbians, gay men, and transgendered people. The more that women are empowered to demand household equity from their male partners, the more straight as well as lesbian and gay couples will be interested in nonmarital options in the state relationship-recognition menu.

Equality practice and the relationship menu could even become a mini-social movement. Such a movement would join lesbians and gay men with a variety of straight women and some of the men who love them. While this possibility is quite utopian, it does suggest ways that same-sex marriage is part of a larger political and social process that joins gay people with others who are open to rethinking their jurisdiction's current menu of relationship options.

3. Tailor-Made Regulatory Regimes. Nitya Duclos's caution that marriage offers risks as well as boons for at least some same-sex couples remains a point worth emphasizing—for straight as well as lesbian and gay couples. Equality practice and the menu of options for state-recognized unions diminish the risks somewhat. In Vermont, a lesbian couple now has a range of options for state involvement in their family:

- If the couple want a minimalist regulatory regime, they can live apart and enter into no agreements. The state will still protect each partner against assault, fraud, and other torts that might be committed by the other partner.
- If the couple want employment fringe benefits for one partner, they can announce themselves as domestic partners, without taking on other obligations or incurring other state benefits.
- If the couple want to live together, they can do so, with the possibility that on breakup one of the partners will seek state-ordered support payments.
- If the couple want authority to make decisions for one another but no more from the state, they can register as reciprocal beneficiaries.
- If the couple want to be co-parents of a the child of one partner, they can petition the state for a second-parent adoption. The couple can jointly adopt a child as well as be joint foster parents.
- If the couple are committed for the long term and want all the state benefits and obligations of marriage, they can join in a civil union. (As discussed in chapter 2, the civil union will not be recognized under federal law or the law of most states in most circumstances.)

Not only is this an impressive array of regulatory choices available to our hypothetical Vermont couple, but these are just the off-the-rack rules. The couple can add and subtract some benefits and obligations through private ordering mechanisms such as wills, joint tenancies, written or implied contracts for mutual support, joint checking accounts, powers of attorney, living wills, employment contracts and collective bargaining agreements, and so forth. (The drawback is that most of these mechanisms require the assistance of a lawyer and so require expenditures as well as careful planning.)

Couples who are committed life partners can choose the last items on the list, while couples whose relationship is more tentative or who do not valorize one-on-one commitment in the traditional way can still obtain some state benefits and protections by opting into one of the first several items on the list. Admittedly, the menu's array of choices does not meet everyone's specifications. For example, two lesbians and a gay man cannot form a family recognized as such by the state—but they can piece together such a family from the menu plus private contracting. Thus, two of the three can either marry or form a civil union, with all the benefits and obligations attendant to that regime. If the two women have children by artificial insemination or intercourse with the man, each of the women can become the second mothers of the child she did not bear; it may be possible for all three persons to have a legal relationship with the children. To assure the man's continued connection, the women might enter into contracts with him promising financial support to his biological children. While this lesbian–lesbian–gay man family's legal foundation would have to be cobbled together piecemeal, it could be done. Equality practice and its menu of state options are contributing to a regime where "families we choose" will have some legal protections.[66]

By no means does equality practice entirely escape the difficulties noted by Duclos, however. With so many choices available, the problem remains that couples—straight and gay and lesbian—will often make bad choices. Bad choices can include (1) overcommitment, as when the couple opt for marriage under the mistaken belief that their current infatuation will last forever; (2) undercommitment, as when one or both partners opt for an arrangement that does not adequately protect one of the partners or reflect their actual yearning for commitment; and (3) the oldest bad choice of all, the lover who is a great date but a lousy partner. It is hard to tell whether equality practice will have an effect on partners' abilities to make good choices.

The case for same-sex marriage can invoke a surprising number of postmodern arguments, which heretofore have been a monopoly of critics. When equality practice and the menu of options are factored in, such arguments multiply. Table 6.3 summarizes the argument flow.

TABLE 6.3. **ARGUMENTS FOR AND AGAINST SAME-SEX MARRIAGE**

Modernist Arguments For Same-Sex Marriage	Postmodern Arguments Against Same-Sex Marriage	Postmodern (Equality Practice) Arguments For Same-Sex Marriage
Formal Equality: Same-sex couples ought to be treated the same as different-sex couples.	*Normalization*: Equal treatment would or could normalize gay couples, denigrate uncoupled gays, and standardize gay lives around an arbitrary norm.	*Homo Normalization*: The same-sex marriage movement has generated experiments expanding lesbian and gay choices. Homosexuality and relationship choices, not marriage, are normalized by the evolving menu.
Critique of Gender Role: Same-sex marriage would help "denormalize" rigid gender roles (woman = wife and child-rearer; man = husband and breadwinner) within marriage. This could have salutary ramifications for straight as well as bisexual and lesbian women.	*Denial*: State recognition of same-sex marriages would have scant effect on gender roles. (Even if it did, what good does that do for queers? argue some radicals.)	*Linkages*: The choreography of woman-woman marriage would be a daily deconstruction of rigid gender roles, as well as of compulsory heterosexuality. Alliances of gay people and straight women represent the best hope for progressive reconfiguration of family law.
Regulatory Benefits: Marriage recognition would assure gay couples of tangible benefits as well as reinforcement of interpersonal commitment. Marriage is not for everyone, however, and couples should weigh the costs and benefits carefully.	*Regulatory Costs*: Marriage recognition would introduce the state into same-sex unions, which would or could undermine the liberty of lesbians, gay men, and bisexuals.	*Regulatory Choice*: The emerging menu of regulatory options empowers the couple to choose which institution best fits its needs. Lesbian and gay partners can alter the "off the rack" legal duties and rights through contract. Caveat: couples will make bad choices.

EPILOGUE

Equality Practice, the Evolution of Social Norms, and the Future of Gay Rights

A COMMUNITY THAT DOES NOT TREAT a productive group of citizens the same as other citizens has some explaining to do. When a state discriminates against a social group for no good reason, it disrespects the dignity owed to members of the group as human beings and as citizens. Such treatment also encourages unproductive rifts in the community fabric. Fifty years ago, however, the state did not have to explain its unequal treatment of "homosexuals," because there was a social consensus that these people were psychopaths and predators. That understanding was deeply erroneous and is now more or less discredited, but only because thousands of lesbians, gay men, and bisexuals have come out of their closets and revealed themselves to be regular persons who lead complete lives. And they are people who participate in politics and will not stand for unequal treatment. Most states have internalized this change in social understanding but still do not treat their lesbian and gay citizens the same as their straight ones. Falling in love and partnering with someone of the same sex is a major life event for lesbians, gay men, and often bisexuals in today's America. That these couples face grossly unequal treatment by the law is no more sustainable in 2001, when I finished this book, than the law's unequal treatment of different-race couples was in 1951, when I was born.

Gay people's politics of recognition insists on equal treatment, but the state is not prepared to do that in the face of a vigorous politics of preservation. The power of that politics would deter any legislature from adopting a same-sex marriage statute like that just adopted in the Netherlands. If any state judiciary insisted on equal rights, a popular majority would rise up and squash the effort. This is the lesson of Hawaii and Alaska, recounted in chapter 1. In the United States, the Vermont Civil Unions Law, described in chapter 2, is the most that even a gay-tolerant state is willing to adopt. The Vermont law, however, changes the dynamics of the same-sex marriage movement. (The Netherlands' new law may also have some effect.) Now that one state has accorded equal benefits and duties to same-sex couples, as a separate institutional form, lesbian and gay activists in other states will be encouraged to seek analogous judicial or legislative recognition of their relationships. Although traditionalists will oppose such recognition, moderates will be more open to it if the Vermont experience turns out all right. The Danish registered partnership law in 1989 had none of the malign consequences predicted by opponents. The law inspired six copy-cat laws within ten years. If this history is any guide, some states in the next decade will create new institutions along lines of the domestic partnership, cohabitation, or civil union models for state recognition.

Which states are likely to follow Vermont and Hawaii with official recognition for same-sex unions? Recall chapter 3's step-by-step model. Just as countries still criminalizing consensual sodomy and failing to protect gay people against discrimination are unlikely to recognize lesbian and gay unions (table 3.1 in chapter 3), so states in this country are unlikely to adopt such recognition as long as they have criminal sodomy laws and no antidiscrimination laws. States that have repealed their sodomy laws and adopted anti-discrimination measures, including hate crime laws, are most likely to take the next logical step and recognize same-sex unions. Table E.1 sets forth the state of the law in the fifty states and the District of Columbia in this regard. The table also reports states in which at least one major municipality or county has recognized same-sex partnerships, endowed them with some benefits, and created a registry for such couples. Finally, the table reports states that have legally allowed gay men and lesbians to adopt the children of their partners and that have created a statewide institution and registry for same-sex couples.

Vermont, Hawaii, California, Massachusetts, and the District of Columbia have already granted formal state recognition of unions by same-sex partners who register with the state, but only Vermont and Hawaii endow those unions with an appreciable number of legal rights and obligations. Only in Vermont does the new institution recognize all the state-assured benefits and duties as the different-sex marriage law does. Which will be the next state to follow Vermont and create an institution for same-sex couples with all or most of the same legal rights and benefits as marriage? According to the table, the best bets are states in New England and the Northeast, states bordering the Great Lakes, and West Coast states: Massachusetts, Connecticut, New Jersey, New York, Illinois, Minnesota, Wisconsin, Oregon, Washington, New Hampshire, Rhode Island, and Pennsylvania.* One of these states or Vermont would also be the leading possibility for the first in this country to recognize same-sex marriage. This event will occur, probably in one of these states, but no one can tell when. Note the bottom as well as the top of the table. States in the South, the border between North and South, the Great Plains, and the Rocky Mountains are highly unlikely to give full recognition to same-sex relationships anytime in the foreseeable future. (States like Georgia, with a mega-urban center, or Kentucky, with a libertarian and relatively pro-civil-rights tradition, might give partial recognition to same-sex relationships through some kind of statewide domestic partnership law.)

★ The table would also suggest Hawaii, California, and the District of Columbia as possibilities. The first two jurisdictions are unlikely candidates, because voter referenda in 1998 (Hawaii) and 2000 (California) hardwired different-sex marriage into the state constitutions, thereby discouraging both judicial challenges (because of new constitutional language) and legislative action (because of legislator fears that voters will retaliate) in the short and perhaps medium term. The District of Columbia would be a highly likely candidate for recognition of same-sex civil unions or even marriage, except that Congress can override the District's substantive laws. When the District adopted a weak domestic partnership law in 1992, Congress, then controlled by the Democrats, enacted a D.C. appropriations law that precluded any public funds from being expended on the law. Similar provisos have been included in every D.C. approppriations law since 1992.

TABLE E.1. **GAY-FRIENDLY LAWS IN THE UNITED STATES, AS OF JULY 1, 2001**

State	Consesual Sodomy, No Crime	Sexual Orientation in Hate Crime Law	Laws Against Public/Private Employment Discrimination	Municipalities with Domestic Partnership Ordinances	Second-Parent Adoptions or Equitable Parenting	Statewide Registration of Same-Sex Partnerships
Vermont	1977	1989	1991/1991	Yes	1993	2000
California	1975	1991	1979/1979	Yes	(1980s)	1999
Hawaii	1972		1991/1991			1997
District of Columbia	1994	1994	1973/1973 1977/1977	Yes	1995	1992 (unfunded)
Massachusetts	(1974)	1996	1989/1989	Yes	1993	1992
Connecticut	1969	1990	1991/1991	Yes	2000	
New Jersey	1978	1995	1991/1991		1995	
New York	1980		1983/None	Yes	1995	
Illinois	1961	1991	1996/None		1995	
Minnesota	(1977)	1989	1986/1993	Yes	2000	
Wisconsin	1983	1991	1982/1982	Yes		
Oregon	1971	1989	1987/None	Yes		
Washington	1975	1993	1985/None	Yes		
New Hampshire	1973	1997	1997/1997			
Nevada	1993	1989	1999/1999			
Rhode Island	1998	1991	1985/1995			
Pennsylvania	1980		1975/None	Yes		
Ohio	1972		1983/None	Yes		
Delaware	1972	1997	2001/None			
Iowa	1976	1992				
Kentucky	1992	1998				
Maine	1975	1995				
Maryland	(1999)		1993/2001			
Nebraska	1977	1997				
Florida	(1971)	1991		Yes		
Alaska	1978					
Colorado	1971			Yes		
Georgia	1998			Yes		

Gay-Friendly Laws in the United States, as of July 2001, continued

State	Consensual Sodomy, No Crime	Sexual Orientation in Hate Crime Law	Laws Against Public/Private Employment Discrimination	Municipalities with Domestic Partnership Ordinances	Second-Parent Adoptions or Equitable Parenting	Statewide Registration of Same-Sex Partnerships
Michigan	(1980)			Yes		
Missouri	(1977)			Yes		
Arizona	(2001)	1997				
Indiana	1976					
Montana	1997					
New Mexico	1975					
North Dakota	1973					
South Dakota	1976					
Tennessee	1996					
West Virginia	1976					
Wyoming	1977					
Louisiana		1997				
Arkansas	(1977)					
Kansas	(1969)					
Texas	(1973)					
Alabama						
Idaho						
Mississippi						
North Carolina				Yes		
Oklahoma						
South Carolina						
Utah						
Virginia						

Sources: William N. Eskridge Jr., *Gaylaw: Challenging the Apartheid of the Closet*, 328–37 (App. A1, collecting sodomy repeals) and 356–61 (App. B2, antidiscrimination laws) (1999); and "Comparative Law and the Same-Sex Marriage Debate: A Step-by-Step Approach Toward State Recognition," 31 *McGeo. L.J.* 641 (2000) (App. II, hate crime laws). Dates in (parentheses) in column 1 mean that the state has not formally repealed its consensual sodomy law but has made some movement in that direction, as by reducing consensual sodomy to a misdemeanor (Arkansas, Florida, Kansas, Missouri, Texas); reducing the penalty to misdemeanor level (Minnesota); nullifying part of the sodomy law by court decision that essentially leaves the law unenforced (Florida, Maryland, Massachusetts, Michigan).

Once a modest but slowly growing number of states recognize same-sex unions and link them with most or all that state's benefits and duties of marriage, there will be some kind of crisis. Part of the crisis will be a technical legal one, as state judiciaries struggle with choice of law issues raised by civil unions and other euphemisms for same-sex marriage. It is possible, for example, that most New England states will adopt some recognition of same-sex unions the way most Scandinavian countries have recognized registered partnerships. Say that, at some point in the not-distant future, Vermont recognizes civil unions, Connecticut and Rhode Island do the same, New Hampshire and Maine have statewide domestic partnership laws like that now in force in California, and Massachusetts recognizes same-sex marriage. If a Vermont lesbian couple joins in a civil union and later moves to Connecticut, the latter would recognize the Vermont union. Would Maine? Probably not, as long as that state has a "junior DOMA," a law explicitly directing non-recognition of same-sex marriages. What if the couple moved to New York, with neither a junior DOMA nor a statewide law? For the reasons developed in chapters 1 and 4, the couple's status would be uncertain under New York law. That state might, by either court decision or legislation, give full or partial recognition to a civil union—a move that, in turn, might place more pressure on the state to create its own civil union law. At the same time, a politics of preservation in New York might persuade the legislature to adopt a broad junior DOMA, preventing recognition of civil unions as well as same-sex marriages. If there were doubt about coverage, perhaps raised by a trial judge somewhere, the thirty four states with junior DOMAs might be pressed to expand their laws to cover civil unions. During this ever-changing kaleidoscope of state civil union or recognition laws, judges all over the country will have to struggle with difficult issues relating to choice of law. Not since the country's division as to different-race marriages will state choice of law rules come under such strain.[1]

Part of the crisis will be a moral one, as ethical thinkers and institutions struggle to determine what stances they must take as to their lesbian and gay partnered brothers and sisters. Much of this debate will be conducted in churches and universities, where it will usually be one-sided, with churches lopsidedly opposed and universities in favor of same-sex marriage recognition. Other important situses for the debate will be the mass media, film and documentaries, fictional and nonfictional books, secondary schools, civic associations, neighborhood barbecues, the watercooler, and the family dinner table. The moral issues that will be in play will be these: What is the essential good of marriage? Do lesbian and gay couples satisfy that essential good? Would state recognition of lesbian and gay unions have symbolic value or generate collateral consequences that are undesirable?

Opponents and supporters of same-sex marriage both realize that the legal debate is strongly connected to the larger normative debate. What is at stake is not just technical legal equality, but fundamental *social norms* and *public values* in the United States. Fifty years ago, American law was consistent with and strongly reinforced the following social norms and public values: (1) The human good of marriage entails the unitive good of interpersonal commitment, actualized through procreative sexual intercourse between the husband and wife. (2) Because "homosexuals" are a degenerate form of human beings, preying on vulnerable people to recruit for their pathetic lifestyle, "homosexuality" should be strongly discouraged, and "homosexuals" should be "cured" of their often-preventable disease. (3) "Homosexual marriage" is not only an impossibility but is an affront to civilized society. These social norms were subsumed under the *meta-norm* that could be termed *compulsory heterosexuality*, as Adrienne Rich has called it, or *malignant sexual variation*, as I have.[2]

The sexual and gay rights revolutions of the 1960s and 1970s challenged these norms and values, as well as their legal supports. As table E.1 reflects, the law has changed dramatically in many states, and not at all in others. Speaking very generally, social norms and public values have also changed, along the following lines: (1) The human good of marriage and other institutions entails the unitive good of interpersonal joy and commitment, typically actualized through penile-vaginal sexual intercourse between the husband and wife. (2) Because gay men and lesbians have an unfortunate mental or genetic disability and lead suboptimal even if sometimes productive lives, homosexuality should be tolerated but should not be promoted. (3) "Gay marriage" is an oxymoron: not only is marriage inherently husband-wife, but gay people are not genuinely capable of the unitive good of interpersonal joy and commitment. These social norms are part of a meta-norm that could be understood as *preferred heterosexuality* or *tolerable sexual variation*. The reader can readily see that this meta-norm is consistent with a legal regime whereby consensual same-sex intimacy is not criminal and where the state and public accommodations and employers do not discriminate against lesbians, gay men, and bisexuals—but also where the state signals young people that homosexuality is not desirable and does not recognize gay marriage.*

Symbolically, the Vermont civil unions law in 2000 and the Netherlands same-sex marriage law in 2001 are inconsistent with the meta-norm of tolerable sexual variation. They are a breach in the regime of preferred heterosexuality. The same-sex marriage movement reflects a different set of social norms and public values than those currently held in most of the United States: (1) The human good of marriage and other institutions entails the unitive good of interpersonal joy and commitment, typically actualized through sexual as well as personal sharing. (2) Because gay men, lesbians, and bisexuals are productive people for whom same-sex intimacy is both natural and joyous, the state should be neutral as to matters of sexual orientation. (3) Because gay people are capable of the unitive good of interpersonal joy and commitment, they ought to have the same choices as to marriage and other relationship institutions as straight people. These social norms are part of a meta-norm that could be understood as *state neutrality as to sexuality* or *benign sexual variation*.

The meta-norm of benign sexual variation is not accepted by most Americans, as my account of the local and nationwide reactions to the lawsuits in Hawaii and Alaska demonstrates. The meta-norm is now tol-

★ The meta-norm of tolerable sexual variation is not accepted everywhere in the United States. In some of the states least likely to recognize same-sex unions or marriages (the epilogue table), the malignant sexual variation meta-norm still holds sway. The new norm better describes the country as a whole. Witness the "don't ask, don't tell" compromise for the federal military exclusion of lesbians, bisexuals, and gay men, and the executive order barring federal government employment discrimination on the basis of sexual orientation and the substantial support for national legislation barring it among private employers as well.

erable sexual variation, and a court cannot change that. Nor can a legislature. But the vision of the Vermont plaintiffs and lawyers is that the meta-norm and its accompanying social norms ought to change. Benign sexual variation is a better norm than tolerable sexual variation, because it more accurately reflects the empirical knowledge and professional consensus that is developing among social scientists about the psychological consequences of homosexuality (few) and closeted homosexuality (many and severe), the ability of gay people to contribute to larger social projects (substantial), the nature and dynamics of lesbian and gay relationships (pretty healthy), and the ability of lesbian and gay households to provide a nurturing home for children (generally quite positive).[3] It is a better norm because it is more consistent with the equality norm that dominates American public law and probably constitutes one of the other meta-norms of our culture. It is a better norm because it would contribute to improved social cooperation among Americans in the long term. There are other kinds of reasons, but these are the main ones. Elaborating on them and responding to reasonable doubts would require another book.

To conclude this book, I want to say a few words about the relevance of the equality practice thesis to theories of social norms. Thinkers in the legal academy have achieved consensus as to the importance of social norms and the difficulty in changing them, even when they have become obsolescent.[4] This is what the academic literature calls the *sticky norms problem*. The meta-norm of malignant sexual variation is clearly obsolescent, and in my view was a bad norm for the entire modern period, but it did not go quickly into the night. Instead, it has gradually waned as the tolerable sexual variation norm has acquired sticking power in our polity. The law played an important role in both the power and the decline of the malignant variation meta-norm, but the primary variable pressing both law and society away from the old norm was the social movement of lesbian and gay liberation and rights. Once lesbians, gay men, and bisexuals came out of their closets in significant numbers, the fate of that norm was sealed. Is the meta-norm of tolerable sexual variation more sustainable? Or is it an unstable transition from the malignant variation to the benign variation meta-norm?

Equality practice of the sort described in chapters 4 through 6 will facilitate further changes in our norms about sexual variation but will not guarantee that change will occur sooner, or even later. But moving step by step in the direction of same-sex marriage, through a series of intermediate reforms and experimental forms, offers three different kinds of advantages for changing this meta-norm.

First, equality practice offers *opportunities for falsification*. An advantage of our federalist system is that one locality or state can adopt a novel legal institution or regulation, and all jurisdictions can benefit from experience with the new form. In the context of same-sex unions, this is a great opportunity, because arguments against legal recognition rest upon extraordinary predictions. So long as the choice for a political system was same-sex marriage versus nothing, the system chose nothing, thereby precluding lesbian and gay activists from disproving predictions about recognizing their relationships. Equality practice makes it easier for one jurisdiction to recognize such relationships. Now that Vermont has followed up on and improved upon the Danish experiment in registered partnerships, moderates can observe for themselves the ramifications of state recognition. While the number of couples taking advantage of these new institutions remains modest, the asserted drawbacks or calamities have been entirely unrealized. And so it shall be for future experiments. As more jurisdictions recognize some form of same-sex partnership, and a few good and no bad consequences occur, the more apparent will be the inconsistency between state discriminations against lesbian and gay couples and the equality meta-norm.

Additionally, equality practice already has and will continue to *open up the normative debate beyond the confines of homogeneous subcultures*. A central problem with the same-sex marriage debate, and a reason it is so polarizing, is that it occurs within subcultures—traditionalist churches, liberal universities, and lesbian and gay communities—whose members start off with relatively homogeneous beliefs. It is unsurprising that deliberation does not always produce better choices. Social scientists have shown that when members of a like-thinking subgroup deliberate about an issue, their group conclusion tends to be more extreme than the tentative conclusion most, and sometimes any, of the individuals had before the deliberation.[5] The deliberation ratchets up the intellectual and emotional precommitments. Thus, when religious fundamentalists skeptical about same-sex marriage deliberate within their subgroup, the group discussion is likely to conclude that such a move is not only dubious but disastrous. Contrariwise, when liberal academics favoring same-sex marriage deliberate within their subgroup, the group conclusion is likely to be that state denial is not only unfair but prejudiced. So long as discussion about same-sex marriage is ghettoized in this way—with supporters and opponents both becoming increasingly fervent—political polarization and even train wrecks will result. Once equality practice brings the issue into public forms such as legislatures and less sectarian groups such as newspapers for a period of time, there is a greater likelihood that people will soften their hard feelings and be more open to understanding other points of view. The ameliorative effects of public discourse will work toward greater equality for lesbian and gay couples if the new institutional forms of recognition are viewed as helping committed couples who contribute productively to the community, people like Holly Puterbaugh and Lois Farnham, Stacy Jolles and Nina Beck, and Stan Baker and Peter Harrigan, the couples who brought the same-sex marriage lawsuit in Vermont. The reason is that once people's precommitments soften and they seek bases for mutual agreement, they will be more willing to look at the actual evidence before them—the couples who join in civil union. And once the focus is on the human beings who happen to be lesbians or gay men, normative thinking will change, slowly but surely.

Finally, equality practice offers *opportunities for cooperation* between subgroup members; these opportunities are useful for both the minority and for the community. Here I appropriate Robert Putnam's distinction between social capital (trust and goodwill) that is *bonding* and that which is *bridging*.[6] Bonding experiences tie you to your subgroup, such as your family, church, and neighborhood. Family reunions, church bingo nights, and block parties build bonding capital. Bridging experiences tie you to people outside your subgroup. Patriotic celebrations such as those on the Fourth of July, political campaigns that engage the citizenry, and the World Series can all build bridging capital. Generally, marriage is the classic situs for bonding capital, but same-sex marriage or civil unions can and do create miniature bridges. The wedding ceremony itself can bring family members, coworkers, and friends of various orientations and backgrounds to be a community of witnesses to the commitment between two women or two men. The choreography obviously has both bonding and bridging features. The couple's everyday life offers bridges. The family reunion, neighborhood cookout, and PTA meeting offer people who have never known a "homosexual couple" the opportunity to witness firsthand the similarities of their relationship with marriages the observers know well. The church bake sale, neighborhood clean-up campaign, and collective efforts to pitch in during times of family crises offer straight people the opportunity to see how lesbian and gay couples can and do contribute to cooperative projects. And so on.

These last examples suggest that equality practice is a day-to-day educational process as much as a long-range political process. Naturally, some people's experiences will be less satisfactory than those hypothesized, and timing is just as important to equality practice as the step-by-step incrementalism. Some state had to go first, and Vermont took the first step because its laws and values were more accepting of lesbians and gay men than most other jurisdictions. Other states will follow, and they will not be those near the bottom of my table. But the educative process I just described for individuals can also work for states: once states in the middle of the table see that those at the top recognize same-sex unions and move forward, they will feel pressure to reform their own laws, including their sodomy and antidiscrimination laws. At some point, perhaps in the distant future, the states at the bottom will follow too, perhaps under the direction of the U.S. Supreme Court, when it finally extends the reasoning and result of *Loving v. Virginia*, the miscegenation case, to same-sex marriage.[7]

There is no force greater than an idea whose time has come. Equality practice is such an idea. There is no intellectual experience more exciting than an idea whose time is coming. That idea may be same-sex marriage.

NOTES

PROLOGUE

1. For accounts of the various country or state moves toward recognition of same-sex unions or marriages, see chapter 3 of this book, as well as *Legal Recognition of Same-Sex Partnerships: A Study of National, European and International Law,* ed. Robert Wintemute and Mads Andenaes (2001).

2. For a brilliant and comprehensive examination for Canada, see Brenda Crossman and Bruce Ryder, *The Legal Regulation of Adult Personal Relationships: Evaluating Policy Objectives and Legal Options in Federal Legislation* (report prepared for the benefit of the Law Commission of Canada, May 1, 2000).

3. See U.S. Census Bureau, *2000 Census of Population and Housing: Profiles of General Demographic Characteristics,* 1 (2001).

4. Ibid.; Eric Schmitt, "For First Time, Nuclear Families Drop Below 25% of Households," *N.Y. Times,* May 15, 2001, at A1, col.2.

5. Between 1970 and 1998, the percentage of women aged forty to forty-four who have not married went up from 5.4 percent to 9.9 percent; for men of the same age, the percentage went up from 7.5 percent to 15.6 percent. See Andrew Hacker, "The Case Against Kids," *N.Y. Rev. of Books,* Nov. 30, 2000, at 12, 16 (table C).

6. Between 1970 and 1998, the number of of children living with unmarried couples went up from 196,000 to 1,520,000. The number of marital births was down by a fifth; the number of nonmarital births more than doubled. Ibid.

7. See Rosalind C. Barnett and Caryl Rivers, *She Works, He Works: How Two-Income Families Are Happy, Healthy and Thriving* (1996); Vicki Schultz, "Life's Work," 100 *Colum. L. Rev.* 1881 (2000).

8. See John P. Robinson and Geoffrey Godbey, *Time for Life: The Surprising Ways Americans Use Their Time* (1997); Joni Hersch, "Marriage, Home Production, and Earnings," in *Marriage and the Economy,* ed. Shoshana Grossbard-Shectman (2001).

9. See Amy Wax, "Bargaining in the Shadow of the Market: Is There a Future for Egalitarian Marriage?," 84 *Va. L. Rev.* 509 (1998).

10. The statement in text is informed speculation, admittedly. There are no systematic data on the sexual orientation of most married people circa 1900. However, leading "inverts" of this period were married: Oscar Wilde, Sir Alfred Douglas, and Virginia Woolf, to name some of the best-known figures.

11. The 1990 and 2000 Censuses reported same-sex households. Because the Census tabulation was based entirely on self-reporting, it greatly understates the number of such households. Still, it is significant that the 2000 Census reported more than four times the number of such households than the 1990 Census.

12. The data on children being reared in lesbian or gay households are critically discussed in M. V. Lee Badgett, *Money, Myths, and Change: The Economic Lives of Lesbians and Gay Men,* 151–55 (2001).

13. For surveys of the evolution of American family law toward private choice and contracting, see Mary Ann Glendon, *The New Family and the New Property* (1981); Jana B. Singer, "The Privatization of Family Law," 1992 *Wis. L. Rev.* 1443. For some moves beyond, see Margaret F. Brinig, *From Contract to Covenant: Beyond the Law and Economics of the Family* (2000).

CHAPTER ONE

1. The shift in homosexuals' understandings of their secrecy from masquerade to the closet is documented and analyzed in William N. Eskridge Jr., *Gaylaw: Challenging the Apartheid of the Closet*, 52–59, 98–101 (1999).

2. Nancy Fraser, "From Redistribution to Recognition? Dilemmas of Justice in a 'Postsocialist' Age," in *Justice Interruptus: Critical Reflections on the "Postsocialist" Condition* (1997) (emphasis in original). For parallel ideas in the legal literature, see, e.g., Richard L. Abel, *Speaking Respect, Respecting Speech* (1997); J. M. Balkin, "The Constitution of Status," 106 *Yale L.J.* 2313, 2321–32 (1997).

3. The term *politics of preservation* is inspired by my reading of Joseph R. Gusfield, *Symbolic Crusade: Status Politics in the American Temperance Movement* (2d ed. 1986).

4. For the politics of protection and the mutually protective closet it engendered, see John D'Emilio, *Sexual Politics, Sexual Communities: The Making of a Homosexual Minority in the United States, 1940–1970* (1983); Eskridge, *Gaylaw*, 80–125.

5. Same-sex marriage was discussed by some; the earliest in print was E. W. Saunders, "Reformers' Choice: Marriage License or Just License?," *One, Inc.*, August 1953, at 10–12.

6. In addition to the sources in note 4, see also David K. Johnson, "'Homosexual Citizens': Washington's Gay Community Confronts the Civil Service," *Wash. Hist.*, Fall–Winter 1994–95, at 50.

7. See Donn Teal, *Gay Radicals* (1971); Kay Tobin and Randy Wicker, *The Gay Crusaders* (2d ed. 1975).

8. "Gay Revolution Comes Out," *The Rat*, August 12–16, 1969, at 7 (interview with members of the Gay Liberation Front); see Ralph Hall, "The Church, State & Homosexuality: A Radical Analysis," *Gay Power* no. 14 (no date, probably 1970) (extending the analysis: "homosexual marriages" aping husband-wife unions are "reactionary").

9. For the feminist critique of marriage, see Shulamith Firestone, *The Dialectic of Sex: The Case for Feminist Revolution* (1970); Sheila Cronan, "Marriage," in *Radical Feminism*, 213–21 (Anne Koedt ed. 1973). See also Alice Echols, *Daring to Be Bad: Radical Feminism in America, 1967–1975* (1989).

10. My characterizations of Nina Beck's views are drawn from my interview with her and her partner Stacy Jolles at their home in Burlington, Vermont, on October 7, 2000. On families of choice that formed in the San Francisco Bay area during the 1970s and 1980s, see Kath Weston, *Families We Choose: Lesbians, Gays, Kinship* (1991).

11. Although gay and bisexual men were the most public practitioners of post-Stonewall sexual liberty (see, e.g., Larry Kramer, *Faggots* [1979]); John Rechy, *The Sexual Outlaw* [1977]), bisexual women and lesbians have been its most articulate theorists in my opinion. See, e.g., Rita Mae Brown, *Rubyfruit Jungle* (1973) (the character Molly Bolt repeatedly rejects the possibility of marriage, whether same- or different-sex); Gayle S. Rubin, "Thinking Sex: Notes for a Radical Theory of the Politics of Sexuality," in *Pleasure and Danger: Exploring Female Sexuality*, 11–34 (Carole Vance ed. 1984) (the best overall theoretical questioning of sex negativity).

12. "An Approach to Liberation," *Gay Liberation: A Red Butterfly Publication*, 12 (no date, probably 1970).

13. This was State Demand Number 8 in the Demands of the National Coalition of Gay Organizations (November 1972). Federal Demand Number 4 was "Elimination of tax inequities victimizing single persons and same-sex couples."

14. See Eskridge, *Gaylaw*, 125–37 (generally), 328–37 (sodomy law repeals), and 356–61 (state and local nondiscrimination rules).

15. See Grace Lichtenstein, "Homosexual Weddings Stir Controversy," *N.Y. Times*, April 27, 1975. The Colorado Attorney General overrode clerk Rorex's interpretation of the state marriage law in Opinion of Att'y Gen. J. D. MacFarlane to Hon. Ruben Valdez, Speaker, Colo. House of Reps., April 24, 1975, "In re: Marriages between two men or two women."

16. Vt. Att'y Gen. Opin. No. 90–75 (April 15, 1975).

17. See Don Kelly, "Homosexuals Should Get Rights," *Los Angeles Collegian*, March 3, 1971, at 2 (student newspaper [L.A. City College] describing the Baker-McConnell story); see generally Tobin and Wicker, *Gay Crusaders*, 135–55 (describing the couple and their story).

18. See *Baker v. Nelson*, 191 N.W.2d 185 (Minn. 1971), appeal dismissed, 409 U.S. 810 (1972).

19. See "Marriage Fight Due: Wisconsin Black Women Slate Christmas Wedding," *Mother*, December 1971, at 1.

20. See *Jones v. Hallahan*, 501 S.W.2d 588 (Ky. 1973).

21. See Kenji Yoshino, "The Assimilationist Bias in Equal Protection: The Visibility Presumption and the Case of Don't Ask, Don't Tell," 108 *Yale L.J.* 485 (1998).

22. *Loving v. Virginia*, 388 U.S. 1, 1–10 (1967).

23. See 118 Cong. Rec. 9096–97 (1972) (Freund's testimony inserted into the Congressional Record); also 9315 (Sen. Ervin, D-N.C., relying on Freund's argument to oppose the ERA); Note, "The Legality of Homosexual Marriage," 82 *Yale L.J.* 573 (1973) (noting Freund's deployment of this argument).

24. See 118 Cong. Rec. 9320–21 (1972) (Sen. Bayh, D-Ind., vigorously denying Freund's analogy between same-sex marriage and different-race marriage).

25. See *Singer v. Hara*, 522 P.2d 1187 (Wash. App.), review denied, 84 Wash. 2d 1008 (1974) (rejecting sex discrimination argument by gay couple seeking right to marry).

26. *Loving*, 388 U.S. at 12.

27. *Jones*, 50 S.W.2l at 589. Other leading cases making the same point were *Bakers*, 191N.W.2d 185, and *Singer*, 522 P.2d1187. For an exhaustive list digesting the pre-1996 same-sex marriage cases, see William N. Eskridge Jr., *The Case for Same-Sex Marriage,* 232–33 n.24, 264–66 (1996).

28. See Didi Herman, *The Antigay Agenda: Orthodox Vision and the Christian Right*, 47–48, 61–63 (1997) (*Christianity Today* was concerned with sexual promiscuity of all sorts before 1969 but focused on predatory homosexuality with increasing alarm only after 1969).

29. See George Mendenhall, "Sex Bill Passes in Historic Senate Tie-Breaker," *The Advocate*, May 21, 1975, at 4.

30. 1977 Cal. Stat. ch. 339, §§ 1–2. For the legislative background of the regendering of the state marriage law, see "Senate Approves Measure Banning Gay Marriages," *L.A. Times*, August 12, 1977; "California Assembly Approves Bill Banning Gay Marriages," *L.A. Times*, August 14, 1977.

31. See *Dean v. District of Columbia*, 653 A.2d 307 (D.C. 1995) (opinion of Ferren, J., recounting the history of the Dixon amendment, which was withdrawn after the churches came out in opposition); Cheryl Kimmons, "The Case for Gay Marriage," *The Blade*, June 1976, at 6 (Kameny's activism on the marriage issue as part of his general politics of recognition).

32. See, e.g., 1984 Md. Sess. Laws 296, codified at Md. Family Law § 2–201; 1975 Va. Sess. Laws ch. 644, codified at Va. Code § 20–45.2.

33. See Eskridge, *Gaylaw,* 106 (Mormon Idaho and Baptist Arkansas unknowingly repealed their consensual sodomy laws when they adopted the Model Penal Code in the 1970s, and both states responded to religious outrage by reenacting a sodomy law) and 328–37 (appendix of state sodomy laws, showing that most states with such laws are in the Baptist south and Mormon west).

34. See generally Anita Bryant, *The Anita Bryant Story: The Survival of Our Nation's Families and the Threat of Militant Homosexuality* (1977); Joe Baker, "Anita with the Smiling Cheek," *The Advocate*, April 20, 1977, at 6.

35. See William N. Eskridge Jr., "No Promo Homo: The Sedimentation of Antigay Discourse and the Channeling Effect of Judicial Review," 75 *NYU L. Rev.* 101, 124 (2000).

36. Ibid., 117–18.

37. See *Marvin v. Marvin*, 557 P.2d 106 (Cal. 1976); see Jana B. Singer, "The Privatization of Family Law," 1992 *Wis. L. Rev.* 1443 (situating *Marvin* as part of a notable shift in different-sex families as they relate to the law).

38. See Eskridge, *Gaylaw,* 125–48 and 356–61 (appendix listing antidiscrimination laws and ordinances as of 1999); James Button et al., *Private Lives, Public Conflicts: Battles over Gay Rights in American Communities* (1997).

39. Excellent overviews of the domestic partnership movement are Raymond C. O'Brien, "Domestic Partnership: Recognition and Responsibility," 32 *San Diego L. Rev.* 163 (1995); Craig A. Bowman and Blake M. Cornish, "A More Perfect Union: A Legal and Social Analysis of Domestic Partnership Ordinances," 92 *Colum. L. Rev.* 1164 (1992) (student note).

40. "San Francisco Mayor Says No to Gay Marriage," *The Blade*, January 26, 1983, at 9.

41. The ultimate policy is set forth in City of Berkeley, "Domestic Partnership Information Sheet," January 1, 1987.

42. See generally Sally Kohn, *The Domestic Partnership Organizing Manual for Employee Benefits* 41–49 (NGLTF Policy Institute June 1999) (appendix of municipal and county domestic partnership policies as they have been applied, with different-sex couples outnumbering same-sex couples).

43. The list in text is adapted from that found in the "Domestic Partnership Listings" portion of Lambda's website, <www.lambdalegal.org> (as of October 26, 2000).

44. See Vermont Labor Relations Bd. Dec., Grievance of B.M., S.S., CC.M., and J.R., Docket No. 92–32, extending medical and dental benefits to domestic partners of state employees.

45. Daniel Weintraub and Bettina Boxall, "Ballot Fallout Expected from Wilson's Veto," *L.A. Times*, September 13, 1994, at 3.

46. 1999 Cal. Stat. ch. 588, codified at Calif. Family Code § 297 et seq.

47. See Memorandum from the Domestic Partnership Comm. of Gay and Lesbian Attorneys of Washington to the D.C. Corporation Counsel, May 12, 1991.

48. Health Care Benefits Extension Act of 1992, Law 9–114, 39 D.C. Reg. 2861 (codified at D.C. Code §§ 36-1401 to 36-1408).

49. The quotations in text are from 138 Cong. Rec. 27,407 (1992) (statement of Rep. Bliley, R-Va.); 139 Cong. Rec. 17,031 (1993) (statement of Sen. Lott, R-Miss.), respectively. They directly echo the position formally written up in Robert H. Knight, "How Domestic Partnerships and 'Gay Marriage' Threaten the Family," *Insight*, June 1994 (Family Research Council).

50. See D.C. Appropriations Act, Pub. L. No. 102–382, tit. I, 106 Stat. 1422, 1422 (1992). Every D.C. appropriations law since the 1992 one has contained similar language.

51. See *In re Kowalski*, 478 N.W.2d 790 (Minn. App. 1991) (court, after years of litigation, finally appoints female partner as guardian of Sharon Kowalski).

52. See Interview with Beck and Jolles.

53. The frequently contentious discussions between Woods and local and national ACLU leaders are recounted, from the "marriage-now" perspective in Hawaii, at the following website: <www.hawaiigaymarriage.com/docs/keydates.html> (as of October 26, 2000). According to Woods, the local and national ACLU branches not only declined to help him with litigation against the same-sex marriage exclusion, but also sought to undermine his efforts within the lesbian and gay community.

54. See Paula Ettelbrick, "Since When Is Marriage a Path to Liberation?" *OUT/LOOK: Nat'l Gay and Lesbian Q.*, Fall 1989, at 8.

55. See Thomas Stoddard, "Why Gay People Should Seek the Right to Marry," ibid. The Ettelbrick and Stoddard essays are reprinted in *Lesbian and Gay Marriage: Private Commitments, Public Ceremonies,* 13–19 (Suzanne Sherman ed. 1992) and William N. Eskridge Jr. and Nan D. Hunter, *Sexuality, Gender, and the Law,* 817–20 (1997).

56. *Bowers v. Hardwick*, 478 U.S. 186 (1986).

57. For a detailed analysis of the Court's precedents and their evolving support for the right of same-sex couples to marry, see Eskridge, *Same-Sex Marriage,* 124–37.

58. *Zablocki v. Redhail*, 434 U.S. 374, 385 (1978), quoting *Cleveland Board of Education v. LaFleur*, 414 U.S. 632, 639–40 (1974). Only Justice William Rehnquist dissented from the Court's judgment, but Justice Lewis Powell vigorously objected to the Court's expansion of the right to marry beyond *Loving* and explicitly feared that a broad right to marry could be invoked by gay people seeking state recognition of their unions. See 434 U.S. at 399 (Powell, J., concurring in the judgment).

59. *Turner v. Safley*, 482 U.S. 78 (1987), emphasizing the expressive goals of marriage and the state benefits associated with it, and omitting procreation as a goal, for some of the prisoners would never be able to consummate their marriages.

60. Ibid., 95.

61. *Watkins v. United States Army*, 847 F.2d 1329 (9th Cir. 1988) (panel opinion by Norris and Canby, JJ.), aff'd on narrower grounds, 875 F.2d 699 (9th Cir. en banc 1989).

62. *Baehr v. Lewin*, 852 P.2d 44 (Haw. 1993).

63. Two of the four participating justices joined the opinion for the court. A third justice concurred in the judgment on the ground that if sexual orientation is hardwired into human beings then this ought to be a suspect classification. A fourth justice dissented. On motion for clarification, five justices participated, and four of them joined a reaffirmance of the earlier opinion. *Baehr v. Lewin*, 852 P.2d 74. (Haw. 1993).

64. Haw. Const. art. I, § 6 (right of privacy "shall not be infringed without the showing of a compelling state interest").

65. See *State v. Mueller*, 671 P.2d 1351 (Haw. 1983).

66. *Baehr v. Lewin*, 852 P.2d at 56.

67. Justice Sandra Day O'Connor's opinion for the Court in *Turner* ruled that prisoners, including those incarcerated for life, had pretty much the same kinds of interests in marriage as other people. These interests include "expressions of emotional support and public commitment"; an "exercise of religious faith"; the potential for sexual consummation; and "government benefits" that are connected with marriage. 482 U.S. at 95.

68. Haw. Const. art. I, § 5.

69. The argument in text was originally made by Professor Paul Freund as a reason for opposing the national Equal Rights Amendment, but has been revived as an argument for same-sex marriage. See Andrew Koppelman, "Why Discrimination Against Lesbians and Gay Men Is Sex Discrimination," 69 *NYU L. Rev.* 197 (1994). See also Eskridge, *Gaylaw*, 218–28, fleshing out this argument.

70. *Baehr*, 852 P.2d at 67.

71. See Defendants' Response to Plaintiffs' First Request for Answers to Interrogatories, 6–10, in *Baehr* on remand (Dec. 17, 1993). These justifications are quoted in Evan Wolfson [co-counsel for plaintiffs], "Crossing the Threshold: Equal Marriage Rights for Lesbians and Gay Men, and the Intra-Community Critique," 21 *NYU Rev. L. & Soc. Change* 567 (1994). See also Richard A. Posner, *Sex and Reason,* 311–13 (1992), and G. Sidney Buchanan, "Same-Sex Marriage: The Linchpin Issue," 10 *Dayton U.L. Rev.* 541 (1985), for similar arguments justifying state bars to same-sex marriage.

72. The state had other arguments: the exclusion of same-sex couples was necessary in order to prevent the degradation of marriage and to head off polygamy, the next step in the "slippery slope."

73. *Baehr v. Miike*, 1996 WL 694235 (Haw. Cir. Ct. Dec. 3, 1996), reversed, 994 P.2d 566 (Haw. 1999) (per curiam).

74. Ibid., slip op., Finding of Fact No.132. See also ibid., Findings of Fact Nos.126–27 (sexual orientation of the parents is not a good indicator of how well children will be raised and how well they will turn out).

75. Ibid., Finding of Fact No. 136.

76. The quotations in text are taken from Beth Robinson, "Same-Sex Marriages in Hawaii" (July 11, 1997) <www.religioustolerance.org/hom_mar5.html> (as of October 18, 2000).

77. See 1994 Haw. Sess. Laws, Act 217, reaffirming marriage as intrinsically limited to one man and one woman and finding that "the question before the court . . . is essentially one of policy, thereby rendering it inappropriate for judicial response."

78. See 1995 Haw. Sess. Laws, Act 5. A commission had been created by Act 217 the year before, but it never met. The new commission met between May and December 1995 and issued its report on December 8, 1995.

79. Thomas Gill, Chair, *Report of the Commission on Sexual Orientation and the Law,* 43–44 (Dec. 8, 1995).

80. Ibid., 45–95 (minority report).
81. 1997 Haw. Sess. Laws 2883, H.B. 117 ("proposing a constitutional amendment relating to marriage").
82. 1997 Haw. Sess. Laws 2786, Act 383 (H.B. 118).
83. Ibid., § 5. The parties could dissolve the relationship either by filing a form of dissolution with the state, ibid., 7, or by one partner's becoming married. Ibid., § 8(c).
84. Ibid., §§ 2 (health care benefits); 22, 31 (funeral leave); 23 (moving expenses); 29, 31, 33 (death benefits).
85. Ibid., §§ 52–55.
86. Ibid., § 56.
87. Ibid., § 57.
88. Ibid., §§ 3, 42–45. See also ibid., § 62 (consent of spouse or reciprocal beneficiary for postmortem examination).
89. Ibid., §§ 46–49.
90. Ibid., § 10.
91. Ibid., §§ 12–18.
92. Ibid., § 58.
93. Ibid., § 20, subject to the liability limits of Hawaii's no-fault insurance rules. See ibid., § 59. See also ibid., § 65 (general responsibility not to commit torts against persons includes duties owed to their spouses and reciprocal beneficiaries as well).
94. Ibid., § 39.
95. Ibid., §§ 66–67.
96. Ibid., § 70.
97. Posner, *Sex and Reason,* 311–13.
98. See Barbara J. Cox, "Same-Sex Marriage and Choice of Law: If We Marry in Hawaii, Are We Still Married When We Return Home?" 1994 *Wis. L. Rev.* 1033, for an excellent introduction to choice of law issues surrounding same-sex marriage—both with and without the new state laws. For further analysis of the new state laws, see Andrew Koppelman, "Same-Sex Marriage, Choice of Law, and Public Policy," 76 *Tex. L. Rev.* 921 (1998); Linda Silberman, "Can the Island of Hawaii Rule the World? A Comment on Same-Sex Marriage and Federalism Values," 16 *QLR* 191 (1996).
99. See Silberman, "Can Hawaii Rule?" responding to Larry Kramer, "Same-Sex Marriage, Conflict of Laws, and the Unconstitutional Public Policy Exception," 106 *Yale L.J.* 1965 (1997).
100. 1993 Utah Laws (2d Special Sess.) ch. 14, § 1, codified at Utah Code § 30–1–2(5).
101. 1995 Utah Laws ch. 146, codified at Utah Code § 30–1–4(1). The new law came in the wake of a 1994 resolution against same-sex marriage by the Church of Jesus Christ of Latter-Day Saints and was drafted by a devout Mormon law professor, Lynn Wardle. See Dan Harrie, "Utah May Ignore Gay Unions," *Salt Lake Tribune,* March 17, 1995.
102. See, e.g., California Proposition 22, adopted March 2000 and codified at Calif. Family Code § 308.5: "Only marriage between a man and a woman is valid or recognized in California."
103. 1996 Mich. Laws Pub. Act No. 324, codified at Mich. Comp. Laws §§ 551.1, 551. 2, 551.3, 551.4.
104. Ibid., codified at Mich. Comp. Laws § 551.272; see also ibid., § 551.271(2) (making certain that Michigan's general rule validating marriages lawfully entered in another state would *not* apply to same-sex marriages).
105. 1996 Ga. Laws, codified at Ga. Code §19–3–3.1. The quote in text is § 19–3–3.1(b).
106. *Romer v. Evans,* 517 U.S. 620, 632, 634–35 (1996).
107. See, e.g., Russell J. Weintraub, *Commentary on the Conflict of Laws,* 525 (3d ed. 1986); Andrew Koppelman, "Dumb and DOMA: Why the Defense of Marriage Act Is Unconstitutional," 83 *Iowa L. Rev.* 1, 10–15 (1997) (applying traditional choice of law analysis to the Georgia law quoted in text). A powerful academic argument for giving full faith and credit and due process scrutiny greater bite in this area is set forth in Kermit Roosevelt III, "The Myth of Choice of Law: Rethinking Conflicts," 97 *Mich. L. Rev.* 2448 (1999).
108. See *Baker v. General Motors,* 118 S. Ct. 657, 663–64 (1998); *Fauntleroy v. Lum,* 210 U.S. 230, 238 (1908); Lea Brilmyer, *Conflict of Laws,* 298–99 (2d ed. 1995).
109. See Douglas Laycock, "Equal Citizens of Equal and Territorial States: The Constitutional Foundations of Choice of Law," 92 *Colum. L. Rev.* 249, 313 (1992). This thesis is applied to same-sex marriage nonrecognition laws in Koppelman, "Same-Sex Marriage, Choice of Law," 992–1001.
110. *Estin v. Estin,* 334 U.S. 541, 553 (1948) (Jackson, J., dissenting).
111. Section 2 has been codified as 28 U.S.C. § 1738C.
112. Section 3 has been codified as 1 U.S.C. § 7.
113. See William N. Eskridge Jr., *New Republic,* June 17, 1996, at 11. Indicting § 2 with somewhat different arguments (which I find quite persuasive as well) is Letter from Laurence H. Tribe, Harvard Law School, to Senator Edward M. Kennedy, May 24, 1996, reprinted in 142 Cong. Rec. 13359–61 (June 6, 1996).
114. See Scott Ruskay-Kidd, "The Defense of Marriage Act and the Overextension of Congressional Authority," 97 *Colum. L. Rev.* 1435, 1449–65 (1997); George P. Costigan Jr., "The History of the Adoption of Section 1 of Article IV [etc.]," 4 *Colum. L. Rev.* 470 (1904). But see Daniel A. Crane, "The Original Understanding of the 'Effects Clause' of Article IV, Section 1 and the Implications for the Defense of Marriage Act," 6 *Geo. Mason L. Rev.* 307 (1998) (arguing for a broader reading of the prescribe effect sentence). On the prescribe effect clause generally, see Michael H. Gottesman, "Draining the Dismal Swamp: The Case for Federal Choice of Law Statutes," 80 *Geo. L.J.* 1, 24–28 (1991).

115. See Act of May 26, 1790, 1 Stat. 122; Act of March 27, 1804, 2 Stat. 298.

116. See *City of Boerne v. Flores*, 521 U.S. 507 (1997) (reading § 5 to allow Congress no room for adding to or taking away rights assured by § 1 of the Fourteenth Amendment). See also *Morrison v. United States*, 120 S.Ct. 1740 (2000) (invalidating the Violence against Women Act on the ground that Congress is not authorized by § 5 to add to the rights protected under § 1); *Katzenbach v. Morgan*, 384 U.S. 641 (1966) (dictum that Congress is not authorized by § 5 to "dilute" the rights protected under § 1).

117. Letter from Andrew Fois, Assistant Attorney General, to Henry J. Hyde, Chair, House Judiciary Commission, May 14, 1996; see Defense of Marriage Act: Hearings on H.R. 3396 Before the Subcomm. on the Constitution of the House Comm. on the Judiciary, 104th Cong., 2d Sess. (May 1996). The only reasoning supporting a broader reading of the prescribe effect sentence came in the statement of Professor Lynn Wardle (who is not an expert on either choice of law or constitutional law), Hearing on S.1740 Before the Senate Comm. on the Judiciary, 104th Cong., 2d Sess. 47 (1996) (the "Senate DOMA Hearing"), and a short letter from Professor Michael McConnell to Senator Orrin Hatch, July 10, 1996, reprinted in ibid., 58. Their analysis was perfunctory and inattentive to the rich history of the full faith and credit clause. See Koppelman, "Dumb and DOMA," 18–24, which responds to the position taken by these professors.

118. See Koppelman, "Dumb and DOMA," 24–32; Senate DOMA Hearing, 46–48 (statement of Professor Cass R. Sunstein, a leading expert on constitutional interpretation).

119. H.R. Report No. 104–664, at 13 (July 9, 1996) (the "DOMA House Report"), reprinted in 1996 *U.S. Code, Cong. & Admin. News* (*USCCAN*) 2905, 2917.

120. See D. Flaks et al., "Lesbians Choosing Motherhood: A Comparative Study of Lesbian and Heterosexual Parents and Their Children," 31 *Dev. Psychol.* 105 (1995) (between 1.5 and 5 million lesbians, many of them in partnered relationships, resided with their children). For a survey of the empirical literature on lesbian and gay families, including families with children, see M. V. Lee Badgett, *Money, Myths, and Change: The Economic Lives of Lesbians and Gay Men*, 146–60 (2001).

121. 142 Cong. Rec. 16801 (July 11, 1996) (colloquy between Reps. Frank, D-Mass., and Largent, R-Okla.).

122. Supporters of DOMA summarily asserted that it was needed to protect marriage. See, e.g., ibid., 22451 (September 10, 1996) (Sen. Coats, R-Ind.) and 22445 ff. (Sen. Byrd, D-W.V.). Critics of DOMA argued that "marriage" was threatened by such things as no-fault divorce, domestic abuse, poverty, and so forth. Why didn't the sponsors try to tackle the real problems? See ibid., 16799 (July 11, 1996) (Rep. Johnston, D-Fla., and Rep. Nadler, D-N.Y.); ibid., 16800 (Rep. Maloney, D-N.Y.).

123. "We all know what is going on here. I regard this bill as a mean-spirited form of Republican legislative gay-bashing cynically calculated to try to inflame the public 8 weeks before the November 5 election." Ibid., 22438 (Sen. Kennedy, D-Mass.).

124. DOMA House Report, 15 n.53 (1996 *USCCAN* 2919 n.53).

125. Ibid., 16 (1996 *USCCAN* 2920).

126. 142 Cong. Rec. 17075 (July 12, 1996) (Rep. Funderburk, R-N.C.).

127. Ibid., 16976 (July 11, 1996) (Rep. Canady, R-Fla.) and 17079 (July 12, 1996) (Rep. Canady, R-Fla, repeating same language from previous day).

128. Ibid., 22451 (Sept. 10, 1996) (Sen. Coats, R-Ind.).

129. See Eskridge, "No Promo Homo," 1381–85.

130. *Evans*, 517 U.S. at 623, quoting *Plessy v. Ferguson*, 163 U.S. 537, 559 (1896) (Harlan, J., dissenting).

131. 142 Cong. Rec. 16972 (July 11, 1996) (Rep. Lewis, D-Ga.). To similar effect was Senator Kennedy's speech in the Senate. See ibid., 22438–39 (Sept. 10, 1996) (Sen. Kennedy, D-Mass.).

132. Ibid., 17070 (July 12, 1996) (Rep. Barr, R-Ga.).

133. Ibid., 16972 (Rep. Coburn, R-Okla.).

134. Ibid., 22447 (Sept. 10, 1996) (Sen. Byrd, D-W.Va.).

135. See *Edwards v. Aguillard*, 482 U.S. 578 (1987) (striking down state "creationism" law because its stated goal, advancement of science education, was a "sham" and its apparent goal was the advancement of a particular religious belief). I do not think that DOMA flunks the *Aguillard* establishment clause test, in large part because its antigay purpose is one shared by many nonreligious and many different religious groups alike.

136. Defense of Marriage Act, Pub. Law No. 104–199, 110 Stat. 2419 (1996).

137. See Chad Blair, "The Gospel According to Gabbard," *Honolulu Weekly*, January 27, 1999 (a detailed retrospective on Gabbard).

138. Mary Adamski, "Christian Groups at Odds over Ads Against Same-Sex," *Honolulu Star Bulletin*, October 1, 1998 (describing several ads and criticism of them by progay churches).

139. "What Do You Think?" *Honolulu Star Bulletin*, December 4, 1996 (quoting ordinary voters, most of whom opposed same-sex marriage). See also Mary Adamski, "Clergy Rebut Charge of Intolerance," *Honolulu Star Bulletin*, October 2, 1998.

140. Mike Yuen, "Same-Sex Marriage Losing Big," *Honolulu Star Bulletin*, August 14, 1998 (reporting big margins in favor of ballot question and quoting voters supporting it).

141. Haw. Const. Art. 23 (adopted 1998).

142. *Baehr v. Miike*, 994 P.2d 566 (Haw. 1999) (per curiam).

143. See Eskridge, *Gaylaw*, 228–31, appreciating and responding to Richard A. Posner, "Should There Be Homosexual Marriage? And If So, Who Should Decide?" 95 *Mich. L. Rev.* 1578 (1997) (reviewing Eskridge, *Case for Same-Sex Marriage*).

144. *Tumeo v. University of Alaska*, 1995 WL 238359 (Alaska Super. Ct. Jan. 11, 1995). Judge Meg Greene not only ruled that the state could not constitutionally discriminate against same-sex couples in providing partnership benefits only to different-sex married state employees, but suggested, in dictum, that the state same-sex marriage bar could be questioned on similar grounds. See ibid., slip opin, 7 n. 8.

145. Alaska Stat. § 25.05.011(a). See 1995 Alaska Op. Att'y Gen. 663–95–0451, 1995 WL 341035 (March 31, 1995) (concluding that the gender-neutral marriage law did not recognize same-sex marriage).

146. *Brause v. Bureau of Vital Statistics*, 1998 WL 88743 (Alaska Super. Ct. Feb. 27, 1998).

147. The details of the Alaska legislative response to *Brause* are set forth, albeit with an antigay slant, in Kevin Clarkson, David Orgon Coolidge, and William Duncan, "The Alaska Marriage Amendment: The People's Choice on the Last Frontier," 16 *Alaska L. Rev.* 213 (1999).

148. Senate Floor Statement in Support of S.J.R. 42, Sen. Loren Leman (R-Anchorage), April 16, 1998, quoted ibid., 232. Senator Leman prefaced this argument with the confession that several members of his extended family, plus some friends, are "homosexual" and that he had "compassion" for these people. Ibid.

149. See Liz Ruskin, "Same-Sex Marriage Foes Given $500,000; Mormon Gift Infuriates Opponents," *Anchorage Daily News*, October 3, 1998, at F2.

150. See, e.g., Maureen Clark, "Bishops Back Single-Sex Marriage Ban," *Anchorage Daily News*, September 8, 1998, at B1.

151. "Opinion—Ballot Measure 2: A Yes Vote—But a Complex Choice," *Anchorage Daily News*, October 25, 1998, at F2.

152. The Alaska Supreme Court deleted a second sentence in the proposed amendment ("No provision of this constitution may be interpreted to require the State to recognize or permit marriage between individuals of the same sex.") on the ground that it violated the single-subject rule. See *Bess v. Ulmer*, 1999 WL 619092 (Alaska Sup. Ct. August 17, 1999) (reaffirming an earlier order of September 22, 1998).

153. *Brause v. Bureau of Vital Statistics*, 1999 WL 619092 (Alaska Super. Ct. September 22, 1999).

CHAPTER 2

1. The account of Holly Puterbaugh and Lois Farnham is taken from an interview I conducted with them at their home on October 6, 2000.

2. "Traditional Marriage Wins Big in Hawaii," *SPHI News*, November–December. 1998, at 1–8 (interview with Michael Gabbard). SPHI is an acronym for Stop Promoting Homosexuality International, and I viewed this newsletter at <www.sphi.com/newsletters/9812> (on October 1, 2000).

3. My references to Nina Beck and Stacy Jolles are taken from an interview I conducted with them at their home on October 7, 2000.

4. The account that follows is largely taken from an interview I conducted with Beth Robinson on October 6, 2000.

5. See 1989 Vt. Sess. Laws (Adj. Sess.) No. 172, codified at 13 V.S.A. § 1455. 1999 Vt. Sess. Laws No. 56, added a new part authorizing injunctions to protect citizens against hate acts, 13 V.S.A. § 1458 et seq., and amending § 1455 to include gender orientation.

6. See 1991 Vt. Sess. Laws Act No. 48, adding "sexual orientation" as a basis for discrimination claims in 9 V.S.A. § 4502 (public accommodations) and § 4503 (housing); 21 V.S.A. § 495(a) (employment).

7. *In re Adoption of B. L. V. B.*, 628 A.2d 1271 (Vt. 1993), codified by 1995 Vt. Sess. Laws (Adj. Sess.) No. 161, 15A V.S.A. § 1–102(b).

8. See Diane Derby, "Political Climate Was Right for Court's Ruling on Gay Rights," *Rutland Herald*, December 26, 1999, at 1. This and other *Rutland Herald* news stories about the ruling can be found on the newspaper's website, <www.rutlandherald.com/vtruling> (as of October 1, 2000).

9. See Vermont Labor Relations Board Dec., Grievance of B.M., S.S., C.M., and J.R., Docket No. 92–32.

10. Interview with Farnham and Puterbaugh.

11. My references to Peter Harrigan and his partner, Stan Baker, are based upon a telephone interview I conducted with them on October 16, 2000.

12. Vermont Freedom to Marry Task Force, Video, *The Freedom to Marry: A Green Mountain View* (Joseph Watson, prod., 1996).

13. Interview with Baker and Harrigan.

14. See Diane Derby, "Same-Sex Marriage Ruling at Issue," *Rutland Herald*, July 22, 1997, at 1, 10.

15. Interview with Beck and Jolles. My notes do not reflect which mother made the statement in text, but she was speaking for both women.

16. *Baker v. State*, No. S1009–97 CnC (Chittenden Sup. Ct. Dec. 19, 1997), rev'd, 744 A.2d 865 (Vt. 1999).

17. Ibid., 15 (first quotation in text), 16 (second quotation).

18. *Zablocki v. Redhail*, 434 U.S. 374, 385 (1978). See also *Turner v. Safley*, 482 U.S. 78 (1987), extending the right to marry to prisoners and rejecting the state's arguments based on administrative considerations in running a prison. Chapter 1 discusses these cases in greater detail.

19. Vt. Const., 1777, ch. I, art. 7.

20. Brief for Appellants, 16–20, *Baker v. State*, 744 A.2d 865 (Vt. 1999) (No. 98–32); Willi Paul Adams, *The First American Constitutions*, 187 (1980) (early common benefits provisions were radically egalitarian).

21. Brief of Appellee State of Vermont, 42–45, *Baker* (No. 98–32). The state's other justifications were: "supporting marriage and protecting it from destabilizing changes," 45–50; "promoting the institution of mar-

riage because it unites men and women," 50–54; "promoting child rearing in a setting that provides both male and female role models," 54–55, similar to the main rationale offered by Hawaii in *Baehr*; "adopting marriage statutes that are aligned with the uniform policies of its sister states," 55–57; and "minimizing the use of surrogacy contracts and sperm donors to avoid, inter alia, the impact and cost of increased child support and visitation disputes," 57–60. Judge Levitt had considered and rejected all these other justifications.

22. Brief of The Roman Catholic Diocese of Burlington and the Burlington Stake of the Church of Jesus Christ of Latter-Day Saints, 2–3, *Baker* (No. 98–32). Accord, Brief of *Amicus Curiae* Peter Brady et al., 24–28, *Baker* (authored by Professor David Orgon Coolidge, Director of the Marriage Law Project at Catholic University); Brief *Amicus Curiae* American Center for Law and Justice, 5–12, *Baker*; Brief *Amicus Curiae* Agudath Israel of America, 3–7, *Baker*.

23. The oral argument, held on November 18, 1998, was videotaped by the Vermont Freedom to Marry Task Force, and a copy of the videotape can be obtained from them.

24. *Perez v. Lippold*, 198 P.2d 17 (Cal. 1948).

25. *Loving v. Virginia*, 387 U.S. 1 (1967), discussed and quoted in chapter 1.

26. The generalizations about the state's oral argument are based upon my viewing of the videotape described in note 23. My comments about the reaction by the state's "friends" are based on conversations (but not formal interviews) I have had with Professor Lynn Wardle and others who worked on briefs supporting the state. For the record, I regard Wardle as a friendly acquaintance.

27. The statements in text concerning the impressions left by the justices' questions are drawn from my interviews with the six plaintiffs (all of whom attended the oral argument) and with attorney Robinson, and from my own viewing of the videotape of the argument.

28. *Baker*, 744 A.2d 864 (Vt. 1999).

29. Ibid., 875–77. Amestoy supported this textual inference with an examination of the historical circumstances surrounding the adoption of the 1777 constitution. Cf. ibid., 877 n. 9 (contrasting less egalitarian construction of common benefits clauses in some other state constitutions).

30. Ibid., 876–77. Concurring Justices Dooley and Johnson followed the tiered approach of the U.S. Supreme Court and, further, would have ruled that sexual orientation classifications require heightened scrutiny of the state exclusion of lesbian and gay couples from marriage. See ibid., 889–97 (Dooley, J., concurring in the judgment); 905–12 (Johnson, J., concurring in part and dissenting in part).

31. Ibid., 879 (opinion for the court).

32. See ibid., 881–82.

33. See ibid., 885–86.

34. Ibid., 887.

35. Ibid., 898 (Johnson, J., dissenting in part).

36. Ibid., 901, citing *Watson v. City of Memphis*, 373 U.S. 526, 532–33 (1963) (requiring prompt remedy for unconstitutional segregation of public parks).

37. See ibid., 887–88 (opinion for the court). See generally William N. Eskridge Jr. and Philip P. Frickey, *Legislation: Statutes and the Creation of Public Policy*, 441–47 (2d ed. 1997) (examples of "prospective" state court decisions, whose effective dates lay in the future so that legislatures could rewrite the statutory scheme).

38. The quotations in text are all taken from the interviews I conducted with the six plaintiffs.

39. See Adam Lisberg and Nancy Remsen, "Legislators Embrace Idea of 'Domestic Partnership,'" *Burlington Free Press*, December 21, 1999. This and other news stories about the ruling can be found on the newspaper's website, <www.burlingtonfreepress.com/samesex> (as of October 1, 2000). For other legislator reactions along the same lines, see John Flowers, "Same-Sex Ruling Celebrated," *Addison Independent*, December 23, 1999.

40. See Lisberg and Remsen, "Legislators Embrace Idea of 'Domestic Partnership.'"

41. See Abbey Duke, "Opponents Gather Forces for Messy Battle with the Legislature," *Burlington Free Press*, Dec. 22, 1999.

42. See Flowers, "Same-Sex Ruling Celebrated" (quoting the bishop).

43. The quotation in text and the remainder in this paragraph are all taken from "Local Reaction to the Vermont State Supreme Court's Decision," *Burlington Free Press*, December 22, 1999.

44. See Jack Hoffman, "Poll: Majority Say No to Same-Sex Benefits," *Rutland Herald*, January 2000.

45. The account of the legislative history of the Vermont Civil Unions Law that follows draws from the public record, most of which is available on the internet, and from interviews I conducted with many of the leading participants. A most useful account that complements mine was published as this book went to press, Michael Mello, "For Today I'm Gay: The Unfinished Battle for Same-Sex Marriage in Vermont," 25 *Vt. L. Rev.* 149–275 (2000).

46. Interview with Thomas A. Little, October 6, 2000.

47. The House Judiciary Committee hearings are listed on the Vermont Legislative Bill Tracking System website for "Civil Unions," <www.leg.state.vt.us/baker/baker.cfm> (as of October 1, 2000).

48. Chair Little's weekly summaries of testimony can be found on the Vermont Legislative Bill Tracking System website for "Civil Unions," <www.leg.state.vt.us/baker/baker.cfm> (as of October 1, 2000).

49. Memorandum from Thomas A. Little, Chair, to House Judiciary Committee Members, January 4, 2000.

50. See Thomas A. Little, "Summary: Work of the House Judiciary Committee for the Week of January 11–14, 2000."

51. See Thomas A. Little, "Summary: Work of the House Judiciary Committee for the Week of January 17–20, 2000." This memorandum not only summarizes the testimony of witnesses but is also an excellent synthesis of the main legal consequences of marriage and, in all probability, domestic partnership in other states.

52. See ibid., 2 (summarizing Cott's testimony, drawn from her then-forthcoming book, *Public Vows: A History of Marriage and the Nation* [2000]); Unofficial Transcript of the Testimony of Professor Nancy Cott to the Vermont House Judiciary Committee, January 17, 2000.

53. See Written Statement of Professor Lynn Wardle to the Judiciary Committee of the Vermont House of Representatives, January 20, 2000, at 3.

54. Ibid., 14.

55. Bishop Angell's letter is excerpted in an editorial, "More Time Is Needed to Cogitate Ruling," *Addison County Independent*, January 27, 2000.

56. Letter from Bishop Mary Adelia McLeod to Vermont Episcopalian Congregations. Stan Baker provided me with excerpts from this letter.

57. See Audiotape of the Joint Public Hearing of the Judiciary Committees of the Vermont House of Representatives and Senate, January 25, 2000 (oral statement of Rev. Lake). The audiotape can be obtained from the Vermont Legislative Council.

58. Ibid. (oral statement of Shirley Garvey, married forty-nine years and mother of seven children).

59. Ibid. (oral statement of Rev. Kowalski).

60. Ibid. (oral statement of Ken Christiansen).

61. See Audiotape of the Joint Public Hearing of the Judiciary Committees of the Vermont House of Representatives and Senate, February 1, 2000 (available from the Vermont Legislative Council); Jack Hoffman, "No Hint of Compromise at Second Hearing," *Rutland Herald*, February 2, 2000 (reporting that second hearing was reprise of arguments and passionate intensity of the first). As before, most of the opponents of same-sex marriage relied on biblical and sectarian arguments: because homosexuality violated the laws of God or was "unnatural," the state should certainly not sanction such unions.

62. See Heather Stephenson, "Big Crowd Rallies Against Gay Marriage," *Rutland Herald*, February 2, 2000.

63. See Carey Goldberg, "Forced to Act on Gay Marriage, Vermont Finds Itself Deeply Split," *N.Y. Times*, February 3, 2000, at A16.

64. Transcript of a Meeting of the Judiciary Committee of the Vermont House of Representatives, February 9, 2000 (oral statement of Rep. Little, Chair).

65. See Greg Johnson, "Vermont Civil Unions: The New Language of Marriage," 25 *Vt. L. Rev.* 15, 40–41 (2000), quoting Representative Michael Vinton, in a colloquy with Professor David Coolidge, who had coauthored the *Baker* brief in support of traditional marriage and was vigorously opposing proposals for state recognition of same-sex marriages or unions.

66. Transcript of February 9 Judiciary Committe Meeting (oral statement of Rep. Edwards).

67. Audiotape of January 25 Public Hearing (oral statement of Kelly Long).

68. Ibid. (oral statement of Donna Lescoe).

69. See interview with Thomas Little.

70. Transcript of February 9 Judiciary Committe Meeting (oral statements of Reps. Lippert, Hingtgen, and MacKinnon).

71. Ibid. (oral statement of Rep. Hingtgen). The separate but equal argument was also the basis for Representative Bill MacKinnon's opposition to domestic partnership. The argument had been mentioned throughout the public hearings, plaintiffs' counsel endorsed it, and its details had been laid out for the committee in testimony by Harvey Golubuck, the executive director of the Vermont Human Rights Commission. See "Summary: Work of the House Judiciary Committee for the Week of February 1–4, 2000," 6.

72. Transcript of February 9 Judiciary Committee Meeting (oral statement of Rep. Cathy Voyer) (emphasis added).

73. Johnson, "Vermont Civil Unions," 44, points out that the term *Contrat d'Union Civil* (contract of civil union) was proposed in a 1992 French bill for recognizing same-sex relationships.

74. See "Summary: Work of the House Judiciary Committee for the Week of February 8–11, 2000," at 1.

75. H. 847, as introduced, § 1 (findings). The bill as passed by the House (with slight changes) can be found on the Vermont Legislative Bill Tracking System website, <www.leg.state.vt.us/baker/baker.cfm> (as of October 1, 2000).

76. See ibid., §§ 3–21 (adding a civil union chapter to the Vermont Code and amending various statutes to conform to the new policy).

77. See ibid., §§ 26–35 (adding a reciprocal beneficiary chapter to the Vermont Code and amending various statutes to conform to the new policy).

78. See ibid., § 37.

79. My discussion of the first day of the House debate is drawn from the Audiotape of the Debate of H.847 by the Vermont House of Representatives, March 15, 2000. The tape can be obtained from the Vermont Legislative Council.

80. Like other legislative proposals, the Robb resolution quoted in the text can be found in the *Journal of the Vermont House*, H.R. 37, 65th Gen. Ass., Bienn. Sess. (Vt.), March 15, 2000. The Journal can be viewed at <www.leg.state.vt.us/2000/journal/hj000315.htm> (as of October 31, 2000).

81. The referendum proposed by Representatives Starr and Schiavone would have posed three questions to the voters: (1) Shall the General Assembly amend Vermont law to allow same-sex marriage? (2) Shall the General Assembly provide for domestic partnership whereby same-sex couples cannot marry but can be given

the same benefits and obligations? (3) Shall the General Assembly initiate an amendment to the Vermont Constitution to provide that marriage is between one man and one woman? The roll call votes for the Starr-Schiavone and other proposed amendments can be found on The Vermont Legislative Bill Tracking System website, <www.leg.state.vt.us/baker/baker.cfm> (as of October 1, 2000). The votes can also be found in the Vermont Legislative Journal.

82. The Town Meeting Day votes are reported in Jack Hoffman, "Reactions Vary to Marriage Votes," *Rutland Herald*, March 11, 2000.

83. Audiotape of the March 15 House Debate (statement of Rep. Flory).

84. Ibid. (oral statement of Rep. Brooks).

85. My account of Lippert's speech is from the Audiotape of the March 15 House Debate, supplemented by a newspaper article, "Plea for Justice," *Valley News*, March 16, 2000.

86. Another amendment, proposed by Representative Perry, would have expanded the committee's bill to allow some blood relatives to enter into civil unions and some nonrelatives to become reciprocal beneficiaries. Representative Little opposed the concededly friendly amendment on the grounds that the committee bill sought to create a big distinction between the romantic civil union and the nonromantic reciprocal beneficiary provisions; moreover, blood relatives already have many legal entitlements. The amendment went down, 16 to 98.

87. Audiotape of the March 15 House Debate (oral statement of Rep. Corren).

88. Ibid. (oral statement of Rep. Nancy Sheltra). Representative Sheltra was the most vigorous opponent of H.847. On February 11, she had introduced a resolution to impeach the justices of the Vermont Supreme Court on the basis of their *Baker* opinion.

89. Ibid. (oral statement of Rep. Mazzariello).

90. Ibid. (oral statement of Rep. Symington).

91. Ibid. (oral statement of Rep. Rusten).

92. My discussion of the second day of the House debate is drawn from the Audiotape of the Debate of H.847 by the Vermont House of Representatives, Mar. 16, 2000. The tape can be obtained from the Vermont Legislative Council.

93. See Nancy Remsen and Adam Lisberg, "Bill Survives Compromise, Delay Tactics; Marriage Defintion Added to Legislation to Gain Support," *Burlington Free Press*, March 17, 2000.

94. Audiotape of the March 16 House Debate (oral statement of Rep. Flory).

95. Ibid. (oral statement of Rep. Kainen).

96. The House vote is taken from the Audiotape of the March 16 House Debate and from the Vermont Legislative Bill Tracking System website, <www.leg.state.vt.us/baker/baker.cfm> (as of October 1, 2000). For analysis of particular groups and members, see "Women Lawmakers Provide Key Votes in Civil Union Passage," *Valley News*, March 19, 2000; "Civil Union Supporters Were a Diverse Bunch," *Valley News*, March 19, 2000.

97. "Civil Unions Bill Clears House," *Valley News*, March 17, 2000 (quoting Rep. Milne).

98. "11 of 18 Valley Members," *Valley News*, March 17, 2000 (quoting Rep. MacKinnon).

99. Mello, "For Today, I'm Gay," 188–212, is an exhaustive and illuminating collection of quotations from letters to the editor, most written in late March, April, and May 2000. The generalizations in text draw heavily from Professor Mello's most useful effort.

100. Blake Frost, "Churches Who Lead People Astray," *Rutland Herald*, March 9, 2000, at 8.

101. See Mello, "For Today, I'm Gay," 189–93.

102. John Lynch, "Fight Sin, Don't Legalize It," *Valley News*, April 12, 2000.

103. See Mello, "For Today, I'm Gay," 193, 202, 204–5 (quoting letters making analogies to Sodom and Gomorrah and forwarding other apocalyptic claims).

104. See S.248 (January 5, 2000). The bill is reproduced on the Vermont Legislative Bill Tracking System website, <www.leg.state.vt.us/baker/baker.cfm> (as of October 1, 2000).

105. Ross Sneyd, "Two Senators Get an Earful on Civil Unions," *Rutland Herald*, April 2000.

106. The Senate Judiciary Committee hearings and the names and organizations of witnesses are reported in the Vermont Legislative Bill Tracking System website for Civil Unions, <www.leg.state.vt.us/baker/baker.cfm> (as of October 1, 2000).

107. See Ross Sneyd, "Clergy Air Views to Senate," *Rutland Herald*, March 30, 2000 (quoting Bishop Angell's testimony, which was not transcribed officially).

108. Ibid. (quoting Rev. Bayley's testimony, which was not transcribed officially).

109. The quotations in text are all from Tracy Schmaler, "Foes of Civil Unions Hold Capitol Rally," *Rutland Herald*, April 7, 2000.

110. See "Summary of Senate Judiciary Committee Strike-All Amendment to H.847" (April 2000). The summary can be found on The Vermont Legislative Bill Tracking System website, <www.leg.state.vt.us/baker/baker.cfm> (October 1, 2000).

111. See Adam Lisberg, "Panel Clears Way for Civil Unions; Senate Judiciary Committee OKs Largely Intact Bill," *Burlington Free Press*, April 14, 2000.

112. My discussion of the Senate consideration of proposed constitutional amendments is drawn from the Audiotape of the Debate of H.847 by the Vermont Senate, April 18, 2000. The tape can be obtained from the Vermont Legislative Council.

113. The constitutional amendments proposed by Senators Canns and Illuzzi are set forth in the Audiotape of the April 18 Senate debate, and in the Vermont Legislative Journal (2000).

114. Ibid. (statement of Sen. Canns).

115. *Romer v. Evans*, 517 U.S. 620 (1996) (invalidating a state initiative depriving lesbians, bisexuals, and gay men a broad range of rights).

116. Audiotape of the April 18 Senate Debate. (statement of Sen. Sears).

117. Robert Bolt, *A Man for All Seasons* 65–67 (1962); see Larry Alexander, "Constitutional Tragedies and Giving Refuge to the Devil," in *Constitutional Stupidities, Constitutional Tragedies* 115–20 (William N. Eskridge Jr. and Sanford Levinson, eds. 1998).

118. Audiotape of the April 18 Senate Debate (statement of a male senator I could not identify).

119. Ibid. (statement of Sen. MacDonald).

120. Ibid. (statement of Sen. Sears, introducing H.847).

121. Ibid. (statement of Sen. Leddy, quoting the letter from Helena Blair).

122. Ibid. (statement of Sen. Ptashnik).

123. Ibid. (statement of Sen. Ready).

124. Ibid. (statement of Sen. MacDonald).

125. My discussion of the final day of the Senate's deliberation is drawn from the Audiotape of the Debate of H.847 by the Vermont Senate, April 19, 2000. The tape can be obtained from the Vermont Legislative Council.

126. Ibid. (statement of Sen. Ankeney).

127. Ibid. (statement of Sen. Rivers).

128. Ibid. (statement of Sen. Illuzzi).

129. Ibid. (statement of Sen. Canns).

130. See Carolyn Lochhead, "Gay Unions Win Final Vote in Vermont/Governor to Sign Measure Extending Rights of Marriage," *San Francisco Chronicle*, April 26, 2000 (quoting some prayers from the vigil).

131. My discussion of the final House deliberation is drawn from the Audiotape of the Debate of H.847 by the Vermont House, April 25, 2000. The tape can be obtained from the Vermont Legislative Council.

132. See "Privately, Governor Signs Civil Unions Legislation Into Law," *Valley News*, April 27, 2000.

133. See Lochhead, "Gay Unions Win Final Vote" (quoting Rep. Lippert)

134. See Tracy Schmaler and Frederick Bever, "Law Praised, Attacked Around Nation," *Rutland Herald*, Apr. 27, 2000 (quoting Robert Knight, speaker for the Family Research Council).

135. See Interview with Puterbaugh and Farnham.

136. See id.; see also Interview with Beck and Jolles.

137. See Interview with Baker and Harrigan.

138. See Jack Hoffman, "Poll Suggests Limited Fallout from Gay Bill," *Rutland Herald*, May 2000.

139. See "Civilly United in Hartland, Vt.," *Valley News*, July 2, 2000.

140. See Interview with Puterbaugh and Farnham.

141. See Interview with Baker and Harrigan.

142. See Interview with Beck and Jolles.

143. See Carey Goldberg, "Old Tensions Surface Over Civil Unions," *Rutland Herald*, September 3, 2000 (quoting Paronto and Weiss).

144. See Jack Hoffman, "Voters Show Anger over Civil Unions Law," *Rutland Herald*, September 13, 2000.

CHAPTER THREE

1. Robert Wintemute of Kings College, London, sponsored the first International Conference on State Recognition of Same-Sex Unions, July 4–6, 1999. More than one hundred scholars and judges from all around the world attended this conference. The conference proceedings are published as *Legal Recognition of Same-Sex Partnerships: A Study of National, European and International Law,* ed. Robert Wintemute and Mads Andenaes (2001).

2. See 1999 Calif. Stats. ch. 588, codified at Calif. Family Code § 297 et seq.; chapter 1's list of municipal domestic partnership ordinances.

3. See Hawaii's Reciprocal Beneficiaries Act, 1997 Haw. Sess. Laws Act 383 (H.B. 118).

4. See Kees Waaldijk, "Small Change: How the Road to Same-Sex Marriage Got Paved in the Netherlands," in Wintemute and Andenaes, eds., *Legal Recognition of Same-Sex Partnerships.*

5. See *Braschi v. Stahl Assocs.*, 74 N.Y.2d 201 (1989).

6. See *In re Kowalski*, 478 N.W.2d 790 (Minn. App. 1991).

7. See *Whorton v. Dillingham*, 248 Cal. Rptr. 405 (Cal. App. 1988). But see *Coon v. Joseph*, 237 Cal. Rptr. 873 (Cal. App. 1987) (no right to sue for emotional distress arising from injury to same-sex partner).

8. The best source for the same-sex marriage struggle in Scandinavia is Darren Spedale, *Nordic Bliss: The Danish Experience with "Gay Marriage,"*chs. 2–3 (a wonderful 1999 book draft still seeking a publisher). Other useful sources are David Bradley, *Family Law and Political Culture: Scandinavian Laws in Comparative Perspective* (1996); B. Hansen and Henning Jørgensen, "The Danish Partnership Law," in *The Third Pink Book* 86 (A. Hendricks ed. 1993); Ingrid Lund-Anderson, "The Legal Position of Homosexuals: Cohabitation and Registered Partnership in Scandinavia," in *The Changing Family*, 397–404 (J. Eekelaar and Th. Nhlapa eds. 1998); Linda Nielsen, "Family Rights and the 'Registered Partnership' in Denmark," 4 *Int'l J.L. & Fam.* 297 (1990).

9. For the early history of lesbian and gay pressure for same-sex partnerships, see Spedale, *Nordic Bliss*, ch. 2.

10. See *First Report of the Marriage Committee,* 19 (1973), discussed in Bradley, *Scandinavian Laws*, 152.

11. See *Eighth Report of the Marriage Committee: Cohabitation Without Marriage* (1980), discussed in Spedale, *Nordic Bliss*, ch. 2.

12. In 1987, the Danish Parliament added sexual orientation to the hate expression crime, Penal Law art. 266, and to the public accommodation Anti-Discrimination Act of 1971. See International Lesbian and Gay Association (ILGA), *World Legal Survey: Denmark,* <www.ilga.org> (as of November 1, 2000).

13. See Commission for the Enlightenment of the Situation of Homosexuals in Society, *The Conditions of Homosexuals* (1988), discussed in Bradley, *Scandinavian Laws*, 152–53; Hansen and Jørgensen, "Danish Partnership Law," 91–92.

14. The quotations from the parliamentary debates are taken from Spedale, *Nordic Bliss*, ch. 2.

15. The Danish Registered Partnership Act, No. 372, June 7, 1989.

16. For the Scandinavian countries, the best sources are Bradley, *Scandinavian Laws,* 95–105, 217–22; and Spedale, *Nordic Bliss*, ch. 9.

17. Norway in 1972 repealed Penal Code § 213, which forbade sexual acts between men. See Bradley, *Scandinavian Laws*, 217–18; ILGA, *World Legal Survey: Norway,* <www.ilga.org> (as of November 1, 2000) (compare the entries for Denmark [age of consent equalized 1978], Sweden [1976], and Finland).

18. See Norway's Penal Code §§ 135a (prohibiting disparagement on the basis of sexual orientation), 349a (prohibiting sexual orientation discrimination by businesses).

19. Norway's Ministry of Children and Family Affairs, *Proposition for a Law on Registered Partnerships,* 42–43 (July 1992), as translated in Bradley, *Scandinavian Laws*.

20. The ministry referred to arguments by opponents that homosexuality was condemned in the Bible, but responded that the few biblical references were critical of sex for its own sake, and not same-sex committed unions. Ibid., 38–39.

21. Ibid., 35.

22. Ibid., 53.

23. See Spedale, *Nordic Bliss*, ch. 9.

24. Sweden's Commission on Homosexuality, *Homosexuals and Society,* 275 (1984), as translated in Bradley, *Scandinavian Laws*.

25. The Homosexual Cohabitees Act of 1987, Lag 1987: No. 813; see ILGA, *World Legal Survey: Sweden* <www.ilga.org> (as of November 1, 2000).

26. Sweden's Commission on Homosexual Partnerships, Report, *Partnership,* 21ff. (1993) as translated in Bradley, *Scandinavian Laws*.

27. Ibid., 30

28. The Registered Partnership Act, Lag 1994: No. 1117.

29. See ILGA, *World Legal Survey: Greenland,* <www.ilga.org> (as of November 1, 2000).

30. See ILGA, *World Legal Survey: Iceland* <www.ilga.org> (as of November 1, 2000).

31. Although the account of the Dutch history in the text is drawn from several sources, the best source for background information is Waaldijk, "Small Change: How the Road to Same-Sex Marriage Got Paved in the Netherlands."

32. See Netherlands Association for the Integration of Homosexuality COC, "Brief Summary of COC's History" (1998), which can be viewed at their website, <www.coc.nl> (as of November 1, 2000).

33. See Law of April 8, 1971.

34. See ILGA, *World Legal Survey: The Netherlands* <www.ilga.org> (as of November 1, 2000).

35. See Commission on Civil Marriage, *Opening Civil Marriage to Same-Sex Couples* (October 28, 1997).

36. As amended by the government on May 3 and August 4, 2000, the proposed Act on the Opening up of Marriage has been translated by Professor Kees Waaldijk and may be found at his website, <www.ruljis.leidenuniv.nl/user/cwaaldij/www/NHR/transl-marr.html> (as of November 1, 2000).

37. Job Cohen, State-Secretary for Justice, "Explanatory Memorandum," Parliamentary Paper 26672, nr. 3, § 1 (July 8, 1999), translated by Professor Kees Waaldijk and accessible on his website, referenced in the previous note.

38. Ibid., § 3 ("Relation to Registered Partnership; Evaluation").

39. Ibid., § 2 ("Equalities and Differences between Marriage for Persons of Different Sex and Marriage for Persons of the Same Sex").

40. *Staatsblad* 2001, nos. 9 and 10 (January 11, 2001). The *Staatsblad* is the official journal of statutes adopted in the Netherlands. I am indebted to Professor Kees Waaldijk of the University of Leiden for the legal cites and for translations of the new Dutch marriage and adoption legislation.

41. The (Same-Sex Marriage and Adoption) Adjustment Law of March 8, 2001, *Staatsblad* 2001, no. 128, can be viewed at <www.minjust.nl:8080/a_BELEID/fact/fact/htm> (as of March 15, 2001), as well as <www.ruljis.leidenuniv.nl/user/cwaaldij/www> (as of March 15, 2001).

42. The Netherlands Civil Code, Book 1, art. 30(1), added by Act of December 21, 2000 concerning the opening up of marriage for persons of the same sex, *Staatsblad* 2001, no. 9 (January 11, 2001). An unofficial translation of the Act on the Opening Up of Marriage can be found at <ruljis.leidenuniv.nl/user/cwaaldij//www/NHR/transl-marr.html> (as of March 31, 2001).

43. There is no absolutely up-to-date source for the legal status of same-sex relationships among the various countries of the world. The best source is the ILGA's *World Legal Survey*, which includes references for

each country and is web-accessible at <www.ilga.org>. The website, unfortunately, runs a year or more behind events. Because this area of law is fast-changing, Arthur Leonard's *Lesbian/Gay Law Notes* are particularly useful, especially now that Professor Robert Wintemute has joined forces with Leonard to give the publication international depth. It can be accessed at <www.qrd.org/www/legal/lgln>.

44. See Elspeth Guild, "Free Movement and Same-Sex Relationships: Existing Law and Article 13 EC," in Wintemute and Andenaes, eds., *Legal Recognition of Same-Sex Partnerships,* discussing the free movement (articles 3, 39–55) and nondiscrimination (articles 12–13, the latter having been rewritten to include sexual orientation, plus article 141).

45. See *Grant v. South-West Trains, Ltd.,* Court of Justice of the European Communities, February 17, 1998, which ruled that denying spousal benefits to a female employee for her same-sex partner, when they were given to female employees with unmarried male partners, was *not* "discrimination based on sex" in violation of article 119 of the treaty. An alternative source of rights for same-sex couples might be the European Convention on Human Rights, which is applicable to most European states and all those in the EU. The convention is a major vehicle for eliminating outlier sodomy laws and offers potentially strong support for same-sex couples as well. See generally Robert Wintemute, *Sexual Orientation and Human Rights: The United States Constitution, the European Convention, and the Canadian Charter,* 91–149 (1995).

46. The history of the New South Wales Property (Relationships) Legislation Amendment of 1999 is told in Jenni Millbank and Wayne Morgan, "Let Them Eat Cake and Ice Cream: Wanting Something 'More' from the Relationship Recognition Menu," in Wintemute and Andenaes, eds., *Legal Recognition of Same-Sex Partnerships.*

47. The background of the French PaCS law is taken from Daniel Borrillo, "The 'Pacte Civil de Solidarité' in France: Midway between Marriage and Cohabitation," in Wintemute and Andenaes, eds., *Legal Recognition of Same-Sex Partnerships.*

48. See Loi no. 93–121, January 21, 1993.

49. *Vilela v. Weil,* Cour de cassation, Chambre civile 3e, 17 Dec. 1997, Bull. Civ. 1997.III.151, No. 225, Dalloz.1998.Jur.111.

50. C. Fourest and F. Venner, *Les anti-PaCS ou la dernière croisade homophobe* (1999).

51. The quotations in the text are from Borrillo, "The 'Pacte Civil de Solidarité' in France."

52. See Conseil Decision No. 99–419 DC, November 9, 1999, which can be found <www.conseil-constitutionnel.fr/decision/1999/99419/index.htm> (as of November 1, 2000).

53. Loi no. 99–944, 15 Nov. 1999, relative au pacte civil de solidarité, <http://www.legifrance.gouv.fr/html/frame_codes_lois_reglt.htm> (as of November 1, 2000) (dossiers législatifs). For a comprehensive analysis of the new law, see Sylvie Dibos-Lacroux, *PACS: Le guide pratique* (2000). For a thoughtful collection of essays, see *Au-delà du PaCS: l'expertise familiale à l'épreuve de l'homosexualité* (Daniel Borrillo et al. eds. 1999).

54. See Code civile new art. 515–1 (added by Loi no. 99–944, § 1).

55. See ibid., new art. 515–4.

56. See ibid., new art. 515–5.

57. See Code général des impôts new art. 6(1). Joint taxation of their combined wealth begins immediately; ibid., new arts. 885A, 1723 ter-00B.

58. See Loi no. 89–462, July 6, 1989, art. 14 (amended by Loi no. 99–944).

59. See Code de sécurité sociale art. 361–4 (amended by Loi no. 99–944).

60. See Suzanne Daley, "French Couples Take Plunge That Falls Short of Marriage," *N.Y. Times,* April 18, 2000.

61. See "German Parliament OK's DP," Nov. 10, 2000, PlanetOut.com, <icq.planetout.com/news/article-print.hmtl?2000/11/10/1> (as of March 14, 2001).

62. See Alon Harel, "Gay Rights in Israel: A New Era?" 1 *Int'l J. Discrim. & Law* 261 (1996); see also ILGA, *World Legal Survey: Israel,* <www.ilga.org> (as of November 1, 2000); Lee Walzer, *Between Sodom and Eden: A Gay Journey Through Today's Changing Israel* (2000).

63. *El-Al Israel Airlines v. Danilowitz,* High Court of Justice 721/94, 48 Piskei-Din 749 (Israel May 4, 1994), translated <www.tau.ac.il/law/aeyalgross/legal_materials.htm> (as of January 31, 2001). For an in-depth discussion of the case, see Aeyal M. Gross, "Challenges to Compulsory Heterosexuality: Recognition and Non-Recognition of Same-Sex Couples in Israeli Law," in Wintemute and Andenaes, eds., *Legal Recognition of Same-Sex Partnerships.*

64. *Danilowitz,* opinion of Barak, J., ¶ 15.

65. Ibid., opinion of Dorner, J. A third Justice, Yaakov Kedmi, vigorously dissented. He maintained that a same-sex partner simply cannot be considered a "spouse." Such a reading does violence to the Hebrew language as well as Israeli tradition; ibid., dissenting opinion of Kedmi, J., ¶¶ 1, 7.

66. See Alon Harel, "The Rise and Fall of the Israeli Gay Legal Revolution," 31 *Colum. Human Rights L. Rev.* 443 (2000), for the political response to *Danilowitz,* and Amit Kama, "From *Terra Incognita* to *Terra Firma*: The Logbook of the Voyage of Gay Men's Community into the Israeli Public Sphere," 38 *J. Homosexuality* 133 (2000), for the media response.

67. *Steiner v. Pensions Officer,* Family Appeal 8/94 (Mag. Court, Tel-Aviv), discussed in Gross, "Same-Sex Couples in Israeli Law."

68. *Steiner v. Israel Defense Forces,* Various Appeals 369/94 (Tel-Aviv Dist. Court 1994), described and discussed in Gross, "Same-Sex Couples in Israeli Law."

69. See ILGA, *World Legal Survey: Israel.*

70. See *Fitzpatrick v. Sterling Housing Ass'n Ltd.*, [1999] 4 All E.R. 705 (H.L.), especially the opinion of Lord Slynn of Hadley.

71. Decision 14/1995, Constitutional Court of Hungary, Mar. 13, 1995.

72. South Africa, Constitution of May 8, 1996, Clause 9(3). A similar provision had been included in the Interim Constitution adopted in 1993. See *National Coalition for Gay and Lesbian Equality v. Minister of Justice*, 1999 (1) SA 6 (Const'l Ct. South Africa, Oct. 9, 1998) (interpreting the constitution to override earlier sodomy and unnatural acts law penalizing gay and bisexual men). The opinion can be viewed at <www.concourt.gov.za/archive.html> (as of January 31, 2001).

73. See ILGA, *World Legal Survey: South Africa,* <www.ilga.org> (as of November 1, 2000) (describing the Pretoria High Court decision).

74. See *National Coalition for Gay and Lesbian Equality v. Minister of Home Affairs*, 2000 __ SA __ (Const'l Ct. South Africa, December 2, 1999). The opinion can be viewed at <www.concourt.gov.za/archive.html> (as of January 31, 2001).

75. See Gary Kinsman, *The Regulation of Desire: Sexuality in Canada* (2d ed. 1996) (account of the 1969 reform bill). See also Donald G. Casswell, *Lesbians, Gay Men, and Canadian Law* (1996).

76. E.g., Ontario Family Law Reform Act of 1978, S.O. 1978, ch. 2. The trend described in the text is elaborated in *Miron v. Trudel*, [1995] 13 R.F.L. 4th 1 (Can. Sup. Ct. 1995), which ruled that the Charter forbade discrimination between married and cohabiting partners for purposes of auto insurance. The Alberta Court of Appeal followed *Miron* to require the province to treat cohabiting partners the same as married spouses for purposes of financial support and alimony. See *Taylor v. Rossu*, [1998] 39 R.F.L. 4th 242 (Alb. Ct. App. 1998).

77. See Kinsman, *Regulation of Desire,* 59–68; Kathleen A. Lahey, "Becoming 'Persons' in Canadian Law: Genuine Equality or 'Separate But Equal'?" in Wintemute and Andenaes, eds., *Legal Recognition of Same-Sex Partnerships.*

78. *Egan v. The Queen*, [1995] 2 S.C.R. 513, 124 D.L.R.(4th) 609 (Can. Sup. Ct. 1995).

79. See ibid., 124 D.L.R.(4th) at 620–27 (LaForrest, J., for a plurality of four justices).

80. See ibid., 653–56 (Sopkinka, J., concurring in the judgment).

81. See ibid., 628–53 (L'Heureux-Dubé, J., dissenting), 656–93 (Cory and Iacobucci, JJ., dissenting), 693 (McLachlin, J., dissenting).

82. See Canadian Human Rights Act, RSC 1985, c. H-6, as amended RSC 1996, Bill C-33, in response to *Haig and Birch v. Canada*, [1992] 9 O.R. 495 (Ont. Ct. App. 1992) (holding that § 15 of the Charter required the Human Rights Act to include sexual orientation as a prohibited category).

83. *Vriend v. Alberta*, [1998] 1 S.C.R. 493, 156 D.L.R.(4th) 385 (Can. Sup. Ct. 1998) (twin opinions of Cory and Iacobucci, J.J.).

84. The statement in text is based on conversations I have had with Ms. Rosen and Ms. Radbord.

85. See *M. v. H.*, 171 D.L.R.(4th) 577, 611–21 (Can. Sup. Ct. Mar. 18, 1999) (Cory, J.), distinguishing and possibly rejecting the plurality opinion in *Egan*, which had argued the different treatment not to be "discrimination" under § 15.

86. See ibid., 634–35 (Iacobucci, J.). The government objected that lesbian and gay couples typically enjoy more egalitarian relationships and so do not need the state's protection as much as straight couples do, see ibid., 650–98 (Gonthier, J., dissenting along these lines). Justice Iacobucci responded that the state should therefore classify according to *dependency* rather than *sexual orientation*. The law as written was way under-inclusive (as to lesbian and gay couples where there was a need for protection) as well as overinclusive (as to straight couples without need for protection). Ibid., 635.

87. Ibid., 635 (Iacobucci, J.).

88. Ontario S.O. 1999, ch. 6, discussed in Martha A. McCarthy and Joanna L. Radbord, "Chartering Family Law" (draft, 2000).

89. See Ontario Ministry of the Attorney General, press release, "Ontario protects traditional definition of spouse in legislation necessary because of Supreme Court of Canada decision in *M. and H.*" (October 5, 1999), and Legislative Assembly, *Ontario Hansard* (October 27, 1999) (debate over first reading of bill).

90. Martha A. McCarthy and Joanna L. Radbord, "A Mirage or an Oasis? Giving Substance to Substantive Reality," 28 (draft 2000).

91. Sup. Ct. Can. Bull. Proc., May 26, 2000 (file 25838), discussed in McCarthy and Radbord, "Chartering Family Law."

92. Modernization of Benefits and Obligations Act, S.C. 2000, ch. 12.

93. On the more liberal treatment of same-sex couples in British Columbia, see Donald G. Casswell, "'Any Two Persons' in Canada's Lotusland, British Columbia," in Wintemute and Andenaes, eds., *Legal Recognition of Same-Sex Relationships.*

94. See In the Matter of Applications For Licenses By Persons Of the Same Sex Who Intend To Marry, and In the Matter of the Marriage Act and the Judicial Review Procedure Act, File No. L001944 (Vancouver Registry). See "B.C. Wants to Legalize Same-Sex Marriages," *Vancouver Sun*, July 21, 2000. A parallel case is *EGALE Canada, Inc. v. The Attorney General of Canada*, File No. L002698 (Vancouver Registry).

95. See Adrian Humphreys, "First Gay Marriage Legal, For Now," *Nat'l Post*, (Toronto), January 15, 2001, at A1.

96. See Elizabeth Young-Bruehl, *The Nature of Prejudices* (1996) (antigay prejudice is a Freudian defense mechanism for people who cannot process their own sexual feelings; require rigid gender roles; or need scapegoats to redeem their own inadequacies in life).

97. The procreative complementarity of the sexes is fundamental to traditionalist thinking, e.g., John Finnis, "Law, Morality, and 'Sexual Orientation,'" 69 *Notre Dame L. Rev.* 1049 (1994), but also to much scientific theorizing about gender and sex, e.g., Robert Wright, *The Moral Animal—Why We Are the Way We Are: The New Science of Evolutionary Psychology* (1994).

98. See also chapter 5 of this book, which discusses the "social endowment effect." On the same-sex marriage debate as an argument about language and people's attachment to old linguistic categories, see Mae Kuykendall, "Resistance to Same-Sex Marriage as a Story About Language: Linguistic Failure and the Priority of a Living Language," 34 *Harv. C.R.-C.L. L. Rev.* 385 (1999).

99. See Waaldijk, "Small Change: How the Road to Same-Sex Marriage Got Paved in the Netherlands."

100. Surveys have found that knowing gay people is negatively correlated with having antigay attitudes. See Gregory M. Herek, "Beyond 'Homophobia': A Social Psychological Perspective on Attitudes toward Lesbians and Gay Men," in *Bashers, Baiters and Bigots: Homophobia in American Society,* 1, 13–15 (John P. DeCecco ed. 1985).

101. On the strong persistence of antigay attitudes notwithstanding gay liberation and thousands of coming out stories, see Albert D. Klassen et al., *Sex and Morality in the U.S.: An Empirical Enquiry under the Auspices of The Kinsey Institute,* 165–84 (Hubert J. O'Gorman ed. 1989).

102. That is, one can logically object to adopting an antidiscrimination law that protects people whose conduct (consensual sodomy) is habitually criminal. E.g., *Romer v. Evans,* 517 U.S. 620, 633–35 (1996) (Scalia, J., dissenting)

103. See Spedale, *Nordic Bliss,* ch. 5 (reporting family data from post-1989 Denmark).

104. See William N. Eskridge Jr., *Gaylaw: Challenging the Apartheid of the Closet,* ch. 6 (1999); Klassen et al., *Sex and Morality,* 225–27, 240–41.

105. Cf. Klassen et al., *Sex and Morality,* 227–28, 238–39 (fundamentalist Protestantism most accurately predicts antihomosexual attitudes).

106. See generally William N. Eskridge Jr., "No Promo Homo: The Sedimentation of Antigay Discourse and the Channeling Effect of Judicial Review," 75 *NYU L. Rev.* 1327 (2000).

107. For the most part, American states impose obligations on cohabiting partners, along the lines suggested in *Marvin v. Marvin,* 557 P.2d 106 (Cal. 1976), and do not confer benefits beyond those conferred by domestic partnership. See generally Jana B. Singer, "The Privatization of Family Law," 1992 *Wis. L. Rev.* 1443, for a discussion of *Marvin* and the post-*Marvin* statutes and other developments.

108. See Louisiana Covenant Marriage Act, 1997 La. Acts No. 1380, amending La. Civ. Code arts. 102–103 and Rev. Statute. 9: 234 and 245 (A) (1), and adding new La. Rev. State. tit. 9, bk. I, tit. IV, ch. 1, pt. VII. For background, see Katherine Shaw Spaht (the principal drafter), "For the Sake of the Children: Recapturing the Meaning of Marriage," 73 *Notre Dame L. Rev.* 1547 (1998).

109. See Martha A. Fineman, *The Neutered Mother, the Sexual Family, and Other Twentieth Century Tragedies* (1995).

CHAPTER FOUR

1. *Baker v. State,* 744 A.2d 864, 902 (Vt. 1999) (Johnson, J., dissenting in part), quoting *Watson v. City of Memphis,* 373 U.S. 526, 535 (1963).

2. Transcript of Hearing Before the Vermont House Committee on the Judiciary, Feb. 9, 2000, at 4.

3. See, e.g., Bruce Ackerman, *Social Justice in the Liberal State,* 349–78 (1980); John Rawls, *The Theory of Justice,* 31 (1971).

4. See John Rawls, *Political Liberalism,* 4 (1993), and "The Priority of Right and Ideas of the Good," 17 *Phil. & Pub. Aff.* 272–73 (1988). See also Will Kymlicka, *Liberalism, Community, and Culture* (1989).

5. See, e.g., John Stuart Mill, *On Liberty,* ch. 4 (1859); Richard A. Posner, *Sex and Reason* (1992) (applying this Millian insight to sexual minorities such as gays).

6. The leading development of this idea among lawyers is Kenneth L. Karst, "The Supreme Court, 1976 Term—Foreword: Equal Citizenship under the Fourteenth Amendment," 91 *Harv. L. Rev.* 1, 5–11 (1977).

7. See Rawls, *Political Liberalism,* 213, and "The Idea of Public Reason Revisited," 64 *U. Chi. L. Rev.* 765 (1997).

8. Rawls, "Public Reason Revisited," 770–71.

9. Rawls says that "the government would appear to have no interest in the particular form of family life, or of relations among the sexes, except insofar as that form or those relations in some way affect the orderly reproduction of society over time." Ibid., 779. He seems to think that marriage can be such an institution. Ibid., 778.

10. See *Loving v. Virginia,* 388 U.S. 1 (1967) (invalidating a state bar to different-race marriages as both an unconstitutional discrimination and unjustified deprivation of a fundamental liberty). The state had made a liberal argument justifying its discrimination: different-race marriages would produce public harms, namely, a "mongrel race." This argument was factually unfounded and was, as the Court held, simply a rationalization for the state's goal of promoting white supremacy. Such a goal is invalid under liberal premises.

11. See Andrew Koppelman, "Why Discrimination against Lesbians and Gay Men Is Sex Discrimination," 69 *NYU L. Rev.* 197 (1994). The main argument against Koppelman's thesis—that the class of people hurt by miscegenation laws (blacks) matches up with the classification (race) and the equal protection goal (anti-racism), while the class of people hurt by different-sex marriage laws (gays) does not match up with the classification (sex) or the equal protection goal (antisexism)—is answered in William N. Eskridge Jr.,

The Case for Same-Sex Marriage, 162–72 (1996); see also 172–82 (arguing that the same-sex marriage bar is also irrational sexual orientation discrimination).

12. See *Turner v. Safley,* 482 U.S. 78 (1987). Consistent with liberal theory, the Court said that deprivation of the right to marry might be justified under some circumstances as part of an appropriate punishment for felons who have harmed others. See ibid., 96–97.

13. *Zablocki v. Redhail,* 434 U.S. 374, 385, 388 (1978), striking down a law requiring dead-beat dads to discharge their outstanding support obligations before they could remarry. The Court in *Zablocki* discussed the family and procreative features of traditional marriage but did not tie marriage to procreation. See Eskridge, *Same-Sex Marriage,* 128–29, discussing *Zablocki* and *Turner,* which failed even to discuss procreation as involved in state-recognized marriages.

14. The old rationale that incestuous marriages would pose high genetic risks is criticized in Carolyn Bratt, "Incest Statutes and the Fundamental Right of Marriage: Is Oedipus Free to Marry?" 18 *Fam. L.Q.* (1984).

15. See David L. Chambers, "Polygamy and Same-Sex Marriage," 26 *Hofstra L. Rev.* 53, 54–60 (1997) (collecting references from opponents of same-sex marriage). See also Maura I. Strassberg, "Distinctions of Form or Substance: Monogamy, Polygamy and Same-Sex Marriage," 75 *N.C. L. Rev.* 1501 (1997) (criticizing the polygamy analogy).

16. See Mill, *On Liberty.*

17. Compare Carol Rose, *Property and Persuasion,* 240–41 (1994) (polygamy would be good for women), and Robert Wright, *The Moral Animal* (1996) (similar), with William N. Eskridge Jr., *Gaylaw: Challenging the Apartheid of the Closet,* 290–92 (1999) (skeptical).

18. See Eskridge, *Same-Sex Marriage,* 148–49 (1996); Robin West, "Universalism, Liberal Theory, and the Problem of Gay Marriage," 25 *Fla. St. Univ. L. Rev.* 705 (1998).

19. For more detailed liberal philosophical and legal arguments for same-sex marriage, see Eskridge, *Same-Sex Marriage*; Morris B. Kaplan, *Sexual Justice: Democratic Citizenship and the Politics of Desire* (1997); David A. J. Richards, *Sex, Drugs, Death, and the Law: An Essay on Human Rights and Overcriminalization,* 29–83 (1982); Mary C. Dunlap, "The Lesbian and Gay Marriage Debate: A Microcosm of Our Hopes and Our Troubles,"1 *Law & Sexuality* 62 (1991); Andrew Koppelman, "Why Discrimination against Gay Men and Lesbians Is Sex Discrimination," 69 *NYU L. Rev.* 197 (1994); and Evan Wolfson, "Crossing the Threshold: Equal Marriage Rights for Lesbians and Gay Men and the Intra-Community Critique," 21 *NYU Rev. L. & Soc. Change* 567 (1994–95).

20. Rawls, "Public Reason Revisited," 779 (first quotation in text) and 778 n. 60 (second quotation).

21. Factual underpinnings for this argument are developed in Lynn D. Wardle, "The Potential Impact of Homsexual Parenting on Children," 1997 *U. Ill. L. Rev.* 833 (criticizing studies finding no impact of lesbian parents on children and invoking social scientists who assert bad influences). But see notes 22–23, below.

22. See *Baker,* 744 A.2d at 881–83; *Baehr v. Miike,* 1996 WL 694235 (Haw. Cir. Ct. Dec. 1996) (state's argument [findings of fact 18, 27, 30] and the evidence refuting it [findings 91, 123], including evidence from the state's witnesses [findings 28, 31, 38, 52–53, 54–55]), *vacated as moot,* 994 P.2d 566 (Haw. 1999).

23. See Carlos Ball and Janice Farrell Pea, "Warring with Wardle: Morality, Social Science, and Gay and Lesbian Parents," 1998 *U. Ill. L. Rev.* 253 (extensively surveying the social science evidence and refuting the claims made in Wardle, "Impact of Homosexual Parenting on Children").

24. See Linda McClain, "Deliberative Democracy, Overlapping Consensus, and Same-Sex Marriage," 66 *Fordham L. Rev.* 1241 (1998); cf. Carlos Ball, "Communitarianism and Gay Rights," 85 *Cornell L. Rev.* 443, 451–57 (2000) (on the whole agreeing with McClain but worrying that Rawls's emphasis on "reproduction of society" is unfortunate language).

25. See Vermont Act No. 91, § 1(3)-(9) (legislative findings).

26. Ibid., § 2(a) (legislative purpose).

27. Ibid., § 1(10).

28. The assertion in text is true as far as formal American law is concerned, but it is not true historically or functionally. Many societies in human history have recognized same-sex unions as marriages (Native American societies within the United States have done so), and same-sex couples have received marriage licenses in the United States by various means. See Eskridge, *Same-Sex Marriage,* ch. 2.

29. 163 U.S. 537 (1896). The parallel between the "separate but different" Civil Unions Law and the "separate but equal" regime in *Plessy v. Ferguson* was much noted during the legislative deliberations and will surely be a big theme of the postenactment commentary. See, e.g., Barbara J. Cox, "But Why Not Marriage? An Essay on Vermont's Civil Unions Law, Same-Sex Marriage, and Separate But (Un)Equal," 25 *Vt. L. Rev.* 113 (2000).

30. *Plessy,* 163 U.S. at 557 (Harlan, J., dissenting).

31. Vermont Act. No. 91, § 1(1).

32. *Plessy,* 163 U.S. at 550.

33. Vermont Act No. 91, § 1(10).

34. The source of the quotation in text is Peggy Cooper Davis, *Neglected Stories: The Constitution and Family Values,* 97 (1997). Mae Kuykendall, "Resistance to Same-Sex Marriage as a Story about Language: Linguistic Failure and the Priority of a Living Language," 34 *Harv. C.R.-C.L. L. Rev.* 385, 424 (1999) quotes this as an example of "unsaying" when states deny the linguistic possibility of same-sex marriage.

35. The thirty-five states with junior DOMA's are listed in footnote on page 38.

36. Choice-of-law precepts for interstate recognition of same-sex marriages are laid down by Barbara J. Cox, "Same-Sex Marriage and Choice of Law: If We Marry in Hawaii, Are We Still Married When We

Return Home?" 1994 *Wis. L. Rev.* 1033; and Linda Silberman, "Can the Island of Hawaii Bind the World? A Comment on Same-Sex Marriage and Federalism Values," 16 *QLR* 191 (1996).

37. Cf. *Commonwealth v. Balthazar*, 318 N.E.2d 478 (Mass. 1974) (narrowly interpreting the state "unnatural acts" crime to be inapplicable to sexual conduct between consenting adults).

38. See U.S. General Accounting Office, Letter to Hon. Henry J. Hyde, Chair, House Judiciary Comm., Jan. 31, 1997, identifying 1049 federal laws and regulations in which rights, benefits, and privileges are contingent on marital status.

39. Public Law No. 104–199, § 3, 110 Stat. 2419, codified at 1 U.S.C. § 7.

40. For arguments that DOMA is unconstitutional, see, e.g., Andrew Koppelman, "Dumb and DOMA: Why the Defense of Marriage Act Is Unconstitutional," 83 *Iowa L. Rev.* 1 (1997); and Evan Wolfson and Michael Melcher, "Constitutional and Legal Defects in the 'Defense of Marriage' Act," 16 *QLR* 221 (1996).

41. Eskridge, *Gaylaw*.

42. See Michael McConnell, "Originalism and the Desegregation Decisions," 81 *Va. L. Rev.* 947 (1995), for an excellent collection of the historical evidence recounted in text—and a controversial thesis that segregation was contrary to the original expectations of the fourteenth amendment ratifiers.

43. *Bowers v. Hardwick*, 478 U.S. 186 (1986).

44. *Dred Scott v. Sandford*, 60 U.S. 393 (1857).

45. *Brown v. Board of Education*, 347 U.S. 483 (1954) *(Brown I)*; 349 U.S. 294 (1955) *(Brown II)*.

46. *Cumming v. Richmond County Board of Education*, 175 U.S. 528 (1899).

47. Vermont Act. No. 91, § 3, adding new 15 V.S.A. § 1204(c).

48. Ibid., § 1204(d), (e)(6).

49. Ibid., § 1204(e)(1), (3).

50. Ibid., § 1204(e)(2).

51. Ibid., § 1204(e)(10).

52. Ibid., § 1204(e)(19).

53. Ibid., § 1204(f).

54. Ibid., § 1204(e)(4).

55. Ibid., § 1204(e)(7).

56. Ibid., § 1204(e)(8)-(9).

57. Ibid., § 1204(e)(12)-(13).

58. Ibid., § 1240(e)(15).

59. Ibid., § 1204(e)(14), (16).

60. David L. Chambers, "What If? The Legal Consequences of Marriage and the Legal Needs of Lesbian and Gay Male Couples," 95 *Mich. L. Rev.* 447 (1996). Chambers's article does not focus on Vermont, but the large majority of his generalizations would apply just as well to that state as to others. My textual discussion changes his categorizations in ways that I find productive but he may not.

61. Ibid., 454.

62. Social scientists separate the emotive component, *prejudice*, from the cognitive component, *stereotyping*, of category-based reactions. See e.g., Susan T. Fiske, "Stereotyping, Prejudice, and Discrimination," in *Encyclopedia of Social Science*, 357 (Daniel T. Gilbert et al. eds., 4th ed., 1998), and references therein.

63. See e.g., John F. Dovidio and Samuel L. Gaertner, "Prejudice, Discrimination, and Racism: Historical Trends and Contemporary Approaches," in *Prejudice, Discrimination, and Racism*, 1, 4–12 (Dovidio and Gaertner, eds. 1986). The data do not help us much in understanding how much of this progress was due to state antidiscrimination policies and how much to other social trends.

64. See e.g., J. B. McConahay et al., "Has Racism Declined in America?," 25 *J. Conflict Res.* 563–79 (1981) (on questionnaires, white respondents will often give answers that make them appear more egalitarian than they actually are).

65. See Roy Brooks, *Rethinking the American Race Problem*, 37 (1990) (notwithstanding decades of progress, the median black family income is only 57 percent of that of a similar white family); "Symposium: The Law and Economics of Racial Discrimination in Employment," 79 *Geo. L.J.* 1619–1782 (1991), especially articles by David Strauss and Michael Gottesman.

66. The sociopolitical impact of *Brown* in either the short or long term remains controversial. Compare Gerald Rosenberg, *The Hollow Hope: Can Courts Bring About Social Change?* (1991) (dubious about any impact), with Michael Klarman, "*Brown*, Racial Change, and the Civil Rights Movement," 80 *Va. L. Rev.* 7 (1994) (persuaded that there was a significant impact), with Gerald Rosenberg, "*Brown* Is Dead! Long Live *Brown*! The Endless Attempt to Canonize a Case," 80 *Va. L. Rev.* 161 (1994) (still dubious).

67. Gordon Allport, *The Nature of Prejudice*, 250–68 (1954). For empirical testing substantially confirming Allport's insight, see, e.g., Y. Amir, "The Role of Inter-Group Contact in Change of Prejudice and Ethnic Relations," in *Towards the Elimination of Racism* 245–308 (P. A. Katz, ed., 1976); Gregory M. Herek and John P. Capitanio, "'Some of My Best Friends': Intergroup Contact, Concealable Stigma, and Heterosexuals' Attitudes toward Gay Men and Lesbians," 23 *Personality & Soc. Psychol. Bull.* 412 (1995); N. Miller et al., "Cooperative Interaction in Desegregated Settings: A Laboratory Analogue," 41 *J. Soc. Issues* 63–79 (1985).

68. See 9 V.S.A. § 4502 (prohibiting sexual orientation [et al.] discrimination in public accommodations) and § 4503 (housing); 21 V.S.A. § 495(a) (employment).

69. See 13 V.S.A. § 1455. Similar state laws including antigay prejudice in their penalty enhancements are collected in William N. Eskridge Jr., "Comparative Law and the Same-Sex Marriage Debate," 31 *McGeo. L. Rev.* 641, 671–72 (2000) (app. 2).

70. 15A V.S.A. § 1–102(b).

71. See, e.g., T. F. Pettigrew and R. W. Meertens, "Subtle and Blatant Prejudice in Western Europe," 25 *Eur. J. Soc. Psychol.* 57 (1995).

72. Transcript of House Comm. on the Judiciary Meeting, Feb. 9, 2000 (Rep. Edwards, R-Swanton).

73. 142 Cong. Rec. 16972 (July 11, 1996) (Rep. John Lewis, D-Ga.).

74. Transcript of House Judiciary Comm. Feb. 9 Meeting (Rep. Little, R-Shelburne).

75. Four committee members openly endorsed same-sex marriage (option A) as the best policy choice: Representatives Bill Lippert (D-Hinesburg), Steve Hingtgen (P-Burlington), Alice Nitka (D-Ludlow), and Bill MacKinnon (D-Sharon). Four committee members emphasized full equality for lesbian and gay couples but were open-minded or uncertain as to whether amending the marriage laws (option A) was a viable idea: Representatives Mike Vinton (D-Colchester), Michael Kainen (R-Hartford), Judy Livingston (R-Manchester), and Diane Carmoli (D-Rutland City). Three committee members expressed strong support for equal benefits and rights but felt that option A was not possible and therefore supported option B, the parallel institution: Representatives Tom Little (R-Shelburne), John Edwards (R-Swanton), and Cathy Voyer (R-Morristown). Ibid. (transcript of committee discussion about the policy to be followed in drafting the bill).

76. Strategic behavior is explained in William H. Riker and Peter C. Ordeshook, *An Introduction to Positive Political Theory* 1–7 (1973), and is applied to courts as well as legislatures in, e.g., "Symposium: Positive Political Theory and Public Law," 80 *Geo. L.J.* 457 (1992).

77. For a theory of constitutional decision making that respects stable political equilibria and imposes changes only where the constitutional court expects protection against political overrides, see William N. Eskridge Jr. and Philip P. Frickey, "The Supreme Court, 1993 Term—Foreword: Law as Equilibrium," 108 *Harv. L. Rev.* 26, 30–56 (1994).

78. *Baehr v. Lewin*, 852 P.2d 44 (Haw. 1993), on remand, *Baehr v. Miike*, 1996 WL 694235 (Haw. Cir. Ct. Dec. 3, 1996), vacated sub nom. *Baehr v. Anderson*, 994 P.2d 566 (Haw. 1999) (per curiam) (trial court injunction overridden by state constitutional amendment ratifying legislative bar to same-sex marriage).

79. *Brause v. Bureau of Vital Statistics*, 1998 WL 88743 (Alaska Sup. Ct. Feb. 1998).

80. *Baker*, 744 A.2d at 902 (Johnson, J., dissenting in part), quoting *Watson v. City of Memphis*, 373 U.S. 526, 535 (1963).

81. *See Brown v. Board of Education*, 349 U.S. 294, 301 (1955).

82. Compare J. Harvie Wilkinson, *From Brown to Bakke* 68 (1979), and Alexander Bickel, "The Decade of School Desegregation: Progress and Prospects," 64 *Colum. L. Rev.* 193 (1964), arguing the pragmatic position, with Derrick Bell, "*Brown v. Board of Education* and the Interest-Convergence Dilemma," 93 *Harv. L. Rev.* 518 (1980), and Robert Burt, "*Brown*'s Reflection," 103 *Yale L.J.* 1483 (1994), taking a much more critical stance.

83. *Naim v. Naim*, 350 U.S. 891 (1955), remanding 87 S.E.2d 749 (Va. 1955).

84. *Naim v. Naim*, 90 S.E.2d 849 (Va.), appeal dismissed, 350 U.S. 985 (1956).

85. See William N. Eskridge Jr. and Philip P. Frickey, "An Historical and Critical Introduction to *The Legal Process*," in Henry M. Hart, Jr. and Albert Sacks *The Legal Process: Basic Problems in the Making and Application of Law*, cx (Eskridge and Frickey, eds. 1994) (1958 tent. ed.).

86. See David S. Schoenbrod, "The Measure of an Injunction: A Principle to Replace Balancing the Equities and Tailoring the Remedy," 72 *Minn. L. Rev.* 627 (1988).

87. See generally Paul Gewirtz, "Remedies and Resistance," 92 *Yale L.J.* 585 (1983).

88. See the debate within the Court in, for example, *Freeman v. Pitts*, 503 U.S. 467 (1992) (especially the sharp exchange among the concurring opinions).

89. The table is taken from William N. Eskridge Jr., "Comparative Law and the Same-Sex Marriage Debate: A Step-by-Step Approach Toward State Recognition," 31 *McGeo. L.J.* 641, 649, 663–70 (2000) (citations for various countries in the table).

90. See Kees Waaldijk, "Small Change: How the Road to Same-sex Marriage Got Paved in the Netherlands," in *Legal Recognition of Same-Sex Partnerships: A Study of National, European and International Law,* ed. Robert Wintemute and Mads Andenaes (2001).

91. The linguistic history of the terminology "coming out of the closet" is briefly recounted in Eskridge, *Gaylaw* 57–58, 99.

92. Rodney Christopher, "Explaining It to Dad," in *Boys Like Us: Gay Writers Tell Their Coming Out Stories* 302–11 (Patrick Merla, ed. 1996). For other examples of accommodation, see William Sterling Walker, "January 18, 1989," ibid., 293–301 (mother accepts her son's homosexuality but does not want him sharing food with his nieces and nephews); Caldwell, "Out-Takes," ibid., 270 (author agrees not to tell his brother until the latter graduates from high school).

93. Philip Bockman, "Fishing Practice," in ibid., 80.

94. See Richard Posner, "Should There Be Homosexual Marriage? And If So, Who Should Decide?" 95 *Mich. L. Rev.* 1578, 1585–86 (1997) (reviewing Eskridge, *Same-Sex Marriage*).

95. Compare *Baker*, 744 A.2d at 885–86 (opinion for the court, rejecting exclusionary tradition as a reason to deny the right), with ibid., 887 (finding tradition not altogether irrelevant in fashioning a remedy).

96. See Rawls, "Public Reason Revisited," 770.

97. Pragmatic liberalism has substantial affinity with the *minimalist liberalism* articulated by Richard Rorty in, e.g., "A Defense of Minimalist Liberalism," in *Debating Democracy's Discontent: Essays on American Politics, Law, and Public Philosophy,* 117–25 (Anita L. Allen and Milton C. Regan Jr., eds. 1998).

CHAPTER FIVE

1. See Michael Sandel, *Democracy's Discontent: America in Search of a Public Philosophy* (1996), and *Liberalism and the Limits of Justice* (1982). See generally *Debating* Democracy's Discontent: *Essays on American Politics, Law, and Public Philosophy* (Anita L. Allen and Milton C. Regan, Jr., eds. 1998).

Communitarianism and critiques of liberalism assume many intellectual forms. Although this chapter will draw largely from Sandel's work (just as the last chapter drew mainly from Rawls), I have greatly profited from *Liberalism and the Moral Life* (Nancy L. Rosenblum, ed. 1989); *New Communitarian Thinking* (Amatai Etzioni, ed. 1995); *The Communitarian Challenge to Liberalism* (Ellen Frankel Paul et al., eds. 1996); Amitai Etzioni, *The New Golden Rule: Community and Morality in a Democratic Society* (1996); Amy Gutmann and Dennis Thompson, *Democracy and Disagreement* (1996); Philip Pettit, *Republicanism: A Theory of Freedom and Government* (1997); Charles Taylor, *Ethics of Authenticity* (1991); and Michael Walzer, *Spheres of Justice: A Defense of Pluralism and Equality* (1983).

2. See Transcript of a Meeting of the Judiciary Committee of the Vermont House of Representatives, Feb. 9, 2000 (oral statement of Rep. Little, Chair); Memorandum from Thomas A. Little, Chair, to House Judiciary Committee Members, Jan. 4, 2000, both of which are quoted in chapter 2.

3. See Brief of Appellee State of Vermont, 42–55, *Baker v. State*, 744 A.2d 865 (Vt. 1999) (No. 98–32).

4. See Audiotape of the Debate of H.847 by the Vermont Senate, April 18, 2000 (available from the Vermont Legislative Council) (oral statements of Sens. Canns and Illuzi in favor of presenting constitutional amendment to the voters to override *Baker* and preserve traditional marriage, discussed in chapter 2).

5. Vt. Const., 1777, ch. I, art. I.

6. See Brief for Appellants, 16–20, *Baker* (No. 98–32).

7. See Audiotape of the Joint Public Hearings Jointly Sponsored by the House and Senate Judiciary Committees, January 25 and February 2, 2000 (available from the Legislative Council), discussed in chapter 2. Almost all the arguments, pro and con, went to the question of whether lesbian and gay unions were good.

8. Audiotape of the Debate of H.847 by the Vermont Senate, April 19, 2000 (available from the Vermont Legislative Council) (Sen. Sears, responding to inquiries from a Rutland County senator). Sears' concession that the bill would "sanction" such unions will be unremarkable to many readers, but in the context of the same-sex marriage debate this is a big step. See William N. Eskridge Jr., "No Promo Homo: The Sedimentation of Antigay Discourse and the Channeling Effect of Judicial Review," 75 *NYU L. Rev.* 1327 (2000) (a history of this kind of "no promo homo" argument).

9. William N. Eskridge Jr., *The Case for Same-Sex Marriage* (1996), responding to the challenge laid down by Michael Sandel, "Moral Argument and Liberal Toleration: Abortion and Homosexuality," 77 *Calif. L. Rev.* 521, 537–38 (1989), arguing that gay people should insist on "at least some appreciation of the lives homosexuals live." See also Carlos A. Ball, "Moral Foundations for a Discourse on Same-Sex Marriage: Looking Beyond Political Liberalism," 85 *Geo. L.J.* 1871 (1997).

10. For an overview of the social science literature on the endowment effect, see Herbert Hovenkamp, "Legal Policy and the Endowment Effect," 20 *J. Leg. Stud.* 221 (1991).

11. See J. M. Balkin, "The Constitution of Status," 106 *Yale L.J.* 2313 (1997); Brenda Major, "Gender, Entitlement, and the Distribution of Family Labor," 49 *J. Soc. Issues* 141 (1993) (endowment effects undermine women's bargaining position within the family and the workplace).

12. See Cass R. Sunstein, "Deliberative Trouble? Why Groups Go to Extremes," 110 *Yale L.J.* 71 (2000).

13. See Eskridge, *Same-Sex Marriage*, ch. 4, and *Gaylaw: Challenging the Apartheid of the Closet*, ch. 8 (1999).

14. See, e.g., Germain Grisez, *The Way of Lord Jesus*, vol. 2, at 633–80 (1993); John I. Finnis, "Law, Morality, and 'Sexual Orientation,'" 69 *Notre Dame L. Rev.* 1049 (1994); Robert P. George and Gerald V. Bradley, "Marriage and the Liberal Imagination," 84 *Geo. L.J.* 301 (1995). See also George, *Making Men Moral: Civil Liberties and Public Morality* (1993).

15. See Stephen Macedo, "Homosexuality and the Conservative Mind," 84 *Geo. L.J.* 261 (1995), as well as Martha Nussbaum, "Integrity," *The New Republic*, November 15, 1993, at 12; Michael Perry, "The Morality of Homosexual Conduct: A Response to John Finnis," 1 *Notre Dame J.L. Ethics & Pub. Pol'y* 41 (1995); Paul Weithman, "Natural Law, Morality, and Complementarity," in *Laws and Nature* (Martha Nussbaum, ed. 1996).

16. See Philip Blumstein and Pepper Schwartz, *American Couples: Money, Work, Sex*, 11–24 (1983) (describing the methodology) and 202–03 (satisfaction with the relationship). See also Alan P. Bell and Martin S. Weinberg, *Homosexualities: A Study of Diversity Among Men and Women*, 219–21 (1978) (close-coupled lesbian and gay people to be happiest).

17. See Blumstein and Schwartz, *American Couples*, 307–08.

18. See Lawrence A. Kurdek, "Relationship Outcomes and Their Predictors: Longitudinal Evidence from Heterosexual Married, Gay Cohabiting, and Lesbian Cohabiting Couples," 60 *J. Marr. & Fam.* 553 (1998), which also surveys the prior literature.

19. Cf. Robert P. George, "Public Reason and Political Conflict: Abortion and Homosexuality," 106 *Yale L.J.* 2475, 2499 (1997) (admitting incommensurability between his natural law worldview and a liberal one but maintaining that liberal theory does not arbitrate comprehensive theories very well either).

20. See Finnis, "Law, Morality, and 'Sexual Orientation,'" 1063–69; George and Bradley, "Marriage and the Liberal Imagination," 314–15.

21. See, e.g., Andrew Koppelman, "Is Marriage Inherently Heterosexual?" 42 *Am. J. Jur.* 51 (1997) (his view is that it isn't); Stephen Macedo, "Reply to Critics," 84 *Geo. L.J.* 329, 334–35 (1995) (resisting natural lawyers' efforts to "carve up basic rights . . . on the basis of reasons and arguments whose force depends on accepting particular religious convictions"); Perry, "The Morality of Homosexual Conduct"; "Is Homosexual Conduct Wrong? A Philosophical Exchange," *New Republic*, November 15, 1993, 12, 13 (statement of Prof. Martha Nussbaum).

22. Mary Becker, "Women, Morality, and Sexual Orientation," 8 *UCLA Women's L.J.* 165, 189–90 (1998) (emphasis in original).

23. See John Rawls, "The Idea of Public Reason Revisited," 64 *U. Chi. L. Rev.* 765, 766–68, 783–84 (1997).

24. See Audiotape of the Joint Public Hearing of the Judiciary Committees of the Vermont House of Representatives and Senate, January 25, 2000 (available from the Vermont Legislative Council) (oral statement of Rev. Jim Lake).

25. Ibid. (oral statement of Shirley Garvey, married forty-nine years and mother of seven children).

26. Ibid., (oral statement of Charles Brett). See also the oral statements of Chris Bixby, who analogized homosexual marriage to incest; Madelyn Hansen, who emphasized that bisexuals as well as gay people violated natural law; a woman named Cindy, who refused to cease her antihomosexual tirade when her time had expired; and many others.

27. Ibid., (oral statements of Tim Mank, making the slavery analogy, and the Reverend Jeffrey Jackson, arguing for abolition of civil marriage).

28. See Audiotape of the Debate of H.847 by the Vermont House of Representatives, March 15, 2000 (available from the Vermont Legislative Council) (oral statement by Rep. Sheltra, interrupted by a point of order that was sustained by the presiding officer).

29. See Brief of Appellee State of Vermont, 42–55, *Baker* (No. 98–32); *Baehr v. Miike*, 1996 WL 694235 (Haw. Cir. Ct. Dec. 1996), reversed, 994 P.2d 566 (Haw. 1999) (per curiam) (extensively summarizing the state's justifications on remand from the state supreme court).

30. See *Baehr v. Miike*, 1996 WL 695235, Findings of Fact ¶¶ 28, 31, 34 (Dr. Kyle Pruett, an eminent child development psychologist now teaching at Yale University); see ibid., ¶¶ 52–53 (Dr. David Eggebeen, a sociologist).

31. Ibid., ¶¶ 126–27.

32. Ibid., ¶ 136; see *Baehr v. Lewin*, 852 P.2d at 59 (listing many of those benefits under Hawaii law).

33. See *Baker*, 744 A.2d at 881.

34. See Charlotte Patterson, "Adoption of Minor Children by Lesbian and Gay Adults," 2 *Duke J. Gender L. & Pol'y* 191 (1995). Leading studies include Patricia Falk, "Lesbian Mothers: Psychosocial Assumptions in Family Law," 44 *Am. Psychol.* 941 (1989); Susan Golombok et al., "Children in Lesbian and Single Parent Households: Psychosexual and Psychiatric Appraisal," 24 *J. Child Psychol. & Psychiatry* 551 (1983); David Kleber et al., "The Impact of Parental Homosexuality in Child Custody Cases," 14 *Bull. Am. Academy Psychol. & Law* 81 (1986); Mary Hotvedt and Jane Barclay Mandel, "Children of Lesbian Mothers," in *Homosexuality: Social, Psychological, and Biological Issues,* 275, 282 (William Paul et al., eds., 1982).

35. See e.g., Susan Golombok and Fiona Tasker, "Do Parents Influence the Sexual Orientation of Their Children?" 32 *Dev. Psychol.* 3, 8 (1996) (on the impossibility of recruiting a random sample of gay parents because of the closetry of most); Charlotte Patterson, "Children of Lesbian and Gay Parents," 63 *Child Dev.*1025, 1036–39 (1992) (survey of the studies, including those of the author).

36. Mike Allen and Nancy Burrell, "Comparing the Impact of Homosexual and Heterosexual Parents on Children: Meta-Analysis of Existing Research," 32 *J. Homosexuality* 19, 28–30 (1996), correcting for some problems identified by Philip Belcastro et al., "A Review of Data Based Studies Addressing the Affects of Homosexual Parenting on Children's Sexual and Social Functioning," 20 *J. Divorce & Remarriage* 105 (1993).

37. Richard Green et al., "Lesbian Mothers and Their Children: A Comparison with Solo Parent Heterosexual Mothers and Their Children," 15 *Archives Sexual Behav.* 167 (1986); Golombok et al., "Children in Lesbian and Single Parent Households," 562–67; Rhonda Rivera, "Legal Issues in Gay and Lesbian Parenting," in *Gay and Lesbian Parents,* 199, 226 n. 79 (reporting unpublished study).

38. On cognitive dissonance, see Leon Festinger, *Conflict, Decision and Dissonance* (1964); Irving Janis and Lawrence Mann, *Decision Making: A Psychological Analysis of Conflict, Choice and Commitment,* 171–72, 212–14 (1977).

39. Lynn Wardle, "The Potential Impact of Homosexual Parenting on Children," 1997 *U. Ill. L. Rev.* 833, 852–57, 865–66.

40. See Carlos A. Ball and Janice Farrell Pea, "Warring with Wardle: Social Science, Morality, and Gay and Lesbian Parents," 1998 *U. Ill. L. Rev.* 253, 272–308; *Baehr*, 1996 WL 694235 (Finding of Fact ¶ 34).

41. See, e.g., Carole Jenny, et al., "Are Children at Risk for Sexual Abuse by Homosexuals?" 94 *Pediatrics* 41 (1994). Other studies are reported in Ball and Pea, "Warring with Wardle," 307 n. 279.

42. On the hysterical, narcissistic, and obsessional features of antigay prejudice, see Eskridge, *Gaylaw,* 211, drawing from the theory of prejudices in Elizabeth Young-Bruehl, *The Anatomy of Prejudices,* 32–36, 157–58 (1996).

43. See H.R. Report No. 104–664, at 13 (July 9, 1996), reprinted in 1996 *U.S. Code, Cong. & Admin. News (USCCAN)* 2905, 2917 (committee report accompanying the Defense of Marriage Act [chapter 1]); Lynn D. Wardle, "A Critical Analysis of Constitutional Claims for Same-Sex Marriage," 1996 *BYU L. Rev.* 1.

44. DOMA House Report, 36, 42–43 (minority views), 1996 *USCCAN* 2938, 2945–46.

45. See Nancy Cott, *Public Vows: A History of Marriage and the Nation* (2000).

46. On the perceived threat to marriage assertedly posed by different-race couples, see Harvey M. Appelbaum, "Miscegenation Statutes: A Constitutional and Social Problem," 53 *Geo. L. J.* 49 (1964); A. Leon Higginbotham and Barbara K. Kopytoff, "Racial Purity and Interracial Sex in the Law of Colonial and Antebellum Virginia," 77 *Geo. L.J.* 1967 (1989); James Trosino, "American Wedding: Same-Sex Marriage and the Miscegenation Analogy," 73 *B.U.L. Rev.* 93 (1993) (student note).

47. See Richard A. Posner, *Sex and Reason,* 311 (1992); G. Sidney Buchanan, "Same-Sex Marriage: The Linchpin Issue," 10 *U. Dayton L. Rev.* 541 (1985); 139 Cong. Rec. 17,031 (1993) (Sen. Lott, R-Miss.) ("no promo homo" as a reason not to fund the D.C. domestic partners law).

48. See Eskridge, *Gaylaw,* 278–80; Balkin, "The Constitution of Status."

49. See Carlos A. Ball, "Communitarianism and Gay Rights," 85 *Cornell L. Rev.* 443, 467–84 (2000).

50. See Ronald Smothers, "Mississippi Governor Bans Same-Sex Marriage," *N.Y. Times,* August 24, 1997, § 13, at 7.

51. Between 1970 and 1998, the percentage of women aged forty to forty-four who have not married has gone up from 5.4 percent to 9.9 percent; for men aged forty to forty-four, the percentage has gone up from 7.5 percent to 15.6 percent. See Andrew Hacker, "The Case Against Kids," *N.Y. Rev. of Books,* November 30, 2000, at 12, 16 (table C).

52. Between 1970 and 1998, the number of children living with unmarried couples has gone up from 196,000 to 1,520,000. The number of marital births is down by a fifth; the number of nonmarital births has more than doubled. See ibid.

53. See Darren Spedale, *Nordic Bliss: The Danish Experience with "Gay Marriage,"* ch. 3 (unpublished manuscript, 1999); Ingrid Lund-Anderson, "The Danish Registered Partnership Act, 1989 – Has the Act Meant a Change in Attitudes?" in *Legal Recognition of Same-Sex Partnerships: A Study of National, European and International Law,* ed. Robert Wintemute and Mads Andenaes (2001) (six-year dissolution rate for registered partnerships, 1990–96, was 9.7 percent, compared with 18 percent divorce rate for married couples at the six-year point).

54. See Lawrence A. Kurdek, "The Allocation of Household Labor in Gay, Lesbian, and Heterosexual Married Couples," 49 *J. Soc. Issues* 127, 135–36 (1993); Letitia Anne Peplau, "Lesbian and Gay Relationships," in *Homosexuality: Research Implications for Public Policy,* 177, 183–84 (John C. Gonsiorek and John D. Weinrich, eds. 1991); N. S. Eldridge and L. A. Gilbert, "Correlates of Relationship Satisfaction in Lesbian Couples," 14 *Psychol. of Women Q.* 43, 44 (1990).

55. See Nan Hunter, "Marriage, Law, and Gender: A Feminist Inquiry," 1 *Law & Sexuality* 9 (1991).

56. See Steven L. Nock, *Marriage in Men's Lives* (1998) (men are much better off, economically and psychologically, if married); Amy Wax, "Bargaining in the Shadow of the Market: Is There a Future for Egalitarian Marriage?" 84 *Va. L. Rev.* 509 (1998) (women make more of the sacrifices in marriage so men are much better off).

57. See Rhona Mahony, *Kidding Ourselves: Breadwinning, Babies, and Bargaining Power* (1995); Carol Rose, *Property and Persuasion,* 240–41 (1994); Wax, "Future for Egalitarian Marriage?"

58. See Robin West, "Sex, Reason, and a Taste for the Absurd," 81 *Geo. L.J.* 2413, 2433 (1993) (the author has no idea what her sexual orientation is). Men don't quite comprehend this phenomenon, as we tend to be pretty sure about our Kinsey numbers; see, e.g., Richard A. Posner, *Overcoming Law,* 573 (1995), who confesses he was "floored" by West's confession.

59. See the exchange of letters between Stanley Kurtz and me in *Commentary,* December 2000, at 5, 10–11.

60. Gutmann and Thompson, *Democracy and Disagreement,* 1–2, 52–54.

61. Compare Rawls, "Public Reason Revisited," with Michael Sandel's comments in "Symposium on [Rawls'] *Political Liberalism*: Religion and Public Reason," 3 *Relig. & Values Pub. Life* 1, 3, 9. Other useful essays drawing from Gutmann and Thompson's book include Edward Foley, "Jurisprudence and Theology," 66 *Fordham L. Rev.* 1195 (1998); George, "Public Reason and Political Conflict," 2501–04; Linda C. McClain, "Deliberative Democracy, Overlapping Consensus, and Same-Sex Marriage," 66 *Fordham L. Rev.* 1241 (1998).

62. Exceptional in interrogating democratic deliberation on grounds of inclusion and fairness are works by critical scholars, including Lani Guinier, *The Tyranny of the Majority: Fundamental Fairness and Representative Democracy* (1994); Melissa Williams, *Voice, Trust, and Memory: Marginalized Groups and the Failings of Liberal Representation* (1998); Iris Young, *Justice and the Politics of Difference* (1990); and Frank I. Michelman, "Law's Republic," 97 *Yale L.J.* 1493 (1988).

63. See Eskridge, *Gaylaw,* 24–34, 60–67; see also ibid., 328–41 (appendices documenting statutes for state and municipal jurisdictions).

64. See ibid., 34–37, 49–52, 67–80.

65. See, e.g., Margaret M. Bierly, "Prejudice Toward Contemporary Outgroups as a Generalized Attitude," 15 *J. Applied Soc. Psychol.* 189 (1985) (homophobia is the most popular prejudice); Gregory M. Herek, "Heterosexuals' Attitudes Toward Lesbians and Gay Men: Correlates and Gender Differences," 25 *J. Sex Research* 451–77 (1988).

66. See Wardle, "Impact of Homosexual Parenting on Children," analyzed above; Posner, *Sex and Reason,* analyzed in William N. Eskridge Jr., "A Social Constructionist Critique of Posner's *Sex and Reason,*" 102 *Yale L.J.* 333, 359–65 (1992).

67. See Diane H. Mazur, "Re-Making Distinctions on the Basis of Sex: Must Gay Women Be Admitted to the Military Even If Gay Men Are Not?" 58 *Ohio St. L.J.* 953 (1997).

68. See Bruce A. Ackerman, "Beyond *Carolene Products*," 98 *Harv. L. Rev.* 713 (1985).

69. 142 Cong. Rec. 16,972 (July 12, 1996) (Rep. Coburn, R-Okla.) (first quotation in the text); and 17,070 (Rep. Barr, R-Ga.) (second quotation).

70. Letter from Pro-Family Hawaii to "Brothers and Sisters in Christ," March 1997, soliciting opposition to same-sex marriage rights, reported at <www.xq/hermp/03–20–97.htm> (as of July 11, 1997).

71. Chad Blair, "The Gospel According to Gabbard," *Honolulu Weekly*, January 27, 1999; see chapter 1 of this book for more on the Hawaii campaign.

72. The quotations in text were taken from HCC's website, <www.hi-christian.com/home-page.htm> (as of February 5, 2001).

73. See Barbara Gamble, "Putting Civil Rights to a Popular Vote," 41 *Am. J. Pol. Sci.* 245, 254 (1997).

74. See, e.g., Derrick Bell Jr., "The Referendum: Democracy's Barrier to Racial Equality," 54 *Wash. L. Rev.* 1, 18–21 (1978). For a comparison of anti-civil rights referenda in the 1960s and 1970s and antigay referenda of the 1970s and 1980s, see Jane S. Schacter, "The Gay Civil Rights Debate in the States: Decoding the Discourse of Equivalents," 29 *Harv. C.R.-C.L. L. Rev.* 283 (1994).

75. See Julian Eule, "Judicial Review of Direct Democracy," 99 *Yale L.J.* 1503 (1990); Hans Linde, "When Initiative Lawmaking Is Not 'Republican Government': The Campaign against Homosexuality," 72 *Or. L. Rev.* 19 (1993).

76. James Madison, *The Federalist* no. 10, at 78 (Clinton Rossiter, ed. 1961).

77. See Reciprocal Beneficiaries Act of 1997, 1997 Haw. Sess. Laws 2786, Act 383 (H.B. 118).

78. See Robert M. Cover, "Obligation: A Jewish Jurisprudence of the Social Order," 5 *J.L. & Religion* 65 (1988); Susan Koniak, "Through the Looking Glass of Ethics and the Wrong with Rights We Find There," 9 *Geo. J. Leg. Ethics* 1 (1995).

79. Cover, "Obligation," 65.

80. Francis Lieber, *Manual of Political Ethics*, vol. 1, at 384 (1838).

81. See *Dred Scott v. Sandford*, 60 U.S. 393, 420 (1857) (Taney, C.J., for the Court).

82. The Fifteenth Amendment assured the right of blacks to vote; the right to serve on juries was assured by the Supreme Court's interpretation of the Fourteenth Amendment in *Strauder v. West Virginia*, 100 U.S. 303 (1879); and military service was opened to African Americans during the Civil War, albeit in segregated units under white commanders.

83. *Dred Scott*, 60 U.S. at 601 (Curtis, J., dissenting).

84. See Lieber, *Political Ethics*, vol. 1, at 102–07; vol. 2, at 65, 110–11, 122–25 (1839).

85. See Maura I. Strassberg, "Distinctions of Form or Substance: Monogamy, Polygamy and Same-Sex Marriage," 75 *N.C.L. Rev.* 1501, 1518–37 (1997), for an excellent and detailed exposition of Lieber, as supplemented by Hegel. See also ibid., 1537–56, updating Hegel's theory to take account of women's equality.

86. Cong. Globe, 39th Cong., 1st Sess. 474 (1866) (Sen. Trumbull, R-Ill., explaining the proposed Civil Rights Act of 1866); see Laura Edwards, "'The Marriage Covenant Is at the Foundation of All Our Rights': The Politics of Slave Marriages in North Carolina After Emancipation," 14 *L. & Hist. Rev.* 81 (1996).

87. See *Reynolds v. United States*, 98 U.S. 145, 165 (1878) (marriage as basis for democracy require suppression of "totalitarian" polygamy); *Maynard v. Hill*, 125 U.S. 190, 211 (1888) (standard cite for marriage as the "foundation of the family and of society"); *Poe v. Ullman*, 367 U.S. 497, 515–22 (1961) (Douglas, J., dissenting) (paean to marriage, a distilled version reemerging in Douglas' opinion for the Court in *Griswold v. Connecticut*, 381 U.S. 479 [1965]).

88. See Philip Bockman, "Fishing Practice," in *Boys Like Us: Gay Writers Tell Their Coming Out Stories*, 80 (Patrick Merla ed. 1996).

89. See, e.g., Janis S. Bohan, *Psychology and Sexual Orientation: Coming to Terms*, 94–110 (1996) (psychological effects of the closet and good effects of coming out); Susan D. Cochran and Vickie M. Mays, "Lifetime Prevalence of Suicide Symptoms and Affective Disorders Among Men Reporting Same-Sex Sexual Partners," 90 *Am. J. Pub. Health* 573 (2000).

90. See Amity Pierce Buxton, *The Other Side of the Closet: The Coming-Out Crisis for Straight Spouses and Families* (rev. ed. 1994) (recounting the pain of marriage between a straight spouse and a closeted lesbian or gay spouse); Jenny et al., "Are Children at Risk for Sexual Abuse by Homosexuals?" 42 (openly gay males do not molest children; male children tend to be abused by men involved in relationships with the children's mother).

91. See *Staatsblad* 2001, no. 9 (the same-sex marriage law) and no. 10 (the adoption law). These statutes are discussed in chapter 3.

92. See Kees Waaldijk, "Small Change: How the Road to Same-Sex Marriage Got Paved in The Netherlands," in Wintemute and Andenaes, *Legal Recognition of Same-Sex Partnerships*.

93. See, e.g., Michelman, "Law's Republic"; Cass R. Sunstein, "Beyond the Republican Revival," 97 *Yale L.J.* 1539 (1988).

94. See Mary Ann Glendon, *Rights Talk: The Impoverishment of Political Discourse* (1991); Suzanna Sherry, "Civic Virtue and the Feminine Voice in Constitutional Adjudication," 72 *Va. L. Rev.* 543 (1986).

95. Cf. David S. Schoenbrod, "The Measure of an Injunction: A Principle to Replace Balancing the Equities and Tailoring the Remedy," 72 *Minn. L. Rev.* 627 (1988).

96. See *Baker*, 744 A.2d at 887 (opinion for the court).

97. On the concept of social capital and America's declining reservoir of it since 1960, see Robert D. Putnam, *Bowling Alone: The Collapse and Revival of American Community* (2000).

98. The account in text of the debate over repeal of consensual sodomy laws is drawn from Eskridge, *Gaylaw*, 156–64, and "No Promo Homo: The Sedimentation of Antigay Discourse and the Channeling Effect of Judicial Review," 75 *NYU L. Rev.* 1327, 1339–46 (2000).

99. 1950 N.Y. Stat. ch. 525, § 15, revamping the state sodomy law to penalize forcible sodomy and sodomy with a minor, both felonies, much more severely than consensual sodomy, recrafted as a misdemeanor.

100. See *People v. Onofre*, 415 N.E.2d 936 (N.Y. 1980). Oddly, the consensual sodomy law remained on the New York statute books until February 1, 2001, the effective date of a statute adopted in 2000 formally repealing it.

101. For laments as to the inefficacy of *Brown* from a variety of perspectives, see, e.g., Jacqueline Irvine, *Black Students and School Failure: Policies, Practices, and Prescriptions* (1990); Gerald Rosenberg, *The Hollow Hope: Can Courts Bring About Social Change?* (1991) (his feeling is that they can't); Raymond Wolters, *The Burden of Brown: Thirty Years of Desegregation* (1984); *Shades of Brown: New Perspectives on School Desegregation* (Derrick Bell Jr., ed. 1980); and Michael Seidman, Brown *and* Miranda, 80 Calif. L. Rev. 673 (1992). An excellent treatment of the remedial problems inherent in the desegregation cases is Paul Gewirtz, "Remedies and Resistance," 92 *Yale L.J.* 585 (1983).

102. For further exploration of the theme that underlying patterns of racist thought undergird the continuing tragedy of efforts to integrate American life, see, e.g., Kimberlé Crenshaw, "Race, Reform, and Retrenchment: Transformation and Legitimation in Antidiscrimination Law," 101 *Harv. L. Rev.* 1331 (1988); Charles Lawrence Jr., "'Justice' or 'Just Us': Racism and the Role of Ideology," 35 *Stan. L. Rev.* 831 (1983). See also T. Alexander Aleinikoff, "A Case for Race-Consciousness," 91 *Colum. L. Rev.* 1060 (1991).

103. See, e.g., Ruth Bader Ginsburg, "Some Thoughts on Autonomy and Equality in Relation to *Roe v. Wade*," 63 *N.C.L. Rev.* 375 (1985); Reva Siegel, "Reasoning from the Body: A Historical Perspective on Abortion Regulation and Questions of Equal Protection," 44 *Stan. L. Rev.* 261 (1992).

104. *Roe v. Wade*, 410 U.S. 113 (1973) (invalidating state laws prohibiting women from obtaining abortions under virtually all circumstances), followed and expanded in *Planned Parenthood v. Danforth*, 428 U.S. 52 (1976), and *Akron v. Akron Center for Reproductive Health*, 462 U.S. 416 (1983).

105. See *Maher v. Roe*, 432 U.S. 464 (1977) (upholding state refusal to pay for abortions by women who could not afford them), and *Webster v. Reproductive Health Services*, 492 U.S. 490 (1989) (upholding a requirement that the doctor test for viability before performing an abortion).

106. For an in-depth examination of the polarizing politics instantiated by the Supreme Court's liberal resolution in *Roe*, see Lee Epstein and Joseph F. Kobylka, *The Supreme Court and Legal Change: Abortion and the Death Penalty* (1992).

107. *Planned Parenthood v. Casey*, 505 U.S. 833 (1992). The judgment of the Court was delivered in a joint opinion authored by Justices Sandra Day O'Connor, Anthony Kennedy, and David Souter. Justices Harry Blackmun and John Paul Stevens agreed with the joint opinion that *Roe* and a woman's right to choose be reaffirmed. Chief Justice William Rehnquist and Justices Byron White, Antonin Scalia, and Clarence Thomas agreed with the joint opinion that most of the state regulations were valid.

108. See Mary Ann Glendon, *Abortion and Divorce in Western Law* (1987).

109. See *Abele v. Markle*, 342 F. Supp. 800, 809 (D. Conn. 1972) (three-judge court) (separate concurring opinion of Newman, J.).

CHAPTER SIX

1. See, e.g., John Finnis, "Law, Morality, and 'Sexual Orientation,'" 69 *Notre Dame L. Rev.* 1049 (1994); Robert P. George and Gerald V. Bradley, "Marriage and the Liberal Imagination," 84 *Geo. L.J.* 301 (1995).

2. See chapter 1's discussion of the 1998 Hawaii referendum overriding the state court decisions requiring heightened scrutiny for the same-sex marriage bar, and chapter 2's discussion of the 2000 Vermont Civil Unions Law. See generally William N. Eskridge Jr., "No Promo Homo: The Sedimentation of Antigay Discourse and the Channeling Effect of Judicial Review," 75 *NYU L. Rev.* 1327 (2000), for an archaeology of the "no promo homo" form of argument and its surfacing as a major reason against same-sex marriage, 1329, 1346–50.

3. See, e.g., Stephen Macedo, "Homosexuality and the Conservative Mind," 84 *Geo. L.J.* 261 (1995); Michael Perry, "The Morality of Homosexual Conduct: A Response to John Finnis," 1 *Notre Dame J.L. Ethics & Pub. Pol'y* 41 (1995).

4. See, e.g., William N. Eskridge Jr. *The Case for Same-Sex Marriage*, chs. 4–6 (1996); Richard D. Mohr, *A More Perfect Union: Why Straight America Must Stand Up for Gay Rights* (1994).

5. See William N. Eskridge, Jr. *Gaylaw: Challenging the Apartheid of the Closet*, 243–92 (1999), showing how American law and theories of sexual consent and family formation rest upon both premodern and modernist ways of thinking.

6. See, e.g., Paula L. Ettelbrick, "Since When Is Marriage a Path to Liberation?," OUT/LOOK, Fall 1989, 8–12, reprinted in *Sexuality, Gender, and the Law*, 817–18 (William N. Eskridge Jr. and Nan D. Hunter, eds. 1997).

7. For a trenchant critique of the law's failure to protect caregiving relationships and an argument that the law should have nothing to do with marriage, see Martha A. Fineman, *The Neutered Mother, the Sexual Family, and Other Twentieth Century Tragedies* (1995). See also Ruthann Robson, *Sappho Goes to Law School* (1998), who argues that the legal categories of *family* as well as *marriage* should be abolished.

8. Cf. Cheshire Calhoun, "Defending Marriage," in *Feminism, the Family, and the Politics of the Closet: Lesbian and Gay Displacement,* 107, 112–15 (2000), who argues that defenders of same-sex marriage are most vulnerable when they insist on one exclusive normative understanding of "marriage" as an overriding goal for lesbian and gay rights.

9. For various arguments for the formal equality of lesbian and gay couples, from various liberal perspectives, see Eskridge, *The Case for Same-Sex Marriage,* 123–91; Morris B. Kaplan, *Sexual Justice: Democratic Citizenship and the Politics of Desire* (1997); Mary Coombs, "Sexual Dis-Orientation: Transgendered People and Same-Sex Marriage," 8 *UCLA Women's L.J.* 219 (1998); Mary C. Dunlap, "The Lesbian and Gay Marriage Debate: A Microcosm of Our Hopes and Our Troubles," 1 *Law & Sexuality* 62 (1991); Nan D. Hunter, "Marriage, Law, and Gender: A Feminist Inquiry," 1 *Law & Sexuality* 9 (1991); Sylvia Law, "Homosexuality and the Social Meaning of Gender," 1988 *Wis. L. Rev.* 187; Evan Wolfson, "Crossing the Threshold: Equal Marriage Rights for Lesbians and Gay Men and the Intra-Community Critique," 21 *NYU J.L. & Soc. Change* 567 (1994–1995).

10. See Richard A. Posner, *Sex and Reason,* 311 (1991), accepting the "stamp of approval" argument against same-sex marriage; G. Sidney Buchanan, "Same-Sex Marriage: The Linchpin Issue," 10 *U. Dayton L. Rev.* 541 (1985), who more enthusiastically supports this argument.

11. See Ettelbrick, "Since When Is Marriage a Path to Liberation?"

12. See Finnis, "Law, Morality, and 'Sexual Orientation,'" 1051–53.

13. See Nancy D. Polikoff, "We Will Get What We Ask For: Why Legalizing Gay and Lesbian Marriage Will Not 'Dismantle the Legal Structure of Gender in Every Marriage,'" 79 *Va. L. Rev.* 1535 (1993).

14. See The Ramsey Colloquium, "The Homosexual Movement: A Response by the Ramsey Colloquium," *First Things,* March 1994.

15. See Nitya Duclos, "Some Complicating Thoughts on Same-Sex Marriage," 1 *Law & Sexuality* 31, 52–55 (1991).

16. This is my view, but the proposition in text receives interesting support from Calhoun, "Defending Marriage," 128–29.

17. See *Romer v. Evans,* 517 U.S. 620 (1996) (measures reflecting antigay animus violate the equal protection clause); *Edwards v. Aguillard,* 482 U.S. 578 (1987) (laws reflecting sectarian religious goals violate the establishment clause of the first amendment).

18. See Carlos A. Ball and Janice Farrell Pea, "Warring with Wardle: Social Science, Morality, and Gay and Lesbian Parents," 1998 *U. Ill. L. Rev.* 253, collecting the social psychology evidence and dismantling the leading account supporting the idea that same-sex marriage would harm the interests of children, Lynn Wardle, "The Potential Impact of Homosexual Parenting on Children," 1997 *U. Ill. L. Rev.* 833.

19. See, e.g., Eskridge, *Case for Same-Sex Marriage,* 87–122, and *Gaylaw,* 271–92.

20. See, e.g., Karen Struening, "Feminist Challenges to the New Familialism: Lifestyle Experimentation and the Freedom of Association," 11 *Hypatia,* Winter 1996, at 135–54.

21. On normalization as a coercive feature of modernism and its obsession with standard deviations, see Michel Foucault, *Discipline and Punish: The Birth of the Prison* 182–84 (Alan Sheridan, tr. 1979 [original, 1975]); and Georges Canguilhem, *The Normal and the Pathological* (Carolyn R. Fawcett, tr. 1989 [1966]).

22. See Ettelbrick, "Since When Is Marriage a Path to Liberation?"; and Polikoff, "We Will Get What We Ask For." See also Claudia Card, "Against Marriage and Divorce," 11 *Hypatia,* Summer 1996, at 1; Duclos, "Complicating Thoughts About Same-Sex Marriage," 35–52.

23. Janet Halley, "Recognition, Rights, Regulation, Normalization: Rhetorics of Justification in the Same-Sex Marriage Debate," in *Legal Recognition of Same-Sex Partnerships: A Survey of National European and International Law,* (ed. Robert Wintemute and Mads Andenaes eds. (2001) (emphasis in the original).

24. The most ambitious polls to this effect, published in the August 1994 (gay men) and August 1995 (lesbians) issues of *The Advocate,* were self-selected and therefore cannot be generalized. Nonetheless, most intellectuals assume their results to reflect the preferences of ordinary bisexuals, gay men, and lesbians.

25. See Calhoun, "Defending Marriage," 121–31.

26. See Act of July 5, 1997, Relating to Registered Partnerships, *Staatsblad* 1997, nr 660, discussed in chapter 3.

27. See Act of 21 December 2000 on the Opening up of Marriage, *Staatsblad* 2001, nr. 9 (January 11, 2001), discussed in chapter 3. An unofficial translation can be found at <ruljis.leidenuniv.nl/user/cwaaldij//www/NHR/transl-marr.html> (as of March 31, 2001).

28. See Hawaii Reciprocal Beneficiaries Act, 1997 Haw. Sess. Laws 2786, Act 383 (H.B. 118), described in chapter 1.

29. Loi no. 99–944 du 15 novembre 1999 relative au pacte civil de solidarité, <http://www.legifrance.gouv.fr/html/frame_codes_lois_reglt.htm> (dossiers législatifs) (as of October 31, 2000).

30. An Act Relating to Civil Unions (H. 847), § 29, 2000 Vermont Statutes No. 91 (adopted Apr. 26, 2000), which can be viewed at <http://www.glad.org> (as of October 31, 2000).

31. See Andrew Hacker, "The Case Against Kids," *N.Y. Rev. Books,* November 30, 2000, at 12, 16.

32. The *channeling* function of law is developed in Eskridge, "No Promo Homo," 1406–10.

33. Hunter, "Marriage, Law, and Gender," 11. See Lisa Duggan and Nan D. Hunter, *Sex Wars: Sexual Dissent and Political Culture,* 101–6 (1995).

34. See Polikoff, "We Will Get What We Ask For," 1538, drawing from William N. Eskridge, Jr., "A History of Same-Sex Marriage," 79 *Va. L. Rev.* 1419–1514 (1993).

35. See, e.g., Marieka Klawitter, "Did They Find or Create Each Other? Labor Market Linkages between Partners in Same-Sex and Different-Sex Couples" (paper presented at the annual meeting of the Population Association of America, 1995); Lawrence A. Kurdek, "The Allocation of Household Labor in Gay, Lesbian, and Heterosexual Married Couples," 49 *J. Soc. Issues* 127, 135–36 (1993); Letitia Anne Peplau, "Lesbian and Gay Relationships," in *Homosexuality: Research Implications for Public Policy* 177, 183–84 (John C. Gonsiorek and John D. Weinrich, eds. 1991); N. S. Eldridge and L. A. Gilbert, "Correlates of Relationship Satisfaction in Lesbian Couples," 14 *Psychol. of Women Q.* 43, 44 (1990). The social science evidence as to the more egalitarian division of labor within same-sex households is surveyed in M. V. Lee Badgett, *Money, Myths, and Change: The Economic Lives of Lesbians and Gay Men,* 144–51 (2001).

36. Dr. John Gottman is a professor of psychology at the University of Washington; Dr. Robert Levenson is a professor of psychology at the University of California at Berkeley. Their study will be published in the *Journal of Homosexuality*, but a preview of its conclusions was published in *Bay Windows*, a Boston gay journal.

37. On the intrinsic value of work outside the home for women generally and wives in particular, see Vicki Schultz, "Life's Work," 100 *Colum. L Rev.* 1881 (2000).

38. Michael Warner, "Normal and Normaller: Beyond Gay Marriage," 5 *GLQ: J. Lesbian & Gay Stud.* 119, 147 (1999).

39. See, e.g., Adrienne Rich, "Compulsory Heterosexuality and Lesbian Experience," in *Blood, Bread, and Poetry: Selected Prose, 1979–1985,* 23–75 (1986).

40. Judith Butler, *Gender Trouble: Feminism and the Subversion of Identity,* 24–25 (1990). I do not know Butler's views regarding same-sex marriage. Her work, *The Psychic Life of Power: Theories in Subjection* (1997), suggests she would be skeptical.

41. Compare Calhoun, "Defending Marriage," 117–23 (viewing homophobia as rooted in rigid gender role as incomplete), with Eskridge, *Gaylaw,* 222–28 (detailed historical case for similar proposition, but concluding, further, that gender role seems to be the main situs of oppression for lesbians and bisexual women and that even for bisexual and gay men gender role is intertwined with anxiety about sexuality).

42. See Coombs, "Sexual Dis-Orientation," 242–65. See also Martha M. Ertman, "Reconstructing Marriage: An InterSEXual Approach," 75 *Den. U.L. Rev.* 1215 (1998), who analyzes marriage from the perspective of people who have ambiguous sex features.

43. See Coombs, "Sexual Dis-Orientation," 244–57 (discussing the cases).

44. See Marjorie Garber, *Vested Interests* (1997) (arguing that the transgendered person's mere presence destabilizes established binary categories).

45. *Littleton v. Prange,* 9 S.W.3d 223 (Tex. Civ. App. 1999).

46. See Duclos, "Complicating Thoughts About Same-Sex Marriage," 52–55.

47. See Eskridge, *Same-Sex Marriage,* 66–71. For a more detailed discussion of the various benefits and costs of marriage, see David L. Chambers, "What If? The Legal Consequences of Marriage and the Legal Needs of Lesbian and Gay Male Couples," 95 *Mich. L. Rev.* 447 (1996).

48. See Halley, "Recognition, Rights, Regulation, Normalization."

49. The state's involvement in custody and visitation disputes between estranged lesbian partners who had been raising the children as a family is a consequence of the law's recognition of second-parent adoptions and *de facto* parenthood. For examples of messy disputes along these lines, see, e.g., *V.C. v. M.J.B.,* 748 A.2d 539 (N.J. 2000); *La Chapelle v. Mitten,* 607 N.W.2d 151 (Minn. 2000) (a three-pronged battle among the child's biological lesbian mother, biological gay father, and de facto lesbian mother).

50. Warner, "Normal and Normaller," 127.

51. Warner's second sentence quoted in the text goes on to say that the state will refuse "to grant them the same rights as those enjoyed by married couples." This is either false or substantially false as to Denmark, whose registered partnership law (as amended in 1999) accords same-sex couples pretty much all the benefits and obligations given to different-sex married couples, and as to Vermont, whose new civil unions law assures exact equality of benefits and obligations for same-sex couples joined in civil union, as for different-sex married couples. (A caveat: the Defense of Marriage Act, Public Law No. 104–109, 110 Stat. 2419 [1996] assures that same-sex couples in civil unions will not be accorded the same federal benefits and obligations as different-sex married couples, but there is nothing Vermont could have done about that, as explained in chapter 2.) As detailed in chapter 3, the Netherlands this year recognized same-sex marriages and equalized rights of same-sex registered partners.

52. See generally, Cassia Spohn and Julie Horney, *Rape Law Reform: A Grass Roots Revolution and Its Impact* (1992); Martha Chamallas, "Consent, Equality, and the Legal Control of Sexual Conduct," 61 *S. Cal. L. Rev.* 777 (1988).

53. On advances and limits in state enforcement of sexual violence and abuse laws, see generally Pat Gilmartin, *Rape, Incest, and Child Sexual Abuse* (1994).

54. See Katherine M. Franke, "Becoming a Citizen: Reconstruction Era Regulation of African American Marriages," 11 *Yale J.L. & Hum.* 251 (1999).

55. See e.g., Michel Foucault, *Introduction*, volume one in *The History of Sexuality* (Robert Hurley, tr., 1978 [orig. 1976]); and Pauline Marie Rosenau, *Post-Modernism and the Social Sciences: Insights, Inroads, and Intrusions* (1992).

56. See Lawrence Kurdek and J. Patrick Schmitt, "Relationship Quality of Partners in Heterosexual Married, Heterosexual Cohabiting, and Gay and Lesbian Relationships," 51 *J. Personality & Soc. Psychol.* 711 (1986), for a sample of the empirical literature that supports the proposition in the text. See also Steven L. Nock, *Marriage in Men's Lives* (1998).

57. I first made the argument in text in Eskridge, "Beyond Lesbian and Gay 'Families We Choose,'" in *Sex, Preference, and Family,* 277 (Martha C. Nussbaum and David M. Estlund, eds. 1996).

58. See Robert Jay Lifton, *The Protean Self: Human Resilience in an Age of Fragmentation,* 1–12 (1993). See also Kenneth J. Gergen, *The Saturated Self: Dilemmas of Identity in Contemporary Life* (1991).

59. See Lifton, *Protean Self,* 120–24; Milton C. Regan Jr., *Family Law and the Pursuit of Intimacy,* 69–88 (1993). See also Regan, *Alone Together: Law and the Meanings of Marriage* (1999).

60. See Regan, *Pursuit of Intimacy,* 119–22 (argument for gay marriage).

61. See William N. Eskridge Jr. and Gary Peller, "The New Public Law Movement: Moderation as a Postmodern Cultural Form," 89 *Mich. L. Rev.* 707, 776–80 (1992).

62. The Vermont Supreme Court construed the state's second-parent adoption statute to be the exclusive mechanism by which a lesbian or gay partner could claim parental rights to the other partner's biological or adopted child. See *Titchenal v. Dexter,* 693 A.2d 682 (Vt. 1997).

63. See Geoffrey Haddock et al., "Assessing the Structure of Prejudicial Attitudes: The Case of Attitudes Toward Homosexuals," 65 *J. Personality & Soc. Psychol.* 1105 (1993). Critique of social science studies of prejudice can be found in Celia Kitzinger, *The Social Construction of Lesbianism* 153–77 (1987).

64. See Gregory M. Herek and John P. Capitanio, "'Some of My Best Friends': Intergroup Conflict, Concealable Stigma, and Heterosexuals' Attitudes Toward Gay Men and Lesbians," 22 *Personality & Soc. Psychol. Bull.* 412 (1996).

65. See generally Jane J. Mansbridge, *Why We Lost the ERA,* 216 (1986) (women who work outside the home were more likely to support the ERA and are much more gay friendly or tolerant than women who work only within the home). For an example closer to the topic of this book, the Vermont Civil Unions Law would have failed in both chambers of the legislature if only men had voted, as they opposed the measure 41 to 60 in the House and 9 to 11 in the Senate. Women supported the measure 35 to 9 in the House and 10 to 0 in the Senate.

66. See Kath Weston, *Families We Choose: Lesbians, Gays, Kinship* (1991), a pioneering work demonstrating that lesbians and gay men often form more informal "families" more like a network of close friends than the living-together "families" of a mom, a dad, and kids.

EPILOGUE

1. For an illuminating survey of the state choice of law experience with miscegenation laws, and how that experience bears on interstate recognition of same-sex civil unions or marriages, see Andrew Koppelman, "Same-Sex Marriage, Choice of Law, and Public Policy," 76 *Tex. L. Rev.* 921 (1998).

2. Compare the "compulsory heterosexuality" idea in Adrienne Rich, "Compulsory Heterosexuality and Lesbian Experience," in *Blood, Bread, and Poetry: Selected Prose, 1979–1985,* 23–75 (1986), with the "malignant sexual variation" idea in William N. Eskridge Jr., *Gaylaw: Challenging the Apartheid of the Closet* (1999), drawing from Gayle S. Rubin, "Thinking Sex: Notes for a Radical Theory of the Politics of Sexuality," in *Pleasure and Danger: Exploring Female Sexuality,* 11–34 (Carole Vance ed. 1984) (coining the term *benign sexual variation*).

3. The social science evidence is collected and analyzed in M. V. Lee Badgett, *Money, Myths, and Change: The Economic Lives of Lesbians and Gay Men,* 144–51 (2001). Among the most useful studies or collections of studies are Philip Blumstein and Pepper Schwartz, *American Couples: Money, Work, Sex,* 11–24 (1983) (the pioneering empirical study on the joys and problems in lesbian and gay relationships); Alan P. Bell and Martin S. Weinberg, *Homosexualities: A Study of Diversity Among Men and Women,* 219–21 (1978) (same); Carlos Ball and Janice Farrell Pea, "Warring with Wardle: Morality, Social Science, and Gay and Lesbian Parents," 1998 *U. Ill. L. Rev.* 253 (success of lesbian and gay households raising children); Lawrence Kurdek and J. Patrick Schmitt, "Relationship Quality of Partners in Heterosexual Married, Heterosexual Cohabiting, and Gay and Lesbian Relationships," 51 *J. Personality & Soc. Psychol.* 711 (1986) (relationship satisfaction among lesbian and gay couples is relatively high).

4. See Eric A. Posner, "Law, Economics, and Inefficient Norms," 144 *U. Pa. L. Rev.* 1697 (1996). On the evolution of social norms and their relationship to law, see generally Robert C. Ellickson, "The Evolution of Social Norms: A Perspective from the Legal Academy," in *Social Norms* (Michael Hechter and Karl-Dieter Opp eds. 2001); Richard H. McAdams, "The Origin, Development, and Regulation of Social Norms," 96 *Mich. L. Rev.* 338 (1997); Symposium, "Law, Economics, and Norms," 144 *U. Pa. L. Rev.* 1643 (1996).

5. See Cass R. Sunstein, "Deliberative Trouble? Why Groups Go to Extremes," 110 *Yale L.J.* 71 (2000).

6. The distinction in text between bonding and bridging social capital is taken from Robert D. Putnam, *Bowling Alone: The Collapse and Revival of American Community* (2000).

7. *Loving v. Virginia,* 388 U.S. 1 (1967). The extension of *Loving*'s equal treatment and right to marry principles to same-sex couples is the project carried out in William N. Eskridge Jr., *The Case for Same-Sex Marriage* (1996).

INDEX